A History of Russian Poetry

A HISTORY OF
RUSSIAN
POETRY

Evelyn Bristol

New York Oxford
OXFORD UNIVERSITY PRESS
1991

Oxford University Press

Oxford   New York   Toronto
Delhi   Bombay   Calcutta   Madras   Karachi
Petaling Jaya   Singapore   Hong Kong   Tokyo
Nairobi   Dar es Salaam   Cape Town
Melbourne   Auckland

and associated companies in
Berlin   Ibadan

Published by Oxford University Press, Inc.
200 Madison Avenue, New York, New York 10016

Oxford is a registered trademark of Oxford University Press.

Library of Congress Cataloging-in-Publication Data
Bristol, Evelyn.
A history of Russian poetry / Evelyn Bristol.
p.   cm.   Includes bibliographical references.
ISBN 0-19-504659-5. — ISBN 0-19-504471-1 (pbk.)
1. Russian poetry—History and criticism. I. Title.
PG3041.B67 1991   891.71009—dc20   89-26602

2 4 6 8 9 7 5 3 1

Printed in the United States of America
on acid-free paper

Preface

Western readers have very little notion of the continuity of Russian poetry. They may have some acquaintance with the poet whom Russians praise above all others, Aleksandr Pushkin in the nineteenth century. Westerners may also know something of the "silver age" at the beginning of the twentieth century, when Boris Pasternak and Osip Mandelstam began to write. They may have heard also of a vigorous avant-garde, which included the enigmatic Velemir Khlebnikov. But the flow of history that ties these poets together has yet to be seen, and that is, in part, why I have written this book. While Soviet scholars have brought out many new editions of poetic works, the actual study of poetry has been somewhat neglected in the Soviet Union. Soviet critics have been wary of lyrical verse, which flourishes not in realistic, but in romantic and neoromantic times. Symbolism, which appeared at the turn of the century in Russia, had metaphysical currents, and the later avant-garde was fraught with individualism. A number of poets, including some who wrote in prerevolutionary times, have been suppressed in the Soviet Union. Some were ignored, for example, because they went into, or wrote in, emigration. The suppression of poets should serve, however, to suggest to the Western reader that poetry has played a more significant role in Russian culture than it has in his own. Indeed, some Russian poets were harassed even under the monarchy, as was Pushkin.

For my knowledge of Russian poetry, I am indebted to my professors at the University of California at Berkeley, particularly to Gleb Struve. I wish to thank my friends at Columbia University, especially William Harkins, for reading my manuscript and for their encouragement and inspiration. I am grateful to the staff of the W. Averell Harriman Institute at Columbia University. In particular, I wish to thank the Director of the Reading Room, Eugene Beshenkovsky, for his sympathetic support. I am grateful also to the staff of the Institute on East Central Europe at Columbia University and to the staff of the Slavic Division of the Library of the University of Illinois. My work was supported in part by a grant from the National Endowment for the Humanities.

The translations of the poems are my own. I have tried above all to be accurate. I have also reproduced the original meter or, in a few cases, offered what seems to me an equivalent of the rhythm in English. I had to sacrifice rhyme, which is quite important in Russian, but which is normally more subdued in English.

Urbana, Ill.   E.B.
January 1991

Contents

Introduction, **3**

I The Early Period

1 The Medieval Era (988–1598), **9**

THE KIEVAN STATE, 9   FOLK TRADITIONS, 10   RELIGIOUS TEXTS, 14
COURT LITERATURE, 15   APPANAGE RUSSIA, 19
THE MUSCOVITE PERIOD, 21

2 Transition and the Baroque (1598–1730), **23**

THE CLIMATE FOR CHANGE, 23   ORAL FOLK GENRES, 25
POPULAR LITERATURE, 27   ORNATE PROSE, 29
PRESYLLABIC VERSE: THE BAROQUE, 30   SYLLABIC VERSE: POLOTSKY, 32
RELIGIOUS CONTROVERSIES, 36

II Classicism

3 The Establishment of Classicism (1730–1762), **45**

THE DESIRE TO CATCH UP, 45   KANTEMIR, 46   TREDIAKOVSKY, 48
LOMONOSOV, 52   SUMAROKOV, 57

4 The Enlightenment (1762–1790), **62**

THE FIRST WAVE: THE SUMAROKOV SCHOOL, 62   MAIKOV, 63
KHERASKOV, 65   BOGDANOVICH, 67   CROSSCURRENTS, 69
THE CRITICAL WAVE: THE LVOV CIRCLE, 70   KHEMNITSER, 71
KAPNIST, 72   DERZHAVIN, 73   HARBINGERS OF THE NEW, 79

5 The Rise of Sentimentalism (1790–1800), **81**

SENTIMENTAL AND PREROMANTIC CURRENTS, 81   RADISHCHEV, 82
KARAMZIN, 84   DMITRIEV, 88

III Sensibility and Romanticism

6 The Era of Sensibility (1800–1820), **93**

AN ECLECTIC PERIOD, 93   ZHUKOVSKY, 94   DAVYDOV, 97
KRYLOV, 98   BATIUSHKOV, 100
KARAMZINISTS VERSUS ARCHAIZERS, 103

7 Pushkin and His Pleiad (1820–1830), **104**

THE GOLDEN AGE GENERATION, 104   VIAZEMSKY, 105   DELVIG, 108
PUSHKIN, 109   BARATYNSKY, 116   IAZYKOV, 118
THE DECEMBRISTS, 121   THE METAPHYSICAL POETS, 123

8 Romanticism (1830–1845), **125**

THE END OF THE GOLDEN AGE, 125   TIUTCHEV, 126   LERMONTOV, 129
KOLTSOV, 133   MINOR ROMANTIC POETS, 135

IV   The Age of Realism

9 The Heritage of Idealism (1840–1860), **139**

THE DECLINE OF POETRY, 139   FET, 140   LESSER PURE ART POETS, 144
POLONSKY, 145   TOLSTOY, 147   LESSER IDEALISTS, 150
THE CIVIC POETS, 152

10 The Ascendancy of Civic Verse (1860–1890), **154**

RIVAL CAMPS, 154   CIVIC POETRY: NEKRASOV, 155
THE RETURN OF POETRY, 159   NEW "AESTHETIC" TRENDS, 161

V   Symbolism

11 The *Fin de siècle* (1890–1905), **167**

THE RISE OF SYMBOLISM, 167   POETS OF THE "AESTHETIC REVIVAL," 169
BALMONT, 172   BRIUSOV, 175   SOLOGUB, 178   HIPPIUS, 181
BUNIN, 184

12 Symbolist Idealism (1905–1912), **186**

SYMBOLISM IN FLORESCENCE, 186   BELY, 187   BLOK, 191
IVANOV, 196   ANNENSKY, 199

VI   Postsymbolist Modernism

13 Tradition and Acmeism (1912–1925), **205**

LITERATURE IN FLUX: ACMEISM, 205   GUMILEV, 207   AKHMATOVA, 210
MANDELSTAM, 214   INDEPENDENT POETS, 218

14 Futurism and the Avant-Garde (1912–1925), **224**

THE AVANT-GARDE FACTIONS, 224   EGO-FUTURISM: SEVERIANIN, 226
KHLEBNIKOV, 227   MAIAKOVSKY, 230   LESSER CUBO-FUTURIST POETS, 233
PASTERNAK, 235   LESSER CENTRIFUGE POETS, 240   TSVETAEVA, 241
IMAGISM, 244   PEASANT POETS, 245   ESENIN, 246

VII   Soviet and Émigré Poetry

15 Between the Wars (1925–1939), 251

SOVIET ROMANTICISM, 251   TIKHONOV, 252   SELVINSKY, 254
BAGRITSKY, 256   LESSER SOCIALIST POETS, 257
UNCONVENTIONAL POETS: ZABOLOTSKY, 259
TRENDS IN EMIGRATION: THE PARISIAN NOTE, 262
THE INDEPENDENT ÉMIGRÉS, 265

16 World War II and Its Aftermath (1939–1955), 267

TVARDOVSKY, 268   BERGGOLTS, 270   SIMONOV, 271
LESSER POETS OF THE WAR THEME, 273   DELAYED CAREERS IN EXILE: IVASK, 274

17 After Stalin (1955–1970), 279

THE OLDER LIBERALS, 280   THE NEW THAW POETS: EVTUSHENKO, 286
TRADITIONALISTS IN THE THAW, 291   BRODSKY, 293
A NEW WAVE IN EMIGRATION, 297

A Postscript on Recent Times, 301

THE SEVENTIES, 301   *GLASNOST*, 305   CONCLUDING REMARKS, 308

Glossary, 310
Metrical Systems, 312
Chronology, 314
Bibliography, 316
Index, 345

A History of Russian Poetry

Introduction

The history of poetry in Russia has differed considerably at times from the course it took in the West. In the first place, Russia was not to have a written tradition of verse until the seventeenth century. The isolation of the nation from the West began with its baptism into Christianity from Byzantium in the tenth century, and was deepened by two centuries of a "Tatar yoke" in the medieval era. The Russians entered the Western intellectual community in the era of the baroque; since then, all of Europe's literary trends, such as neoclassicism, romanticism, and realism, have had a reflection in Russia. Those currents have been influenced, however, by Russia's own historical circumstances. Romanticism, for example, scarcely had time for a florescence in Russia; it lost out in a period of rapid transition from the Enlightenment to realism. Russia's greatest poetic age came in the early twentieth century, just at the point when symbolism was challenged by an avant-garde. The poets of both generations were exceptional; Boris Pasternak was among them. The era has been neglected, however, by Soviet literary historians. Its ideologies were alien to them. Poetry in Russia has always been more visibly linked with political sentiments and destinies than in the West. This engagement has contributed, of course, to the Russians' great love for poetry.

Medieval Rus had only one artistic tradition that could have a deep influence on the poetry that was to come—its own folklore. The literature that the medieval land, whose capital was at Kiev, received from Byzantium consisted of chronicles, saints' lives, and other Church-sponsored works. There was no written poetry. A written epic, *The Tale of Igor's Campaign*, appeared in the twelfth century. Despite its having been written in prose, it has influenced later poets, especially since the romantic period. During the Mongol invasion in the fourteenth to sixteenth centuries, written traditions began to decline, and folklore flourished. There were folk epics, called *byliny*, that described legendary wandering champions (*bogatyri*); they usually served the prince at Kiev. These epics were improvised chants that were performed to the accompaniment of a musical instrument. They, too, have been imitated by modern poets, but not nearly so often as the "slow" songs, often plaints about love, that were sung by peasant women. In addition, there may have been an oral tradition of verse that was in the hands of the wandering players, called *skomorokhi*, who were discouraged by the Church.

The secularization of Russia's written culture began in the seventeenth century after the rise to power of Moscow. It was the northern city that defeated the Mongols and reunited the other Russian cities, but under a regime so rigid and xenophobic that it was shattered at the beginning of the seventeenth century by the Time of

Troubles. That brief period after the reign of Ivan the Terrible saw peasant revolts, nineteen pretenders to the throne, and invasions by Poland and Sweden. The Time of Troubles itself was to inspire a number of later literary works, such as Aleksandr Pushkin's play *Boris Godunov*. When a new dynasty had been established, the Ukraine was returned to Russian suzerainty after a century of union with Poland. Jesuit schools had been founded in the Ukraine, and a Latin literary culture initiated. Ukrainian clerics brought poetry, and drama, to Moscow, where the new learning found favor with the Romanov rulers. A period of Westernization began.

In the eighteenth century, all the fine arts began to serve as showcases for an empire on the rise. Peter the Great founded a new capital, St. Petersburg, in the north. He broke the power of the Church, encouraged translations, and sent young Russians to study in the West. They returned already acquainted with Western intellectual currents, literary fashions, and new rules for versification. By mid-century, a neoclassical literature was settling in, and poetry was its chief means of expression. Laudatory odes, to the rulers and to the nation, were more common than in the West. Satire also enjoyed a large success, whether in imitations of Horatian satires, in Aesopic fables, in comedies, or in prose essays. At first, the targets of ridicule were the conservative opponents of Peter's reforms. But as the century wore on, as the tsars became more jealous of their power, and as the seeds of the Enlightenment grew, the satirists turned against the court. A liberal intelligentsia was born. The towering genius of eighteenth-century Russian poetry, Gavrila Derzhavin, appeared just on the threshold of the sentimental movement in the last years of the century.

The age of sensibility, a brief and transitory period in the Western literatures, was in Russia an era of stable eclecticism that the Russians have called their "golden age" of poetry. The best poets were Pushkin and members of his school, or "pleiad," who surveyed the resources of neoclassicism, sentimentalism, and romanticism and used them as they saw fit. They still valued the critical impulse of the Enlightenment. Yet they also admired and imitated Byron, in whom they saw not only a champion of liberty, but a dark, rebellious, and enigmatic spirit. The atmosphere of this period was abruptly altered by the occurrence of an abortive coup d'état, which is now called the Decembrist Revolt of 1825. It signaled the extent of gentry opposition to the monarchy. The spirit of resistance was exemplified for many in Pushkin's poems, especially in a lyric called "The Prophet," where God is seen to send His inspiration from on high: "Arise, O prophet, heed, give witness. . . ." Urbane as he was, Pushkin's works were nevertheless to become popular in the West in the form of romantic operas, *Boris Godunov* by Moussorgsky, and *Eugene Onegin* and *The Queen of Spades* by Tchaikovsky. This golden age of poetry was followed by a brief period of authentic romanticism. Its leading poet, Mikhail Lermontov, remained close to Byron, but he cultivated the English poet's cynicism. The Russian romantic poets were drawn, probably following after Byron, to depict the exotic landscapes of the Caucasus and Crimea.

In the era of realism, the fortunes of poetry declined. The period was dominated by the great novels, first of Turgenev, and then of Dostoevsky and Tolstoy, and the spirit of intellectual inquiry went into prose fiction. The leading poet of mid-century, Afanasy Fet, represented the beginning of an art for art current. But all those writers who were not realists, in prose or in verse, were harassed, and sometimes silenced, by a series of powerful utilitarian critics. They tended to despise poetry as unfit for the reflection of contemporary issues. By 1860, there was a camp of "civic" poets whose aim was the cultivation of a social conscience. Russia did not have poets of the stature of a Browning of a Tennyson in the 1860s and 1870s. There was no equivalent of the Parnassian movement in France, or of the decadence initiated by Baudelaire and continued by Verlaine.

The era of modernism, called the "silver age," benefited from a swing of the pendulum. The florescence of the arts, including literature, painting, and music, was unprecedented in the history of the nation, and poetry was popular again. In the 1890s came a first wave of new poets. They were the heirs of Baudelaire and Verlaine, but they also learned from Fet and the Russian romantic Fedor Tiutchev. The new Russian poets were decadents and usually complained of a metaphysical malaise. In the second wave of symbolists, the religious nature of the Russian movement became apparent. The newer poets combined German romantic philosophy with millenarian political hopes. Their greatest poetry was written after the failure of the Revolution of 1905, in a period of irony and pessimism. The symbolist movement collapsed around 1910 and was followed by schools with a less religious coloration.

Among the modernist successors to symbolism, there were two factions of approximately equal importance: the moderates, called acmeists, and the rebel futurists. The acmeists rejected the mystical aspect of symbolism, but availed themselves of the great cultural history of the West. The greatest poet of the group was Osip Mandelstam, although he was not its leader. The acmeists were comparable in the breadth of their historical interests and psychological subtlety to Paul Valéry or T. S. Eliot. The Russian avant-garde encompassed a wide spectrum of poets, the most dynamic of which were the cubo-futurists, so called to distance them from the Italian futurists and to emphasize their affiliation with Russian painters. The Russian futurists were utopian idealists who looked with favor on the coming political revolution and believed, again, in a natural alliance between politics and art. They rejected the past and coined words. The most radical wrote verse that is unintelligible. Other futurists, such as Boris Pasternak, were less outspoken as rebels.

The Soviet period has brought great differences between the literatures of the East and of the West. Russian literature has been divided into Soviet and émigré camps. The Soviet poets, although they have constituted the mainstream, have been subjected to the constraints of socialist realism. Meanwhile, a small number of poets, writing in exile, have been deprived of their natural audience. In the early years of the Soviet period, the best poetry was still written by the giants of pre-revolutionary poetry. It was the futurists who tended to remain at home, led by Vladimir Maiakovsky. The émigrés came more often from the acmeist camp, and they settled especially in Paris and Berlin. By the 1930s, the newest Soviet poets were socialists who wrote about their memories of the Revolution and the ensuing civil war. In 1932, the Union of Writers was organized, and in 1934 socialist realism became the only officially permitted literary method. World War II brought patriotic poetry in the homeland; its appeal has proved to be primarily national. The émigrés, meanwhile, were preoccupied with philosophical subjects and had broad cultural horizons. They have not been deeply affected, however, by the Western poetry around them. After World War II, new émigrés arrived in the West, and still others have come in more recent years. A new period of Soviet poetry came with the first decade of de-Stalinization, or the "Thaw." The young Soviet poets attempted to rediscover the currents of futurism and acmeism and to widen the scope of Soviet poetry. The gap between Soviet and émigré poetry has narrowed somewhat in principle, but the current differences may remain in place for some time. Meanwhile, the most original, and the most outstanding, of Russian poets, Joseph Brodsky, resides in emigration.

I

THE
EARLY
PERIOD

1

THE
EARLY
PERIOD

1

The Medieval Era
(988–1598)

Medieval Russian culture began in the tenth century with Christianization from Byzantium. During the subsequent six centuries, Russia was relatively isolated from the West. The natural community of Kievan Rus was the Orthodox Slavic states of south central Europe. The kinds of literature typical of the Kievan state—the chronicles, which were initially kept at monasteries, the saints' lives, sermons, and liturgical texts—were to change in style during the medieval period, but not in essential genre. The influence of the Church on written culture was strong throughout the medieval era. A vigorous popular culture was expressed almost entirely in anonymous folklore. From the thirteenth through the fifteenth century, the Mongols dominated Russia. Territories in the south and west, including Kiev itself, were temporarily lost. At home, Orthodoxy became the sign of the Russian as opposed to the Muslim intruder. Folk genres proliferated. In the fifteenth century, Moscow began the reunification of the Russian lands and assumed the powers of a new central government. Its autocratic rule was to be epitomized by the reign of Ivan the Terrible. Its culture was Orthodox, and its written literature was meager. The medieval period was brought to a close at the beginning of the seventeenth century by political upheavals called the Time of Troubles.

The Kievan State

The Orthodox Slavic states of central Europe included Moravia, Bulgaria, Serbia, and Macedonia. The first missionaries to the Slavs, Saints Cyril and Methodius, had reached Moravia in the ninth century. They made use of a Slavic dialect that is now known as Old Church Slavic and wrote their texts in the Cyrillic alphabet, which legend has attributed to Saint Cyril. Prince Vladimir of Kiev was baptized on behalf of Rus in 988. Translations of Byzantine Greek texts appeared in Rus, often by way of the other Slavic states, but sometimes directly from Byzantium. Ecclesiastical literature was favored, but some secular tales, such as the *Alexandreis,* the story of Alexander the Great, were known. Contacts with the Latin traditions of the West were minimal. New texts, such as chronicles, sermons, and liturgical texts, were written in Old Church Slavic on Russian soil. The liturgy contained translations of Byzantine Greek verse, but it was not imitated in Kiev, and perhaps was not perceived by many as verse. Old Church Slavic continued as the official written language until the eighteenth century, although it had begun to be Russified immediately after it was introduced.

Kievan Rus was limited in the kinds of literature it had to offer. Folk songs apparently flourished in Kievan times, but their forms cannot be described without conjecture because they were not recorded until the seventeenth century. It seems that they had an impact on the written literature of the period. In modern times, the songs have been documented in such abundance, and in such a great variety of types, as to suggest a long history and a robust culture. As for the epics, or *byliny,* about 100 basic stories have been recorded, and each performer had his own variants of the *byliny* in his repertory. The culture of the wandering players called *skomorokhi* has been lost. It is known almost entirely by inference from the deprecations of clerics. Other songs were sung, according to chronicle accounts, by bards at the courts of princes. These songs are described as celebrations of military victories and eulogies for the rulers. Russia's national "epic," *The Tale of Igor's Campaign,* is perhaps related to these lost court songs. The *Igor Tale* was written, on internal evidence, in the twelfth century, but it was lost from sight and rediscovered only in the eighteenth century.

Folk Traditions

The lyric folk songs are more timeless in appearance than the *byliny,* and richer in variety. The oldest of the lyrics apparently originated in pagan rituals, while the later ones are urban songs. The lyrics have been described in a wide array of categories, some of which are overlapping. There were ritual songs and nonritual songs; "slow" or "drawn-out" (*protiazhnye*) songs, usually sad, and "quick" (*chastye*) songs to accompany dances and games; songs about love and marriage; songs about the occupations of men; children's songs; satirical songs; and laments.

Rituals marking the dates of a prehistoric agricultural calendar seem to have given rise to the oldest surviving songs. The rituals became mere seasonal social events and were attached, with their songs, to the Christian calendar. One winter ritual was transformed into an occasion for group caroling; its songs were called *koliadki,* a word whose root is related to "calendar." Fortune-telling rituals at the new year were accompanied by songs:

> Death comes walking down the street
> Bearing pancakes on a plate. . . .[1]

The spring rituals were more numerous. At the pre-Lenten festival, which in Russian is called *maslenitsa* (*maslo* means "fat"), there were songs to be sung for the ritual death of an effigy figure. At the vernal equinox, "spring songs" (*vesnianki*) were sung to welcome the returning birds. Yet other songs were sung at a post-Easter celebration called *semik* (seventh week), during which girls joined in circle dances called *rusalii* (*rusalka* is a water nymph). The songs of the *rusalii* have been imitated by twentieth-century poets in search of the primitive. At the summer solstice came a celebration that is now connected with a figure called Ivan Kupala, a folk name for John the Baptist. In the fall there were songs, apparently unconnected with any ritual, that were sung simply to mark the beginning and end of the harvest season.

It is the great body of lyric songs that concern love and marriage, however, that has been taken as best representing the achievements of Russian folk art. Some of these songs also derived from rituals, namely the ceremonies of matchmaking and weddings. These marriage songs were sung on various occasions, such as at traditional parties and for the giving of gifts. The most common kind of song was the lament of the bride-to-be. She begs not to be given away from her home and complains of what her fate will be in a new household. Her laments were sung at meetings of the two families, at the bride's party for girls, and on the wedding day. Other songs about love and marriage were independent of any ritual and can be divided into the "drawn-out" and "quick" categories. Here is a "drawn-out" song on one of the most typical subjects of Russian folk lyrics, a woman's regret at her marriage:

> Had I known, had I learned,
> As a young girl foreseen
> My own bitter fate,
> The grief of marriage,
> I would not have wed,
> My fortune to lose!
> I'd have scattered my fortune
> Through the open field,
> Scattered my bridal wreath
> Through the pale blue flowers,
> Given my black eyebrows
> To the bright falcon:
> Be pretty, my bridal wreath
> In the pale blue flowers,
> Go, go, my freedom
> Through the open field.
> Be white, my fair skin
> On the white birch tree,
> Be black, my eyes
> On the black crow.[2]

Other love songs were of the "quick" variety intended for activities and some were not only joyful, but humorous and satirical.

Songs on other subjects fall outside the designations "drawn-out" and "quick." The purpose of some songs was satire. Women were ridiculed, for example, for being lazy or mincing, while men could be portrayed as drunken husbands; other satires were aimed at priests and monasteries. There were children's songs, and some lullabyes. Songs reflecting the preoccupations of men, or their sources of livelihood, could be on occasion as melancholy as the "drawn-out" songs. Some men's songs were complaints about the hardships of serfdom and the desire for freedom. The boatmen who pulled barges on rives had their own songs. The songs of robbers and of convicts were of particular interest to the poets of the nineteenth century. Robber songs sometimes spoke with joy of the choice for freedom, while other, sad, songs pictured the probable results of crime, capture, and execution. Military service also elicited songs; some were about the suffering it entailed, but others expressed an enthusiasm for battle. There were women's laments for men who had gone as soldiers. Still other songs were those of exiles and runaways.

It is the melancholy songs, whatever their subject, that have seemed to Russians to typify their peasant culture. These sorrowful songs are often first-person outpourings of emotion; the narratives at which they hint remain in the background. Humans are pervasively symbolized by the phenomena of nature. The man may be a falcon; the girl, a birch tree. Technically these parallels may be comparisons, metaphors, or plain juxtapositions. Syntactically, the songs favor parallel phrases and repetitions. Their rhythm tends toward the trochaic. Rhymes may appear, but they are usually the simple result of grammatical parallels.

The *byliny* were apparently created most abundantly in the Kievan era. They describe the exploits of rough-hewn popular heroes called *bogatyri,* who possess prodigious, supernatural strength. Seldom are princes of other rulers the protagonists of the *byliny,* nor are the tales chivalric in character, as are Western adventure romances of the medieval period. The *bogatyri* typically wandered alone on horseback, however, through the "open field" in search of adventure. Such popular heroes as Ilia Muromets were the subjects of several *byliny.* The epics were recited by performers called *skaziteli* to the accompaniment of a stringed instrument. Phrases and details were improvised at each recitation. *Byliny* have been recorded since the seventeenth century. They first won the admiration of a literary audience when they appeared in the collection attributed to Kirsha Danilov. Known since the 1760s, this collection was first published in 1804. The epics have been called *byliny* by literary historians since the middle of the nineteenth century. To their performers, they were *stariny,* or "songs of old times."

The *byliny* have a distant and tenuous connection with historical events. The enemies whom the heroes met and conquered, usually in single combat, included various brigands and marauders, some in fantastic shapes. Others were the real foes of Kievan Rus, such as Turks or Mongols. Among the earliest heroes was a Prince Volkh Vseslavevich of Kiev, who was able to assume the shape of any animal. He was sired by a snake, and when he was born,

> The damp earth trembled.
> The great kingdom of India shook,
> And the blue ocean rocked
> Because of the *bogatyr* birth,
> Birth of young Volkh Vseslavevich.[3]

Audacious exaggeration is a feature of the *byliny*. Volkh's feat was in leading his retinue to India, the conventional name for any fabulous land, where he stormed the palace, killed the king, and became tsar. Several heroes are attested in chronicle accounts, as is Alesha Popovich of Rostov, who in the *byliny* is the conqueror of the dragon Tugarin Zmeevich. In the chronicle account, Alesha is called by the proper form of his name, Aleksandr.

Ilia Muromets (of Murom), who is the subject of the largest number of epics, encounters some legendary and some historical foes, such as the Mongols. Here Ilia sets out from home on his first adventure, which will be the defeat of the familiar villain Nightingale the Robber, who sits on seven (or twelve) oak trees. Ilia's strength is extended to his horse:

> Ilia Muromets bowed to the ground before his father,
> Sat himself on his good horse,
> Rode out into the open field.
> He strikes his horse on its steep flanks,
> Pierces the skin to the black flesh:
> His spirited horse grows angry,
> Divides himself from the earth,
> He jumps higher than the upright tree,
> Just lower than the passing cloud.[4]

The *byliny* are studded with dialogues that contain challenges and boasting, and sometimes elements of broad humor. Here is an exchange between Prince Vladimir of Kiev and Nightingale the Robber before the latter is dispatched by Ilia Muromets:

> Prince Vladimir, our father, began to speak:
> "Well done, Nightingale the Robber!
> How was it that Ilia Muromets captured you?"
> Nightingale the Robber makes his answer:
> "Because at that time I was roaring drunk,
> It was my eldest daughter's name day."[5]

Ilia Muromets is also the vanquisher of Idolishche, another well-known dragon. Tugarin, Idolishche, and Nightingale the Robber are all as familiar, and as harmless, as fairy-tale villains.

The onslaught of the Mongols is a recurring topic in the *byliny*. This historical process is crystallized, for example, in "The Battle of Kama," a narrative about a legendary confrontation in which the Mongols are turned back by the *bogatyri*, with Ilia Muromets at their head. Historical Mongol leaders such as Mamai can be recognized in some of the *byliny*. The heroes sometimes fight for the Christian faith, as well as for the land of Rus. Well-known *byliny* that describe contests between the *bogatyri* and the Mongols include "Vasily Ignatevich and Batyga" (a reference to the Mongol Batu Khan) and "Alesha Popovich Kills a Tatar."

The political, and even spiritual, center in most of the *byliny* is Kiev. The *bogatyri* characteristically owe fealty to the prince at Kiev, who is always called Vladimir, and he is the recipient of conventionally eulogistic phrases. He is shown, however, to be an indifferently effective ruler. A longstanding conflict between the prince and Ilia Muromets emerges in several *byliny*. In some *byliny* about the Battle of Kama, Ilia Muromets, who has been insulted, is reluctant to fight, and in some of the later *byliny* the struggle between the two becomes overt. The towns usually mentioned in the *byliny*, such as Chernigov, indicate a Kievan orientation, as does the mention of the river Dniepr. Foreign countries may be named, but their location is often unrealistic. Kiev is also seen to be the heart of the genre in that no *byliny* depict the fall of Kiev in 1240, or the "Tatar yoke," or the subsequent liberation under Moscow. In fact, some *byliny* composed well after the fall of Kiev even adopt the conventions of the Kievan setting as appropriate to the genre.

Some *byliny*, however, are associated with other ancient towns, principally Novgorod. The *byliny* concerning Novgorod are of indeterminate age. The chief hero at Novgorod is Sadko the merchant. Stories about him reflect the fishing and commercial interests of the city. Sadko is not a combative *bogatyr*. He wins a large fortune as a result of his adventures in a kingdom under the waters of Lake Ilmen. He and the other hero of Novgorod, Vasily Buslaev, are competitive in spirit: Sadko succeeds by acquiring goods, while Buslaev leads his retinue against the town itself. Moscow emerges as a locale of several later *byliny*—for example, "The Invasion of the Lithuanians."

The *bogatyri* were normally invincible, and the *byliny* are robust in tone. The Russian *byliny* are probably related historically to the Serbian folk epics, which have an equally long tradition. Both are frequently violent in subject, and their methods of composition are similar. The Serbian epics also make use of formulaic phrases to construct rhythmic lines. The Serbian epics have regular ten-syllable lines, which may have been an archaic Indo-European form. The Russian language, however, changed in the Kievan period so that many words had fewer syllables. Thus verse lines that had once been equal in length would cease to be equal. In their recorded form, the *byliny* have lines that vary in length from eleven to thirteen syllables. They are trochaic in tendency and have dactylic line endings. The line endings sometimes rhyme, but on grammatical suffixes. Although they must have originated in the southern, Kievan territory, the *byliny* continued to be performed longest in the far north. Recordings were frequent in the eighteenth and nineteenth centuries. Literary imitations became popular in the nineteenth century, and the influence of the *byliny* can be seen on some avant-garde works of the twentieth century.

Religious Texts

It was discovered at the end of the nineteenth century that some Old Church Slavic religious texts that were known in Kievan Rus and thought to be in prose were actually written in verse. By now, hundreds of such texts have been reexamined and also seen to be in verse.[6] Most were hymns or other parts of the written Church service, and had been translated from Byzantine Greek. Their system of versification was syllabic. A few religious texts that were written in verse came from other

Slavic countries and were independent of the service. Among the earliest were two poems attributed to St. Cyril. One is a Prologue to the Gospels, and the other is a eulogistic poem that was found in a life of the saint composed in Pannonia in the ninth century. Other texts were by a Bulgarian bishop, Konstantin Preslavsky, who wrote an "Alphabet Prayer" and a service to Saint Methodius in which the saint's name appears as an acrostic. The extent to which these liturgical and independent texts were recognized as verse in Kievan times is not known. They were copied correctly by Russian scribes over a period of several centuries, but by the seventeenth century even the clerics did not know that the hymns were in verse. Original Church services that included hymns were written on Russian soil in Kievan times, for example, for the Russian saints Boris and Gleb, but the Byzantine prosodic tradition was not transferred to them.

There are several reasons why Byzantine versification might have been gradually obscured. First, the Byzantine system of syllable counting, with a caesura, was complex and might have been too elusive for the uninitiated. Second, most of the hundreds of texts now known to be poetry were, as parts of the Church services, tied to melodies that may have masked their poetic structure. Moreover, the Russian language, which was kin to Old Church Slavic, was in the process of dropping some short syllables. An artificial pronunciation was therefore developed in the Church services, and the weak vowels were preserved. The system could then have been perceived as archaic and pertaining only to Old Church Slavic, not to Russian. This case would have been the opposite of that of the *byliny*, where the sense of syllable counting was wholly lost and the lines became free.

The Psalter was well known in Kievan Rus and exerted a considerable influence on the written literature of the period. The psalms were seen as poetic in the broad sense: they were rhythmic in tendency and were associated with a melodic line. Their vivid vocabulary and figures of speech made them fitting examples of an elevated style. They also had occasional rhymes, if only in cases of parallel phrasing. They had a rhetorical influence on Old Russian literature whether they were known to be versified or not, and they continued to stimulate the poetic sense in later centuries.

Court Literature

The courts of the princes, both at Kiev and at the regional capitals, were centers of literacy, but not of literature. The princes and their retinues, called the *druzhiny,* composed such documents as letters and legal codes. The first secular autobiography, the *Testament of Vladimir Monomakh,* appeared in 1125. Nevertheless, the greatest piece of Old Russian literature, the work esteemed as the national epic, *The Tale of Igor's Campaign,* is ascribed by scholars to the courtly milieu. Historical evidence indicates that there were court singers, although no one can say who they were. The "creators of songs" at court were commended by a famous bishop, Cyril of Turov, Metropolitan of Kiev from 1243 to 1250, who wrote that they would glorify the princes and "crown them with praise" for their courageous deeds in battle.[7] Chronicle accounts from the eleventh through the thirteenth century mention celebration feasts where eulogistic songs were addressed to the princes. But it is not known whether the singers were members of the *druzhina* or wandering performers, or even whether they had the accompaniment of a stringed instrument.

The Tale of Igor's Campaign is often called an epic, and it has played the role of a national epic in Russian culture, but it is plainly a piece of erudite literature. It is the twelfth-century account of the defeat of a Prince Igor of Novgorod-Seversk at the hands of a Turkic tribe, the Cumans, whom the Russians call Polovtsy. The campaign is also known from two different chronicle accounts.[8] The *Tale* can therefore be dated, on internal evidence, between 1185, the date of Igor's departure, and 1187. The work has a clear political message: the need for cooperation among the Russian princes in the face of a Turkic menace. This patriotic appeal in the name of the Kievan state makes the work unique in the literature of the period. Although the *Tale* was written in prose, it is close in some of its phrasing to the *byliny* of its time, and it was probably influenced by folk lyrics as well. The *Igor Tale* is regarded as a composition that is deeply poetic, and it has even been the object of attempts to make it scan as verse.

The *Tale* is an impure epic in that it consists of narrative, argumentative, and lyrical parts. The title calls the work a *slovo,* a word that meant "speech" and also appeared in the titles of sermons. The author opens his work with a comment on his chosen genre: he does not intend to imitate the great singer of yore, Boyan, presumably a court singer. This Boyan was to be evoked with considerable reverence by romantic poets of the nineteenth century. His existence is unattested, however, elsewhere in Old Russian literature. There follows an account of the military events, after which come the political argument and, finally, the lyrical portion.

The unsuccessful military campaign is described in extremely ornate terms. An eclipse of the sun (somewhat displaced for this tale) precedes the departure of Igor, who is accompanied by his brother Vsevolod. After an initial victory, they sustain a defeat and Igor is captured. The narration shares stylistic traits with the *byliny*. The epithet "golden" marks the loyal Kievan faction: "he steps into his golden stirrup." The battle is not described, but is reported in terms of long and colorful metaphors from peasant life: "The black earth under the hooves was sown with bones and watered with blood; a harvest of sorrow came up over the Russian land"; or, elsewhere, "Here the brave Russians ended the feast: they plied the wedding guests with wine and themselves were laid low for the land of Russia." The narrative is interrupted, however, by a refrain, "seeking honor for themselves and glory for their prince," which has a somewhat more chivalric ring than the tone of the *byliny*. The *Tale* is truly differentiated from the *byliny* in that it is pathetic in the best sense: it is a solemn, elevated, and humorless work. Its narrative style, moreover, resembles that of the chronicle accounts.

The political exhortation is spoken by the reigning prince at Kiev, Sviatoslav. His practical message is equally ornate in the telling. He begins, in fact, with the relation of a prophetic dream, one of the many signs and omens in the work:

> Early this evening they were clothing me, he says, in a black shroud on a bed of
> yew, they poured for me blue wine mixed with sorrow, they dropped on my chest
> large pearls out of the empty quivers of pagan strangers.[9]

The prince's elegant style is undifferentiated from that of the author: "Then the great Sviatoslav let fall a golden word, mingled with tears, and he said, O my nephews, Igor and Vsevolod." Now Sviatoslav urges mutual respect among the overly independent princes at other cities, a cessation of their territorial quarrels, and a concerted military action. The speech concludes with epic comparisons. Legendary heroes are addressed, and appeals are made immediately afterward to the contemporary princes:

> You, bold Riurik, and David! Did your armies not swim through blood in their gilded helmets? Does your brave *druzhina* not roar like bison wounded by tempered sabres in an unknown field? Step, my Lords, into your golden stirrups, for the insult to these times, for the land of Rus, for the wounds of Igor, the bold son of Sviatoslav![10]

The political argument resembles chronicle accounts in its detailed allusions to the histories of princely families. And the insertion of verbatim oratory was in itself a feature of the chronicle style.

The aesthetic climax of the work is not in Sviatoslav's political harangue, but in a "lament" by Igor's wife, Iaroslavna. Her complaint is believed to derive from folk lyrics:

> On the Danube Iaroslavna's voice is heard, like an unknown cuckoo she cries early in the morning: "I shall fly," she says, "like a cuckoo along the Danube, I shall wet my beaver sleeve in the river Kayala, I shall wipe the prince's bloody wounds on his strong body."
>
> Iaroslavna laments early in the morning on the rampart of Putivl saying, "O Wind, Wind! Why, O Lord, do you blow so hard? Why do you carry the Huns' arrows on your light wings against the warriors of my beloved? Was it too little for you to blow on high beneath the clouds, rocking the ships on the blue sea? Why, O lord, did you scatter my happiness along the feather grass?"[11]

In further "stanzas" she addresses the sun and the river Dniepr. Iaroslavna's lament may also reflect a folk tradition of keening that was done by professionals who were always women. These laments were extemporaneous, unlike the lyrics, and had no fixed texts. The occasions for mourning were not only death, but also the recruiting of soldiers and other losses.

As the *Tale* concludes, the mood is artfully lifted to optimism. Igor escapes from captivity with the help of the forces of nature. The account is swift and jubilant, and the author ends the work in phrases close to the parting message of Sviatoslav's "golden word": "Long live the prince and the *druzhina,* who fight for the Christians against the pagan troops! Glory to the princes and to the *druzhina.* Amen."

The *Tale* is radically different from any other literature extant from Kievan times in that it is profoundly national in spirit. It is practically devoid of Christian sentiment. The first appearance of the word "Christians" is at the end, near the "amen" proper to the closing of a *slovo* in the sense of sermon. In general, the work extols a military sense of honor that is not Christian. It is also close to the world of nature in a way that is alien to early Christian literature, which usually called on nature only for allegories. In the *Igor Tale,* nature is prominent as a setting, but is even more important as the ultimate ideological framework for the events. Nature is sympathetic to the Russian cause and participates in the military occurrences. The eclipse of the sun at the beginning of the campaign is a warning to Igor; the trees and the grass droop in sorrow when he is defeated; the river Kayala wraps Igor in warm mists for his escape. Iaroslavna addresses the wind, the sun, the river as though they were pagan deities in charge of human events. In this context the many tropes in which man and nature are blended become especially convincing. The Russians are identified with falcons, and the Cumans with swans and jackdaws. Elsewhere, people are compared to wolves, ermines, ducks. These are rhetorical devices, but animals are also prominent in their own right throughout the work: the foxes watch and bark.

The *Igor Tale* also has a worldly sophistication beyond that of other works of Kievan literature. Literary allusions to the pagan Slavic pantheon appear throughout the narration. Lower embodiments of evil, called Div and Deva-Obida, both bird-like creatures, call out from the trees or dip their wings in the sea. The Slavs are identified as the "grandchildren of Dazhbog" (wind); Boyan is the "grandson of Veles" (sun). The author may have believed, as did some contemporaries, that pagan gods originated in the idealized remembrances of former rulers.[12] If so, he was a knowledgeable, learned person. His purview is cosmopolitan; he mentions foreign peoples more often than is common in other Kievan texts. He speaks of Gothic maidens in the Crimea (with Russian gold), Frankish steel, virgins on the Danube, as well as Greeks, Moravians, Germans, and Venetians.

In sum, the *Igor Tale* is unique and even puzzling in its farsighted political message, its extensive knowledge of history, its literary expertise, and its cosmopolitan grasp. The work was discovered by a collector of manuscripts, Count Aleksey Ivanovich Musin-Pushkin, and published in 1800. The copy he found apparently dated from the late fifteenth or early sixteenth century and was imperfect. The text of the *Tale* as published contained further distortions. The original was destroyed, along with an entire library and many other rare manuscripts, when Moscow was burned before the advancing troops of Napoleon. As a result, the text is irrevocably obscure in some places.

The claim has been made that the *Tale* is a forgery composed in the eighteenth century. In particular, it is said to have been adapted from a fourteenth-century military narrative called *Zadonshchina,* a work that records a victory over the Mongols, rather than a Russian defeat. The two texts are plainly related to each other, but the *Zadonshchina* is considered by most scholars to be the later one. The *Zadonshchina* is weak from the literary point of view and has never appealed to later poets. All attempts at verse scansion of the *Tale,* even of Iaroslavna's lament, have been rejected by scholars. The fact that *The Tale of Igor's Campaign* was not intended to be verse is, from the point of view of the history of Russian poetry, now beside the point. Precisely this work entered the popular mind as "poetic" and had a powerful influence on later poets, especially in romantic times. The *Tale* was translated into English by Vladimir Nabokov, but the West knows it primarily as *Prince Igor,* an opera by Borodin.

Another work of Old Russian literature, *The Supplication of Daniil the Prisoner,* while not regarded as poetic in itself, is thought to reflect a strain of folk poetry that is now lost. The *Supplication* is believed to owe much to the so-called declamatory verse (*govornyi stikh*) used by the *skomorokhi* for a tradition of comic storytelling. These "merry men" staged various kinds of performances, both with and without musical instruments. Their stories were sometimes termed "blasphemous," and they were often criticized or even banned by churchmen.

The Supplication of Daniil the Prisoner is in form a petition for patronage addressed to a prince from a courtier or would-be courtier. The form, however, is a pretext for a rambling discourse that is a display of wit. The *Supplication* was written not very long after *The Tale of Igor's Campaign,* in the early thirteenth century. But the later work is cynical in tone and often in substance. An opening appeal to the prince is characterized by exaggerated humility. The body of the work consists of mock advice to the prince and sarcastic comments. Almost all the statements are aphoristic: "If the clothes are beautiful, the words are honorable." Many of these comments and adages are quotations. Among their sources are the Bible, a book of proverbs called the *Collection of 1076,* the *Physiologus,* a translated bestiary, and the chronicles. The ornate language of the *Supplication* includes many literary allusions and striking figures of speech. Its form is so open-ended and the work was so popular that successive scribes added their own contributions to the adages, and now the work's original form cannot be reconstructed.

All the quotations in the *Supplication* are from written texts, but its cynical tone and abundant rhymes suggest the "declamatory verse" of the *skomorokhi.*[13] Its features were apparently a loosely rhythmic line, imaginative rhymes, and many parallel constructions: "For some people the town is Pereslavl, for me it is Woeslavl." This popular aspect of the work perhaps explains why it was copied and embellished with additional quotations.

Appanage Russia

The Mongols were not sedentary rulers, but their continuous presence during two and one-half centuries resulted in unprecedented destruction. The invasion meant for the Russians the loss of a central government and economic ruin. A decisive defeat was inflicted on them at the river Kalka in 1223; Kiev fell in 1240. Kiev and other towns were devastated and their populations decimated. An excessive tribute was demanded of the entire Russian territory. Yet the period of the "Tatar yoke" was characterized by nearly ceaseless feuding among the princes. The southern and western lands drifted away into the political sphere of Lithuania and Poland. They developed new ethnic identities separate from the Great Russian and emerged, respectively, as the Ukraine, with its capital at Kiev, and White Russia. The northwestern territory, whose leading city was Novgorod, was not physically devastated by the Mongols and leaned toward trade with the West. Novgorod participated in the Hanseatic League. But this area was weakened in its turn by battles with the Teutonic Knights, Livonian Knights, and Swedes. The eastern, Muscovite region entered a period of deep isolation and distrust of the West.

Literature was in decline during the thirteenth and fourteenth centuries. The subjugation of Russia by the Mongols was described in written narratives of the thirteenth century; some borrowed traits from the *byliny*. *The Tale of the Ruin of Riazan by Baty* is the story of the martyrdom of a Russian hero, Evpaty Kolovrat. *The Tale of the Destruction of the Russian Land* has been noted for its use of rhymes. Here is its beginning:

O, brightly bright and beautifully beautiful Russian land! You are astounding with many beauties: You are astounding with many lakes, with rivers and springs in hallowed places, with steep mountains, high hills, pure groves, wonderful fields, a variety of animals, innumerable birds, great cities, wonderful villages, abundant gardens, church buildings, dreadful princes, honorable boyars, many courtiers. You are full of everything, O Russian land, O Orthodox Christian faith![14]

This *Tale* is now extant only as a fragment found with *The Life of Aleksandr Nevsky*. Nevsky, who was a prince of Novgorod, is lauded in the *Life* as a hero both of this struggle against the Mongols and of the wars with the Teutonic Knights. He died in 1263.

Ballads apparently replaced the *byliny* during the appanage period as the most characteristic form of oral narrative.[15] The ballads were stories of individuals rather than heroes. The protagonists might be named or unnamed; the drama of their situation was the point of the song. In "The Robbers and a Sister" the brigands are about to do in an unknown girl in whom they suddenly recognize their only surviving sister. Stories of family conflicts, mistaken identity, and other errors are common. Many ballads are about violence done to the defenseless: children are destroyed at the hands of parents, or women by men, and wives may be unjustly slandered. The ballad form is thought to have arisen in the thirteenth and fourteenth centuries and to have waned during the seventeenth and eighteenth centuries. An early, and popular, example of the ballad is "Vasily and Sophia," in which the poison intended for a bride by her mother-in-law is shared by the young couple. The details of their burial will be familiar from ballads in English:

Vasily's coffin was gilded,
Sophia's coffin was painted.
Princes and boyars carried Vasily,
Beautiful maidens carried Sophia.
They buried Vasily on the right hand,
They buried Sophia on the left hand.
On Vasily's grave a golden willow grew,
On Sophia's grave a cypress tree.
Root grew together with root,
Switch intertwined with switch,
Leaf clung to leaf.[16]

A number of ballads depicted Russians held in captivity by Mongols. Women were shown as married to Muslims, or forced to live in harems or as servants. Some ballads apparently derived from *byliny,* and others were close in subject to the genre called historical song (*istoricheskaia pesnia*), which also arose during the Mongol period. In the fifteenth century, Orthodoxy came to be identified with Russian culture. The intensification of religious, pious sentiment within the culture was reflected in the appearance of ballads with religious subjects. The ballads of later centuries saw the development of the robber theme, however, and by the seventeenth century satirical ballads had begun to appear. Generally, the ballads are not as striking aesthetically as are the *byliny*. One reason is that the form entailed a great deal of progression by repetitions. Although the ballads gave rise to some literary imitations in the romantic era, they have never stimulated popular awareness to the same extent as the "drawn-out" songs or the *byliny*.

The Muscovite Period

During the fifteenth century, Moscow managed to throw off enough of the Mongol dominion to establish a new central government. The first decisive victory for the Russians had been won by a Muscovite prince, Dmitri Donskoy, at Kulikovo field in 1380. Moscow extended its influence over other regions partly through its economic aggressiveness. Ivan III was the first Grand Prince (from 1462), and Ivan the Terrible the first tsar (from 1547). By the sixteenth century, it would become clear that Moscow's political policy was to be the absolute rule of the autocrat, over the Church, over the other princes, and over all territories. The imposition of this harsh rule was the more feasible because the Russian land was still impoverished.

Russian culture was subjected in the fifteenth century to waves of fundamentalist religious movements, which tended to come from the West. Their essential impulse was opposition to a powerful and worldly Church, with its ownership of considerable wealth. Prominent among these groups were the Judaizers, who rejected the New Testament. The cultural life sanctioned by Moscow in the sixteenth century was little open to the West, deprived of some of its own scanty heritage, and arid. Compilations of legalistic state documents and Church literature were its major achievements. Literature came under strict state control. An unofficial doctrine arose that identified Moscow as the "Third Rome," since Constantinople had fallen to the Turks in 1453. Moscow was seen, despite Russia's poverty and deprivations, as the last bastion of true Christianity and the religious superior of a West that was little known. These convictions were to surface time and again throughout the future course of Russian literature, philosophy, and popular sentiment.

Religious culture had its own vitality at the popular level. By the sixteenth century, original songs had emerged from the liturgy. These began as lyrical passages that were inspired by moments of heightened emotion in illustrative stories. These extra sections, called "added verse" (*pribyl'nyi stikh*), were written into the Church services, although not as an essential part, and had musical notations. An example:

> If I had known, O soul,
> The vanity of this world,
> I would have ascended a high mountain,

And seen my coffin,
And I would have sighed and said:
O coffin, coffin, take me
Like a mother her child,
My coffin is my eternal home,
And worms are welcome guests.[17]

The inserted sections were rhythmic, in imitation of the hymns. In time, they left the service to travel on their own as anonymous songs. A literature of "repentance poetry" (*pokaiannyi stikh*) that developed from them was particularly popular in the seventeenth century among schismatics.

Notes

1. *Narodnye liricheskie pesni*, 2nd ed. (Leningrad: Sovetskii pisatel', 1962; Biblioteka poeta, Bol'shaia seriia), p. 81.

2. Ibid., pp. 320–21.

3. *Byliny*, 2nd ed. (Leningrad: Sovetskii pisatel', 1957; Biblioteka poeta, Bol'shaia seriia), p. 53.

4. Dmitri Obolensky, ed., *The Heritage of Russian Verse* (Bloomington: Indiana University Press, 1976), p. 24.

5. Ibid., p. 31.

6. A. M. Panchenko, "Istoki russkoi poezii," in *Russkaia sillabicheskaia poeziia XVII–XVIII v.v.*, 2nd ed., ed. V. P. Adrianova-Peretts (Leningrad: Sovetskii pisatel', 1970; Biblioteka poeta, Bol'shaia seriia), pp. 7–8.

7. A. M. Panchenko, "Knizhnaia poeziia drevnei Rusi," in *Istoriia russkoi poezii*, ed. B. P. Gorodetskii (Leningrad: Nauka, 1968), vol. 1, p. 27.

8. The *Igor Tale* is known from the Hypatian and Laurentian Chronicles. See Dmitrij Čiževskij, *History of Russian Literature from the Eleventh Century to the End of the Baroque* (The Hague: Mouton, 1963), p. 113.

9. Obolensky, *Heritage of Russian Verse*, p. 10.

10. Ibid., p. 13.

11. Ibid., p. 18.

12. Čiževskij, *History of Russian Literature from the Eleventh Century to the End of the Baroque*, p. 117.

13. Panchenko, "Knizhnaia poezii drevnei Rusi," p. 29.

14. N. K. Gudzii, *Khrestomatiia po drevnei russkoi literature XI–XVII vekov*, 7th ed. (Moscow: Gos. Uch-ped. Izd., 1962), p. 155.

15. A. M. Astakhova, ed., *Narodnye ballady*, 2nd ed. (Moscow and Leningrad: Sovetskii pisatel', 1963; Biblioteka poeta, Bol'shaia seriia).

16. Ibid., p. 50.

17. Panchenko, "Knizhnaia poeziia drevnei Rusi," p. 35.

2

Transition and the Baroque
(1598–1730)

Russian culture began to assume modern Europe an forms and to discard its medieval traits in the course of the seventeenth century. At the beginning of the century stands the Time of Troubles, a period of violent political events that included an interregnum and invasions by Poland and Sweden. The Muscovite regime was so shaken that it could not have endured without change. The Romanov dynasty, which was established after the turmoil in 1613, favored Western acculturation. The new tsars centralized the administration of the government and began to create a new landed aristocracy. The acquisition of Western ideas was considerably furthered by the return of the Ukraine, with Kiev, from the Polish-Lithuanian state during the seventeenth century. New currents within the Church brought the influence of Jesuit scholasticism and the Counter Reformation. A permanent schism between the new and the old resulted. A flood of translations from Western literature brought new genres, including medieval chivalric romances and tales, or short stories. Written traditions began to merge with folklore. Finally, Western poetry and drama appeared, brought by the Latin schools that had been founded in the Ukraine. A taste for the baroque was born.

The Climate for Change

The Time of Troubles (1598–1613) had complex causes, among which were economic straits, famine years, and the ending of Ivan the Terrible's family line. Civic disorders commenced with the reign of Boris Godunov. The interregnum that followed his death brought almost a score of pretenders to or near the throne, drastic political realignments, successive peasant uprisings, and the foreign incursions. Even before these upheavals, the boyars had contended with the monarch for power. Rival candidates for the throne were supported by the interventions of Poland, which hoped to Catholicize the nation, and Sweden. In 1610 Poland held Moscow, while Sweden occupied Novgorod. These disruptive events were to be the subject of a number of literary works in the nineteenth century. After the Romanov dynasty was established by the election of Mikhail in 1613, the power of the boyars was systematically supplanted by that of a lower service gentry. It was from this social class that almost all of Russia's authors were to come for the next 200 years or more. The process of administrative Westernization was to reach a high point in the reign of Peter the Great (1689–1725).

The return of the Ukraine, which was now a source of both scholasticism and popular literary currents, was gradual. During the sixteenth century, many peasant refugees from Great Russia had fled to the south. This new population gave rise to a Cossack ethnic group, which maintained itself thereafter as a military elite. In 1569 the Ukraine entered, together with Lithuania, into a union with Poland. An aggressive policy of Polonization was applied to the new lands; a Uniate church was founded, as were Latin schools. The Ukrainians began to feel oppressed as an ethnic minority. The Cossacks were able, through political and military actions, to facilitate the return of the territory to Russia. In 1654, they declared their own suzerainty to Moscow, and in 1667 the eastern part of the land, up to the Dniepr River, was, in fact, returned through an agreement with Poland. The restitution was completed in 1709, when Peter the Great won the west bank during one of his many conflicts with Sweden. Despite their ethnic and patriotic loyalties, the educated members of the Ukrainian population did not relinquish the cultural advantages of their Western schooling; Latin was retained, and with it Western literary traditions and some Jesuit influence.

The official culture of Russia continued to be dominated by the Church throughout the seventeenth century. Secular powers were interlocked with those of the Church hierarchy. Under the early Romanov tsars, the centuries-old proscription of the *skomorokhi* was finally enforced. The players were suppressed as primitive, secular entertainers, while the pious new literature of the Latin schools was encouraged. In 1636, all private musical instruments were required to be forfeited, and they were burned.[1] The most energetic steps in remolding Russia were taken during the reign of Tsar Aleksey Mikhailovich (1645–1676), whose appellation was "most quiet." The reforms in Church ritual and doctrine that were to result in a permanent schism were introduced by Patriarch Nikon in the 1650s. In themselves, the reforms were only trivial corrections of small Russian deviations from Greek Orthodox canon: three fingers were to be used to make the sign of the cross, for example, instead of two. The changes were opposed with fanaticism, especially at the popular level. Some dissenters, in the spirit of the doctrine of Moscow as the Third Rome, feared that compliance would result in personal damnation. The lower priests tended to oppose the hierarchy as representatives of a worldly Church. Further, an attempt was made by Nikon to centralize Church authority at the expense of the parish priests. The religious community was implacably divided. The Archpriest Avvakum, a leader of the schismatics, wrote the most outstanding piece of seventeenth-century Russian literature, his *Life*, and he was executed. The struggle led to self-immolations by whole congregations. The Old Believers were not to disappear from Russian life; they receded to the forests and maintained a culture that became increasingly divorced from reality. In addition to their religious beliefs, they preserved customs and folklore that were to inspire some modern literature. Meanwhile, the religious controversies were of immediate and practical concern to the new poets, since many of them were clerics.

At the beginning of the seventeenth century, Russia was not prepared to acquire the literary fruits of the Renaissance. Both the humanistic currents that occupied Europe in the fifteenth century and the Reformation of the sixteenth were remote from Russian concerns. In the sixteenth century, Shakespeare brought English literature to its florescence, and in the seventeenth Milton wrote *Paradise Lost*. But Russia's literary needs were more elementary, and its borrowings were at first medieval, popular, or provincial in character. Medieval romances and tales were translated into Russian just before and after the turn of the seventeenth century. An Italian adventure romance called "Buovo d'Antona" became a Russian folk tale, "Bova the King's Son," and Aesop's fables appeared. In mid-century, a Printing Office was established, and somewhat more learned translations were published. Among them were Aristotle's *Physics* and other scientific and philosophical works, travel accounts, foreign chronicles, political tracts, and some practical handbooks. The major literary translations of the century included Ovid's *Metamorphoses* and, near the end, the great medieval story collections, *Speculum Magnum* and *Gesta Romanorum,* as well as picaresque novels with love plots. These translations had an effect on popular, anonymous literature in Russia, as well as on the more elegant works.

Oral Folk Genres

The folklore genres known since Kievan times survived intact and gave rise, at the same time, to newer forms. The historical song, which arose during the Tatar yoke in the fourteenth century, gained popularity at the expense of the older *byliny*.[2] The historical songs portrayed known figures and identifiable events, and they had greater pretensions to accuracy and realistic description. In the sixteenth century, some told of the military exploits associated with Ivan the Terrible. Others originated in the Cossack community. Although this colorful ethnic group governed itself outside territorial Russia, its songs described the defense of the Russian borders from Turks and Mongols. There were also songs about Ermak, the Cossack commander who was credited with the "conquest of Siberia" in the sixteenth century. The following song is about the appearance of the first false Dmitry in the Time of Troubles:

> There laments a small bird, a white quail:
> "Ah, young men, I must grieve,
> they want to set on fire the green oak,
> to destroy my poor nest,
> to slay my little children,
> to snare me, a mother quail."
> There laments in Moscow a tsar's daughter:

"Ah, young men, I must grieve,
for a traitor rides to Moscow,
Grisha Otrepev named, the Unfrocked."[3]

Other songs were called forth by the appearance of yet other contenders for the throne and by the will to defend the country from foreign invaders. The great peasant rebellion of 1670 to 1671 led by Stepan (Stenka) Razin, a Don Cossack, during the reign of Aleksey Mikhailovich was the subject of many songs. Razin never ceased to be a popular hero, and he was portrayed by the poets of later times, particularly by the iconoclastic avant-gardists of the twentieth century. Eighteenth-century historical songs describe the wars of Peter I in the north, especially his decisive defeat of Charles XII at Poltava, and, finally, the peasant rebellion led by Emelian Pugachev in 1773 to 1774.

The seventeenth century also saw the florescence of religious narratives, which were called ecclesiastical poems (*dukhovnye stikhi*).[4] The first recorded example was "The Lament of Adam Outside Eden" in the fifteenth century. The genre was derived from written literature that had descended to the folk level. Many songs were folk renderings of legends from the apocrypha or saints' lives.

Joseph's Lament

To whom shall I relate my grief,
To whom call out that he may weep?
To Thee alone, my Lord!
My Maker, my Creator,
Who giveth all good things.
I shall plead for mercy
With my entire strength.
Who would give me a well of tears?
I would cry both day and night,
I would weep for my sins,
I would pour tears forth from my eyes
Like the streams of Paradise.
I would quench the fire of Hell.
Who would give me a she-dove,
Prophetic in her speech?
To Jacob I would send it,
To my father Israel:
O Father, Father Jacob,
Holy man of the Israelites!
Shed tears unto the Lord
For your son Joseph's sake![5]

These ecclesiastical songs were sung by special singers who had no other trade and who were called "blind men" (*sleptsy*) or "pilgrims" (*kaleki*; from *caligae*, or "pilgrim's shoes"). They appeared in Russia, in White Russia, and in the Ukraine, where they had their own guild and schools. Individual songs tended to remain in the territory of their origin, however. In some areas the songs were sung to a musical instrument, but they had no meter; some lines ended in rhymes. These songs had their greatest success among the Old Believers in the seventeenth century.

Popular Literature

The intermingling of folk literature with written genres, some of which had recently been introduced from the West, led to a new kind of literature—anonymous works for a reading audience. This new type of literature is described as "democratic" (*demokraticheskii*) by Soviet scholars in order to distinguish it from the "folk" (*narodnyi*) genres. The new works bore the imprint of folk forms, but their substance was new. Among them was the anonymous tale, written to be enjoyed as fiction. Most tales were written in prose, but one, called *The Tale of Woe-Misfortune,* was composed in a verse form that was derived from the *byliny.* In spirit this *Tale* remains cautionary and medieval. (Some prose tales had a ribald character.) Its subject is the religious consequences for mankind of original sin, and it opens with the Biblical account of Adam and Eve and their expulsion from Eden. Its hero is a Russian youth, who remains a nameless everyman; he is tempted by drink into a life of revelry. His entire story is told with anonymity: he crosses "a river," comes to "a town," speaks with "good people" or with evil ones. His fate, which will bring about his downfall, is personified in the style of folk lyrics or ballads. Here are the words of that evil power, called "Woe-Misfortune," as it warns the youth:

> Do not boast, young man, of your good fortune,
> do not take pride in your riches.
> I, Woe, have had to do with people
> wiser than you are and richer,
> and I, Woe, outwitted them:
> I caused them great misfortune:
> they struggled to the death with me,
> in evil misfortune were they shamed,
> they could not escape me, Woe,
> but settled of themselves into their coffins,
> covered themselves then with earth to be rid of me forever,
> they were rid of their nakedness and barefootedness
> and I, Woe, departed from them,
> but misfortune stayed on their graves.[6]

This young man, however, escapes his fate by entering a monastery. In its religious nature, this *Tale* brings to mind the tradition of ecclesiastical narratives. The form, however, has the unmistakable traits of the *byliny:* a free line length, trochaic patterns with dactylic endings, and occasional rhymes resulting from parallel phrases. The vocabulary is sometimes that of the *byliny:* "And he drank green wine." Although this work shares features with folk literature, it was apparently the creation of one author and intended to be read rather than performed. Only one manuscript copy was found. The abstract nature of the story has prompted some Soviet scholars to see in it a parallel to the Faust legend in the West.

The seventeenth century is known for its rich vein of anonymous satires. In form they were parodies of nonliterary writings, such as the Church service or the alphabet. The first extant popular satire dates from the fifteenth century, but it was an isolated event. The satires of the seventeenth century gave expression to a new spirit of social cynicism that had appeared in Russian culture and that was accompanied by actual unrest. The parodies were written in a racy, aphoristic kind of language that sometimes allowed rhymes. Some had variant versions that featured a humorous, doggerel kind of verse. The "Tale of Ruff, Son of Ruff" (the ruff is a fish) is a well-known example. It satirizes corrupt legal practices, and its verse is a parody of the lawsuit. The Ruff is accused by the Bream of monopolizing the waters of Lake Rostov:

> If some fish he oppress,
> That fish will find no rest,
> Nor be able to live.
> A tsar's saber is sharp, and so are Ruff's bristles. . . .[7]

Through chicanery, the despotic Ruff is awarded the right to pursue his illegal advantages. The verse is marked by colloquial language, rhythmic but unmetered lines, and prominent rhymes. The same style of verse appeared in "The Cock and the Fox" and in "The Tale of the Priest Savva," which depicts a worthless, shamming lout who takes advantage of the priestly calling.

The verse form that appeared in the poetic variants of the satires had its own extraordinary development in the seventeenth century and beyond. It was called *raeshnyi* verse, a name that reflects its use in a folk theater where a narrator showed pictures (*raiki*). The pictures had once been religious and pious, but they had become grotesque and farcical, sometimes topical. The narrator's verse style was witty and aphoristic. Sharp contrasts and parallels were common, as well as conspicuous rhymes and exaggerated figures of speech. The form spread rapidly to various genres and eventually appeared in both elevated lyrics and hawker's cries. Some scholars believe that the style derives from none other than the declamatory verse of the *skomorokhi,* which once left its mark on *The Supplication of Daniil the Prisoner,* and that it was the normal folk form for spoken, as opposed to sung, lines.[8] *Raeshnyi* verse was adopted by the narrators of the puppet theater (*balagan*), which was introduced from the Ukraine in the eighteenth century. The lively verse form was used by Pushkin for his "Tale of the Priest and His Servant Balda," which is an imitation of popular poetry. Eventually, it even reappeared in avant-garde poetry of the twentieth century.

The "drawn-out" folk lyric ascended briefly to the level of written literature, in part because it offered a form in which to speak of love. The peasant genre was taken up in the towns and transformed into urban folklore. The poems were also collected, and apparently composed, by the provincial gentry. The evidence consists of discovered manuscripts in which what was simply recorded cannot always be distinguished from what was created. Here is a song that is thought to have been composed by Petr Andreevich Kvashnin, who lived at the end of the seventeenth century:

> O blow, stormy winds,
> blow, scatter my great grief and sorrow,
> blow, carry away my grief, sorrow
> to the dark forests,
> drown my sorrow there in deep waters
> weigh down my sorrow with yellow sand,
> give me peace if only for one, one short hour![9]

The literary songs left by Kvashnin and others are melancholy and picturesque. They share features with genuine folk songs: persons are blended with the phenomena of nature; some prepositions are repeated to achieve a rhythmic effect; there are parallel phrases; the lines are trochaic in tendency and have some dactylic endings. These seventeenth-century imitations of folk songs were done by naive authors. In the nineteenth century, the "drawn-out" songs were to foster a new genre—the literary folk song written by the best poets.

Ornate Prose

Literary taste in the seventeenth century called for the ornate, even before the introduction of the baroque. By the end of the sixteenth century, prose itself was expected to display the rhetorical devices that are now considered poetic. Metaphors, parallel structures, rhythmic cadences, and sometimes rhyme and near-rhyme appeared in all works with serious intentions. A *Tale* written by a monk, Avraamy Palitsyn, uses rhymes to punctuate a description of the violence inflicted by the Poles during the Time of Troubles. Here the besieged men at the Holy Trinity–St. Sergius Monastery reject a Polish offer of rewards for conversion to Catholicism in a high-flown letter:

> Be it known to your dark kingdom, you proud leaders Sapega and Ligovskoy and the rest of your *druzhina,* that in vain do you entice us, a Christian flock of Orthodox Christians. . . . What would it gain a man to love darkness more than light and to prefer the lie to truth instead of honor to dishonor and freedom to bitter slavery? How could we abandon our eternal, sacred, true Orthodox Christian faith of the Greek law. . . . But we would not take the wealth of all the world in exchange for the oath with which we kissed the cross. . . .[10]

Palitsyn's tale was, with other records of the events of the Time of Troubles, a step in the direction of modern history writing.

Several military tales of a later date describe how the Don Cossacks seized the Turkish fortress of Azov in 1637 and defended it from a Turkish attack in 1641. One variant of the story has traditionally been called the "poetic" version. Here is the beginning of the siege as it was reported to Tsar Mikhail by the Cossacks themselves:

> Where we had open steppes, there appeared in one hour, because of their many people, as though great and impenetrable dark forests. Because of their large

armies and the riding of their horses, our earth began to shake and quake near Azov; and because of their great weight the waters of our Don River stepped out onto its shores.[11]

The work has antecedents in both written and oral epic traditions. The tsar ordered the return of the fortress to the Turks.

Presyllabic Verse: The Baroque

When poetry in the Western tradition appeared in Russia during the Time of Troubles, it was called by the Ukrainian word *virshi* (from Polish *wiersz,* meaning "verse"). Among the early writers of *virshi* were nobles who were military men and members of the Church hierarchy. Their poems included panegyrics to the tsar or to princes, requests for patronage, theological disputes, and exhortations. In form, these poems were usually epistles or prayers, especially at first. They derived from the traditions observed at the Latin schools, where poetry was written as a part of the curriculum and as recreation. Authors of *virshi* also included commoners and civilians—for example, the employees at the Printing Office, which had a school. Their epistles included not only requests for patronage, but also advice to students and even notes on trivial domestic affairs. By the mid-seventeenth century, collections of these epistles came into being, and since the poems were letters, they also found their way into letter-writing handbooks. These early *virshi* had a free line length and were rhymed in couplets. Their rhymes were almost always feminine—that is, trochaic—because Polish words are stressed on the penultimate syllable. Acrostics and anagrams were a common feature. In composition, the *virshi* were distinguished by their intellectual nature as well as by their formal experimentation.

The baroque mentality that the *virshi* brought into Russian literature was in many ways in agreement with views already present in Old Russian literature. The new poems were shaped in nearly every statement by Christian piety and zeal. Strife and danger are rampant in the world they paint. Appeals for help, whether to heaven or to highly placed men, are common. Panegyric statements appear to be indispensible. An "Epistle" written by the boyar Semen Shakhovskoy to Prince Pozharsky opens with praise for the prince, although Shakhovskoy's immediate cause for writing was to request food for himself and his household during the Time of Troubles. He opens his poem with praise for Pozharsky's outstanding virtues, his courage in battle, his habits of prayer, and his generosity. The author's tribulations are said to be the means by which God aids mankind to attain salvation:

> It is in His mercy that the Lord our God sends on us these sorrows and attacks,
> To keep us all from falling, for our evil deeds, away from Him at last.[12]

Our own misfortunes are said to lead to acts of brotherly help and love, and so we are led to God. Instability and violence are accepted by Shakhovskoy as the way of the world. Shakhovskoy, who was an acknowledged master of *virshi,* served several contending factions during the Time of Troubles.

The importance of *virshi* in the political and religious conflicts of the times is demonstrated by the unhappy case of Ivan Khvorostinin, who was imprisoned and tortured for his writings. He was once a favorite of the first false Dmitry, and his contemporaries considered him to be an arrogant follower of Western manners. After his imprisonment in monasteries, he became an Orthodox monk. His celebrated "Prayer to Christ the Lord" is an attack on Catholicism. The poem opens with a call for faithfulness to the Orthodox Church despite the oppression of "tsars and unwise rulers."

> Abel the holy Eastern church we designate,
> But Cain we name the fatal Western church.[13]

Other clerical poets of *virshi* included the priest Ivan Nasedka, who had been on a diplomatic mission to Denmark and who warned against the menace of Lutheranism; the monk Avraamy, who was persecuted as a close friend of the leader of the Old Believers, Avvakum; and the monk Savvaty, who worked at the Printing Office and wrote exemplary epistles that were included in letter-writing handbooks. The lay poets included Ivan Katyrev-Rostovsky, who was personally related to a number of rivals for the throne and who lauded the emergence of Mikhail Romanov as tsar, and Timofey Akundinov, a low-born adventurer and the last of nineteen pretenders, who wrote a political "Declaration" to the Muscovite Embassy.

New baroque genres followed the appearance of epistles. Some poems were descriptions of heraldic signs in which the holders of those signs were flattered. These poems were printed in a reference work called the *Governmental Big Book,* also known as the *Royal Title Handbook.*[14] Religious songs in the form of *virshi* were written at the Voskresensky (New Jerusalem) Monastery outside Moscow, where the Patriarch Nikon founded a school for the cultivation of Western arts. The monks who were his followers became adept at *virshi* and wrote religious songs in imitation of Polish examples. They published collections of their songs and sometimes included pieces that were translated or adapted from Polish. A noted poet of Nikon's school was the monk German. He composed an Easter song that opens thus:

> O come, let all exalt
> Angelic joy today
> And mankind's joy. Let all
> Hear tidings of this day.
> Hallelujah, hallelujah, hallelujah.[15]

German was among the first to observe a constant number of syllables in each line. Icon painting and other graphic arts were also fostered by Nikon.

Syllabic Verse: Polotsky

A new wave of *virshi* whose novelty lay not so much in their substance as in their versification came to Russia in the second half of the seventeenth century. Their lines were based on the counting of syllables. This change, apparently so slight, would cause future generations to date the advent of Russian poetry itself from the introduction of syllabic verse. The new *virshi* acquired prestige by the example of a court poet, Simeon Polotsky, who was Russia's first poet of consequence. His was the first large body of poems known to belong to one individual poet. The concept of versification, which had come late to Russia, was poorly understood at first. At the turn of the seventeenth century, the idea had been introduced through Ukrainian and White Russian grammars. But in 1618, an authoritative grammar of Old Church Slavic, which was written by a Russian, Melety Smotritsky, described versification in Slavic poems as based on the same opposition of long and short syllables that is found in ancient Greek and Latin. By the second half of the seventeenth century, Russia had Polish handbooks for syllabic versification, however. In the new style of *virshi,* each line had a fixed number of syllables and was divided in two parts by a caesura. Rhymes continued to be in couplets and feminine.

Simeon Polotsky (1629–1680) was a monk and a White Russian, a refugee from his native Polotsk after it was invaded by Poles in 1661. Polotsky brought a panoply of new genres into Russian literature; his poetry was not dominated by epistles and panegyrics. He was the first poet to collect his works in separate volumes and see to their publication. His books include *The Garden of Many Flowers* (1678), which is an encyclopedia in verse; a complete Psalter in which the Old Church Slavic hymns are rendered in Russian syllabic poetry; and a *Rhythmologion* (1678) containing the panegyrics he wrote for occasions at court. The new style did not immediately replace the old-fashioned *virshi,* with their unfettered lines. The latter were still written throughout the century, but Polotsky set an example. He was to be followed by a remarkable series of court poets, most of them also monks, who wrote syllabic verse.

Polotsky was a dedicated educator. He had received his own schooling in Kiev at the Peter Mohila Academy, which was to send several other influential Western-izers to Moscow. Before fleeing to Russia in 1664 he had written panegyrics to Tsar Aleksey Mikhailovich. After his arrival, he taught Latin at the Zaikonospassky Monastery. He soon had other duties at court. He was tutor to the two royal heirs, Aleksey and then Fedor, as well as to other noble children at court. A high point of his career was an ideological debate with Avvakum, the spokesman of the schismatics. In his several activities, Polotsky's aim was to lift his chosen homeland out of its backward state of learning.

As an encyclopedia, *The Garden of Many Flowers* has a vastness of purpose that was in itself baroque. The attempt it makes to bring system and order into the world of knowledge was new as a form of Christian didacticism. The poems appear in alphabetical order by entry. They progress, for example, from Alexander to Augustus to Bdenie (Watchfulness), and later from Gordost' (Pride) to Gost' (Guest). The entries are diverse: they include human attributes, states of mind, and activities (Drunkenness); ancient and mythical rulers; the occupations (the merchant, the monk); women; the fauna that filled medieval bestiaries; and other miscellaneous topics. Some entries include several poems. Here is one of the early lyrics:

Worldly Goods Entice

The speechless fish is pleased by the food
upon the hook it is wont to seize.
Not knowing what lies concealed therein,
    poor fish is fooled.

For later on the fish will be torn,
the fisherman does draw in his hook,
and so in pain the fish will be caught
    and turned to food.

A like case holds in the world of men,
of those who think its goods are its bliss,
for when they strive to collect these well,
    they take the hook.

When in their hearts they rejoice for these,
in life's wide sea they swim with a hook,
which later on will carry them in,
    caught by the foe.

And at that time they most clearly see
how the world's goods are a lure for them,
but now they have no time to take ease,
    they are hell's food.[16]

The goal of comprehensiveness could scarcely be realized in this encyclopedia. The whole is characterized by a certain lack of logic. The categories of poems are ill-assorted, and the sequences among them mildly unexpected. The poems are diverse in style; by no means does an elevated tone prevail.

The Garden of Many Flowers has solemnity, humor, and not a few cautionary horror tales. Polotsky's best-known poem is perhaps "Merchantry," a satirical depiction of the seller's methods of chicanery. The world is a dangerous place in Polotsky's art, and this poem warns of only one of its practical pitfalls. The didactic case is presented in "The Official," which describes a model leader: he is a good shepherd, a rational Christian, a firm ruler, and a humble man. One of the general lessons of the volume is that the temptations of Satan and the flesh are everywhere at hand. Polotsky is severely intolerant of the senses and the passions, as we see from his cycle "The Proximity of Women." His attitude toward women is in itself unthinkingly medieval. Under the general title "The Woman," he relates a legend of guile and cruelty. Wealth is another temptation of which he frequently warns; in "Do Not Believe Good Fortune," he tells the story of Croesus.

There is a general ideology in Polotsky's work, and an inner coherence to this volume, although the separate poems might seem superficial. The one goal worthy of human endeavor, according to his poetry, is the achievement of Christian virtuousness and, eventually, salvation. In "Our Life Is Mist" all else is shown to be transient. His work illustrates how to be virtuous and proper; for example, in "Aid" brute elephants are more ready to help one another than are humans. Evil is often shown in his cautionary examples to be ridiculous or silly. Life's pitfalls are for him a motivation for constant didacticism. As in "The Goods of the World Entice," worldly circumstances can be illusory and unpredictable. Our attainments depend only partially on our own morality, and for the rest we must rely on God's mercy. Polotsky's real subjects were what were for him the commonplaces of human experience. If he had a tendency that set him apart from the baroque mentality, it was his instructor's zeal and energy; it ultimately belied the pessimistic philosophy of the baroque view. Polotsky believed in a world where change is possible, and to that extent he left medieval views behind. It was his vision that led to the foundation of a Slaviano-Greco-Latin Academy at the Zaikonospassky Monastery.

The poems in *The Garden of Many Flowers* go far toward illustrating a gamut of poetic genres. His shortest poems are mere couplets:

Rank

Pride and humility are not from station:
The great may be humble and the lowly proud.[17]

Some statements resound like folk adages. His longest poems are narratives, often of mythical or Biblical stories. "The Lion" is the tale of Androcles, and the animal is again shown to be superior to men. Contrasts and parallels are regular features of his mentality and of the poems' structure. Life is often contrasted with death. Polotsky's way of speaking to the reader is unwaveringly gracious and intelligent. Even natural horrors, as in "The Snake," can be depicted primly. Wit is an essential element of his style. His extended metaphors and balanced repetitions are engaging. Acrostics and other tricks of reading appear. A few poems are written so that the lines create an image; one forms a leaf. His studied arrangements and general ornateness were attempts to entertain as well as to instruct. His forms suggest a sunny mind. He was avuncular, not fanatic.

The Psalter is a collection of more majesty. For these hymns, he renders the magnificence of the divinity and of the universe. He praises God for His grace and mercy, and he voices the gratitude and supplications of man. He begins Psalm 100:

Your mercy and judgment, O Lord, I praise
As I walk my pure path, I sing, I know. . . .[18]

Adaptations from the psalms continued to play a role in Russian literature after the period of the baroque. In the eighteenth century, the hymns of Polotsky's Psalter became popular as set to music by the composer V. P. Titov. The collection also served as an example of stately poetry for the neoclassical poets. They also made adaptations from the psalms when they wanted to express philosophical views or even opinions about political causes and government. The psalms were suitably clouded in their message for controversial issues, and their effect was gained through their forthright vocabulary. Polotsky was also responsible for popularizing the creation of part songs which were called *kanty*. They were composed on religious subjects in the seventeenth century, but in the eighteenth their sphere was widened to include love and other themes.

Panegyric poems were to play a relatively large role in Russian baroque poetry. Polotsky provided with apparent good will the many laudatory poems and elegant "greetings" for people at court that his duties demanded. *The Russian Eagle* (1667) was composed to celebrate the naming of Tsar Aleksey Mikhailovich to the throne. Yet the laudatory poems were the last of his works that he attempted to collect and have printed before his death. The encomiums and advice that appear in his *Rhythmologion* are sanguine in a conventional way. He praises the rulers and the nation. The cautionary horrors of *The Garden of Many Flowers* are absent. The *Rhythmologion* consists of several large cycles that he called "booklets." The earliest was for Tsar Aleksey Mikhailovich on the birth of a son (1665); a "Threnody" was written on the death of the Tsaritsa Maria Ilinichna (1669); "The Last Voice to God . . . " marked the death of Aleksey Mikhailovich (1676); while "The Harmonious Gusle" was for the coronation of Fedor Alekseevich (1676). This poem from the last booklet is preceded by a hint that it reads "Rule many years" if begun at the center and read outward in all directions:

```
S r a e y y n y y e a r S
r a e y y n a n y y e a r
a e y y n a m a n y y e a
e y y n a m e m a n y y e
y y n a m e l e m a n y y
y n a m e l u l e m a n y
n a m e l u R u l e m a n
y n a m e l u l e m a n y
y y n a m e l e m a n y y
e y y n a m e m a n y y e
a e y y n a m e n y y e a
r a e y y n a n y y e a r
S r a e y y n y y e a r S 19
```

The *Rhythmologion* features elaborate verse pictures; two poems, one depicting a cross, the other a heart, are especially well known. Polotsky compared the addressees of his poems with figures from myths, from the Bible, and from the history of states and rulers. The disparate sources mingled indiscriminately in his verse, all serving the purposes of didacticism. His panegyrics are more elevated in style than his encyclopedic lyrics, but they are all of a piece in their advocacy of Christian virtue.

Polotsky also left, mostly in manuscript, school handbooks, two volumes of sermons, and two school dramas, *The Comedy of the Prodigal Son* and *The Tragedy of Nebuchadnezzar*, both written in syllabic verse. The comedy opens, after a prologue, with the good advice of the father. The epilogue states not only that youth should learn from age, but that older people should be good teachers. The tragedy shows in one act the story in which three young men are saved by an angel in the fiery furnace. Its moral is the efficacy of faith. Polotsky did not equal a Dante or a Chaucer, but his poems are the beginning of the continuous tradition of a national poetry.

Religious Controversies

The several poets of note who followed Polotsky were almost all clerical men who were also court poets. Most were Russians, but some had studied in the south or abroad. Their poetry was essentially religious, and even of secondary concern to them. The Church hierarchy was split between the Catholic sympathizers, or Latinizers, and proponents of Orthodoxy, or Grecophiles, and the conflicts impinged on the careers of all. Some took one side or the other; some hoped to avoid the issues. The Latinizers sought to increase the Church's power at the expense of the state. The linkage of theological parties with factions at court made life precarious. Nikon, who was ambitious for secular power, was deposed by a Council of 1666 to 1667 and replaced by Orthodox traditionalists.

Silvester Medvedev (1641–1691) was a pupil of Polotsky and later his editor, secretary, and friend. After his mentor's death, he assumed Polotsky's role at court. Medvedev was a diligent follower. The fundamental purpose of his poetry was that of Polotsky, the teaching of Christian virtue. He also showed an admiration for learning as such. Medvedev was less prolific than Polotsky, and his poems were less intellectual and brilliant in technique. He was also more directly motivated by court occasions and the religious calendar; his work was to a great extent congratulatory, or panegyric. His "Epitaph" for Polotsky enumerates his mentor's outstanding traits, and serves to teach his virtues as well:

> Wisdom was well kept by him, and justice,
>> Measure too observed with zeal, and courage.
> God endowed him with his many talents,
>> Adorned him with his mind without anger.[20]

Medvedev's patron was the Regent Sophia, whom he describes in his poems as an exemplary, wise, and benevolent ruler. One of the great political struggles of Medvedev's life was for the founding of the academy that Polotsky had envisioned. He believed, as he wrote in a poem addressed to Sophia, that the enlightenment taught by the academy would be the practice of Christian virtue. He was more narrowly scholastic than Polotsky in that he equated goodness and learning. Polotsky had understood, in "Reason," for example, that logic without faith is dangerous. Medvedev was a simpler man, who seldom rose to abstractions like faith and reason.

Medvedev's ordinary strengths as a poet were his steadfastness in his purpose and his occasional touches of humility. In "Virsha on Passion Saturday," where he depicts the sufferings of Christ, he rose to tragedy. Here is the lament of Mary:

> Light of my eyes, why did you set like a sun,
>> Why take me to grave and hell? Without you
> The sun is darkness, you were light in dark,
>> I lived with you here as though in heaven. . . .[21]

The poem ends with expressions of joy for the Christian salvation that has been won through the Resurrection. Precisely this victory of Christian humility over willful evil epitomizes Medvedev's message in his work as a whole. Medvedev lost his life in the rivalry between the Regent Sophia and the family of the young Peter I, the Naryshkins, who formed an alliance with a Grecophile, Patriarch Ioakhim. Medvedev was forced to flee to a monastery, where he lived for one year under the guard of loyal streltsy troops. Forced to take refuge in a second monastery, he was twice betrayed, finally charged with imaginary crimes in documents that were scarcely literate, and beheaded.

In the poetry of Karion Istomin (c. 1650s–1717/1722) can be seen a Christian didacticism without the aim to enlighten. The recurrent themes of his work are the incomprehensibility of the world and its destiny in the grave. Istomin was a protégé of Patriarch Ioakhim and a Greek instructor. Istomin it was who betrayed the location of his "uncle" Medvedev before his final capture and execution. As court poet, Istomin wrote panegyrics, epitaphs, epigrams to heraldic signs and icons, and spiritual lyrics. He professed a neutrality in politics, and served both Sophia and the Naryshkins. Istomin wrote an imitation in poetry of a depressing sixteenth-century work called the *Household Guide* (*Domostroy*). This didactic handbook, attributed to the Archpriest Silvester of Moscow, even advises brutalities to family members. Istomin's poem describes how the family must observe the customs of each day, from rising in the morning to retiring at night. He emphasizes piety, discipline, and cleanliness. The young people must pray:

> With prayers wash yourself, then dress
> Comb hair, wash mouth, and do not laugh. . . .[22]

Next they must bow to their parents and greet everyone in the house. He closes each stanza with a prescribed punishment for disobedience and with exhortations to reverential bowing.

Istomin's lyric poetry combines warnings about the transitory nature of the world with praise for religious rejoicing. In his poems, it is precisely the instability of the world that evokes awe. In "Verses to Remember Death with Greeting," he begins:

> I look on the sky—my mind knows not
> How I shall go there, but God calls me.[23]

The world that Polotsky and Medvedev depicted could be improved through learning, but in Istomin's verse earthly affairs remain static. Another subject of his spiritual lyrics is the passions. In "Verses Cautionary against Sinful Delusion," he discourages any admiration of fairness of face by describing how flesh decays. Istomin was also the author of sermons, a translator from Latin, and a historian. He served as director of the Printing Office and as secretary to Patriarch Adrian until 1700.

Ian Belobotsky, a Polish émigré to Russia, was the poet who best understood the effectiveness of art as spectacle. His long poem "Pentateugum" (five books) succeeds in part through its strikingly dramatic scenes of hell and the Last Judgment.

Belobotsky had lived and studied in France, Italy, Spain, and other Western countries for fifteen years before fleeing to Russia in 1681. He entered the Church hierarchy in Moscow, but Medvedev feared him as a rival for the directorship of the Slaviano-Greco-Latin Academy. In 1686 Belobotsky was forced to join a diplomatic mission to China as a translator of Latin texts; after six years spent in China, he returned in 1691. His major works were "A Short Dialogue between Mercy and Truth" (1685) and "Pentateugum" (1690s).

The "Pentateugum" stands out from the literature of its time as an exhilarating emotional experience. Its message, a warning against the dangers of spiritual lassitude and sin, is platitudinous enough. But Belobotsky stimulates the imagination. He does not exhort with didacticism; he frightens. The work is adapted, however, from the Latin poems of various German poets of the late sixteenth and early seventeenth centuries.[24] Belobotsky's five sections are the following: on death, on the Last Judgment, on the torments of hell, on the glory of the saints, and on the state of man. His imagery is unabashedly overpowering. The fires of hell, the melting of human bodies, and the gems that on earth were the signs of hedonism are typical examples. Here are some torments of the damned:

> Their neck's chain is of grass snakes; serpents near their throat a necklace.
> On their backs a filthy bast; over their whole bodies reptiles.
> Their feelings are now so much changed, which were by nature so pleasant.
> Like hard marble they've become, their desires are now for nothing.[25]

His repugnant scenes of hell are followed by descriptions of the cool, distant stars of the zodiac in his section on sainthood. His erudition is considerable. He makes many allusions to the figures of Greek mythology, particularly the events of the *Iliad,* and he closes the "Pentateugum" with references to the successive rulers of Rome as that capital approached irrevocable decline. The "Pentateugum" is bold and audacious in its differences from other Russian works of the time. Belobotsky also wrote a treatise on rhetoric. His many translations include several works by the Catalan philosopher Raymond Lully, including the *Ars Magna.*

Stephan Iavorsky (1658–1722) was a scholarly monk from Galicia. He was forced to serve, against his principles, as president of the Holy Synod that Peter I brought into being to replace the patriarchate. He wrote verse in Latin and Polish as well as in Russian; most of his poems are panegyrics. His language is quite archaic, but he expressed sentiments more freely than his predecessors. His "Emblemmata et Symbola" (1797) is an epitaph for the Metropolitan of Kiev and Galicia; it reflects affection as well as admiration. In the section of "emblems," the deceased metropolitan, Varlaam Iasinsky, speaks to inform us of his transfiguration into a better world. His images include Jacob's ladder, the dying moon, the eternal sun, and the ship at harbor. In "Verses on the Betrayal of Mazeppa," Iavorsky denounces the Cossack leader who deserted Peter to join Charles XII during Russia's wars with the Swedes. Russia speaks as a mother who has been wounded by a snake or by a wolf hiding in sheep's wool. Iavorsky's poems are written in a greatly purified Old Church Slavic. This archaic quality gives his epitaph to the metropolitan an airy remoteness from life, and his denunciation of Mazeppa a solemnity. Iavorsky also wrote sermons and theological works, some as polemics with the Old Believers, and others against the Protestants.

Feofan Prokopovich (1681–1736), a monk from Kiev, was an energetic supporter of Peter's subjugation of the Church to the secular government. In his hands, poetry advanced somewhat toward classical times. It became less an instrument for the salvation of the soul, and more nearly recognizable in its modern guise—as an artistic endeavor with its own honor to serve. Prokopovich began to write less on religious and philosophical topics. His motivations were often practical, especially when he wrote on current events and the politics of the day. While he was a committed author, in fact a propagandist, he avoided the appearance of didacticism in his poems. He is best known for a play called *Vladimir* (1705) written in syllabic verse. The priests who opposed Saint Vladimir's Christian baptism are satirized in it, but the play is an obvious reference to the resistance to Peter's reforms. Prokopovich had a long career, and the cultural life of the nation changed significantly in the meantime. He introduced new genres of poetry as well as new subjects. He also wrote handbooks on poetics and rhetoric.

Prokopovich wrote as a man prepared for combat. The expectation of strife runs like a thread through his early poetry. Fears seem to lie just under the surface of man's awareness, and God is his sole recourse. In "Epinicion" (1709), a monumental celebration of Peter's victory over Charles XII at Poltava, God is seen as quite literally and personally involved in the war on the side of the Russians. The fighting is described as enveloped in smoke and fire, as though a hell, and some details are chilling. Death is personified and stalks the field. The closing eulogy for the victory is elevated and rhetorical. The poem does anticipate newer intellectual times in that its local geography is real. An entirely different genre was introduced by Prokopovich in "The Penitent of Zaporozhe," where he expresses the wistful sentiments of a Cossack, presumably one who after Poltava wishes to renew his fealty to Russia.

In later years Prokopovich's poems were noticeably less militant, and he chose lighter genres. "The Shepherd Weeps in Long Bad Weather" is, in form, a simple pastoral, a lament for inclemency. It may be a veiled complaint about political difficulties that Prokopovich had during Anna's reign, but it is made to stand on its own:

> Shall I survive until good weather
> And lovely days.
> Will the kind mercy of clear heavens
> Appearance make?
> Light is not seen from any quarter
> All is foul grey.
> Hope there is none. O much defeated
> Is my good luck![26]

Even Prokopovich's panegyrics for Anna could assume a pleasant, songlike character. In "Away, depart, away" the passing of night and coming of day is a stylized metaphor for her ascension. New intellectual activities are mentioned by Prokopovich in some later poems. He praises a "satire" by an anonymous author, actually his protégé, Antiokh Kantemir, whose poetry would surpass his own. In other poems, Prokopovich speaks of the composition of "lexicons" and even of atheism. His "Thanksgiving from the servitors. . . ." expresses the gratitude of the inhabitants of an estate for the installing of a beer-making apparatus.

Prokopovich occasionally wrote adaptations of psalms and spiritual songs, a form that called for greater depth and an outlook that remained closer to the baroque. The following poem became a popular song in the eighteenth century:

> He who firmly relies on God
> 　　He looks unmoved on all that's wrong:
> Not the poor wrath of popular storm
> 　　Nor bestial tyrant frights him,
> Nor thunder frights that soars from clouds
> 　　Nor wind from south lands making noise
> When it comes full of mortal awe
> 　　To stir the Finno-Baltic waves.
> The world might fall in shattered parts
> 　　Not even then would this man start;
> A fierce blow bursts the flesh to dust,
> 　　But cannot even move the soul.
> O Lord, who are our one firm strength,
> 　　This circumstance is Yours alone:
> Without you we in vain take fright,
> 　　With You not fright itself brings fear.[27]

In "Each giving himself to service of the highest," which is an adaptation of Psalm 90, the adversities of man are symbolized by the asp, the basilisk, and the lion.

Prokopovich was not a great lyricist or poet, but he was a tasteful and intelligent one. He differed from the poets of Polotsky's generation in that he indulged in no piteous calling out to God. But the time had not yet come for that ordered universe in which classicists of the next era saw God as the supreme watchmaker. Prokopovich's language was at first studiously archaic, but it also changed with time and gradually became more contemporary. The traits of the baroque were to survive well into the classical era, however. Russians were not puristic in regard to literary schools. They tended rather to intermingle the currents of successive movements.

Notes

1. A. M. Panchenko, "Knizhnaia poeziia drevnei Rusi," in *Istoriia russkoi poezii*, ed. B. P. Gorodetskii (Leningrad: Nauka, 1968), vol. 1, p. 41.

2. *Narodnye istoricheskie pesni* (Leningrad: Sovetskii pisatel', 1962; Biblioteka poeta, Bol'shaia seriia).

3. *Demokraticheskaia poeziia XVII veka,* 2nd ed. (Moscow and Leningrad: Sovetskii pisatel', 1962; Biblioteka poeta, Bol'shaia seriia), p. 66.

4. P. Bessonov, *Kaleki perekhozhie,* 2 vols. (Moscow, 1861–1864; reprint, London: Gregg International Publishers, 1970).

5. Ibid., vol. 1, p. 187.

6. N. K. Gudzii, *Khrestomatiia po drevnei russkoi literature XI–XVII vekov*, 7th ed. (Moscow: Gos. Uch-ped. Izd., 1962), p. 392.

7. *Demokraticheskaia poeziia XVII veka*, p. 125.

8. V. P. Adrianova-Peretts and D. A. Likhachev, Introduction to *Demokraticheskaia poeziia XVII veka*, pp. 10–11.

9. *Demokraticheskaia poezii XVII veka*, p. 104.

10. Gudzii, *Khrestomatiia po drevnei russkoi literature XI–XVII vekov*, p. 330–31.

11. Ibid., p. 358.

12. V. P. Adrianova-Peretts, ed., *Russkaia sillabicheskaia poezii XVII–XVIII v.v.*, 2nd ed. (Leningrad: Sovetskii pisatel', 1970; Biblioteka poeta, Bol'shaia seriia), p. 46.

13. Ibid., p. 64.

14. Panchenko, "Knizhnaia poeziia drevnei Rusi," p. 45.

15. *Russkaia sillabicheskaia poezii XVII–XVIII v.v.*, p. 97.

16. Ibid., pp. 119–20.

17. Ibid., p. 137.

18. Ibid., p. 173.

19. Simeon Polotskii, *Izbrannye sochinenii* (Moscow and Leningrad: AN SSSR, 1953), p. 121.

20. *Russkaia sillabicheskaia poezii XVII–XVIII v.v.*, p. 188.

21. Ibid., p. 199.

22. Ibid., p. 206.

23. Ibid., p. 211.

24. The first four sections are adapted from the German poets M. Rader and I. Niess in the Polish translation of Z. Brudecki. The fifth is derived from a poem by Jacob Walde, which was known both in Latin and in German, besides being translated into Polish. See ibid., pp. 382–83.

25. Ibid., p. 233.

26. Ibid., p. 275.

27. Ibid., p. 286.

II

CLASSICISM

3

The Establishment of Classicism (1730–1762)

Peter I's victories in the Great Northern War with Sweden were followed by a century of imperial expansion and growing Russian political influence in Western Europe. His successors on the throne endeavored to stimulate a culture worthy of a European power. A Westernization of the gentry class had been initiated by Peter's reforms, and, inevitably, a reading public had appeared. Foreign literatures, especially French, were to exert an influence throughout the century. The reign of Empress Anna (1730–1740) brought an era of German ascendancy at court and in high positions. Secular writers replaced the literary clerics of the past during her rule, and the baroque began to be supplanted by classicism. The Russian aristocracy regained their control at court during the reign of Elizabeth I (1740–1762). Literature was now written in the awareness that a new national culture was in creation. A poet of European stature, Mikhail Lomonosov, appeared. Laudatory odes seemed to be in order, and a viable literary language was created from elements of Russian and Church Slavic. By mid-century, European Classicism—with its taste for rules and harmony, its veneration of antiquity, and its reliance on reason—was accepted among Russian authors.

The Desire to Catch Up

By the 1730s the new men in literature felt Western Europe to be their natural intellectual community. But its humanist traditions were as yet unfamiliar. The Russian bureaucratic administration had been modernized, as had the army and navy. Schools had been opened, translations fostered, and young Russian men sent abroad to study. Trade and industry were newly encouraged. The best writers were ready to imitate Horace and other Latin poets, as well as French writers of the seventeenth century, such as Nicolas Boileau. But it would be decades before Russia would be able to share in contemporary European culture. The French were at the threshold of the Enlightenment; Voltaire's *Lettres philosophiques* were published in 1734.

Empress Anna, who ruled in the 1730s, introduced conservative policies that countered the democratic tendencies of Peter's reforms, and her actions were resented by Peter's followers, among whom were literary men. A distinguished young author of Moldavian extraction, Antiokh Kantemir, ridiculed the new opponents of Western reforms in Horatian satires. He became the Russian ambassador to London and to Paris. The presence of Germans at court did not have much influence on Russian literature during Anna's reign because Russian writers had looked to France from the beginning. French poetry of the seventeenth century, from love songs to odes, was imitated by Vasily Trediakovsky, the first native Russian to be named a professor at the newly opened Academy of Sciences. These two poets put an end to the dominance of the Ukrainian baroque in Russian letters.[1]

Elizabeth I brought about a relaxation of the political climate and returned Russians to the court during the 1740s and 1750s. Patriotic feelings began to surge, while the interest in French culture intensified. An extraordinary florescence of panegyric odes appeared in Russia that had no real precedent in Western Europe. François de Malherbe and Boileau had written odes, but not in abundance. In contrast, Russian monarchs were virtually adulated in verse, and the nation itself was extravagantly praised. Meanwhile, Russian had to be established as a literary language, and a system of versification had to be chosen. Such technical matters had occupied French writers at the end of the sixteenth century and the beginning of the seventeenth. In both fields it was Lomonosov who found suitable solutions. He introduced a syllabo-tonic system of prosody based on German verse, and it was welcomed as symbolic of new times. A full repertory of classical genres was established within the next decade by a writer, Aleksandr Sumarokov, who assumed the role that Boileau had played in French literature with his *Art poétique* in 1674. Sumarokov was adept at love songs, fables, and the lighter genres of poetry. When these had made their appearance beside Kantemir's satires and the prevalent laudatory odes, it seemed that the classical movement had arrived and acquired an original, Russian, character. Classical taste still reigned in France, but in England the newer poetry of sentimentalism had already found acceptance; James Thomson's *The Seasons* appeared in 1730. In forty years sentimentalism would undermine the Enlightenment itself and appear in Russia as well.

Kantemir

Antiokh Kantemir (1708–1744) was the first modern author of note and a major pioneer of classicism. He was the first Russian author to turn directly to the writers of classical antiquity for guidance. His major poems, nine Horatian satires, were written in part to defend Peter's Westernizing governmental reforms. The poems had more than a narrow political aim, however; they were broadly philosophical. In praising the classical ideals of reason, moderation, and learning in them, Kantemir showed himself to be a forerunner of the Enlightenment. He also wrote Horatian odes and epistles, as well as fables and epigrams. His verse was written, however, in the old syllabic system of prosody.

Kantemir brought an immense erudition to his poems. His father, Dmitri Kantemir, was a former governor (*hospodar*) of Moldavia and the author of a history of the Ottoman Empire in Latin. The family came to Russia, as did other prominent Moldavians, in 1711 after an unsuccessful attempt by Peter I to wrest Moldavia from Turkish rule. Among Kantemir's early works was a Russian translation of Bernard de Fontenelle's *Entretiens sur le pluralité des mondes* (1686), a popular exposition of the Copernican system. His first satire brought him an acquaintance with Feofan Prokopovich and other supporters of Peter's policies. Under Empress Anna, Kantemir served as ambassador to England (1732–1738) and then to France (1738–1744), where he joined European intellectual circles that included Montesquieu. In Russia, however, his satires were denied publication during his lifetime; they first appeared in a French translation of 1749.

Kantemir's early satires consist of lampoons of some universal stereotypes, such as the hypocrite, the miser, the dandy, and the drunkard. He gave them Russian social positions, however, as well as dress and voice, in order to make them appear to impede Russian progress. Some were apparently drawn from life, a fact that brought him enemies. The Horatian satire was conceived as a rambling monologue or dialogue designed to entertain by its sarcasm while being instructive. Boileau had written Horatian satires in French. Kantemir's first satire, "On the Detractors of Learning. To My Mind" (1729 in its first version), leads off with a caricature of the nearly illiterate priest Criton, who opposes education in the name of superstitions. Religion is for this cleric only its empty shell—the ritual:

> "Your heresies and schisms are children of learning.
> He speaks the most nonsense who has fathomed the most;
> He loses religion who pores over volumes,"
> Sighs Criton, and grumbles, with his prayer beads in hand,
> And he pleads, holy soul, bitter tears in his eyes,
> That the evil be seen brought by science's seed.[2]

Young people, Criton laments, have been tempted to acquire knowledge through reading the Bible: "They reason, want to know the cause and why of all, / Extend but little faith to rank within the church." Worse, they question the Church's ownership of "estates and manses." A second caricature is of the provincial landowner who resists scientific agricultural advances; he is also greedy and stubborn. After him comes the carouser, always inebriated, always belching; he is the vulgar hedonist who pursues only pleasure. The dandy embraces new currents, but he sees in them mere haberdashery and haircuts; he prides himself on vanities. These few types were to be enduring targets of eighteenth-century Russian satires, in prose and drama as well as in verse. The title of the first satire is a reference to Boileau's ninth. Like all the others, this satire is furnished with footnotes in which Kantemir patiently explains ancient myths, European legends and history, the branches of modern science, his own opinions on fundamental matters, and all his figures of speech.

All of Kantemir's first five satires consist of picturesque verbal cartoons. The second satire, "On the Envy and Pride of Wicked Aristocrats," assails the arrogance of noble birth; Filaret, a lover of virtue, converses in it with Evgeny, the well-born. The third satire, "On the Variety of Human Passions," depicts a variety of unpleasant types, including the merchant obsessed with money, the prying gossip, the self-centered neighbor, and the pious fanatic. The hero of the fifth satire, "On Human Wickedness in General," is an engaging satyr who quits the great, but evil, city to return to a more innocent life in the forest; the poem is based on Boileau's Satire VIII. Kantemir's first five satires are extant in shorter, original, versions that were passed in manuscript.

The four later satires, written in England, are more abstract, and Kantemir's outlook is stated in more positive terms. "On Education" is a lament that men's efforts to bequeath riches to their children deprive them of examples of love and moral behavior. "On True Bliss" is an argument for moderation in desires. "On Shameless Impertinence" is reserved for remarks about authors. His ninth (probably seventh in order of composition), "On the State of this World," is addressed to the sun, the source of light or, allegorically, of enlightenment. Kantemir aimed to write in a new, bracing, and colloquial way, but his Russian was mixed with archaic forms and his syntax was sometimes ponderous. He preserved nearly intact the syllabic verse forms of the baroque poets who preceded him. All nine satires were published in Russian only in 1762.

A still clearer idea of Kantemir's philosophy can be had from his lesser poems. Religion and science went hand in hand for him because he viewed the divinity as the origin of a transcendent reason. "Against the Godless" is an argument that God resides in His physical creation—in the sun, moon, earth, rivers, and animals. God's care, as of the lilies of the field, is the theme of "On Reliance on God." The wisdom that has guided mankind through the ages of civilization is the subject of "In Praise of Science." Both heavenly Reason and earthly wisdom are extolled in a birthday ode (1731) for Empress Anna. Kantemir was a fighter: his fable "The Fire and the Wax Figure" depicts an artist who has failed to defend his creation from his enemies. His last epistle, "To My Verse," is the touching farewell of a sick man to the calling of literary labors. In these lesser poems he sometimes experimented with rhyme schemes. He was also a translator of Anacreon, Horace, and Boileau.

Kantemir opposed the introduction of metrical feet into Russian verse. When he encountered Vasily Trediakovsky's *New and Short Method for the Composition of Russian Verse* in Paris, he saw in it only an eccentric attempt to resurrect the quantitative system devised by Smotritsky in the seventeenth century. He answered in "Letter by Khariton Makentin to a Friend on the Composition of Russian Verse" (1744), suggesting that stresses be placed before the caesura and on the penultimate syllable, and he revised his own satires accordingly. Even communications about prosody were difficult at first for Russian poets.

Trediakovsky

The first Russian poet on whose work the imprint of French culture was strong was Vasily Trediakovsky (1703–1769). He was the court poet of Anna's reign, a translator of French literature, and a theoretician of Russian versification. He was a productive innovator. His love songs, for example, were Russia's first taste of French salon poetry, while his laudatory odes initiated a tradition. He opened the controversies that were to alter Russian prosody. It was his misfortune that he was surpassed as a poet and theoretician by Lomonosov. All too often Trediakovsky has been remembered as a stubborn ideologue.

Trediakovsky rose from humble beginnings to be a legislator of his nation's culture. Born the son of a priest, in Astrakhan, he bolted at age twenty from his ecclesiastical milieu and entered the Slaviano-Greco-Latin Academy in Moscow. Two years later he made his way to The Hague, where he lived with the Russian ambassador, and then to Paris, where he studied philosophy at the Sorbonne. On his return to Russia in 1730, he made a name with his translation of *Voyage à l'isle d'amour* (1663), a novel in the style of *les précieuses* by Paul Tallemant. Trediakovsky's *New and Short Method for the Composition of Russian Verse* appeared in 1735. He became a professor at the Academy of Sciences in 1745. His last literary work was a translation (1766) of Fénélon's *Les Aventures de Télémaque* (1699), a utopian novel in which despotism is satirized. The work was ridiculed at Catherine II's court, and Trediakovsky's reputation has never recovered.

Trediakovsky was generally attracted to the formative period of French classicism in the seventeenth century. His *Voyage to the Isle of Love* delighted the Russian public. It was the first book in Russian devoted almost entirely to love; it was also the first whose stylistic aim was merely graceful verse, without depth or realism. Tallemant's original is a frivolous allegory in prose and verse; it depicts love as a journey, which all must take, to a pastoral island of shepherds and shepherdesses. Its protagonist, a Thyrsis, is enslaved to his love for an Aminta until her infidelity; when freed from the tyranny of love, he quits the island. Trediakovsky's volume includes a number of his own poems. The first several are patriotic, including a "Song" on the coronation of Anna Ioannovna and an elegy on the death of Peter I. A "Song" expressing Trediakovsky's homesickness while abroad became quite popular. Here is the first stanza:

> Sad lines I open upon my flute,
> From countries distant I view my Russia.
> Desire so fills me throughout this day
> To dwell in spirit on all her virtues.

Most of the poems are in the rococo style of Tallemant. Half were written by Trediakovsky in French and printed with his own translations into Russian. Here is the first stanza of his "Petition to Amour":

> O halt, Amour, your arrows!
>   We are no longer whole,
>   But poisoned, if so sweetly,
> By shafts that come all golden
>   And bear desire from you;
>   We are to love submissive.

An important aim of the book was, as Trediakovsky stated in a preface, to replace Church Slavic with everyday Russian. Many songs, both by Tallemant and by Trediakovsky, were set to music and led an existence apart from the whole.

When Anna Ioannovna ascended the throne, Trediakovsky took the occasion to write the first proper laudatory odes in Russian; they were published in *Panegyrics* (1732). In the early seventeenth century, Malherbe had remade the Pindaric ode into a vehicle for the praise of monarchs; his later follower was Boileau. In a central ode Trediakovsky welcomed the future monarch to St. Petersburg; she is pictured as the protector of the sciences and the muses. Two years later, when the Russians had won a victory over the French fleet in the War of the Polish Succession (1733–1735), Trediakovsky wrote an even more influential laudatory piece, "Triumphal Ode on the Surrender of the City of Danzig . . ." (1734). His rhetorical extravagances set precedents. Praise for the monarch was henceforth to be hyperbolic:

> Of European skies and Asian,
> O lovely sun, magnificent!
> O autocrat above all Russia!
> Beneficient how many times!

Battle scenes were to be described in a tumultuous, epic style:

> Lightnings issue from dense explosives,
> And break asunder all that's known.
> You have no way to make resistance,
> And thunder cannot fail to come,
> No shield have you against its flashes.
> Earth sunders in abysses deep;
> A building soars into the ether,
> And many walls are broken down.

In an afterword entitled "Discussion of the Ode in General," Trediakovsky wrote a brief history of the ode, naming as his own models Boileau's ode on the taking of Namur and Prokopovich's Latin ode on the coronation of Peter II. Other odes of historic interest were the one he wrote for the coronation of Elizabeth in 1742 and a congratulatory piece on the fiftieth anniversary of the founding of St. Petersburg (1752). Trediakovsky also wrote spiritual odes, a kindred genre, which Boileau described as having its precedent in the psalms of David. Accordingly, Trediakovsky paraphrased ten psalms; other spiritual odes were based on Deuteronomy and on the writings of Avvakum, the Old Believer.

General technical problems such as versification and the introduction of a genre system were Trediakovsky's next concerns. In *New and Short Method for the Composition of Russian Verse,* he suggested that metrical feet, namely iambs and trochees, be observed in the writing of long verse lines. He argued that the syllabic system, being Polish, was unnatural for Russian. He favored trochees over iambs because he saw their prevalence in folklore. His views were opposed not only by Kantemir but also by the younger poets Lomonosov and Sumarokov, who argued for a fuller metrical system. After a three-sided controversy, the poets published

Three Odes (1744), in which each contributed his own adaptation of Psalm 144. Trediakovsky was the first to describe a complete genre system and to give examples of such forms as the sonnet, the rondo, the epistle, the elegy, the madrigal, and the epigram, but his efforts were ignored and virtually forgotten. His later theoretical works included "A Conversation . . . on Orthography" (1748), in which he proposed a phonetic system of writing; "View on the Origin of Poetry and Verse" (1752), in which he outlined a classical theory of literature; and "On Ancient, Middle, and New Russian Verse" (1755).

Trediakovsky set some precedents for Russian literature in his translations and adaptations from classical authors. These included his fifty-one fables based on those of Aesop. His predecessor had been Jean de la Fontaine, whose fables, also often inspired by Aesop, were avidly read at the end of the seventeenth century. Trediakovsky's fables were sometimes Russified; for example, Aesop's "The Man and the Satyr" became "The Wood Demon and the Peasant," and Trediakovsky omitted Aesop's moral lessons at the ends of his poems. In the eighteenth century, the fable was to have a renaissance in Europe, and especially among Russians. Trediakovsky introduced Horace's pastoral theme with his adaptation of the second epode, in which Horace praised his ancestral country home. Trediakovsky's title was "Strophes in Praise of Rural Life" (1752). The idealization of the bucolic life was to traverse Russian poetry of the eighteenth century and enter into the nineteenth-century novel as well.

The interests of Trediakovsky's later years were weighty, philosophical, and earnestly felt. In the 1750s he translated the complete Psalter—all the psalms of David—to demonstrate, as he said, the beauties of "God's language." However, the Holy Synod suspected that the work had deist leanings and banned its publication (after the first ten psalms, which now appear as spiritual odes). A twin project was a series of six philosophical epistles, collectively called *Theoptia* (1754), in which the physical world is interpreted as a proof of God. It was also banned by the Holy Synod, chiefly on the grounds that the universe was depicted according to the Copernican system.

The morality of government, however, was the most constant concern of Trediakovsky's later works. In 1751 he had published a translation of *Argenis* (1617), a historical novel in Latin by John Barclay, in which the absolute monarchy of France is satirized. This was a first step toward Trediakovsky's translation of Fénélon's *Les Aventures de Télémaque,* the novel that was to be disastrous to his reputation. In *Deidamia* (1755), a verse tragedy, he depicted a conflict between love and duty. The young Achilles, hidden by his mother, Thetis, on the island of Skyros in women's clothes to prevent him from entering the Trojan War, forsakes his love at the play's end to fulfill his obligation to join the Greek forces. By 1766 Trediakovsky had finished his *Telemachiad,* a verse translation of Fénélon's prose. Under the guidance of the wise Mentor, Telemachus, the son of Odysseus, seeks his wandering father after the Trojan War. Fénélon used the form to satirize the French monarchy under Louis XIV. Telemachus is advised, for example, to shun militarism and vainglory. This ideology was resented at Catherine's court, where Trediakovsky's work was ridiculed, ostensibly only for its style and meter. Trediakovsky's dactylo-trochaic hexameter was borrowed from the German poet Wilhelm Klopstock, who had invented it to imitate a Classical meter. Later poets have used the meter with success, but Trediakovsky became, and has remained, an object of derision.

Quite apart from his poetic activities, Trediakovsky translated extensive histories of Classical antiquity written by his former professor at the Sorbonne, Charles Rollin, and by his student Jean Baptiste Crevier. Between 1749 and 1762, he translated the ten-volume *Histoire ancienne* and the sixteen-volume *Histoire romaine* by Rollin. Between 1761 and 1767, he translated *Histoire des empéreurs romains* in four volumes by Crevier. All Trediakovsky's work in the fields of philosophy and government were intended to bring Russia abreast of contemporary thought abroad. He did not create any Russian masterpieces, but his work in its totality is distinguished by an innovative spirit and by a concern for wider perspectives.

Lomonosov

Mikhail Lomonosov (1711–1765) is often described as the father of Russian literature, and his contributions to science were equally imposing. He wrote the first Russian poems that deserve to be called great. His finest pieces were philosophical odes in the grand style. In his laudatory odes he combined a patriotic enthusiasm with contemporary European thought. He confronted the problems raised by the use of Russian as a literary language, and he brought the Russian system of versification into consonance with a European system. He was simultaneously a professor of chemistry at the Academy of Sciences and the unofficial court poet of Elizabeth's reign. He also wrote lighter lyrics and tragedies in verse.

Lomonosov devoted his prodigious creative energy to the furtherance of Russia, primarily in science but also in literature. He rose, like Trediakovsky, from a lower-class family. Born near Archangel into the family of a peasant fisherman, he too left home abruptly and entered the Slaviano-Greco-Latin Academy in Moscow; he had to pose as an impoverished gentleman's son, since peasants were excluded by rule. He was selected for further study in St. Petersburg and was sent, with other Russians, to learn mining at the universities at Marburg and Freiburg. He was impressed by the rationalist philosophy of his professor at Marburg, Christian von Wolff, who had been a student of Leibnitz. Lomonosov's "Letter on the Rules of Russian Versification" was sent from Freiburg in 1739 to the Academy of Sciences in St. Petersburg. In 1741 he was married in Marburg and returned to Russia. He became a professor of chemistry at the Academy in 1745. He was also active in the fields of geology, geography, astronomy, and the applied sciences; he founded a glass factory and learned the art of mosaics. He was instrumental in the founding of Moscow University in 1755. His language studies included the first Russian grammar (1755) and an influential stylistic essay on the use of Church Slavic and Russian (1757).

In his laudatory odes, all addressed to present or future monarchs, Lomonosov portrays Russia as a new, not an old, nation. The country is seen as a young giant whose resources are as yet unplumbed and whose spiritual capacities promise extraordinary achievements. Russia's rulers are heroes worthy of the vast nation. His first piece, "Ode . . . on the Seizure of Khotin," was sent with his rules for versification to the Academy of Sciences and has become famous as the first ode written in regular iambic feet by a Russian poet.[3] His typically vigorous style still recalls elements of the baroque, which he found to be in vogue in Germany. Lurid figures of speech suggest the horrors of conflict: "The darkest smoke will cover earth, / Moldavian mountains drown in blood." But Lomonosov was devoid of the religious dread characteristic of the baroque; the poem ends, as all his odes do, with optimism. He looks forward to peace and well-being: "The dreadful gaze of mighty Anna /Is quick to comfort those who ask."

Lomonosov usually selected peaceful occasions, such as anniversaries, birthdays, and name days, for his odes. Only three of the twenty odes he wrote between 1739 and 1769 celebrate military victories. His ode of 1747 for the anniversary of Elizabeth's ascension of the throne was one of his best and most typical. It opens with an address to Peace, under whose dominion Russia will flourish. He praises Peter I as a source of great energy, as he does in other odes, and Elizabeth as a guardian of her father's legacy. Russia is portrayed as vast in space and limitless in potential wealth from ores, forests, and animals.

> Your nation with its spacious lands
> Must offer you how many thanks!
> Regard your mountains, how they tower,
> Regard your meadowlands, how wide,
> Where Volga flows, the Ob, and Dniepr.
> The riches that therein now hide
> Through science will be brought to light,
> That you, beneficent, will guide.

Lomonosov's enormous faith in the efficacy of learning is also characteristic. The world itself is seen as not yet sufficiently comprehended, but subject to reason. In all, seven odes were devoted to anniversaries of Elizabeth's ascension of the throne, and half of all his odes are to her. He also wrote odes for Ivan VI, Peter III (once on the occasion of his wedding to Catherine, who was to depose him), and Grand Duke Paul.

Lomonosov's grandiloquent style was to be widely imitated. His verse is studded with elaborate figures of speech. His allusions to the mythic figures of Classical antiquity are frequent, as are references to the giants of European and Russian history. Through Lomonosov's example, the ten-line stanza employed by Boileau became standard for odes in Russian.

Lomonosov's most enduring poems are his sacred odes; in them he extolls the grandeur of nature and the power of God. The genre dated, like modern laudatory odes, from the seventeenth century; Malherbe had written a paraphrase of Psalm 146, and Boileau had cannonized the form in his *Art poétique*. In his youth Lomonosov had owned only three books, one of which was Simeon Polotsky's Psalter translated into Russian verse. (The others were Smotritsky's grammar and a book on mathematics.) Lomonosov's sacred odes included eight paraphrases of psalms, including Psalm 144, adapted for his competition with Trediakovsky and Sumarokov, and Psalm 146, a Russian favorite, on God's omnipotence and mercy.

His greatest poem is called "Ode Selected from Job, Chapters 38, 39, 40, and 41."
In the following passage God describes His works: the stars, the ocean, the storm,
the eagle, behemoth, and leviathan.

> See behemoth within the forests,
> I made him, too, when I made you.
> He tramples thorny bushes, harmless,
> When he desires, beneath his foot.
> His tendons lace, like ropes, his body,
> Then match with his your puny power.
> His ribs resemble molded bronze,
> Who could his dreadful horn remove?

In "Evening Meditation on God's Greatness on the Occasion of the Great Northern
Lights," Lomonosov combined scientific curiosity with religious awe:

> The day now hides its face from us;
> Dark night has blanketed the fields,
> Black shades ascend the sides of hills,
> And rays of light are bent away.
> A chasm of stars has opened up,
> The stars lack count, the chasm end.
>
> A grain of sand in ocean waves,
> A tiny spark in endless ice,
> A fine dust in a raging wind,
> A feather in a savage fire
> Am I, within this chasm sunk,
> I falter, staggered by my thought!
>
> From mouths of wise men we are told:
> There hosts of diverse worlds exist,
> And countless are the suns that burn,
> And tribes are there, and circling years,
> And nature's force is just the same
> For common glory unto God.
>
> But where, O nature, is your law?
> A dawn appears from midnight lands!
> Then does the sun place there his throne?
> Do icy seas cast up a fire?
> For lo, a cold flame covers us!
> For lo, day came at night to earth!
>
> O tell us, ye whose rapid glance
> Can pierce the book of perfect truth,
> For whom the smallest sign in things
> Reveals the system of the whole,
> Ye know the paths that planets take,
> Then say, what's this that makes us start?

What brings clear rays to wave at night?
What lights a slender fire on high?
Why lightnings without stormy clouds
That from the earth at zenith strike?
How can it be in winter's midst
That icy steam gave birth to fire?

Thick fog and water fight out there,
Or solar rays do shine, but bent
By passing through dense air to us,
Or peaks of massive mountains burn,
Or out at sea the zephyr ceased,
And waves to ether smoothly rise.

And if our answer's full of doubt
About what lies at nearest hand,
Then say, how wide's the universe?
And what's beyond our smallest stars?
Is creatures' end to you unknown?
Then say, is He who made them great?

The poem has proved to be his most popular. A twin piece to this poem is "Morning Meditation on God's Greatness."

Lomonosov's most effective essays on the literary language were terse. His "Letter on the Rules of Russian Versification" outlines in a mere ten pages a metrical system that is still in use, with few changes. Taking German prosody as his model, he described the use of iambs, trochees, anapests, and dactyls. His proposal, which the Academy of Sciences received in 1739, was more sweeping and more rigorous than Trediakovsky's had been, and the ensuing controversy was brief.

Lomonosov's longer treatises had less direct impact on literature, but his penetrating theoretical mentality is evident in them. His rhetoric, *Short Handbook on Eloquence* (1745), opens with a discussion of the question What is an idea? and the work is in part an epistemology. His *Russian Grammar* (1757) begins with a linguistic introduction, "On Human Speech in General."

He outlined a useful reconciliation between Church Slavic and Russian in a preface to his collected works. The essay, "Introduction on the Use of Church Books in the Russian Language" (1757), proposes that some Church Slavic words be retained in elevated styles of Russian for the sake of solemnity. Classical doctrine usually called for three stylistic levels—high, middle, and low—to each of which certain genres were assigned. Odes were to be written in the highest style, epistles in a middle style, and comedies in a lowly style. Lomonosov divided Church Slavic and Russian words into five layers of formality and prescribed their blending to achieve the three styles. His own practice went far toward culling out a welter of foreign words that had become fashionable in Russian.

Lomonosov's concerns in the lesser genres were essentially the same as those in his grand odes, but his style was, indeed, pleasantly varied according to his purpose. Akin to his odes is an idyll called "Polidor" (1750), written to honor Kiril Razumovsky when he was named hetman of the Ukraine; the poem features Calliope, the muse of epic poetry. "Letter on the Use of Glass" (1751) is a veritable treatise in verse, an apologia for glass from the point of view of an appreciative scientist. The poem opens with a mythic image: Ocean gave birth to glass in volcanic action. Glass has moral advantages; it has not fostered greed, as has gold, or caused atrocities like those of the *conquistadores*. The possessors of glass— Prometheus, for example, or the later students of astronomy—have been unjustly persecuted by bigots. Here Lomonosov boldly defends the Copernican system and celebrates the circumnavigation of the globe. The telescope, he says, reveals not only the heavens but God, while through microscopes we see all His otherwise invisible creatures. As a verse letter addressed to Ivan Shuvalov, the rector of Moscow University, the poem is in the middle style. Other poems are satirical or amusing, and are written in a wholly unpretentious style. "Hymn to the Beard" (1757) is a famous spoof of reactionary clerics; it was written when the Holy Synod had banned a translation of Alexander Pope's "Essay on Man" (1734).

The role of art occupied a number of eighteenth-century poets. Lomonosov was the first of several Russians to paraphrase Horace's "Exegi monumentum" (Book 3, ode 13), a poem in which the Latin poet celebrates poetry and his own contribution to its history. In "Dialogue with Anacreon" (1756–1761) Lomonosov explained his differences from the Greek epicurean poet of light verse; his own grand style, Lomonosov said, reflected his patriotic aims.

Lomonosov's light style can be seen, however, in "Verses Composed on the Road to Peterhof in 1761," in which he envies the freedom of the lowly cricket: "O cricket by the road, are you not blest! / How much more happiness have you than men." The poem's concluding lines:

> An angel in the flesh, or no, but air!
> You hop and sing, are free, and have no care.
> All you survey is yours, home's everywhere.
> You no petitions bring, and no debts pay.

Peterhof was the royal palace where Lomonosov went to present his own petitions.

His duties as court poet led him to compose poems of the type called "inscriptions" (*nadpisi*) for special occasions. Some appeared on statues displayed in conjunction with fireworks at court festivities. Others simply marked lesser court events. Lomonosov also wrote translations and paraphrases of verse by Homer, Virgil, Ovid, Lucretius, Calpurnius, Martial, Juvenal, and others.

Lomonosov was the author of two tragedies in verse. *Tamira and Selim* concerns the defeat of the Tatar leader Mamai by Dmitri Donskoy in 1380; it incorporates a fictitious love story. *Demofont* is the tale of Theseus' son, who was blown off course while returning to Greece from the Trojan War.

To read Lomonosov's sacred odes is to forget that meters were once a matter of controversy and that words could be deliberately layered into three styles. His best poems retain their power. His laudatory odes have suffered the general fate of all odes; a reaction against the genre had set in by the early nineteenth century, and they have never regained the favor of the public. The appeal of Lomonosov's verse derives in part from a nearly constant enthusiasm, whose source was a faith in universal order and harmony, an inheritance from Leibnitz. Lomonosov's contribution is undiminished by the fact that his French contemporary Voltaire was about to disparage that optimism in *Candide* (1759). Lomonosov created a body of verse whose excellence was unprecedented in his own language, and he did so in the metrical system of Western Europe.

Sumarokov

Aleksandr Sumarokov (1718–1777) was the final lawgiver of Russian classicism, a vigilant defender of its rules. He was a purist who took on himself the role of a Boileau in the *Art poétique* (1674). He also tried to give every classical genre its legitimate place in Russian literature. In other respects he resembled Voltaire: he excelled in songs, satire, and verse tragedies. He was among the first Russians for whom literature was a primary career, although he also served as a military adjutant. To the extent that he was able, he sought to free literature, as a profession, from the influence of the court.

Sumarokov was the first of the many gentry authors who were to dominate literature throughout the nineteenth century. The son of a military officer, he was educated at the Cadet Corps school in St. Petersburg and served under General A. G. Razumovsky, a favorite of Elizabeth. His love songs first brought him popularity. In "Two Epistles . . . " (1747) he established himself as a literary legislator. As a playwright Sumarokov was so successful that a troupe of actors was brought from Yaroslavl to found a theater at the Cadet Corps school; Sumarokov served as its director from 1756 to 1761. In 1759 Sumarokov initiated a literary magazine, the *Industrious Bee,* in which he introduced Russia's first regular literary criticism. By the early 1760s, he was known for his fables, a form he used for satire. Having lost favor at court, he moved to Moscow in 1769, where he was impoverished in a dispute with the local commander. Some of the best younger writers considered themselves to be of his "school." His major collections of poetry during his lifetime included three volumes of *Fables* (1762–1769), *Miscellaneous Poems* (odes, elegies, eclogues, 1769), *Eclogues* (1769), and *Satires* (1774).

Sumarokov altered the grand style in which Lomonosov wrote odes. The younger poet favored the language of everyday. Sumarokov declined to be the court poet of any reign, but he was to write eleven secular odes in praise of military victories and benign eras of peace under Elizabeth. His first odes, written for Empress Anna in 1740, were reminiscent of Lomonosov's, but Sumarokov soon began to dispense with elaborate figures of speech and mythological allusions. His new style never rose to the ecstasy of high rhetoric, but it was more modern and it proved to be exemplary for future authors. His addressees included Elizabeth I, Catherine II, and Grand Duke Paul. But Sumarokov was increasingly critical of autocrats, and he gave ever less attention to laudatory odes.

Sumarokov's spiritual odes show him not to have had a philosophical mentality; they are cautionary and religious. Although original rather than adapted from Biblical texts, they take the form of prayers, admonitions, meditations, lamentations, and hymns. Their titles are indicative: "On the Vanity of Mankind," "The Hour of

Death," "Ode on Virtue." Only in "Hymn on God's Wisdom in the Sun" is nature seen as the mighty sign of a greater creator. The fourteen poems, written at the turn of the 1760s, are generally about sin and salvation, and their style is elevated and archaic.

The song was well established in Russia as a genre because it derived from folklore. Sumarokov added to this tradition the influence of elegant French salon poetry. His subject was usually an unhappy love. He learned emotional expansiveness from the "drawn-out" song. "Do not grieve, my love, for I do grieve" is close in spirit to folklore; it is the complaint of a woman who has been married against her will:

> Do not grieve, my love, for I do grieve,
> It has been so long since I saw you.
> Jealous is my man, he keeps me home;
> When I try the door he meets me there.

Sumarokov avoided the long parallels between humans and plants or animals that characterize the folk song, and his language was more refined. From the French tradition he took a playfulness and a capacity for irony that had no place in Russian love songs.

> O fly, my sighs, to her, whom I adore
> And paint for her my grief, relate my pain.
> Stay in her heart, assuage her haughty gaze
> And afterwards fly back again to me,
> But bring me only news that I desire.
> O, say that hope for love remains to me.
> My nature bids me sigh, but not for long—
> Another can be found, fair maids abound.

From the French songs he also took choruses, nonsense words, and other whimsical elements of composition. The song was not esteemed in classical doctrine, and Sumarokov, unfortunately, published only a few of his approximately 150 songs.

Like Trediakovsky, Sumarokov turned for authority to seventeenth-century French literature. His didactic poem on genres, written in imitation of Boileau's *Art poétique*, has a long title: "Two Epistles. The First Treating of the Russian Language, and the Second on Poetry" (1748). The first epistle is a plea that the Russian language be respected and developed carefully. He urged Russian writers to think clearly, translate skillfully, and use Church Slavic sparingly. (He did not mention Lomonosov's three styles.) In the second epistle he describes, as does Boileau in *Art poétique*, the appropriate use of all the classical genres. He emphasizes the song and the satire, genres already at home in Russian literature, and devotes less space to sonnets and other special forms which had yet to take hold in Russia. Sumarokov's genre distinctions proved somewhat precious for Russia. The spirit of genre divisions was caught by other Russian poets, but they were more concerned with larger modes, such as praise or satire. Twenty-six years later, Sumarokov collapsed his two verse epistles into an article in prose called "To Those Wishing to Write."

Tragedy, too, had reached its peak with Corneille and Racine in the seventeenth century. Sumarokov's nine verse tragedies were an integral part of his own development as a poet and of the evolution of drama in Russia. (He also wrote prose comedies.) Sumarokov discarded the baroque school drama and wrote the first proper plays according to classical canons. He observed the three unities and the custom of depicting high-born characters. His early successes were *Khorev* (1747), *Hamlet* (1748), and *Sinav and Truvor* (1750). His tragedies depict cruel tyrants and destructive passions and now seem overly didactic. He showed virtue triumphant, moreover, so that his tragedies have eccentric, happy endings. (His *Hamlet* obviously differs from Shakespeare's.) His plays are no longer staged. They seem stilted and unconvincing (tragedies were thought to require the most elevated style). *Dmitri the Pretender* (1771), however, deserves mention as being among the first of many Russian works to depict the Time of Troubles as a crucible of the nation. In his later years, Sumarokov fought the staging of new, tragicomic forms such as *la comédie larmoyante* and Diderot's *le drame*.

By the 1760s and 1770s Sumarokov's popularity was rather for genres based on satire, sarcasm, and criticism—the fable, poems he called "choruses," and Horatian satires. Sumarokov began to endow the fable, popular since La Fontaine, with a newer spirit of political and social commentary. Some of his more than sixty fables were based on Aesop and other fabulists such as Phaedrus (a first-century Roman), La Fontaine, and Christian Gellert (1715–1769), who wrote in German. Sumarokov told again such well-known stories as "The Fox and the Crow," in which the fox steals a cheese through flattery. Other fables were turned into lampoons of the corrupt lawyer, the venal judge, and other age-old professional stereotypes. One particularly popular fable, called "The Dummy" (1760), ridicules blind despotism; here are its opening lines:

> A so-and-so was chosen as a god:
> He had a head, he had two arms, and feet
> And form,
> A mind alone was lacking in the stick,
> And wooden was his little soul.
> He was an idol, simply put: a Dummy.

In "The Flea" (1769) the arrogance of the blooded aristocracy is the target:

> A flea raised up a haughty brow—
> It's noble blood he carries,
> Seeks a ranking military,
> "I'm worthy," he exclaims, "the blood in me's all noble."
> The answer he received: "What's that for noble fame?
> You need nobility of mind and noble judgments."

Sumarokov's language is thoroughly colloquial. His iambic lines of free length and arbitrary spacing were copied from the *vers libre* of La Fontaine, and all Russian fabulists followed his example.

The poems that Sumarokov called "choruses" were facetious satires, written with nonsense words and refrains, in 1762 and 1763. The most famous, "Second Chorus to a World Backwards" (1763), is a playful description of a utopia:

> And pride beyond the sea is banned,
> And flattery's not heard at all,
> And baseness there is never seen,
> And lies are quite against the law.

In his Horatian satires, most of which were written in the 1770s, he dispensed with veiled humor and made caustic observations on social customs, morality, and the state of literature. Sumarokov also wrote a number of small poems in the classical forms that embody wit—the epigram, the pseudo-epitaph, and the parody.

Sumarokov first developed certain classical genres devoted to the private emotions—the elegy, the idyll, and the eclogue. All were somewhat experimental in his hands. The elegy was ultimately to have an important role in Russian poetry, but Sumarokov's were still overly solemn and archaic, as is "On the Death of the Author's Sister E. P. Buturlina" (1759). Their heavy hexameter lines are more rigid than the four-foot lines of his odes. In Sumarokov's mind, idylls called for love stories in pastoral settings. His, begun in the 1750s, are also very elevated; "O tortuous thought, cease to rend me" (1755) is an indicative first line. High human tensions are contrasted with the innocence of nature. The eclogues, which he had begun writing by the 1760s, are frivolous, elegant, and rococo, however. They are also pastorals, but their shepherds and shepherdesses indulge in trivial loves; examples are "Doriza" (1768) and "Clarisa" (1768). The urbanity of these poems, as well as their touches of irony, would reappear in the lighter genres favored by future poets.

Finally, Sumarokov tried the forms that were as yet rare in Russia, including the sonnet, the rondo, the madrigal, the ballad, and the verse tale. He was also a translator of Corneille, Fénélon, Fontenelle, and others, including Paul Fleming, a German diplomat and poet who wrote sonnets in and about Moscow.

The virtue of Sumarokov's efforts was that Russian classicism began to seem "complete." Most of his work, however, has the mark of conventionality on it. He wrote well-made pieces, few of which are memorable. His love songs were innovative, but he is scarcely remembered now for any warmth of feeling. His black and white tragedies were too schematic. His unabashed assumption of the position of a Boileau in Russian literature gave him the dubious appeal of a schoolmaster. His fables and satires were important for their combative skepticism and caustic wit. They were to have the most influence on the course of Russian literature. His best followers, younger poets who professed their admiration for him, are all known, however, for one genre of which he left them no examples—the long narrative poem.

Notes

1. On the boundaries between the baroque and classicism, see John Bucsela, "The Problems of Baroque in Russian Literature," *Russian Review* 31, no. 3 (July 1972): 760–71;

and Harold B. Segel, "Baroque and Rococo in Eighteenth-Century Russian Literature," *Canadian Slavonic Papers* 15, no. 4 (December 1976): 556–65.

2. Antiokh Kantemir, *Sobranie sochinenii* (Leningrad: Sovetskii pisatel', 1956), p. 57. Because the works of Kantemir and other eighteenth-century poets are readily available, there will be no further citations to individual poems.

3. The first syllabo-tonic poems in Russian were written much earlier by Germans and Swedes in Russia. Johann Werner Paus wrote an iambic ode to Peter I in 1714. See Boris Unbegaun, *Russian Versification* (Oxford and London: Oxford University Press, 1956), p. 25.

4

The Enlightenment
(1762–1790)

The reign of Catherine the Great brought the most extensive territorial gains of the century, but it also saw signs of widespread unrest and the formation of a liberal intelligentsia. At first the empress herself fostered the critical attitudes of the Enlightenment. She encouraged the anticipation of liberal reforms when she called the Legislative Commission in 1767 to reform the legal system, but the commission was dismissed little over a year later in the face of a Russo-Turkish War. In 1773 a peasant uprising, led by the Cossack Emelian Pugachev, spread over the Urals and vast areas in the south, as in medieval times. The revolt was suppressed in 1774, but public opinion was split thereafter between conservative and liberal tendencies. Freemasonry spread among the liberals. Catherine's fear of the new political and cultural trends led to her first efforts at containment. Russia gained the lands adjacent to the Black Sea in two wars with Turkey (1768–1774 and 1787–1792), and Polish territory was added through partitions. The best writers responded but little to these imperial successes, however, since they felt a greater concern about the tighter laws regulating serfdom.

The First Wave: The Sumarokov School

The Enlightenment was seen by Russians as a constructive intellectual movement; they were interested in improvements and progress. They ignored the notes of philosophical skepticism that had already been seen in France. Voltaire had published his satirical *Candide* in 1759. Diderot was airing doubts about the moral nature of man in *Le Neveu de Rameau* (1762), and Rousseau had warnings to make about the nature of civilization and the effects of learning. Catherine II corresponded with Voltaire, however, and she invited both Diderot and d'Alembert to Russia, the first to publish his *Encyclopédie* in St. Petersburg when it had been banned in France in 1759, and the second as tutor to the Grand Duke. In the early years of her rule, she "considered it her main mission to civilize Russia."[1] Catherine was eager to participate in the Enlightenment as an author. For her Legislative Commission she composed an *Instruction* (1767), which followed, if distantly, Montesquieu's *L'Esprit des lois* (1748). In 1769 she founded a mildly satirical magazine, *All Sorts and Sundries,* with which she hoped to engender a current of critical thought. But Russia's authors had already outstripped her in critical fervor. Four writers quickly founded satirical magazines. The most radical was Nikolay Novikov, whose *The Drone* (1769–1770) took up such serious issues as the institution of serfdom. In the course of an ensuing controversy with Catherine's magazine, he was forced to abandon *The Drone,* as well as three subsequent magazines. By 1774 (the end of the Pugachev Revolt) all satirical magazines had been suppressed. This series of events proved to be a minor watershed in Russian culture. Catherine's subsequent writings were intended for only private circles.

The young poets who formed the Sumarokov school were moderate in their aims and not associated with any program for practical action. They proposed to instill new attitudes through the practice of literature; they avoided writing laudatory odes, and they altered the genre system. They were brought together in the early 1760s by Mikhail Kheraskov, who by virtue of his administrative position at Moscow University was able to found several literary magazines. He was a prominent Freemason, and his activities reflected that order's pedagogical aims. Those writers who were more inclined toward politics were drawn to the circle of Nikita Panin, who was head of the Foreign Office from 1763 to 1781. The Sumarokov poets worked in accord among themselves, unlike the earlier generation of founding titans. The most effective among them were known for long verse tales, which appeared in the 1770s and 1780s. A ribald mock epic called *Elisey, or Bacchus Enraged* (1771) was published by Vasily Maikov. His narrow purpose was to satirize a new state liquor monopoly, but the spirit of defiance reflected in the work is much broader. After the suppression of the Pugachev Revolt the literary climate changed, and less critical works became the rule. A patriotic epic, *The Rossiad* (1779), was published by Kheraskov. He celebrated the fall of Kazan to Ivan the Terrible in 1552, but his "epic" included elements of the medieval romance. The most urbane work of the entire century was a verse tale about love, called *Dushenka* (1783), by Ippolit Bogdanovich. His story is based on the ancient legend about the marriage of Psyche and Cupid. The Sumarokov school was touched in some respects by the English school of sentimentalism. Samuel Richardson's *Pamela, or Virtue Rewarded* (1740) had set off a wave of new prose, and a sentimental novel, Fedor Emin's *Letters of Ernest and Doravra* (1766), had even appeared in Russia.

Maikov

The spirit of irreverence that informs his *Elisey, or Bacchus Enraged* is now remembered as the chief accomplishment of Vasily Maikov (1728–1778). His work was the first mock epic in Russian literature and the first poem to descend to low comedy and farce. Its liberating influence on subsequent authors continued to be felt into the nineteenth century. Maikov was also the author of fables, odes in the grand style, epistles, and dramatic works. He was a civil servant, but he devoted his chief efforts to literature. His father was a provincial landowner, an army officer, and patron of the actors' troupe at Yaroslavl. Maikov became acquainted with Sumarokov through members of the troupe after their move to St. Petersburg, where Maikov lived when attached to the Semenovsky Regiment of the Guards. He began to contribute to Kheraskov's literary magazines in 1762. His first literary success came with a satirical verse tale called *The Ombre Player* (1763), a lampoon of the aristocracy's pastime of gambling. His *Fables* appeared in 1766 and 1769. In 1767 he served as secretary to Catherine's Legislative Commission and met Novikov, to whose magazine *The Drone* he later contributed. His last major satirical work was *Elisey, or Bacchus Enraged* (1771). After the Pugachev Revolt his works tended to be morally instructive in the spirit of Freemasonry.

Maikov was an extremist, whatever his genre. *The Ombre Player* was a tale calling for humor, barbs, and racy language. His protagonist is the aristocrat Leander, who loses all his possessions, including his estate, through his bets. The gaming itself is described in grandiose, nearly epic terms. Maikov's fables reflect an Enlightenment mentality. Reason tends to be equated in them with virtue; vices and foibles seem to flow from either a lack of intelligence or faulty logic. About half the fables had their source in the works of earlier fabulists, including Aesop, Phaedrus, La Fontaine, the Dane Ludvig Holberg, Sumarokov, and Trediakovsky.

Maikov's ostensible targets in *Elisey, or Bacchus Enraged* are the wine merchants who implemented the monopoly in alcoholic beverages. His accusations extend, however, to all those who prey on society. His Elisey is at once a victim, a hapless peasant, and a rogue, a bellicose St. Petersburg coachman who is inspired to revenge by Bacchus. His epic feat will be the destruction of a wine cellar. The opening lines are as follows:

> I praise the clink of glass, I praise that special hero
> Who caused, when he was drunk, catastrophes most dreadful
> At Bacchus's behest, who went from inn to inn,
> Who fought and furnished drinks for waiters and for louts.

The opening is followed by an epic invocation to Paul Scarron, whose travesty of the *Aeneid,* called *Le Virgile travesti* (1659), is hailed here as the first mock epic. Maikov probably also knew Voltaire's *La Pucelle* (1755), a burlesque about Joan of Arc. Maikov's immediate predecessor in bawdy scenes was certainly the contemporary translator Ivan Barkov, whose original verse tales were thought too suggestive to be printed. Certain episodes in Maikov's works are distant travesties of the *Aeneid.* Some of these were probably spoofs of recent translations made by Catherine's court poet, Vasily Petrov, whom the Sumarokov school disdained as a tasteless writer and ambitious climber.

The spirit of *Elisey* arises to a great extent from sexual innuendo and descriptions of violence. Its hero is a drunkard, a lecher, and a brawler. He is dressed by Bacchus as a woman and locked in a correctional home for prostitutes, where he has an affair with its directress. In other episodes Elisey rescues his own wayward wife from her attackers, and spends a night with the wine merchant's wife. The strife seen between two villages appears to be a reference to the Trojan War. Elisey's destruction of the wine cellar is a climactic episode:

> In infamous defeat the cellar fell entire,
> Its phials all aboil, its bottles upside down.
> All vessel hoops were burst, the wine flowed out of vats,
> And not a drop was left that anyone could find,
> So then the end had come of that most noble feat.
> They came up from the vault, and left a pool of wine.

In a final battle, the merchants are pitted against the coachmen. Elisey is then sentenced by the Olympian gods to serve in the army as a penance. The fights are given a heroic cast, while the erotic anecdotes are presented as low comedy. The bawdy scenes can be compared with those in *The Fair Cook* by Maikov's contemporary, the satirist Mikhail Chulkov. Maikov also protested in this work against many forms of injustice, whether in laws, social conventions, or even literary canons. Zeus is made to inveigh against "unjust judges, thieves, and perfidious friends." The narrator holds up public fistfights and bear baiting to scorn. The cautionary thread traversing this work ties it to Maikov's odes, but *Elisey* was perceived as refreshing and taboo-lifting. The poem's overall tone is deliberately crass, although its verse form is the elevated Alexandrine, or iambic hexameter.

Maikov was one of the first to write odes that marked solemn occasions without being laudatory. He commemorated such historic events as the naming of deputies to the Legislative Commission, Russia's military victories over the Turks, and the concluding of peace treaties with the Ottoman Empire. One ode, called simply "War" (1773), describes the carnage of the Pugachev Revolt. His few sacred odes until that year had been paraphrases of psalms, but in "On the Last Judgment" (1773) he describes skeletons as gripped by fear while God's righteous anger is delivered in fire. Afterward Maikov turned to pietism; in "Happiness" (1778) he exhorts the reader to a life of humble virtue in a particularly ornate and solemn style. His epistles and occasional poems were also rhetorical in tone. Some are private in subject, while others express patriotic feelings on state and military occasions. Maikov was also the author of two tragedies in verse, *Agriopa* (1767), set in the Trojan War, and *Themistus and Hieronyma* (1772), set in fifteenth-century Constantinople. Both have complicated plots and lots of adventure. His last major piece was a pastoral comic opera, *A Country Holiday, or Virtue Crowned* (1777), in which relations between landowners and peasants are idealized.

Kheraskov

The Sumarokov school had an energetic leader in Mikhail Kheraskov (1733–1807). He was a tireless organizer in the service of the Enlightenment and literature. He wrote *The Rossiad* (1779) to fill a longstanding need for a national epic. (*The Tale of Igor's Campaign* would be discovered only in 1796.) His epic depicts the fall of the Khanate of Kazan to Ivan the Terrible in 1552 as the decisive battle in the liberation of Russia from the "Tatar yoke." Kheraskov also wrote lyric poems, numerous long narrative poems, plays, and novels. He was as prolific in prose as he was in poetry. Kheraskov was born to a nobleman of Wallachian extraction at Pereslavl, educated at the Cadet Corps school in St. Petersburg, where he knew Sumarokov, and began his literary career as a translator of articles from Diderot's *Encyclopédie*. His administrative post at Moscow University enabled him to direct the library, the press, and the theater; he founded and edited the literary magazines *Useful Entertainment* (1760–1762) and *Free Hours* (1763). Three collections of his verse appeared in 1762 and 1764. He was transferred to a position in St. Petersburg to lessen his effectiveness as a Freemason, but once there he organized the magazine *Evenings* (1772–1773), established a salon, and befriended Ivan Novikov. In 1779 he was returned to Moscow University as the rector; he rented the university press to Novikov, who published a stream of periodicals and books compatible with the benevolent goals of Freemasonry. In 1791 Kheraskov aided Nikolay Karamzin in the production of the first sentimental magazine in Russia, *The Moscow Journal*.

Kheraskov's works are generally informed by a Christian rationalism and gentle didacticism. He espoused the Enlightenment, but he understood "light" as a quality that would reveal and teach only what is good. He became a bridge from classical optimism to sentimental idealizing. The critical aspects of the Enlightenment were essentially alien to him. He skewed almost every genre he touched in the direction of an uplifting tendency. He first succeeded with short lyrics that he called "Anacreontics" and published under the title *New Odes* (1762). His poems breathe the atmosphere of rectitude and miss the bittersweet clasping of life that characterizes the genuine Anacreontic. Friendship and learning are extolled, as well as the enjoyment of beauty and rustic life. One Anacreontic is called "On Wisdom," and another is entitled "On the Importance of Poetry." In general, his Anacreontics are close in mentality to the sentimental prose *Idylls* (1756) of Salomon Gessner. Kheraskov's *Didactic Fables* (1764) are almost all original. Several protest class differences, as does "Two Dogs," in which the working dog is contrasted to the pet. His style is graphic and rather lacking in humor. Kheraskov once acknowledged his lack of talent for the comic in an epistle called "To the Muse of Satire." His *Didactic Odes* (1764) are similar in subject to his "Anacreontics," but are not stylized like pastorals. In "Well-being" he praises the pure heart; in "Riches" he condemns wealth; in other odes he lauds wisdom and disparages facial beauty.

Kheraskov's narrative poems are patriotic, with the exception of the first, "Fruits of Science" (1766). *The Battle of Chesme* (1771) celebrates in five cantos a Russian victory over the Turkish fleet in the Aegean Sea on June 26, 1770. He wanted to write an epic, but that genre called for a historical subject, not a current event. Kheraskov chose the fall of Kazan for *The Rossiad* because, as he explained in an introduction, he saw in it the beginning of a centralized government in Russia. He related for his readers the history of the epic genre beginning with the *Iliad*, and he named Voltaire's *La Henriade* (1728) as his immediate model. Henri IV (1553–1610) had brought order to France after a period of disruptive wars and had introduced religious tolerance through the Edict of Nantes in 1598. In *The Rossiad*, Ivan the Terrible is presented as an energetic young tsar with whom Peter I might be compared. Canto I opens thus:

I sing of Russia freed from her barbarian yoke,
Of Mongol reign in dust and arrogance laid low,
Of ancient states' campaigns, of bloody battles, feats,
Of Russia in ascent, the ruin of Kazan.
The start of peaceful years began at these times' end,
And like a radiant dawn shone forth in Russian lands.

Kheraskov also reminded his readers that Tasso's *Jerusalem Delivered* (1575) was an epic depiction of Christians set against Muslims. In *The Rossiad* the Russians are portrayed as heroic, while the Khanate of Kazan is the site of chivalric incidents typical of medieval romances. The Khanate's queen, Sumbeka, is seen in her intimate life and loves. Magic events occur, and folkloric figures, such as the evil sorcerer Kashchey, appear. But at the fall of Kazan, God comes to the aid of the Russians, while the Islamic forces are seen to have been allied with Satan. Here, in the twelfth canto, is the catastrophic event:

At once the ties to hell were loosed beneath the city,
The mountains and the fields were wrecked below and shaken,
A dreadful thunder struck, the earth was moved awry;
And all things shook, and rushed, the air itself grew thick.
The world, it seemed, was turned to chaos by its Lord.
A gloomy crack appeared whence issued smoke and fire,
And though the sky was clear, the sun was hid at day.

The meter is the solemn Alexandrine. The poem appeared in an era of anti-Turkish feeling, just before Catherine's seizure of the Crimea, the last land held by the descendants of the Golden Horde. Later, *The Rossiad* was seen as an embodiment of the outmoded, creaky machinery of classical literature. Kheraskov's subsequent narrative poems were yet more religious; they include *Vladimir Reborn* (1785), about the Christianization of Russia.

Kheraskov's verse plays and novels were also successful in their day. The first of his nine tragedies was *The Venetian Nun* (1758), a popular love story. The other tragedies depict the Christian Church or the Russian nation in struggles with foes; the most popular was *Moscow Delivered* (1798), about the Time of Troubles. His two classical comedies had contemporary subjects. His five sentimental dramas concern families in moral dilemmas. His three novels are utopian or symbolic works; *Cadmus and Harmony* (1786), for example, is a story of the progression of the soul to marriage with Harmony. Kheraskov's erudition was enormous. His earnest concern for culture was appreciated in his time, but his conception of moral issues was not deep, and eventually his patriotism ceased to be stirring.

Bogdanovich

The literary reputation of Ippolit Bogdanovich (1743–1803) now rests on his one verse tale, *Dushenka*, a Russian version of the classical legend about the marriage of Psyche and Cupid. Bogdanovich's tale has the grace and playfulness of French classical literature because his immediate predecessor was La Fontaine's *Les*

Amours de Psyche et de Cupidon (1669). The Russian word *dushenka* renders the
Greek word *psyche,* but it is also a play on words because it also means both "soul"
and "darling." Bogdanovich's tale was still admired for its light, elegant verse by
the poets of the golden age in the early nineteenth century. Bogdanovich was also
the author of lyric poems in various genres. He was a civil servant, a translator, and
an editor. Born into an impoverished gentry family in the Ukraine, he was brought
to Moscow at age ten to work. He introduced himself at age fifteen to Kheraskov,
who helped him through Moscow University. His first literary success was a translation (1763) of Voltaire's "Poème sur le désastre de Lisbonne en 1755," widely
considered the protest of a religious free thinker against universal evil. Bogdanovich
had political interests, joined the circle of Nikita Panin, and served as a translator in
the Foreign Office; he was secretary of the Russian legation in Dresden from 1766 to
1769. His lyric poems appeared in *The Lyre* (1773), and *Dushenka* brought fame in
1783. At the behest of Catherine II, he published in 1785 a *Collection of Russian
Proverbs.* Until 1795 he worked in the government archives.

Bogdanovich's unpretentious lyric *oeuvre* consists of a mere seventy-five
poems. He was among the first Russian poets of note to dispense with odes. Instead,
he wrote pastorals, paraphrases of psalms, epistles, fables, eclogues, epigrams,
Anacreontic odes, an idyll, and songs. His lyrics, although few, strike an original
note. They make an overall impression of sadness. His early poems include several
paraphrases of psalms, some of which are lamentations, while others are songs of
praise and gratitude. He was alone in writing candidly about money. In "Epistle"
(1760) he describes a miserly father who denies his son an education. In "A Fable"
(1761) he describes a poor ass who died while trying to reach grass that is greener—
he tried for the superfluous. Bogdanovich's love poems are so completely couched
in pastoral conventions as to seem impersonal. Yet several suggest a painful intensity of heat, as does "A Dangerous Occasion" (1763), where Amor is seen as a
blacksmith forging his own arrows. A fable called "The Honey Bees and a Bumble
Bee" (1783) apparently reflects his relationship to official circles; the Bumble Bee
values his freedom and declines to join a hive. Bogdanovich's lyrics have a coherence, but each one seems to be an occasional piece, as though he were not
concerned with forming an *oeuvre.*

Dushenka was somewhat eccentric in the context of the didacticism of Russian
classicism: it celebrates passion. The legend was first told, with a tongue-in-cheek
tone, by Lucius Apuleius in his prose novel *The Golden Ass* (A.D. 130). The tale is
not attested before Apuleius, and he may have invented it. Although the story is
inherently moral, it is always told with ironies and innuendoes. Psyche, or Dushenka, the fair youngest daughter of a Greek king, is destined to wed a rapacious
monster whose identity must remain unknown; in short, he is Amor. Prompted by
her wicked elder sisters, she approaches her sleeping husband, alleged to be a
serpent, with lamp and sword. She finds the god instead:

> It was—but who?—Amor himself,
> The lord, the god of all creation,
> To whom all cupids owe obeisance.
> He slept for fair, was nearly bare,

He lay, spread out across the bed
And covered by the finest gauze,
And it had slipped aside and down,
So only part concealed his frame.
His face was bent and turned aside,
His arms were open far and wide.
It seemed as though he sought in sleep
For Dushenka on every side.

Cast out into an earthly wilderness for her transgression, Dushenka must then perform the penitential tasks required by Venus. When reunited with Amor, she ascends to Olympus as a deity herself. The tale has always invited mythic interpretations. In Apuleius' time it was said by some to be an allegory of the rise above animal nature to Platonic intelligence. La Fontaine's version, written in prose and verse, has solemn parts. Bogdanovich's happy ending leaves the interpretation of the tale to the reader:

Amor and Dushenka became like to each other,
And all the gods on high joined them as one forever.
A daughter came along, like mother in good looks,
        But what to call her name
Is still unknown, alas, to those who write in Russian.
For some this daughter's name is Pleasure, simply put,
For others, it is Joy, or even Life, at last.
        So let each wise man have his way
And call her by the name he chooses.
For nature can't be changed by any name you give her.
Our reader knows himself, and so does all the world,
        What kind of issue must be born
        To Dushenka and to Amor.

Bogdanovich Russified his tale. His heroine is a spirited, slightly vain, curious, and loyal girl, who was declared by his audience to be entirely Russian. Her palatial surroundings when married are described so as to resemble the royal gardens of Tsarskoe Selo. There are touches of Russian folklore. Among her tasks, Dushenka must fetch "living and dead waters" guarded by the snake Zmey Gorynych, and she must bring golden apples from the garden of the Tsar-Maiden. The narrator's voice is confiding, experienced, and entertaining; it resembles the style of Ovid in his *Metamorphoses,* a work that was translated by Bogdanovich's friend Maikov. For his meter Bogdanovich chose the *vers libre* that Sumarokov had popularized in fables. The work was, like Alexander Pope's *Rape of the Lock* in English, the new norm for polished and whimsical elegance.

Crosscurrents

The mainstream of Russian poetry was defined by the work of the Sumarokov school; it had both allies and enemies. Among its lesser representatives was Aleksey

Rzhevsky (1737–1804), a poet who foreshadowed sentimentalism. He wrote only in genres calling for the middle style—elegies, stanzas (an Italian Renaissance form), light odes, fables, and epigrams. He began to popularize sadness; he wrote of hopeless loves and earthly vanities. He experimented with unusual forms, such as the sonnet and the madrigal, and with some graphic features of mannerism. His style eventually came to seem overwrought and mincing. Ivan Barkov (1731–1768), whose risqué works opened up the field of ribaldry, was a translator of Horace and Phaedrus. His original satires and parodies have survived in manuscript copies of the eighteenth and nineteenth centuries, but most have yet to be printed anywhere. The literary foe of the Sumarokov school, Vasily Petrov (1736–1799), wrote the laudatory odes that those poets were reluctant to write, and even called himself Catherine's "pocket poet." Almost all his poems were occasional pieces for important events at court; for example, he wrote a lament for the death of Grigory Potemkin in 1791.

The Critical Wave: The Lvov Circle

In the late 1770s and the 1780s, social criticism became much more visible as an element of Russian classicism. The skeptical disciples of Diderot appeared. Sentimental tendencies were more often seen, and preromantic notes were introduced. In England, James Macpherson's Ossianic work, *Fingal, an Ancient Epic Poem* (1761), was believed to be old Celtic poetry, and it was much imitated on the Continent. Russian writers were more widely affected by Rousseau's *Le Contrat social* (1762), which called for a new understanding of the relationship between peoples and their governments; man was said to be born free. The moral tendency of Russian literature remained intact and was even intensified, in part because of the opposition of intellectuals to Catherine's new conservative directions. Satires were common, as were all the classical genres conducive to it. The fable enjoyed a special vogue, and comedies replaced tragedies in popularity. One of the great works of the century was a comedy satirizing the provincial gentry—*The Minor* (1782) by Denis Fonvizin. The optimistic aspect of the Enlightenment had a stubborn adherent in Gavrila Derzhavin, the greatest poet of the century. He limited his criticism to courtiers and high-ranking officials, but he loosened the genre system.

The writers of the era were drawn into wider intellectual circles, which for the most part were liberal. Among the liveliest was the St. Petersburg salon of Nikolay Lvov (1751–1803), a prominent architect who was a dilettante in art and poetry; he was also talented in the fields of opera and the comic opera. His salon was intended for artists, but the writers who reached maturity at the end of the 1770s also met in his circle. Among them was the pessimistic fabulist Ivan Khemnitser, an admirer of both Diderot and Rousseau. The group also included Vasily Kapnist, a lyricist and playwright; he began his career with an accusatory epistle, but was to be a pioneer of the cult of melancholia. Derzhavin, the greatest, retained the profound spiritual optimism of the first builders of classicism in Russia, but it was he who was most susceptible to preromantic influence. Literary schools were of curiously little importance to these writers. They were eclectic and crossed the boundaries of Western schools.

Khemnitser

The fable became a vehicle for social satire and a more general cynicism in the hands of Ivan Khemnitser (1743–1784). His predecessor in fables, Sumarokov, had been gifted in the art of caustic observations, but the older poet had ridiculed in order to inspire improvement. Khemnitser's bitterness set him apart from all earlier fabulists. For Khemnitser, vices such as stupidity and greed were not the faults of a few, but the norm for society. The object of his chastisement was not the individual, but the social fabric and conventional wisdom. He was the philosophical follower of Diderot. He was also the author of now forgotten laudatory odes and Horatian satires, as well as of original poems in French and German. Khemnitser was well acquainted with Western literature by reason of his origin and his interests. Born near Astrakhan, he was the son of an army officer from Saxony. He enlisted illegally in the army at age thirteen and retired in 1769 to become a translator in St. Petersburg. In 1776 and 1777 he undertook, with Nikolay Lvov, a lengthy tour of Germany, France, and Holland to observe at first hand the state of Western art, literature, and the theater. His *Fables and Tales* in two volumes appeared in 1779 and 1782. In the latter year, he was named consul general in Smyrna, where he died of an illness in 1784.

Khemnitser wrote several laudatory odes before settling on satire as his specialty. He celebrated Russian victories on the field during the first Russo-Turkish War (1768–1774) and praised the armies themselves, rather than Catherine as monarch or the commanding generals. His style was ponderous. Popularity came in 1779 with two Horatian satires called "On Bad Judges" and "On the Shortcomings of Civil Service. . . ." Judges are seen to be venal or doltish, and the bureaucracy is said to be motivated by greed. The poems were too acrimonious to be published and were circulated in manuscript. His other satirical poems were written in diverse genres. Most are criticisms of the bureaucracy, but several are general denunciations of crooked dealing and miserliness. Khemnitser also wrote a number of short, humorous poems in the form of epigrams, epitaphs, and inscriptions.

Khemnitser's fables do not appear to flow from any coherent philosophical system, but seem instead to be motivated by an impatience with stupidity and greed. In form he was inspired by the Saxon fabulist Christian Gellert, a classical rationalist who had also been a source for Sumarokov. Like Gellert, Khemnitser combined ageless animal fables with narratives about humans in modern life; a number of his 105 anecdotes were adapted from Gellert's. In Khemnitser's fables the intelligent are made to suffer from the rule of the stupid. In "The Dying Father" the parent even leaves all his money to his intelligent son, knowing that he will need it more: "About your brother, said the father, do not fret, / For any fool can find the way / To happiness on earth." In "The Parrot" the bird, which can speak, nearly perishes when he falls into the hands of superstitious peasants. Stupidity in the strong can lead to arrogance and greed, thus, in "The Horse and the Donkey" the snooty horse must finally carry not only the donkey's burden, but the donkey's skin as well. In "A Wolf's Opinion" the predator is ridiculed for killing the sheep, which might otherwise have been periodically fleeced. Some of Khemnitser's most daring fables are about the lion, which as king of beasts is a rapacious, but in no way stupid, animal. In "The Lion's Share" the king explains by what rule he takes all:

> And then I'll also take the fourth part as my due
>   By right of who it is beats who,
> And if some one should reach to take the final part,
>   Well, that will be his farewell act.

In "Privilege" the lion has allowed the "freedom" of preying to some lesser beasts, but the clever fox understands that the king means to feed on these fattened subjects.

It was a virtue in Khemnitser that he never suggested acquiescence in evil. In some fables he counsels pride and independence. In "Freedom and Unfreedom" the wolf chooses to go hungry rather than pay the dog's price for his life of comfort. In "The Trap and the Bird" a bird at liberty can hear that a caged bird sings differently. Khemnitser wrote very few harmless tales such as that of the ant and the grasshopper (here "The Dragonfly"), known from Aesop. A favorite tale with Khemnitser's readers was "The Metaphysical Student," in which school learning is seen as the epitome of stupidity. A student, having fallen into a ditch and being thrown a rope, exclaims, "What is the nature of a rope?" Khemnitser's fables are not precisely funny, but they are knowing, ironic, amusing, and well written. Their casual language is worlds apart from his stilted Horatian satires. His verse form in the fables is the *vers libre* popularized by Sumarokov.

Kapnist

Vasily Kapnist (1758–1823) was a pessimistic author of melancholy lyrics in the sentimental vain. He was known in his own time for more notorious works—his bitter social commentary and his classical comedy, *A Case of Calumny* (1789). His treatment of traditional classical genres was high-handed; he altered them to accommodate either his critical tendency or his sentimentalism. He was also a celebrated translator of Horace.

Kapnist was a Ukrainian landowner who valued above all his place in literature and close ties with his literary colleagues. As a young man, he served in the Preobrazhensky Guards in St. Petersburg, where he joined the Lvov circle. In his "First and Last Satire" (1780) he assailed all highly placed "thieves"; the poem was widely appreciated for its political tendency, but it also necessitated his retirement to his estate in the Ukraine. A collection of his lyrics appeared in 1789. From 1799 to 1801, he served as director of the imperial theater in St. Petersburg. In the same period he assisted Nikolay Karamzin, the chief sentimentalist, in the publication of his periodicals. Kapnist was a brother-in-law of Derzhavin, as was Lvov.

Kapnist wrote two particularly outspoken expressions of social indignation. His "First and Last Satire" is a broadside in which he attacks corrupt judges, bribe takers in general, and the climbing authors of laudatory odes at court. His targets appear in caricatures, as in Kantemir, and his narrative tone is confiding and colloquial. He also wrote "Ode to Slavery" (1783) on the occasion of Catherine's arbitrary extension of Russian serfdom to the peasants of the Ukraine. The poem is an elevated and protracted lament; here Kapnist pictures the stunned suffering of the new serfs:

> In chains of slavery they sadden,
> Nor dare to overturn the yoke. . . .

In other "Solemn Odes" he made disparaging comments on the career of Catherine II. Thus "ode" began to signify any deeply felt statement, even an ironic one.

Kapnist continued to use the classical genres, the Horatian ode and the Anacreontic, but he poured into them his sentimental melancholia, his laments for loved ones, and graveyard meditations. His so-called "Didactic and Elegiac Odes" introduce new pessimistic currents. In "Ode on Hope" (1780), for example, he gives vent to a sadness that is said to be both causeless and implacable. "Ode on Happiness" (1792) shows that earthly life is a vale of tears alleviated only by faith and virtue. Other "odes" are laments for those who have died—a son, a beloved, a friend. His "Anacreontic Odes" retain an attentiveness to nature and a suggestion of rococo stylization, but they are not at all epicurean in substance. Among them is "On the Death of Julia" (1792), a lament for a dead daughter:

> Since night has brought its darkness,
> A stillness has spread round.
> Out of the forest rises
> A melancholy moon.

Elsewhere he wrote on friendship, the renunciation of vainglory, fate. His titles are indicative: "The Refuge of the Heart" (1806), "Idle Tears" (1806). His "Sacred Odes" are adaptations of psalms made at the turn of the nineteenth century. They are full of pathos and reminiscent of Lomonosov in style.

In the early nineteenth century, Kapnist became a literary conservative. His "Ode on the Death of Derzhavin" (1816) is written in the grand style of the mideighteenth century. His verse play, *A Case of Calumny*, is a lampoon in the spirit of his "First and Last Satire"; the plot is based on a lawsuit over land in which Kapnist and his family were parties. The portrayals are sharply drawn; the verse dialogues are crisp, witty, and effective. A verse tragedy, "Antigone" (1815), is a dramatization of the myth known from Sophocles. His later translations of Horace, made between 1814 and 1821, were closer to the original than his earlier transpositions, which had been paraphrases.

Derzhavin

One of Russia's greatest poets was Gavrila Derzhavin (1743–1816), who excelled in Lomonosov's genre, the ode. He was the true poet laureate of Catherine's age. He is remembered nevertheless as the poet who loved "truth" more than he loved "kings." He was a defender of justice and an independent spirit. He was an admirer and close follower of Horace, who did not consider the ode a laudatory form. Accordingly, Derzhavin made no distinction between laudatory odes and "Horatian" odes. The subject of Derzhavin's Horatian poems are diverse, from war and peace to love and dining. It was part of his greatness that he was at ease with various philosophical perspectives. He was a man of the Enlightenment. As for literary schools, he was open to the influence of all contemporary currents. He was the only major Russian poet to write a large body of original Anacreontics, in the authentic spirit of the genre.

The excellence of Derzhavin's poetry opened up high positions in the civil service for him. He was born in Kazan, the son of an impoverished provincial army officer. He was indifferently educated at a newly opened gymnasium and served as a common soldier in the Preobrazhensky Guards; he was the poet of his regiment. During the Pugachev Revolt, he acted as an intelligence officer and was rewarded with an estate. In St. Petersburg he joined the artistic salon of Nikolay Lvov; he began to take his poetry seriously, he said, from the year 1779. In 1783 his "Ode to the Wise Princess Felitsa" reached Catherine, to whom it was addressed, and his career in the civil service began. He was governor of Olonets and then of Tambov, but his administrative zeal brought him into conflict with his superiors; he was even tried by the Senate for insubordination and cleared in 1789. In 1791 he was appointed secretary to Catherine and in 1793, became a senator himself. He was later protected by Paul I, and in 1801 Alexander I named him a Minister of Justice. He retired in 1803 to his estate in the Novgorod region, Zvanka, where he wrote, primarily Anacreontics, and was esteemed by a grateful nation as its foremost writer.

Derzhavin was best known for his "laudatory" odes, but his praises were usually complemented by some unexpected contamination of genre. The conventions he flouted were those recently created by neoclassicism, however. He praised the worthy, he expressed his love for harmony, and he was aware of the inevitability of death. His talent for sustaining the grandiloquent style in odes was equal to Lomonosov's, but in all his better pieces Derzhavin introduced some surprising stylistic twists. He brought in elements of the elegiac, for example, or of the satirical; he included sentimental or preromantic imagery. In his first significant ode, "On the Death of Prince Meshchersky" (1779), he spoke in elegiac tones on the transience of epicurean delights. The poem has textual similarities both to Horace, the poet of *carpe diem,* and to Edward Young, the sentimentalist poet of death and the afterlife. In all, Derzhavin wrote about a dozen laudatory odes. His most famous innovations were the satirical touches he introduced in "Ode to the Wise Princess Felitsa." First, he praised the sovereign not with awe, but with easy, Horatian familiarity, and then he satirized her allegedly worthless courtiers, one of whom he pretended to be:

> But I, when I have slept til noontime,
> Drink coffee and enjoy a pipe,
> For I make holiday of weekdays.

My mind revolves in endless dreams:
I bring back captives from the Persians,
I turn my arrows on the Turkish,
Or if I'm sultan in my dream,
My glance would scare the universe.
But all at once I crave new clothes
And dash out for an ethnic shirt.

His name for Catherine, Felitsa, is a reference to a figure in Catherine's story "The Tale of Prince Khlor," written for the instruction of her grandson, the future Alexander I. She drew herself as the Khan's daughter, who sends Reason to accompany the hero on his search for the rose without thorns, or virtue. In Derzhavin's poem, Felitsa is a plain and forthright Oriental princess, while he is her lazy, card-sharping *murza*. Other poems in a "Felitsa" series followed. In "The Vision of the *Murza*" (1783) Derzhavin rejected a charge of sycophancy; in "A Portrait of Felitsa" (1789) he likened Catherine to the idealizations of art.

Derzhavin's most admired laudatory ode was "The Waterfall," which commemorates the death of Catherine's favorite, General Grigory Potemkin, in 1791. The poem opens with sentimental descriptions of an actual location—the cataract called Kivach on the Suna River near Olonets. The waterfall is seen to attract untamed animals—the wolf, the deer, the wild horse, and it serves throughout the poem as a symbol of earthly glory and its transient fate. The battle scenes take place in a visionary atmosphere that is reminiscent of Macpherson's Ossian poems. These scenes include the pale or the bloody moon, burning sunsets, and the flashes of lightning typical of preromanticism.

When shines a crimson-colored moon
Into a night of misty darkness,
And Danube River's murky waves
Do glint with blood, and through the forests
That circle Izmail winds howl,
And groans are heard—what thinks the Turk?

Some details, such as the worms that gnaw the dead, are baroque; so are the glints of color that are seen as gems in the falling water:

O Suna, how you sparkle high
In air—when lit by evenings' glow,
You seethe and scatter round a rain
Of sapphires and of purple flame.

The poem ends on a note of serenity when the river enters its placid lake: "O what a spectacle to see! How like the heavens are you now!" Derzhavin's associations are fluid and unpredictable.

His sacred odes are his finest, as was the case with Lomonosov. "To Rulers and Judges" (1880) is a paraphrase of Psalm 82, but it was immediately sensed to have a political significance.

Almighty God arose in judgment
On earthly idols in their sum.
'Til when, said He, will ye the wicked
And the unjust, 'til when, condone?

Your duty: guard the laws' observance,
Not shed your favor on the strong,
Nor widows, orphans, undefended,
To leave without your sheltering arm.

Your duty: innocents to rescue
From harm, give roof to those deprived,
Protect the weak from who is mighty,
To wrest the poor out of their chains.

They heed not! see not, are unknowing!
Their eyes are shaded by their gain:
The earth is shattered by malfeasance,
Injustice shakes the very skies.

O kings! I thought you gods in power,
With none above to be your judge,
But ye, as I, are prey to passions,
And ye, as I, will face life's fate.

And ye will likewise fall, no different
Than withered leaf falls from a tree!
And ye will likewise die, no different
Than your least slave when he does die!

Arise, O Lord! God of the righteous!
And hearken to the prayers they make:
O come, and judge, cast down the wicked,
And reign, the only king on earth!

Paraphrases of psalms were thereafter to be pressed into political use by a number of Russian poets.

Derzhavin's greatest poem is a sacred ode called "God" (1784); too long to reprint here, it expresses metaphysical wonderment, as had Lomonosov's paraphrase of excerpts from Job. Derzhavin's viewpoint is Christian, yet the poem also speaks for the eighteenth-century deist. The divinity is seen as the substance of the universe, of cosmic spaces, and of earthly creatures, large and small. The poet, not God, is speaking:

To dust I do decay in body,
In mind am I the lord of thunder.
I am a king—slave—worm—a god!
But if I be so full of wonder,
Whence came I then? No one can tell me,
Nor could I be were I alone.

Edward Young's *The Complaint, or Night Thoughts on Life, Death, and Immortality* (1745) has a similar passage. Derzhavin ends his poem with a humble expression of willingness to enter the stuff of the cosmos:

> They can no other way praise Thee
> Nor rise to share Thy spirit holy
> Than all diversity to enter,
> And weep their tears of gratitude.

This was the first Russian poem to be translated into Western languages.

Derzhavin's Horatian odes are characterized by his rough-hewn honesty and quickness of feeling. His observations are subtle, and his language is strong. He was courageous both in his criticism and in his praise. In "The Courtier" (1794) he assailed the vain, self-seeking, and decorated "donkey" of high rank; the poem hit its mark at the time, but is ageless in application. When the great general Aleksandr Suvorov had died out of favor at court, Derzhavin addressed his genuine sorrow to a pet bird and called his small poem "The Crossbill" (1880); it has outlived many laudatory odes. Derzhavin described his own odes in his paraphrase of Horace's "Exegi monumentum," which he called "The Monument" (1795). Where Horace boasted that he brought Greek meters into Latin, Derzhavin asserts, "I was the first who dared in Russian style diverting / The virtues to proclaim that our Felitsa has, / To chat of God as with a friend in heartfelt candor, / And tell the truth with smile when speaking up to kings." The poem has been understood by the Russian intelligentsia as a declaration of the independence of any poet from the rule of despots. Derzhavin's view of art was, in fact, nearly romantic; in lesser poems he held poetry to be divine in origin.

Derzhavin was the first to write memorable Russian poems celebrating the rustic home, and in other poems he was the first to depict impressive nature scenes. In "Invitation to Dinner" (1795) he offered his homespun hospitality in a genuine letter in verse. In "To Eugene, or Life at Zvanka" (1807) he enumerates the simple pursuits of the locality, which are fishing, walking, and serving home-grown meals. Now he describes hams, fish, and cabbages as having the colors of radiant gems. The ruling spirit at Zvanka is *carpe diem*. But at the end of the poem stands a sentimental depiction of the grave of the poet, about whom it will be said, "Here lived the singer of God, and of Felitsa." When Derzhavin described nature, he always added notes of human interest, as James Thomson had in *The Seasons*. "The Swallow" (1794) is airy and grand, but ends with a plaintive lament for his deceased first wife, the beloved Plenira of many poems. A series called "Winter," "Spring," "Summer," and "Autumn" (1803–1804) speaks of loneliness, plenty, and harvests. The poems called "The Cloud," "The Thunder," and "The Rainbow" (1806) resemble religious odes in their allusions to earthly tsars, God's omnipotence, and the covenant.

The Anacreontic was always a lighter form than the Horatian ode, but its characteristic theme, the transience of earthly pleasure, was congenial to Derzhavin in any genre. Many of his nearly 100 Anacreontics were paraphrases of translations published by Lvov in 1794. Most were written in his later years, and at Zvanka. "Nightingale in a Dream" (1795) is both well known and typical:

> I lay sleeping on a hillside,
> Nightingale, but heard your voice,
> Even in my deepest slumber
> It was singing in my soul:
> Loudly first, and after softly,
> Sobbing first, and after laughing,
> As if coming from afar.
> Fair Calisto did embrace me,
> Yet your songs, sighs, calls, and whistles
> Sweeter made my sweetest dream.
>
> If when I exist but yonder
> In some dull and endless sleep,
> Ah, I may no longer hearken
> To these songs as now I do,
> And the sounds of joy and playing,
> Dances, triumphs, and of glory
> Never will I hear again,
> So I'll take in life my pleasures,
> With my sweetheart kiss more often,
> Listen to the nightingale.

He avoided the sound *r*, which he believed to be harsh, in this and nine other poems. One aim of his Anacreontics was to show the Russian language to be as capable as any other of tender emotions and soft sounds. His original Anacreontics were sometimes Russified; he occasionally replaced the Olympian gods by Slavic gods— for example, Lel, the god of love. In "Russian Girls" he wishes that Anacreon had seen them dance, with their "speaking shoulders" and "falcons' eyes." "Gypsy Dance" describes a tavern entertainer, but the poem is in form a Bacchic dithyramb. Gypsy dancers and singers were to appeal to Russian poets well into the twentieth century.

At his death Derzhavin left unfinished a characteristic poem about the passage of time:

> Time's river in its onward current
> Will sweep away all men's affairs,
> And sink in chasms of nonbeing
> All nations, kingdoms, and their kings.
> And if a thing should seem to linger
> Through sounds of trumpets and of lyres,
> In jaws eternal it will vanish,
> The common fate will be its lot.

Its tentative title was "On Transience."

Derzhavin's poems often feature large contrasts in theme, as between life and death, luxury and modesty. He was proud, too, that he mixed the solemn and the mundane. His syntax was sometimes unexpectedly terse and elliptical because of his intellectual leaps. Aleksandr Pushkin was to say of him, "I swear, his genius thought in Tatar and did not know Russian grammar for lack of time."[2] Derzhavin's poems bespeak a high intelligence in his instinct for the crux of the matter. His style was rugged, although the tendency of the age was toward a smoother manner. His contrasts in theme and style often led in the end to a sense of resolution and harmony. At the end of "The Waterfall" an atmosphere of peace follows scenes of tumult. In all, his work embodied so much energy, ardor, and optimism that it masks the true character of a transitional period during which other poets were turning to irony, cynicism, and sadness.

Harbingers of the New

Nikolay Lvov has a place in the history of Russian poetry apart from the fame of his salon in St. Petersburg at the end of the 1770s. His original poetry, which included fables and epistles, is conventional, but his collection of Russian folk songs, published in 1790, was an important sign of preromantic interests. His translations from Anacreon (1794) were in keeping with the general tendency to develop the lighter genres.

Iury Neledinsky-Meletsky (1752–1828) was once known almost exclusively for his original songs. An aristocrat, he served in the army and at court; poetry was an avocation. His songs sometimes resemble the "drawn-out" folk song, and some were set to music. Among Neledinsky-Meletsky's conventional genres were odes, epistles, and fables. He had in common with the sentimentalists of the 1790s a predilection for the theme of friendship and a graceful, unassuming style, and his work appeared in the magazines of the new movement.

Mikhail Muravev (1757–1807) was an enthusiastic partisan of sentimental poetry in the late 1770s and the 1780s. In the early 1770s he had published relatively conventional books. The innovative later poems appeared only in magazines, sometimes anonymously, and were circulated in manuscript. The son of a provincial bureaucrat, Muravev studied at Moscow University and at the Academy of Sciences. He was acquainted with Kheraskov, Novikov, and the Masonic circles. He was the tutor of Grand Duke Alexander. In 1801 he became a Trustee of Moscow University, a post he used to support the publication of journals and to enable Karamzin to begin his *History of the Russian State* in 1804. Younger poets, who were followers of Karamzin, first published the collected works of Muravev in 1819 and 1820.

Muravev's early books, published when he was but fifteen to eighteen years old, already showed the influence of sensibility. They include *Fables* (1773), in which his anecdotes are seldom biting, and *Odes* (1776), whose themes include the lamentable transience of earthly life and the heavenly nature of poetry. Among early poems that he did not publish were such sentimental titles as "Friendship," "The Rustic Life," and "The Lament of Dido," written because of an "obsession," as he called it, with tragedy.

In form Muravev's later poems are odes, epistles, pastoral tales, and philosophical meditations. But some are landmarks in the new treatment of nature and of personal experience. In "Night" (1776) the misty setting is essential, and his subjects are mere transitory moods and reveries. In "The Grove" (1777) the trees are addressed as a sheltering refuge for the ennobling release of his inner self.

> Since I have entry in peace to your quietly shimmering shadows,
> Forest, the poet can scarcely disturb your so sanctified refuge. . . .

Among the 100 or so poems are tales of pastoral love, poems in praise of his rustic home, and poems on the passing of youth.

Muravev's lyrics on literature are outspoken, like manifestos. In "The Good Fortune of the British Muse" (1778) he admires the poetry of Dryden, Milton, Shakespeare, Pope, and Thomson. In "Letter . . . " (1783) he welcomes the new religious and philosophical trends set by Edward Young and Rousseau. "Epistle on Light Poetry" (1883) was written to hasten the end of odes and the rise of minor genres. "The Power of Genius" (1785) was an early sign of the preromantic adulation of the superior individual. Muravev's poems are often in praise of other poets and of painters, such as Lomonosov, Bogdanovich, and Correggio. Muravev was a translator of Homer, Sappho, Anacreon, Virgil, Horace, Petronius, Tasso, Boileau, Voltaire, and others.

Notes

1. Nicholas V. Riasanovsky, *A History of Russia,* 3rd ed. (New York: Oxford University Press, 1977), p. 292.

2. Letter to A. A. Delvig, not later than June 8, 1825, in *Polnoe Sobranie Sochinenii* (Leningrad: Akademia Nauk SSSR, 1937), vol. 13, p. 181.

5

The Rise of Sentimentalism
(1790–1800)

In the decade after the French Revolution of 1789, the Russian monarchy became a bulwark of conservatism both at home and in Europe. The Jacobin terror and the execution of Louis XVI embittered Catherine and appalled many of the gentry, who had been so long accustomed to admire French culture. As an empire the nation thrived. The wars with Turkey were successfully concluded. Poland was swallowed by Prussia, Austria, and Russia in two final partitions, which took place in 1792 and 1795. Catherine turned against the liberals inside Russia, but Western ideas continued to enter the country, and at an accelerated rate. The influence of English and German preromanticism became more palpable, and the impact of French literature was undiminished. A republican sentiment that favored political change inevitably arose. The suppression of books and authors began. Private melancholia and, to a lesser extent, democratic sympathies became fashionable themes in Russian literature. In 1796 Paul I succeeded Catherine on the throne and pressed Russia into a military coalition with Great Britain and Austria against France. Russian troops were sent to fight in northern Italy, and the international prestige of the nation was high.

Sentimental and Preromantic Currents

The unfettered spirit of preromanticism appeared in Russia while the more moderate sentimental movement had only begun to run its course. The two currents could thus be found side by side, and some Russians did not distinguish between them, seeing in all the new literature an affirmation of the private emotions and a reverence for nature. Rousseau's influence began to flow not only from his ideas on government but also from his novel *Julie, ou la nouvelle Héloise* (1761). The book tended to sanctify passion at the expense of the circle of social virtues and to enhance the stature of prose. The *Sturm and Drang* movement, which flourished in Germany in the 1770s, carried the seed of political rebelliousness. Along with the influence of English literature, it fostered the appearance of ballads and the Gothic mode.

A new period in Russian literature was abruptly opened by the appearance of two works. One was a novelistic diary called *Journey from St. Petersburg to Moscow* (1790) by Aleksandr Radishchev. Patterned in form on Sterne's *A Sentimental Journey* (1768), the work unexpectedly showed the sufferings of the serfs and was a veiled call for the end of the autocracy. Another work calling for social compassion was a short story, "Poor Liza" (1792), by Nikolay Karamzin. His heroine was a peasant girl who was loved and deserted by an aristocrat, and the story aroused a cult of admiration. Rebellious works such as the *Journey from St. Petersburg to Moscow* could scarcely have fostered much literary progeny, and indeed Radishchev was arrested for writing it. Even classical literature of a critical or satirical tendency was suspect in these new times. The comic playwright Denis Fonvizin, for example, was excluded from literature, as was a budding fabulist, Ivan Krylov. Sentimentalism, with its private tears and social sympathy, became a leading literary current, championed by Karamzin. In the long run, the Russians were to embrace sentimentalism and find it more congenial than political extremism.

In the 1790s a number of poems were written about the history of poetry or the faculty of the imagination. They served the purpose of manifestoes, especially when written by Karamzin. Through them the philosophical premises of sentimentalists and preromantics alike were disseminated. In other respects, the poetry of the 1790s was cautious and selective when set beside the new developments that were taking place in prose. Reason, in any case, was challenged as the ultimate criterion of behavior and morality, and was replaced by intuition. The keynote of sentimental poetry was melancholia. Muravev had already written about sentimental sorrows that were irrational in origin. In the works of Karamzin and others, sadness is again shown to well up in the self and to be its own cause. There were also meditations on the loss of youth and on the coming of winter. A number of new poems were set in graveyards; Thomas Gray's "Elegy Written in a Country Churchyard" (1750) was well known in Russia. Nature had acquired new philosophical dimensions since James Thomson. Now landscapes were endowed with gentle emotions and were approached with a sense of awe. Russian poets imitated not only the English sentimentalists but also their later Continental counterparts, such as Charles-Hubert Millevoye and Salomon Gessner. The somewhat precious pastoral style that resulted can be seen in the poetry of Ivan Dmitriev.

Since political invective was not permissible, preromanticism was limited to the creation of a national aura and the imitation of folklore. The national past began to be seen in an emotional, popular light, rather than from the standpoint of politics and expediency, particularly in Dmitriev's work. Ballads and other imitations of folk narratives appeared as a novelty. Some new notes were inspired by the Gothic current, with its emphasis on the supernatural.

Radishchev

The role of Aleksandr Radishchev (1749–1802) in Russian literature has been greater than what his creative works alone would merit. He was the first distinguished proponent of egalitarianism and republicanism. He endeavored to be the first firebrand, the first revolutionary to make a mark on Russian culture, and he was the first martyr of the radical intelligentsia. His *Journey from St. Petersburg to Moscow* epitomizes the spirit of all his works. In form it is a fictional diary, but it dramatizes, under the guise of sentimentalist compassion, the injustices of serfdom. Catherine considered the author of this work "worse than Pugachev." Radishchev was also the author of lyric poems, as well as essays and notes on political and philosophical subjects.

Radishchev was a high-ranking civil servant for whom literature was an instrument of culture, and sometimes of his cause. An aristocrat born in Moscow, he was educated at the elite Page Corps school and studied law, with a small group of other young Russian men, at Leipzig University between 1766 and 1771. His political ideas and literary tastes were formed in Germany. During the Pugachev Revolt, he served in the army in Finland. He was acquainted with Ivan Novikov and other Freemasons, but he opposed their pietism. He was stirred by the American Revolution. Although *Journey from St. Petersburg to Moscow* was published anonymously in 1790, its author was arrested. Radishchev was sentenced to be executed, but the judgment was commuted to ten years of exile in Siberia; he was released by Paul I in 1796. In 1801 Alexander I named him to a commission on law, for which he wrote proposals for the abolition of serfdom, of class privilege, of arbitrary rule, and of physical punishment. When he was rebuked for these projects, he feared a second exile and he took a lethal dose of poison in September 1802.

Radishchev's most celebrated poem was an ode, "Freedom" (1790), in which he called for the assassination of tyrants. The poem was published as a prologue to *Journey from St. Petersburg to Moscow*, although it had been written separately. In the ode he praises both Brutus and William Tell, a hero of the *Sturm und Drang* movement, as exemplary political rebels. The hypothetical despot is addressed with threats:

> O villain, fiercest of all villains,
> Your evil towers above your head,
> O criminal and first among them,
> Then cease, I call you up to doom!
> Your crimes I've massed into one circle
> So that no one shall pass you by
> Of all your punishments, O foe!
> You dared to sink in me your stinger,
> One death alone for that is little,
> Then die, O die, one hundredfold!

Cromwell is commended in the following stanza for the execution of Charles I. The poem imparted an unmistakably revolutionary meaning to the tearful series of sketches of Russian life in the *Journey*. Among the scenes of suffering that Radishchev depicts is an auction of serfs that will separate family members. In a central "vision," moreover, a tyrant is shown to be blind from cataracts; his courtiers stand nearby in bloodied clothes; his people are in rags. The introductory ode recalls the political rhetoric already seen in Kapnist's "Ode to Slavery."

Radishchev's "Freedom" was written in an elevated style, with archaic words and syntax. His invective was to influence the civic poets of the early nineteenth century, particularly those who were to perpetrate in December 1825 the first attempt at a coup d'état to limit the power of the autocracy.

Radishchev's small poetic legacy was in keeping with the ideas and moods of the *Sturm und Drang* movement. His first preserved poem, "Song," expresses the desolation of an unrequited love. An oratorio, "The Creation of the World" (1782), suggests through its bleak cosmic imagery the omnipotence of an austere, unloving God. Most of Radishchev's lyrics were written after his arrest and exile. He continued to be optimistic about the possibility of good governments. In "Historical Song" (1796) he relates the mythic and civil histories of Greece and Rome in their entirety in order to end with Marcus Aurelius, the perfect ruler. "The Eighteenth Century" (1802) celebrates the good works of both Peter I and Catherine II. In "Bova" (1802?) Radishchev wrote an imitation of a Russian folk tale; his rough-and-ready hero longs for an ideal, the princess Meletrissa Kirbitevna. In contrast, Radishchev was pessimistic in poems that touch on more personal subjects. His private pain as a citizen is rendered in "For what, my friend?" (1791). In other poems he pictures birds as victims of circumstance. In "The Crane" (1800) a wounded bird is taken to heaven, while in "Idyll" (1800) a captive bird is able to escape. In his philosophical poems, Radishchev was concerned with earthly pain. Death is seen as a release from sufferings in "The Epitaph" (1783), but in "Prayer" (1791?) he fears that pain may not vanish even in the afterlife. As a stylist Radishchev preferred to give the impression of strength rather than of melodiousness. He sought harsh sounds through colliding consonants and the use of spondees.

Although Radishchev's egalitarian and philosophical views had no systematic airing in his verse, they were important to the poets who were his followers. His deistic premises appear in his essay "On Man, On His Mortality and Immortality" (1792), written in Siberia. All his writings were banned in Russia before 1905, but they were known in manuscript and in editions printed abroad, and they exerted a continuous if indirect influence on Russian culture and literature.

Karamzin

The high road to the future of Russian literature was opened by the first works of Nikolay Karamzin (1766–1826). An epistolary report called *Letters of a Russian Traveler* (1792) brought illuminating observations of cultural trends in Western Europe. His short story "Poor Liza" was taken as proof that "a peasant also can love." Karamzin wrote the first enduring sentimental prose and established the first sentimental periodicals, beginning with *The Moscow Journal* in 1791. Yet Karamzin was as eclectic as any other writer of his day. His best story, "Bornholm Island" (1794), is a Gothic tale about incest, and his lyrics include cynical remarks that undercut the idealistic tendency of his sentimentalism. He was innovative in the use of lyrical genres. Karamzin was as great a linguist as Lomonsov; the literary language of the nineteenth century was essentially his creation. He devoted the second half of his career to the monumental *History of the Russian State*. In sum, he introduced the age of sensibility; he upheld the promptings of taste and innate morality in a period of transition; and he created a literary school.

Karamzin expended considerable energy in furthering new currents, especially sentimentalism, which he was to desert in later life. He was a landowner of Simbirsk, a Volga city that was to produce several poets of note. He was schooled in Moscow and joined the Preobrazhensky Regiment of the Guards in St. Petersburg. His first literary circle was that of Ivan Novikov and the Freemasons, for whom he translated a number of works, including Shakespeare's *Julius Caesar* in 1787. In May 1789 he began an eighteen-month tour of Germany, Switzerland, France, and England that would lead to his *Letters of a Russian Traveler*. During his tour he interviewed a number of writers, including Kant, Herder, and Wieland; he also observed governmental bodies, such as the Constitutional Assembly in France, and social institutions, including Newgate Prison and Bedlam Hospital in England. In *The Moscow Journal* he published his translations of Sterne and Macpherson (the Ossian poems), as well as his own first works. He edited the literary anthologies called *Aglaia* (1794, 1796) and *Aonides* (1797–1799). A crisis of outlook in the mid-1790s led him to sympathize with monarchist views. In 1801 he married Elisaveta Protasova, whose family were prominent Freemasons. A literary and political magazine, *The Herald of Europe* (1802–1803), reflects his later views. In 1803 he was appointed an official historiographer and devoted himself to his twelve-volume *History of the Russian State,* which would provide the golden age of poetry with a wealth of stories from the Russian chronicles.

Karamzin's poetry evolved from sentimentalism to conservatism. His more than 150 poems include odic meditations, epistles, elegies, songs, tales, and even epigrams. In his early poems, these genres were adapted to sentimental trends. In "Poetry"—written in 1787, before his European tour—poetry is said to be a hymn to God, divinely inspired. The poets of classical antiquity are praised, as are many poets of modern Europe, including Thomson, Young, and "Ossian"; Klopstock, he said, "soared higher than them all." (No Russian poets are mentioned.) He popularized the nature poem with philosophical or private meditations. Here is his "Autumn" (1789), written in Geneva and included in the text of *Letters of a Russian Traveler:*

Winds of the autumn are blowing
    Through the dark oak grove.
Earthward the yellowing leaves fall,
    Noisily scattered.

Empty are gardens and grain fields,
    Hills are in mourning,
Songs in the forests are ended,
    Birds have departed.

Geese in a flock lately risen
    Hurry to southward,
Smooth in their flight they go soaring
    High in the heavens.

Strands of grey mists in wreathes wander
    Through the still valley,
Merge with the smoke from the village,
    Upwards to flutter.

Gloomy, a wayfarer gazes
    Down from the hilltop,
Seeing the pallor of autumn
    Sighs as though weary.

Wayfarer sad, O be solaced!
    Nature will falter
Only for this little season.
    All waits the future.

All is renewed with the springtime:
    Proudly and smiling,
Nature arises all vital,
    Bridal in clothing.

Mortals, alas, fade forever!
    Men old at springtime
Feel in themselves the chill winter—
    Ancient in lifetime.

The poem was written in dactyls without rhymes, an example of Karamzin's experiments in prosody. These elegiac nature scenes gradually disappeared from his verse in the mid-1790s, when he lost faith in sentimental premises.

Many of Karamzin's meditations on man's place in the earthly order are more stylized, and more distant, in manner. An arresting elegy called "The Graveyard" (1792) poses a religious dilemma in the form of a dialogue between two disembodied voices that speak from beneath the earth. One describes the grave as a refuge in the afterlife, the site of doves and flowers, while a cynical respondent describes death as an extinction amid worms, snakes, and nettles. Karamzin ended an Anacreontic called "To a Nightingale" (1793) with a note of nostalgia at the grave:

Painful is the heart alone,
Earth is wilderness, and dark.

Will your singing soon win over,
O my pretty nightingale,
Passersby, their hearts enchanting,
As you perch above my grave?

Among his new genres was the literary ballad, and he created a taste for imitations of folk narratives. In "Raisa, an Ancient Ballad" (1792) he turned a classical legend into a sentimental story in the spirit of Gessner's idylls. The bereaved girl ends her life by drowning in a lake—a conclusion he used in the same year for "Poor Liza." Karamzin's love poems were always somewhat rococo and pastoral. Whatever their occasion, they all feature cupids and nightingales. His emotions flowed readily, even when his circumstances were melancholy. His beloved in "Farewell" (1792) will wed a rival; in "To Her" (1796) he declared that love comes only once; in "The Nightingale" (1796) the bird sings alike for grieving and for happy lovers; "To Emilia" (1802) was written for a new wife.

A failed utopianism was the key to much of Karamzin's disillusionment. His first balled, "Count Gvarinos" (1789), was based on an old Spanish epic extolling Christian faith and chivalric courage. In his "Song of Peace" (1791) he anticipated a brotherhood of man; the poem is close to Wilhelm Schiller's "An die Freude." Skepticism about the political capacities of men came after the revolutionary Terror in France. In an epistle to a Simbirsk countryman, "Letter to Dmitriev" (1794), he complained: "Ah, evil is eternal under the sun." His epistle to Aleksandr Alekseevich Pleshcheev is equally telling. In both poems he concludes that the moral person must be content to seek friendship, love, and virtues only at home. He argued in "Epistle to Women" (1795) that females have a superior capacity for intuition and discernment, for wisdom springing from the heart.

This crisis of political belief led Karamzin to lower his ideas about the nature of art; creation became for him the mere exercise of the sensitive imagination. In 1795 he evoked a new goddess, Untruth, as he began "Ilia Muromets, a *Bogatyr* Tale." The chivalric hero of this poem is unlike those of the genuine *byliny,* and his feat is drawn from fairy tales: Ilia awakens a Sleeping Beauty, a symbol of the ideal. The narration is marred by a mincing style in the rococo fashion. In "The Gift" (1796) Karamzin described poetry as that civilizing force within an evil world that imparts to man his feeling for nature, morality, love, religion, and heroism. By the end of the 1790s, Karamzin's aesthetic had made of art a simple romantic nostalgia for what cannot be. In "Proteus, or the Disharmony of Poets" (1798) he regrets that truth and divine inspiration are not accessible to man: poetry records the mere whims of the soul:

> And where is the key to Nature kept for me?
> On earth the heart speaks, but truth is mute.

His "Melancholia" (1880) is an adaptation of Jacques Delille's "L'Imagination," in which the habit of dreaming and longing is described as a source of solace and healing:

> Your joy—it is to ponder, to be silent,
> And turn upon the past your gentle gaze.

The heart still reigns, as in sentimentalism, but its sorrow is only private and its comfort is from illusions.

From the mid-1790s on, Karamzin wrote cynical epigrams and humorous inscriptions like those of almost any classical poet. Several were witty philosophical statements that could be reduced to aphorisms: "Inconstancy" (1795): fate is inconstant, but so are we; "Time" (1795): times kills us, but so do we kill time; "Last Words of a Dying Man" (1797): life brings lies for the mind and suffering for the heart; "Passions and Indifference" (1797): life is either desires or boredom. A fable, "The Owls and the Nightingale" (1805), is a spoof of creatures who shun the light, enlightenment.

Karamzin was, meanwhile, increasingly concerned with the practical world; he had become a conservative and a patriot. An old-fashioned, classical pride in country had appeared in "Volga" (1793), a laudatory poem for the river. In 1796 he welcomed a new autocrat in "Ode on the Occasion of the Oath of Moscow's Residents to Paul I." In 1801 he wrote two odes for the accession of Alexander I; the Napoleonic Wars inspired "The Liberation of Europe and the Glory of Alexander I" in 1814. The odes are a forgotten part of Karamzin's *oeuvre*. By 1803 he quit literature for his *History of the Russian State*, the first systematic survey of material in the various Russian chronicles of the medieval period. Karamzin's *History* was to be the source of Pushkin's *Boris Godunov* and other works of a more romantic age.

Karamzin opened the age of sensibility if he did not sustain it. His mind was ever searching and restless. He could be touched only temporarily by sentimental compassion or by a preromantic longing for ideals. His verse bears the imprint of thought as much as of feeling. He paid homage to the emotional life, but his poems are in fact rather cold. There is, however, a pathos in the incessant searching that characterizes his career as a whole. Karamzin's work was influential in part because he vastly enlarged the vocabulary of the literary language and thereby gave it the capacity to express a multitude of new Western concepts. He translated French roots into Russian and gave French meanings to Russian words.

Dmitriev

The persistence of classicism can be seen in the work of Ivan Dmitriev (1760–1837). He cultivated melancholia and tears, yet was adept at satire and preserved the genres of classicism—the song, the epistle, the fable, and others. He wrote nothing with a heroic tone, however. He was a native of Simbirsk and a lifelong associate of Karamzin. He entered the Guards in St. Petersburg at the age of fourteen and became the disciple of Derzhavin. It was through Dmitriev that Karamzin first learned of sentimental trends. Dmitriev's first collection of poems appeared in 1795. His career took a strange turn when he was falsely charged in 1797 with complicity in an attempt to assassinate Paul I. But Alexander I advanced him to high offices, and in 1806 he was named Minister of Justice. He retired in 1814 and settled in Moscow.

In his youth Dmitriev was popular for his stylized songs. "Sweet the little dove that moans" was set to music and brought him fame; it tells of a bird that died of a broken heart. The song is clearly derived from folklore. Generally, his songs have such subjects as love, the passing of youth, and the presence of sadness in beauty. Many other songs were set to music, but few were published in his collections of verse. The melancholia in Dmitriev's published lyrics is more urbane and is sometimes colored by a gentle didacticism. In "Two Graves" (1789) the dread tomb of the tyrant is contrasted with the benign grave of the shepherd. "Meditations on the Occasion of a Storm" (1796) reflects the power of nature. Dmitriev helped to make introspection fashionable in Russian poetry, as well as the view that life is naturally sad. His sorrows are stylized, however, and probably owe as much to Continental writers as to the English sentimentalists.

Dmitriev's most ambitious poems were preromantic re-creations of moments in the national past. The poems are democratic in tendency and full of pathos. In "Ermak" (1794) two Siberian shamans lament the conquest of their land in the sixteenth century by the Don Cossack "conqueror of Siberia." The exotic landscapes on the distant river Irtish recall the "Ossian" atmosphere. "The Liberation of Moscow" (1795) celebrates the expulsion of the Polish intervention forces during the Time of Troubles in 1612. Moscow itself is the hero of this work; the commanding military officer willingly yields his power to the young Mikhail Romanov, the elected tsar. Dmitriev was also the author of an adaptation of Psalm 50 and a "Hymn to God" that suggests deism.

His satirical vein appeared as early as his sentimentalism and lasted longer. In a worldly verse tale called "The Fashionable Woman" (1791) he describes a wealthy old man who marries a young woman, only to discover that she is as selfish, demanding, and vain as he had been in his youth. The lesson is that matches should be based on inclination rather than on wealth. In "Boredom" (1805) the poor man is shown to be more fortunate than the rich:

> When boredom comes, desire itself goes flying,
> But hope will wipe the tear away from sorrow.

Dmitriev could be sarcastic; in "The Camel and the Rhinoceros" (1810) the camel is successful because he has learned not only to work but also to bend the knee. Dmitriev also wrote witty poems in genres that he called madrigals, epitaphs, and epigrams.

III

SENSIBILITY
AND
ROMANTICISM

6

The Era of Sensibility
(1800–1820)

The major Russian writers of the nineteenth century were to be, with some exceptions, liberal in sentiment. The monarchy, in contrast, was usually conservative and sometimes repressive. In the earliest years of the century, the intellectuals hoped that Alexander I, as a new tsar, would eventually introduce a constitution from above. The rapid influx of romantic currents into literature began to be resisted, and fashion began to favor a partial return to liberal classicism. However, political expectations were to be thwarted again. During the Napoleonic Wars, which were seen by the monarchy as a consequence of the French Revolution, the government turned conservative. After Napoleon's invasion of Russia was repulsed at Moscow in 1812, Russia entered the Holy Alliance, a European pact formed to avert further revolutions. Reactionary domestic policies were inaugurated by Alexander's most active minister, General Aleksey Arakcheev. The liberals did not relinquish their aspirations, and Russian army officers who had been stationed in the West returned with a fresh enthusiasm for republican ideas. A political opposition arose that was sometimes reflected in literature.

An Eclectic Period

The outstanding Russian writer of the early years of the new century, Vasily Zhukovsky, was attracted to romanticism. The writers who acknowledged his leadership did not follow him, however, in that direction. In an era when Wordsworth and Coleridge were bringing a renewal of Christian vitality to English literature and when much of European thought was influenced by Schelling's *Naturphilosophie,* the leading Russian writers remained eclectic. Zhukovsky's followers, the former Karamzinists, were sentimentalists at best. They enjoyed an ascendancy in Russian literature that might be said to have begun with Zhukovsky's translation in 1802 of

Gray's "Elegy Written in a Country Churchyard." Sentimentalism itself was placed on a new, moral plane by Zhukovsky: he avoided the teary excesses of the 1890s, spelled out the aesthetics of the movement, and developed its themes—virtue, friendship, nature. He was soon to perform similar services for the romantic current. His followers remained essentially urbane, and sometimes classical, well into the 1820s. They continued to write "light poetry" (*poésie légère*), which usually meant epistles and elegies, and to criticize society in their satires. A suggestion that this literary grouping was, at its core, a political alliance can be seen in the fact that an ally of Zhukovsky's in the new era was a liberal general, Denis Davydov, who was in literature an old-fashioned epicurean.

There were literary conservatives who opposed the Karamzinists, and it was evident that their reasons were partly political. Their spokesman was Admiral Aleksandr Shishkov, who advocated, in "Discussion on Old and New Styles of the Russian Language" (1803), a return, not precisely to classicism, but to Church Slavic. In 1811 Shishkov brought the conservative authors together in the Circle of Lovers of the Russian Word. Members of his group included Derzhavin, who was at the height of his powers, and the fabulist Ivan Krylov, who was to become a perennial favorite of Russians. The moral tenor of his animal stories is broad and universal, and the fables are written in a racy, semi-peasant style. The peasant colloquial was favored by the conservatives because it was free of Western influence.

The period after the War of 1812 brought conflicting inclinations. The defeat of Napoleon at Moscow engendered patriotic feelings and inspired some important poems. The longlasting literary effect, however, was to strengthen the hand of the liberals, or Karamzinists. Zhukovsky began to be fascinated by preromantic ballads, with their emphasis on mystery and horror. He translated a number, sometimes quite freely, from Schiller, Southey, Uhland, and others. The form became very popular in Russia. But the characteristic traits of the new era were embodied in the poems of Konstantin Batiushkov; he combined the restraint of classicism with the vision and warmth of sentimentalism. He fostered a reliance on personal taste and a reverence for the imagination. In 1815 the Karamzinists formed a literary society whose purpose was to spoof the solemn literary gatherings of Shishkov's circle. The new society was called Arzamas, after an insignificant provincial town near Karamzin's estate. Its initial aim was humor, but political discussions were inevitably introduced. The Arzamas encouraged the younger poets who were to create the golden age.

Zhukovsky

The sentimentalism of the 1790s was brought into the nineteenth century by Vasily Zhukovsky (1783–1852), but he subsequently popularized preromantic ballads and then introduced the other-worldly nostalgia of romanticism itself. He was known as an extraordinary translator, particularly of English and German sentimentalists and romantics. He once wrote, "Nearly everything of mine belongs to someone else, or is in response to someone else," but this statement was unjustly modest. Most of his ballads are adaptations, but the majority of his lyrics are original. He is credited, in fact, with pioneering the lyricism of personal confessions. The poems of his old age, written in Germany, are marked by an unusual religious serenity.

Zhukovsky was the illegitimate son of a gentry landowner (Afanasy Bunin), an influential figure at court, and a mentor to a generation of poets. He was born near Tula (to a Turkish captive) and reared as an adoptive Zhukovsky. He was educated at home and in Moscow, and assumed, in 1808, the editorship of Karamzin's literary magazine, *The Herald of Europe*. Renown came with the appearance of a wartime poem, "The Bard in the Camp of the Russian Warriors" (1812). His personal lyrics stem in part from his unhappy love for Maria Protasova. In 1813 his marriage proposal to her was rejected by her mother, who was, as he did not know, his own half-sister. In the same year he became a court reader, and he later tutored members of the royal family, including the future Alexander II. Zhukovsky was a principal founder, in 1815, of Arzamas, whose aim was to read new literary works and to further Karamzin's literary language. In 1839 Zhukovsky retired and traveled abroad; in 1841 he married in Germany, where he remained until his death.

In his early verse, Zhukovsky was a talented proponent of Karamzin's sentimentalism. His themes were the transience of earthly life and the inevitability of melancholia. His philosophical inclination was evident in two lyrical essays on morality, both called "Virtue" (1798). His poem called "Man" (1801) contains many of the thoughts expressed by Edward Young in *The Complaint, or Night Thoughts on Life, Death and Immortality*. It was thus in keeping with his own themes that Zhukovsky approached his translation of Gray's "Elegy Written in a Country Churchyard," in which the virtue of the melancholy shepherd is extolled. Art was seen by Zhukovsky as God's consolatory gift to man in a world of sorrow ("To Poetry," 1804). Virtually the whole mentality of sentimentalism can be seen in "The Singer" (1811), in which he describes the grave of a poet who wrote of friendship, love, and life's losses.

Zhukovsky created a romantic persona, the hero of his own verse, in the poems that appeared from 1806 on. He complained of an ill-starred love. He translated Pope's "Letter of Heloise to Abelard," a turbulent lyric by Sappho, and a love poem by Schiller. Then came original lyrics in which passion can be seen to have an autobiographical origin—his love for Protasova. For two decades his poems recorded his faithfulness to this unhappy love. In 1823 he wrote this response to the news of Maria's death:

March 19, 1823

You stood before me,
And you were silent.
Your gaze was mournful
And full of feeling.
It brought remembrance
Of days loved dearly. . . .
Your last appearance
In this existence.

> You have departed—
> A silent angel—
> Your grave is quiet,
> Like heaven, peaceful!
> It holds my earthly,
> Fond recollections,
> It holds my holy
> High hopes of heaven.
>
> Stars in the sky,
> Silence at night. . . .

Afterward Zhukovsky's thoughts about this love were inseparable from his meditations on death and a longing for spiritual perfection or for heaven. Love, however,
was not the only new theme to appear in 1806. In "Evening" (1806) he describes
nature as a refuge for solitary reverie. The same year brought Zhukovsky's first
Ossianic poem, "The Song of the Bard." The singer here is Boian, the legendary
Russian bard from *The Tale of Igor's Campaign*. He is both a poet and a military
hero, and he was to appear again in "The Bard in the Camp of the Russian
Warriors" in 1812.

Meanwhile, Zhukovsky had not deserted the classical genres. He was still
writing fables in 1806, usually adaptations from the French of La Fontaine or Jean
de Florian; he even wrote humorous epigrams. This classical side of his talent led to
a number of friendly epistles, written in 1812 and 1813, which were true verse
letters, not stylized sentimental complaints. Some were addressed to fellow Karamzinists, among them Batiushkov and Petr Viazemsky. Literary criticism of an
amiable, constructive sort was included in these poems, as well as some quite
ordinary talk about the techniques of poetry. Zhukovsky even wrote humorous
poems for the meetings of Arzamas. His classicism had a more serious facet,
however. When odes had gone out of favor among his literary party, he commemorated historic and court occasions in respectful epistles addressed to the members of
the royal family ("To the Emperor Alexander," 1814).

Zhukovsky wrote narrative poems in various genres, but only the ballads, with
their violent crimes and air of the uncanny, were popular. He began with a translation from Gottfried Bürger's "Lenore," a poem that had become a symbol of
religious defiance among the German *Sturm und Drang* poets. Zhukovsky made
two adaptations of this poem, the first of which, called "Ludmilla," appeared in
1808. The second, "Svetlana" (1812), inspired a flood of ballad writing in Russia.
In Zhukovsky's poem the heroine does not curse God when she has followed her
ghostly lover:

> What? a coffin in the hut,
>   White the shroud upon it,
> Christ's own image at the foot,
>   High above, an icon. . . .
> O, Svetlana, what's awry?
>   Whose is this the dwelling?
> Dreadful in this empty hut

Is its silent dweller.
Tearful, trembling, she goes in,
Falls before the Christ to earth,
Prayers to icon offers.
Then her cross in hand she takes,
Timidly, and under saints,
In a niche she cowers.

The apparition turns out to have been a nightmare. Evil prevails in Zhukovsky's other translations. In "The Forest King" (1818), which is an adaptation of Goethe's "Erlkönig," a malevolent spirit takes the life of a child. Feuds and revenge are the topics of other ballads. Some are set in exotic southern countries or in ancient times.

Zhukovsky's original ballad "Twelve Sleeping Maidens" (1817) is about the triumph of good over evil. The hero of this poem saves a sinner from eternal damnation and wins the love of a perfect maiden for himself. Zhukovsky also wrote "epics and stories," a more literary category of narrative. His 1821 translation of Byron's "The Prisoner of Chillon" was a milestone in the progress of romantic awareness in Russia. In the 1830s he made a charming translation of "Undina," La Motte Fouqué's story of a mermaid. In the same period Zhukovsky turned to verse adaptations of prose folk tales. Among them is a "Puss in Boots" story and a very familiar Russian folk tale, "Ivan Tsarevich and the Gray Wolf." The six stories were written in a friendly competition with Aleksandr Pushkin. The poets hoped to further the national spirit, but some of their tales were international in origin.

By the 1820s Zhukovsky had become inspired by a religious idealism that placed him far in advance of his urbane followers. Such themes as love and art were colored by his nebulous religiosity. He praised the conception of a spiritualized femininity in Thomas Moore's "Lalla Rookh: An Oriental Romance" (1817) in a new poem, "Lalla Rook" (1821). In "Prevision" (1823) the trembling veil suggests the nearness of divine inspiration. In "The Secret Vision" (1824) love, poetry, and presentiment are all said to flow from a single intuitive source. He adapted some of these poems from originals by Schiller, Goethe, and Uhland. In Zhukovsky's last poem, "The Swan of Tsarskoe Selo" (1851), the dying swan is, as in Greek myth and romantic literature, the symbol of the soul's return to ineffable spheres.

Davydov

The classical pole of the eclectic age was represented by General Denis Davydov (1784–1839). Davydov is now remembered for his "hussar poems," which depict the roistering off-duty camp life of line officers. He was first known for his political lampoons, however, and he also wrote a small body of conventional lyrics. He was a dedicated army officer for whom poetry was a second interest. During the War of 1812, he introduced partisan tactics into the activities of the regular army. His liberal sentiments were, however, a detriment to his career. He was among the first members of Arzamas and was later close to Decembrist circles. He published a treatise on guerrilla warfare in 1821 and a collection of his verse in 1832. During the 1830s he wrote memoirs that contain portraits of other Russian military leaders.

Davydov wrote the old-fashioned poetry of a soldier unconcerned for new literary movements. His satires were entirely in the tradition of the eighteenth century. "The Head and the Feet" (1803) is a fable in which the feet are no longer subservient to a despotic head; the feet speak:

> And if you are, by right, the one in charge,
> Then we can also have the right to stumble,
> And sometime it might happen—no intention—
> That you, Sir, could get broken on a rock.

Catherine II and her ineffectual successors are ridiculed in "The She-Eagle, the Ruff, and the Grouse" (1804). In other satires Davydov criticized both urban society and the military command. This spirit of defiance also informs his "hussar poems" in that he praises the men who fight rather than the great military leaders. In "To Burtsov. An Invitation to Punch" (1804), Davydov describes his own plain soldier's home and hospitality. The typical "hussar poem," with its images of camping, drinking, and fighting, can be found in another piece, "To Burtsov" (1804):

> At a smoky field encampment,
> Sitting by a blazing fire,
> I see that the nation's saviour
> Is the good *arak* we drink.
> Let us gather in a circle,
> True believers, one and all!

Unexpectedly, the men are called back into battle: "Fate has sent a different feast, / One that's hotter and that's wider. . . ." The festive meal was also a metaphor for battle in the *byliny* and in *The Tale of Igor's Campaign*.

In his conventional lyrics, Davydov began as the epicurean who thinks above all about love. His poems contain avowals of dedication, admiration, and passion, as well as his expressions of regrets and fears; his style is utterly simple. Sentimental notes began to enter his work in the 1820s. In "Half-Soldier" (1826) he pictures the fighting man whose heart is always with his family in the Caucasus Mountains. "The Partisan. A Fragment" (1826) is a recollection of Moscow in flames in 1812; the comparison of the soldiers to "hungry wolves" is Ossianic in style. In "The Field of Borodino. An Elegy" (1829) he remembers a decisive battle with Napoleon; he recalls his former comrades, the generals Petr Bagration, Nikolay Raevsky, Aleksey Ermolov, all famous men.

Krylov

The fables written by Ivan Krylov (1769–1844) have been venerated as the best of the genre and are the only Russian fables that are still widely read. His anecdotes are close in spirit to those of Aesop; many were adapted from the fables of La Fontaine and others. The virtues they uphold include not only common sense, honesty, and ordinary decency, but cleverness as well. Some fables once had a contemporary, topical meaning, but these are now forgotten by the general public. Krylov also wrote prose satires, plays, and a number of lyrical poems.

Krylov was an editor, a publisher, and then a librarian. He was born in Tver, the son of an army captain, and was largely self-educated. In 1782 he moved to St. Petersburg, entered the theatrical milieu, and wrote plays. He started two liberal satirical magazines, *The Spirits' Mail* (1789) and *The Spectator* (1792), as well as a newspaper, the *St. Petersburg Mercury* (1793), but he was forced from the field by political pressure. For a decade he worked in the provinces as a tutor and secretary. In 1806 he returned to the theatrical circles of St. Petersburg, now with more conservative views. In 1809 his first book of fables appeared, and in 1811 he joined Admiral Shishkov's Circle of Lovers of the Russian Word. From 1812 to 1841, he was employed at the St. Petersburg Public Library, whose director, Aleksey Olenin, was active in literary circles.

Krylov's liberal imagination produced works that were laudable in intent but not memorable in themselves. His prose satires were patterned on those of Ivan Novikov and other men of the 1770s. Krylov's targets were the landowners and their abuse of serfs, theater people, authors, women, urban night life, and the world of fashion and snobbery. *The Spirit's Mail* consists entirely of arch letters from the sylphs, nymphs, and gnomes who are the spirits of the air, water, and earth to an Arabian philosopher and magician. "Laudatory Speech to the Memory of My Grandfather" is more down-to-earth; the deceased was "dog's best friend," a typical landowner. "Kaib. An Eastern Tale" depicts an idle potentate. Krylov's dramatic works include tragedies and comedies in prose and verse, as well as a comic opera. The despotism of Paul I is ridiculed in *Trumf,* in form a tragedy. A satire of Russian Gallomania called *The Boutique* was his most popular play. His other comedies are classical plays about love and marriage among typical gentry families.

Krylov's lyrics, over fifty in number, are curiously prosaic and flat compared with his fables. The philosophy of Rousseau is reflected in the love he expresses for the rustic life and in his distrust of civilization and urban life. In "Epistle on the Utility of Desire" and "Epistle on the Utility of Passions" he ridicules the classical adulation of reason. In form the poems are odes, epistles, songs, and epigrams.

Krylov's fables are distinguished as art and unassuming in manner. His animal characters have the folksy traits of a provincial population, and his narrator seems to share their humble origin. The critical attitude behind the fables is moralistic; they oppose such vices as greed. They appear to be quite uncontroversial now that their topical references have lost their meaning. The targets, usually stupidity and ineptitude, are more universal than in Krylov's earlier satires, and his tone is more mischievous. In "Quartet" the monkey, donkey, goat, and bear presume to form a string ensemble:

> The Monkey, little prankster,
> The Ass,
> The Goat,
> And Mishka-Bear, the clumsy,
> Resolved to render a quartet,
> Brought scores, a cello, violins, viola,
> And took the lea beneath the lindens

To capture with their art—the world.
They strike their bows and saw away, but have no luck.
"Wait, brothers, wait," the Monkey cries, "hold on a minute,
How can the music come? For you are sitting wrong.
Your cello faces the viola, Mishka mine,
     And I, as First, must face the Second;
     The groves and hills will soon be dancing!"
     They sat, and the quartet began,
     But still no harmony came forth.
     "Wait now, for I've the secret found,"
The ass cries out, "we'll get it right now, surely,
     If we sit singly."
They did as said the Ass, sat singly in a row.
  And yet the whole quartet was out of tune.
And so the argument seethed on still more than ever,
     And quarrels,
     On how to sit and where.
Once Nightingale heard all their noise and came on wing.
All turned to ask him, please, to settle their discussion.
"Give us," they say to him, "a little of your patience,
Fix up the order of our poor quartet:
We have our scores, and each has got his instrument,
     Just tell us how to sit!"
"If you would be musicians, you must have some learning,
     And ears more tender than are yours,"
     Responded Nightingale to them,
     And you, with any seating, friends,
     Are not to be musicians fit."

For today's readers, Krylov's fables are no longer truly didactic; they are playful exercises on truisms. Their ridicule, as a necessary ingredient of the genre, is harmless. A fundamental reason for their durability has been Krylov's clever imitation of peasant speech. His phrases are witty, his intonations are subtle, and many of his lines have become genuine proverbs in that their authorship is lost to the unknowing. His contemporaries perceived in his folksy viewpoint and his colloquial phrases an example of "nationalness" (*narodnost*)—a trait much discussed by Russians during that period when romanticism flourished in the West.

Batiushkov

Konstantin Batiushkov (1787–1855) was an excellent representative of some aspects of an age of sensibility—its weary sophistication, its tender emotions, and its love of art. He was the champion of "light verse," that poetry which is private but not deeply confessional. He also wrote as the modern man at war, seeing both its grandeur and its pathos. He was a translator of Greek, Roman, Italian, and French poets who were in harmony with his times. He was the mentor to whom the younger poets of the golden age owed most in interests, tone, and technique.

Batiushkov was an aristocrat, an army officer, and a diplomat, but his primary vocation was as a poet. He was born in Vologda, a nephew of the sentimentalist poet Nikolay Muravev, with whom he went to live in 1802. Batiushkov was educated in St. Petersburg at private French and Italian *pensions,* and admired those languages. The Napoleonic invasion in 1812 initiated a depression from which he never completely recovered. He served in military campaigns across Europe and was in the occupying army in Paris in 1814. In 1815 he returned to Russia and suffered a nervous breakdown on being refused in marriage by A. F. Furman. In the same year he was a principal founder of the Arzamas literary club. In 1816 he moved to Moscow and joined a group called the Society of Lovers of Russian Letters, to which he read an influential address, "Speech on the Influence of Light Verse on Language." Batiushkov served from 1818 to 1821 as a diplomat in Italy, where his depression deepened into an incurable insanity with hereditary causes. His career was cut short in 1822 at age thirty-three.

Batiushkov's poetry is a relatively seamless blend of the several currents of his age. He projected a character that is melancholy but not inclined to isolation. His personal crises in 1812 and 1815 intensified his work, but left the essential directions of his talent unchanged. He appeared in his early verse as that modest figure who shuns fame and seeks friendships. He described his rustic cabin and humble dedication to verse. He addressed epistles to a fellow poet, Nikolay Gnedich, who was to be a translator of the *Iliad.* Batiushkov was an admirer of Tibullus, a Latin poet who also posed as a modest rustic, and translated three substantial elegies by him. Among the French poets, Batiushkov was close to Evariste Parny, the gentle epicurean and elegist. Batiushkov's "Madagascar Song" (1810), a poem in praise of the carefree life, was translated from one of Parny's Madagascar songs in prose. "My Penates" (1812) epitomized for Batiushkov's younger contemporaries the virtues of light verse; it begins: "Penates of my fathers, / O guardians of mine! / You are not rich in gold"; the poem is an epistle addressed to Zhukovsky and Prince Petr Viazemsky. "Friendship" (1812) was adapted from the Greek poet Bion. After 1812 Batiushkov wrote quite practical and realistic verse letters to his friends, including Zhukovsky, Andrey Turgenev, and Karamzin.

Batiushkov's love poems were to embody in turn nearly every literary trend of the day. At first he wrote about love in a self-indulgent and mildly epicurean manner. "Elegy" (1804 or 1805) and other translations from Parny are sentimental in tone. "Recovery" (1807) is a sensuous, classical description of a beauty with "crimson lips" and "shining eyes"; the poem was a favorite among the younger poets. Batiushkov began to idealize love in his adaptations from Petrarch on the death of Laura. Among all these stylizations, a few poems were realistic: in "The Departure" (1810?) he complains about his many rivals in love. The great poems on the subject came after 1812. These include the oddly cold "Bacchante" (1814), which describes an encounter at an orgy. One of the best is "The Awakening," which hovers between classicism and sentimentalism; it reflects the crisis of 1815:

> A zephyr blew the last of sleep
> From off my lashes, rapt in visions,
> But I—was not to fortune roused

By gentle touch of winged Zephyr.
For neither bliss of rosy rays,
Forerunners of the morning Phoebus,
Nor timid gleam of azure heavens,
Nor fragrance blowing from the fields,
Nor flight of steed with spirit rapid
Along the slope of velvet leas,
With baying hounds and hunting horn
Flung round the bay without a dwelling—
For nothing makes my heart awake,
A heart that in its dreams is troubled,
And no proud mind can overtake
A love—with cold words' empty prompting.

In 1816 he wrote "The Song of Harold the Brave," an adaptation of an old Scandinavian poem in which the hero is rejected by a Russian girl.

War was seen by this gentle man of sensibility in its historical context and as cause for elegiac meditations; he saw the exorbitant sufferings of those who fight. He began with picturesque depictions of Christian heroes translated from Tasso's *Jerusalem Delivered*. But he soon condemned the horrors of war in an epistle to Gnedich. In 1811 he translated excerpts from Parny's versions of Scandinavian myths: in "The Warriors' Dream" the war dead are forever frustrated in their desires, although in "The Scald" the past is glorified. The ruin of Moscow in 1812 is recorded in an epistle, "To Dashkov" (1813): "A sea of evil I have seen, My friend, and vengeful heaven's anger"; Batiushkov decried his own former use of the Anacreontic mode as frivolous. In later pieces he depicted men captured or wounded in war. In "The Shade of a Friend" (1814) he describes a clouded vision of a comrade killed in battle. The greatest of Batiushkov's war poems is an elegy, "The Crossing of the Rhine. 1814," written in 1817. The river is seen in the history of its populations, in the panorama of its shores and hills, and finally, during the triumphant fording by the army. No moral comment intrudes.

The romantic veneration of poetry and the other arts was convincing to Batiushkov, as it was to all the younger poets of the golden age who came after him. In "The Dream" (1802) he loves fantasy, as Karamzin had loved Untruth. He describes the poet as being always close to nature (an epistle to I. M. Muravev-Apostal, 1814). The crowd's insensitivity to genuine poetry is shown in "Hesiod and Homer—Rivals" (1817), in which the great artist is ostracized in favor of the merely popular. In "The Dying Tasso" (1817) the crowd is forgiven by the genius, who departs admiring the sun and anticipating heaven. Finally, the imagination is seen as a gift from heaven in "The Dream" (1817). These romantic views in no way precluded his return to *The Greek Anthology*, from which he made thirteen translations in 1817 and 1818; imitations that he made in 1821 were among his last poems. Batiushkov was not to be known as a translator, although about one-quarter of his lyrics are either translations or adaptations. Despite its eclecticism, Batiushkov's work has a coherence as a whole; it bears the stamp of a melancholia that is tastefully expressed. It is irreproachable in tone; its sole drawback is that it is faintly abstract.

Karamzinists versus Archaizers

Among the many active members of the Turgenev family was Andrey Turgenev (1781–1803), who in 1801 organized one of the early Karamzinist circles, the Friendly Literary Society, in Moscow. He wrote poetry close to the sentimental example of Dmitriev and died young. The inner circles of the Karamzin school included Vasily Pushkin (1770–1830), an uncle of Aleksandr Pushkin. Vasily Pushkin is best known for a satirical verse narrative called "A Dangerous Neighbor" (1810), a ribald tale spoofing the provincial gentry. Pushkin was also the author of a number of lyrics—including elegies, romances, songs, and album verse—most of which were written between 1810 and 1815. His poetry is not exceptional, but his presence on the literary scene is not forgotten. He was the friend and ally of Zhukovsky, a member of the Arzamas literary club, and the first literary mentor of his famous nephew. A collection of his verse appeared in 1822.

The archaizers generally subscribed to Admiral Aleksandr Shishkov's view, expressed in "Discourse on the Old and New Style in Russian Language" (1803), that Church Slavic words should be preserved for the sake of solemnity and because they embody the national spirit. Shishkov believed that Karamzin's neologisms carried in them the seeds of revolution. In their purism, the archaizers also favored the use of the peasants' Russian. Eventually, the members of the group included political liberals, if not potential revolutionaries, whose populist view of language was romantic. Among them was Nikolay Gnedich (1784–1833), who was primarily a translator. In addition to the *Iliad,* he translated works by Schiller, Voltaire, Shakespeare, and Macpherson, seeking in every language its own popular element. He was the friend both of Batiushkov and of Krylov. Pavel Katenin (1792–1853) was a political rebel and the author of civic poetry in the 1810s and early 1820s. In 1814 and 1815, he also wrote imitations of folk ballads with a religious point of view. He was a follower of Krylov, and he in turn influenced the poets who were to be among the perpetrators of the Decembrist Revolt in 1825. Katenin was banned from St. Petersburg in 1822 and was thus unable to participate in the revolt himself.

7

Pushkin and His Pleiad
(1820–1830)

The most significant political event in the life of the new literary generation was the Decembrist Revolt, a coup d'état attempted by liberal aristocrats on December 14, 1825. The occasion chosen by the conspirators was the passage of power from the conservative Alexander I to his brother, Nicholas I. In the last years of his reign, Alexander had fostered an atmosphere of superstition-ridden mysticism. Liberal public opinion, which had once been stirred by the republican ideas brought back from Europe by veterans in the wake of the Napoleonic Wars, were now aroused by the Greek war of independence from Turkey. The cause was popular in the West, especially after Lord Byron died at Missolonghi in 1824. Secret insurrectionist societies had been formed in Russia in the early 1820s. The gentry enthusiasts who perpetrated the Decembrist Revolt were punished by execution or exile to Siberia. The revolt, although small and initially without public support, quickly became a symbol of resistance and engendered a tradition of popular remembrance. Nicholas I formed his policies in fear of violent disturbances. Liberal tendencies were held in check after 1826 by the newly created Third Department, or secret police which was responsible only to the tsar.

The Golden Age Generation

The Russian poets who came to maturity in about 1820 were influenced by Byron, as were poets on the Continent, but they could not be called a totally romantic generation. They admired in Byron his rebellious, self-lacerating hero, as well as his exotic Eastern settings. Byron's contemporaries, Percy Bysshe Shelley and John Keats, who embodied the romantic impulse toward mystical affirmation, had no echo as yet in Russia. The Karamzinists, who still occupied the central place in Russian literature, came to be known in the course of the decade as the Pushkin pleiad, or Pushkin party. They remained as eclectic as their mentors. They still rallied to the banner of "light poetry" bequeathed to them by Batiushkov, and they were still indebted to the elegist Evariste Parny and others of his period. They excelled at small elegies in a minor key, and at friendly epistles; even pastoral idylls were written. Some wrote political invective and satire in a classical style. Notable among these poets was Petr Viazemsky, whose targets were not only the court and bureaucracy, but Russian culture as a whole. The Pushkin poets kept alive a feeling for the classical genres and their proper subjects. But the literary decade was dominated by a series of Byronic narratives written by Pushkin, who imitated the Eastern Tales. The *mal du siècle,* with its psychic poisons, was also reflected in the works of the Pushkin group. However, romanticism was primarily a banner of literary freedom for these poets. They also thirsted for political liberty, but they kept that need subdued in their verse. Pushkin wrote *Boris Godunov,* a Shakespearean study of usurpation, on the eve of the Decembrist Revolt.

Those poets who remained outside the Pushkin party included the archaizers, who in the early 1820s still opposed Karamzin's language reform and who urged the use of both Church Slavic and folk Russian. Some hoped to see a new civic literature. Vilgelm Kiukhelbeker, for example, endeavored to create a new high style for solemn, public themes. There were poets for whom the civic theme was paramount, regardless of language and vocabulary; they are now considered "Decembrists." The leader of the Decembrist Revolt was a minor poet, Kondraty Ryleev, who wrote romantic narrative poems on historical subjects. His execution and the exile of many other Decembrists to Siberia dismayed their literary foes.

The post-Decembrist era brought a chill to literature and the beginning of a shift in direction. Satire begin to decline, and, in general, a sense of immediacy, or even of play, receded from poetry. Pushkin's major works were sober and anti-Byronic. His narrative poem *Poltava* (1828) is an intensely patriotic study and an emotional argument against rebellion. In the final chapters of his verse novel, *Eugene Onegin,* his once-Byronic hero faces a muted fate. The Pushkin group was in time challenged by others. The group's party almanac, *Northern Flowers* (1825–1832), was attacked by bourgeois journalists. Philosophical subjects became more common. Even a major poet of the Pushkin group, Evgeny Baratynsky, wrote metaphysical elegies about reason and the passions. German romantic philosophy, particularly Schelling's *Naturphilosophie,* was reflected in the work of other poets.

Viazemsky

The contradictions of the 1820s are exemplified in the work of Petr Viazemsky (1792–1878). The poems for which he is usually remembered are classical in their dependence on wit and intellectual acumen, and often satirical. Yet he was the theoretical defender of romanticism in the golden age, and his admiration for Byron was genuine. He was at heart an ideological combatant, and was always in the thick of any of the controversies surrounding the Pushkin pleiad. During a long career he also wrote sentimental and romantic verse, and finally became a realist in an age of prose.

Viazemsky was an aristocratic liberal, a somewhat reluctant diplomat who was devoted to his literary activities. He was born in Moscow; on the death of his father in 1807, he moved in with Karamzin, his brother-in-law. He was educated in St. Petersburg and was an original member of Arzamas. He fought at the Battle of Borodino in 1812 and later served the Foreign Office in Warsaw. He was dismissed in 1821 for having participated in a government-inspired project for a Russian constitution in 1820. His romantic manifesto, "A Conversation between a Publisher and a Classicist from the Vyborg District or Vasilevsky Island," appeared as an introduction to Pushkin's Byronic narrative, "The Fountain of Bakhchisaray," in 1822. He was an active contributor to Pushkin's periodicals, *The Literary Gazette* and *The Contemporary*. He survived all the other members of the Pushkin group and lived to oppose both the conservative Slavophiles and the radical Hegelians in the 1840s and the 1850s. During 1850s he was a censor; after his retirement in 1863, he lived abroad. His memoirs, written in the 1860s and 1870s, illuminate the golden age.

Viazemsky delighted his audience in the 1810s with bracing lyrics that were nearly devoid of sentimentalism, a current that he ridiculed in epigrams. In epistles written to Zhukovsky, Batiushkov, Davydov, Fedor Ivanovich (the "American") Tolstoy, and others, he pictured himself as an active, somewhat eccentric person. His occasional love poems were Anacreontics (he was particularly fortunate in his happy marriage). Those satires in which he attacked tyrants, bureaucrats, and the institution of serfdom were especially admired; but he also spoke out against drunks, fools, hypocrites, slanderers, and lovers of rank. His political invective was occasionally elevated. In "Indignation" (1820) he anticipates the punishment of political malefactors: "Of fear and shame the icy sweat / Will bead upon their gloomy foreheads." His satires appeared throughout the 1820s. Among the most popular was "The Russian God" (1828):

> Would you like an explanation
> Of the term, "our Russian god"?
> Here is my delineation,
> These are traits that I have found:
>
> God of snowstorms, god of potholes,
> God of miserable roads,
> Stations that are cockroach bureaus
> That's him, that's our Russian god.
>
> God of hungry men and freezing,
> Beggars standing on all sides,
> God of farms that earn no income,
> That's him, that's our Russian god.
>
> God of hanging breasts and asses,
> Shoes of felt and swollen feet,
> Sour cream and bitter faces,
> That's him, that's our Russian god.
>
> God of aperitifs and pickles,
> Peasant souls tied up in pawn,

Brigadiers' wives of both sexes,
That's him, that's our Russian god.

God of men with court medallions,
God of doormen without boots,
Peers in sleighs with two postilions,
That's him, that's our Russian god.

Full of grace for every moron,
Hard as nails if you are smart,
God of everything that's backward,
That's him, that's our Russian god.

God of everything that's foreign,
Does not fit, is out of place,
God of mustard after dinner,
That's him, that's our Russian god.

God of aliens in transience,
All who come to us by chance,
God especially of Germans,
That's him, that's our Russian god.

This was, however, one of his last satires, and by the 1830s all his criticisms of the government had ceased.

Sentimentalism appeared in Viazemsky's verse in the 1820s. His "The First Snow" (1819) is a genre painting reminiscent of Thomson's *The Seasons;* Viazemsky shows the gentry at their winter pastimes, such as ice skating. He described himself as alienated from society and preferring country life. Even so, the persona he created seemed somewhat cynical and witty. He also wrote in admiration of Byron. It was in "Byron" (1827), his response to the poet's death, that he made his most concise statement of romantic doctrine: the poet's gift is said to be inborn, not learned as a craft; the poet is drawn to nature and creates in isolation. Byron himself is described as "the genius of emotions." But Viazemsky's own poetry remained more sentimental than romantic; in "My Parents' House" (1830) he wrote about his family memories. In other poems he described tears as healing, and earthly transience as a cause for nostalgia.

In the 1830s Viazemsky portrayed himself as a lonely Russian nomad in Western Europe, a man who indulges in meditations, melancholia, and hypochondria (his keen sense of irony never left him). His homesickness appears in "The Samovar." But his descriptions of the sea were romantic, sometimes Byronic. In "Brighton" (1838) the ocean speaks to us about the mystery of existence, but we, limited humans, fail to understand. In subsequent years, Viazemsky wrote many travel impressions—of Reval, Rome, the Bosporus, Palestine, France, Carlsbad, Venice, Baden-Baden, Nice, Ferney—and made pensive commentaries about the peoples, histories, and landscapes of the places he visited. In "The Graveyard" (1864) an Italian cemetery is described as the locale of grandeur, purity, and respite from the passions. He also found a note of utmost candor, which is reflected, for example, in "Our life when we are old is like a worn-out robe" (1877).

Delvig

The life of the classical genres was prolonged in the verse of Baron Anton von Delvig (1798–1831), but almost as an affectation. At the heart of his poetry was a sentimental susceptibility to tender emotions, particularly to friendship and love. He brought the idyll to a late flowering, wrote memorable sonnets, and imitated the "drawn-out" folk song, as Sumarokov once had. As the chosen editor of the Pushkin group, he maintained impeccable standards of taste and intelligence in the periodicals he published.

Delvig dedicated his short career as much to the successes of the Pushkin pleiad, or "gentlemen's party," as to his own verse. He was born in Moscow to a Russified German family. He was educated at an elite gymnasium newly opened at Tsarskoe Selo, the summer palace; Pushkin was his classmate, and the distinguished faculty fostered humanistic studies and liberalism. Delvig was a member of the Arzamas literary club and of a political discussion group called the Green Lamp. He was the editor of *Northern Flowers* (1825–1831), a literary miscellany, and of the *Literary Gazette* (1830–1831), which was closed after a false denunciation to the secret police. Delvig died soon afterward of a respiratory illness.

At the core of Delvig's poetry there is a sadness or nostalgia, but his old-fashioned and carefully preserved genres are quaint. It seems that he has inherited the shell of an epicurean outlook, but has discovered life to be difficult. In "My Hut" (1818) he appears to be the fortunate, and familiar, lover of the modest, rustic life. Yet he wrote in the same year that only his verse is happy, while his life is sad ("In this book, this heap of verse"). He opens "To Krylov" (1820) with the line, "I am no more that carefree poet." Delvig, as a sentimentalist, made friendship an indispensable aspect of his identity, and many of his poems are epistles, often to fellow poets. These verse letters describe not only his own joys and sorrow but also the pathos he found in the tie of friendship itself. He wrote an idyll, "Friends" (1826), in which two Roman men recall the childhood they spent together and anticipate their reunion after death. In the other world they will question new-comers: "Do friends still love one another, as once they did in the old years?" Delvig's poems seem to suggest that some once-cherished ideals are passing in a noisier age, and his antiquated forms add to that impression. Yet Delvig could also be light and frivolous. He wrote readily for the albums of friends, annually cele-brated the graduation anniversary of his Tsarskoe Selo class, composed drinking songs, and even honored his friends' pet dogs in his verse. All his imitations of Russian folk songs were, however, melancholy in mood. In "No quick autumn rain, and fine, is it / Falling, falling, through the fog" (1824), the rain will be a simile to tears. As early as 1824 he anticipated an early death—for example, in "Your friend has gone, despairing of earth's days."

Love poems were also an essential element in Delvig's *oeuvre*, but this theme is always expressed in somewhat impersonal stylizations—the inconsequential Ana-creontic, the conventional lover's plaint, the idealizing idyll, and imitations of the folk song. His early poems are often addressed to the anonymous Liletas, or shep-herdesses, of youthful adventures, and some have pastoral settings. "Vision" (1818 or 1819) is a description of the deification of Psyche through the love of Eros.

Delvig's contemporaries especially admired an idyll called "The Bathing Girls" (1824), in which a satyr spies on the naked young women and reports their conversations about love. Among Delvig's best poems were avowals of love in sonnets; this example was written in 1822:

> Your golden curls, their fortunate disorder,
> Your azure eyes, their greeting, as in dream,
> Your lips' sweet sound, if only in dissent,
> Give birth to love with hopelessness together.
>
> Was it for this the gods sent me my caring,
> That I should faint while still in early years—
> But I forsee, I drink the cup of tears—
> The misstep in the future brings no fear;
>
> I can no more win back my peace again,
> I have forgot a free life's sweetness,
> My soul's afire but in my heart joy's silent.
>
> My blood in me does seethe and then grow cold.
> O love, is it then grief, or joy, you be:
> For death or life have I my youth entrusted?

Occasionally his stylizations were put aside; in "Disillusionment" (1824) his soul, having been deceived, is now closed to love. His imitations of "drawn-out" songs were usually devoted to love's sorrows; an example is "Nightingale, O nightingale" (1825). The same can be said of his "romances," a somewhat more literary form. Many of his songs were set to music. In his idyll "The End of the Golden Age" (1828) the familiar sentimental tale of an abandoned girl is transferred to a Greek setting. In "Death" (1830 or 1831) Delvig asks that the grim reaper come for him only at night, in place of love.

Those poems that appear to be the least stylized and to speak most directly for Delvig are the ones that concern literature and the other arts. Among them are workaday epigrams attacking literary enemies (often Dmitri Khvostov, an old-fashioned odist). Art itself, however, is depicted in romantic terms, as a priesthood. In "The Poet" (1820) art takes precedence over mere happiness. In "Inspiration" (1820) the moment of poetic inception is a martyr's moment. In the idyll "The Attainment of a Sculpture" (1829) a Greek artist receives a sacred vision of Olympus and the gods. And in "The Poet" (1830) the artist is always a sacrifice because it is his turmoil that brings beauty to the world.

Pushkin

Aleksandr Pushkin (1799–1837), by consensus Russia's greatest writer, was at his best as a poet. In an eclectic age he was the most versatile, and ultimately the most elusive and inscrutable, poet. His novel in verse, *Eugene Onegin,* is a pastiche of classical, sentimental, and romantic elements; its hero is a Childe Harold. Pushkin's narrative poems span an evolution from classical wit through Byronic romanticism to unique works. He was impatient to test the capacities of many different literary tendencies. Yet he created with his diverse tales and lyrics what some romantic poets did: a legend of his own life, a story inferred by the reader. His dramas, all in verse, fall within this circle of intimate meaning and are similar in theme to his poems. His Shakespearean play, *Boris Godunov* (the origin of Mussorgsky's opera), was but one of his studies of political power. But his prose fiction was written as though beyond the reach of his lyric thrust. The motivational springs of his romantic short story "The Queen of Spades" (Tchaikovsky's *Pique dame*) are hidden, as is the case with his Scottian historical novel, *The Captain's Daughter*.

Pushkin was an aristocrat who became for Russians a symbol of the civilizing function of literature. He survived a political exile when young and lived thereafter as a famous, but suspect, man of letters. Born to Moscow, he was educated at an elite gymnasium at the summer palace, Tsarskoe Selo. He was a member, like his colleagues, of Arzamas and of the Green Lamp circle for political discussion. He was appointed to the Foreign Office, but in 1820 he was "transferred" to Kishinev because of his political verse. He was later moved to Odessa and, in 1824, to house confinement at a family estate, Mikhailovskoe, near Pskov. The early chapters of *Eugene Onegin* brought fame, and he assumed the leadership of the Karamzinists. In 1826 he was released from Mikhailovskoe by Nicholas I on the basis of a secret agreement. Pushkin was thereafter directly monitored by the Third Department, forbidden to travel, and hindered in the publication of certain works. In 1831 he married Natalia Goncharov. He was the principal founder of the *Literary Gazette* in 1830 and of *The Contemporary* in 1836. He hoped to become a historian, like Karamzin, and was permitted to research the era of Peter the Great and the Pugachev Revolt, the subject of *The Captain's Daughter*. As a result of his wife's flirtations he was killed in a duel with Baron George D'Anthes, the adopted son of the Dutch minister in St. Petersburg.

Pushkin's earliest verse at the gymnasium was already eclectic and in part experimental. He earned the attention of the public with political statements. In a brief ode, called "Freedom" (1817), he calls for the assassination of tyrants, as Radishchev once had. In a pastoral elegy called "The Village" (1819) he complains that the Russian countryside fosters slavery. In other poems, however, Pushkin is the modest epicurean poet, attentive to friends and to colleagues—Zhukovksy, Batiushkov, and Delvig. He is then the humble inhabitant of a rural abode; in "To a House Sprite" (1819) he pleads, as to lares and penates, for the protection of his rural patrimony. The masterpiece of his early years, *Ruslan and Ludmila* (1820), is a spoof of knightly romance and fairy tales. The story, with its *bogatyr* setting and three suitors for the daughter of Prince Vladimir, owes much to Ariosto's *Orlando Furioso*, Tasso's *Jerusalem Delivered*, Bogdanovich's *Dushenka*, and Voltaire's *La Pucelle*. It was also reminiscent of the French ballets staged in St. Petersburg by the choreographer Charles Didelot. This work is the subject of an opera by Glinka.

In the south, Pushkin's poetry acquired a seething, Byronic element that was general, not merely political. He wrote narrative poems that were candid imitations of Byron's Eastern Tales, especially "The Giaour" (1813) and "The Corsair" (1814). The appearance of Pushkin's *The Captive in the Caucasus* (1821) can be taken as the opening date of Russian romanticism. Its protagonist was the first alienated hero, and its heroine was an innocent Circassian maiden. The poem depicts the craggy, stormy Caucasus Mountains, newly won from Turkey and quite unlike the plains and rivers of Russia proper. The apogee of Pushkin's Byronic tendency was *The Fountain of Bakhchisaray* (1822), whose plot turns on a love triangle among Moslems and Christians and whose heroine, a harem favorite, is murdered by drowning. A step toward the sentimental depiction of women was made in the character of her unwilling rival, the chaste, bewildered Christian captive, Mary. At the end of the poem comes a tourist's view of the harem fountain, now dry after the passage of years. The Easter season of 1821 had meanwhile brought forth from Pushkin a Voltairean travesty called "The Gabrieliad." The archangel Gabriel is seen in it to have been the first lover of the Madonna. The poem is utterly light, tastefully insinuated, and still durable as ribald literature. It could not be published, however, and was circulated only in manuscript; it was to be held against Pushkin by the secret police in his later years.

The lyrics of Pushkin's southern period were usually elegies, and in some he began to use local color. The first was an enigmatic and hotly felt elegy, "The Diurnal Orb Has Died" (1820), in which he describes the sea and speaks of betrayals. But his former St. Petersburg persona reappears in a small, polished elegy with a cool style, "I have outlived my own desires" (1821), whose tone is close to that of the fashionable Parny. "The Demon" (1823) is a Byronic confession of spleen and blasphemous tendencies. In "The Prisoner" (1822) Pushkin describes the mascot eagle that he saw in jail when he was confined for his insubordination. While in the south, Pushkin wrote a number of poems about love in a variety of styles, but they were not as memorable as his later love poems would be.

At age twenty-five, Pushkin was transferred to the family estate at Mikhailovskoe, where, after a heated fight with his father, he lived alone and was limited to visits to the neighbors. There he completed *The Gypsies* (1824), a new kind of Byronic narrative in which the rebel hero is stripped of sympathy and viewed as a common criminal. He is a renegade Russian who travels with a Gypsy tribe and murders his lover in a jealous rage. The Gypsies are themselves the less than happy representatives of Rousseau's natural man: "And everywhere are fateful passions, / And from the fates there's no defense." *Boris Godunov*, written in 1825, stems from Pushkin's preoccupation with tyranny and usurpation. Its form resulted from his reading of the historical plays of Shakespeare while in Odessa, and it is an attempt to break classical tragedy's hold on Russian drama. Boris had come to power through assassination (as Pushkin believed Alexander I had consented to do), and was thereafter unable to rule well, despite good intentions. The false Dmitri had fewer scruples and was even more quickly destroyed; would a moral rule win the favor of the fates? of the population? On finishing *Boris Godunov*, Pushkin turned immediately to an ironic piece of nonsense, "Count Nulin" (1825). This frivolous narrative was based, however, on Shakespeare's murky *The Rape of Lucrece*, in which Brutus summons the Roman populace to resist tyranny. "Count Nulin" is an arch tale about a spunky wife, but it happened to be written during the few days before the Decembrist Revolt.

The lyrics that Pushkin wrote at Mikhailovskoe began to suggest an autobiographical story. He bid farewell to the south in an elegy, "To the Sea" (1824). In

"Winter Evening" (1825) he established a new image; he is alone now but for the brisk old woman who had once been his peasant nurse; he listens as an artist to the folk tales presumably heard before. His love poems were now among his greatest. An intensely jealous inner monologue, "The cloudy day has died, the cloudy dark of night" (1824), is devoted to his memories of Amalia Riznicz, a lover in the south. Lines of airy idealization appear in his most famous love poem, "To . . ." (1825); it is addressed to a neighbor's guest, Anna Kern, whom he had known in St. Petersburg.

> I now recall a wondrous moment:
> When you appeared before my eyes,
> You were a vision seen in passing,
> An angel in your beauty pure.
>
> When in the toils of hopeless sorrow,
> In noisy vanities' alarms,
> Your gentle voice was my companion,
> And I did dream of your dear charms.
>
> Years passed. A burst of storms in tumult
> Did scatter all my former dreams,
> And I forgot your voice so gentle,
> Forgot what heaven sent, your charms.
>
> Afar, and in the dark of prison,
> In endless silence passed my days,
> With aught divine, or inspiration,
> Devoid of tears, of life, of love,
>
> But now my soul has been awakened:
> And you have once again appeared—
> You are a vision seen in passing,
> An angel in your beauty pure.
>
> And my heart beats in exultation
> And for it there do live anew
> Divinity and inspiration,
> And life itself, and love, and tears.

"Beneath the azure skies, home in your native land" (1826) is both a response to news of the death of Amalia Riznicz and a veiled allusion to the recent execution of the convicted Decembrists.

The political rebel also appeared in the lyrics written at Mikhailovskoe. In a series of poems called "Imitations of the Koran" (1824) Pushkin developed a new, authoritative style—the equivalent of the Biblical. In 1825 he translated the great elegy written by André Chenier, the epicurean poet turned revolutionary, on the eve of his execution by Robespierre in 1794. In the wake of the Decembrist Revolt, in 1826, Pushkin embarked on an imitation of the Book of Isaiah, from which only one famous poem survives—"The Prophet." It concludes:

Upon the sand, corpse-like, I lay,
And then God's voice within called out:
"Arise, O prophet, see, and hear,
Fulfill from now what is my will,
And, circling round the earth and seas,
Sear with your words the hearts of men."

This poem has always been understood as a statement of the independence of the poet. Pushkin took it with him to freedom when released by Nicholas I; according to legend, he carried it in his pocket during his secret interview with the tsar.

When Pushkin had been freed from Mikhailovskoe, he was determined to take a responsible attitude toward the government, but he was also wary. He was to write one more narrative that grew out of the Byronic inspiration of his southern years. In *Poltava* (1828) he portrays the Cossack hetman Mazeppa, who joined Charles XII of Sweden and betrayed his fealty to Peter I. Now it is Mazeppa, who lives in the south and resembles the Byronic character, who is the immoral tyrant, while Peter I is described in odic terms. The author's passion in this poem seems strangely frenetic. Tchaikovsky used the work as the basis for his opera *Mazeppa*.

The novel in verse, *Eugene Onegin* (1831), is a more distant landing of the Byronic wave. Two currents germane to Pushkin's verse are brought together in it. Eugene is a Childe Harold, while the heroine, Tatiana, is a sentimental or romantic heroine, a Clarissa Harlowe or new Heloise. A narrator tells their bleak and eventless story with sympathy. Tatiana, a reclusive provincial girl, writes a love letter to the haughty Eugene, and he rejects her. Years later she rules the *haut monde* in St. Petersburg, and he writes a love letter to her. Having married a conventional general, Tatiana, in pain, rejects Eugene. When Pushkin once brought Byron's and Rousseau's ideas together in *The Gypsies,* it was to criticize both philosophies. In *Eugene Onegin,* the protagonists are sympathetic, almost the only interesting characters in a sea of nonentities. The conventional general, in particular, is a cipher who scarcely merits description. The narrator has much to say in his digressions, and is easily the least schematic and most attractive figure. But he does not exemplify life's mistakes, as do the two characters he presents, and he is easily forgotten. The tone of the work changes imperceptibly from mirthful and insinuating to somber and elegiac.

The spirit of youthful defiance remained alive in the *Little Tragedies,* Pushkin's miniature plays. They were conceived at Mikhailovskoe in the wake of his fight with his father. They were not written until the autumn of 1830, when Pushkin, who was preparing for his marriage to Natalia Goncharov, was quarantined at a family estate, Boldino, by a cholera epidemic. The small plays were suggested by the *Dramatic Sketches* of Barry Cornwall, now forgotten. All have Mediterranean settings. In *The Miserly Knight* a stingy father is challenged by his free-handed, resentful son. In *Mozart and Salieri* (the basis for an opera by Rimsky-Korsakov) the same pair is transformed into Salieri, the musical drudge, and Mozart, the carefree genius. As the miser's speech steals the show in the first piece, so does Salieri's smoldering, calculating envy in the second. In *The Stone Guest,* a Don Juan story, Pushkin made an unexpected alteration: Don Juan has tasted an irrevocable love for Donna Anna before the stone commander comes to drag him down to hell. The young man has learned a lesson here. The fourth play—*Feast in the Plague*—is an accurate translation of one interlude selected from John Wilson's *The City of the Plague* (1816); the leader of the street revelers stands up to the priest as corpses are rolled through the streets. These compact plays were followed by a relaxed, humorous narrative poem, "The Little House in Kolomna": the daughter of a widow hires a new cook, who is a man passing as a woman but is caught shaving. At Boldino, Pushkin also wrote the five prose stories that compose his *Belkin's Tales*.

The lyrics that Pushkin wrote after his release from Mikhailovskoe were those of a man who wished to settle down and to marry. He wrote few introspective elegies, but those he did write were among his greatest poems. "Memory" was written in 1828:

> When for the mortal man the noisy day does end
>   And when the city's squares are silent,
> Half in transparency night's shade comes down to rest,
>   And sleep, reward for each day's labor—
> For me that is the time when in the silence drag
>   The hours of my tormenting vigil:
> In idleness at night more lively burn in me
>   The constant bites of my heart's serpent;
> My daydreams roil, and in my mind, crushed down with grief,
>   Crowd thoughts excessive and too weighty,
> Then does my memory in silence for my eyes
>   Unwind a scroll that seems unending;
> And with revulsion deep, as I do read my life,
>   I tremble and I curses utter,
> And bitterly complain, and bitter tears I weep,
>   Nor wash away one line of sorrow.

The elegy called "When through the noisy streets I wander" (1829) is an expression of the classical philosophy: death is an unfeeling rest amid a grand but indifferent nature.

Pushkin's lyrics about love contain the story of a difficult period in his life. "The Winter Road" (1826) suggests a longing for domestic warmth. "O do not sing, fair maid, for me" (1828) is a confession that his heart is still drawn to Georgia and the south. In 1829 he proposed to Natalia Goncharov and was refused. He bolted from St. Petersburg and traveled without permission to the south, where he rode with the Russian army against the Turks. Here he wrote descriptions of nature unprecedented in his *oeuvre*. "The Caucasus" is a panoramic sweep from the sky down into a mountain abyss where the river Terek rages like a wild beast. On the same day in September, he wrote "Monastery on Kazbek," in which a religious retreat attracts the eye upward like the peace of a heavenly ark. A commitment to his desire to marry Natalia brought farewells to older memories. "I loved you once; that love perhaps does linger" (1829) is admired for its brief elegance. In 1830 came a last goodbye to the memory of Amalia Riznicz, "Unto your distant homeland's shores." Also in 1830 he wrote "Madonna," comparing Natalia, now his fiancée, to a painting by Raphael. After his marriage he ceased to write love poems. "The Beauty" (1832) is a cool admiration of a physical perfection.

Several of Pushkin's poems on general issues turned on the role of art. He adopted the romantic view of art as a priesthood, but for him this view seemed to be a guarantee of artistic freedom. In "The Poet" (1827) the artist is lifted above trivial pursuits by the divine and irresistible inspiration of Apollo. In "The Poet and the Mob" (1828) the poet rejects the crowd's demand for the conventional homilies that it believes suitable to art. Pushkin had meanwhile confirmed his liberal outlook with an epistle (1827) sent in secret to the exiled Decembrists in Siberia. In a bleak parable on statehood, "The Upas Tree" (1828), his message is austere: tyrants send slaves to collect poison for their warfare, and the slave who obeys will die.

The poetry written by Pushkin after his marriage seemed increasingly impersonal to his readers. In his greatest narrative poem, *The Bronze Horseman* (1833), the rectitude of the monarch, Peter I, is placed on the moral scale opposite the rights of one insignificant subject whose dreams cannot rise above the mediocre—and the scales will not budge in either direction. The poem depicts a flood of 1824 during which citizens of St. Petersburg perished while Peter's descendant, Alexander I, looked helplessly on. The statute of Peter is threatened by a gesture from a lonely clerk, Eugene; the gesture is so far impotent, but it symbolizes, as does the flood, revolution. Pushkin had reached the stage of wanting to be a historian and had researched the Pugachev Revolt on its sites as well as in libraries.

Pushkin's energies were devoted in part to his imitations of folklore, which were written in the spirit of romantic nationalism. "The Tale of the Priest and His Servant Balda" (1830) is an escapade showing how one Russian peasant can outwit the kingdom of Satan (or the upper classes). "The Tale of Tsar Saltan" (1831), a story in which the youngest sister marries the king, is believed to be Pushkin's honeymoon work, or epithalamion. His last, "Tale of the Golden Cockerel" (1834), was adapted from Washington Irving's "The Legend of the Arabian Astrologer" in *The Alhambra*. The magician of Pushkin's tale is able to destroy the entire royal family through the creation of a phantom beauty, a princess. Several of these tales were written because of a controversy with Zhukovsky. Rimsky-Korsakov utilized the most famous of them for his operas *Czar Saltan* and *Le Coq d'or*.

In the lyrics written after Pushkin's marriage in 1831, the autobiographical threads are all but lost. He is still appreciative of life and its ordinary joys, for example in "Autumn" (1833). But other, unpublished poems, such as "O God, don't let me go insane" (1833), throw light on a hidden anguish. He also wrote a prayer, "Hermit Fathers and Chaste Women" (1836), which was to be included in a small cycle of poems on authority and morality. A bitter note appears in "The Monument" (1836), his adaptation of Horace's "Exegi monumentum"; Horace knows that his work will endure, and so does Pushkin, so he can disdain the harassment of contemporaries. Pushkin's work does in fact outlast every interpretation that is put on it. In every age he has been the symbol of his nation's literature.

Baratynsky

The only philosophical poet among the urbane Pushkin poets was Evgeny Baratynsky (1800–1844). He has been regarded as a poet's poet, and admirers place him among the very best. He was the most convincingly melancholy of the group, and the most nearly romantic. Caught between two ages, he dismissed the reason as a meaningless faculty, but he was not yet able to trust the passions. He was the first major poet to feel the influence of Schelling. He also wrote the light poetry, the epistles and love poems, that were typical of the Pushkin group. And he was the author of sentimental and romantic narrative poems.

Baratynsky began as a willing composer of light verse; good times among good friends is the whole subject of his first long poem, "The Friends" (1821). His epistles soon became nostalgic and apprehensive, however. He spoke of being deprived of happiness and driven by fate. He wrote with youthful earnestness about his friends' careers and about the value of industry and ambition. He was to write especially moving epistles to Delvig, as Delvig did to him. Friendship itself is idealized in a meditation called "Star" (1824). It was in part through Baratynsky's conscientious letters that a feeling of close alliance among the Pushkin pleiad was maintained. In the 1830s epistles went out of fashion as a genre.

His introspective lyrics were closer to his metaphysical poems than were his epistles. His melancholia at first appeared to be merely conventional. He complained of the losses sustained in youth, of being alone in Finland. A deeper and more causeless sadness appeared in "Elegy" (1821), where his hopes and happiness recede like a friend departing by sea. He welcomed death. In "Hopelessness" (1823) he seeks peace in resignation. But within his solitary self there was a conflict. He was stirred in "The Waterfall" (1821) by the power of nature's violence to attract him, and again in "The Storm" (1824) he discovered a sense of challenge. His introspective elegies took on the character of intellectual poems and began to register life's dilemmas.

The intellectual poems for which Baratynsky is remembered pertain especially to the pain of the inner life. His poetry emanates not from a system of thought, but from a romantic distrust in its own guide—the search for happiness in the emotions. He discovered, as did some other romantics, the futility of that search. He recorded the impasses he encountered, and the springs of his melancholia. In general, the vital forces, sometimes seen as passions, seemed to him the polar opposite of the reason, often viewed as mere logic, and he felt constrained to choose between them. An early elegy on this subject is "Two Fates" (1823):

> By providence two fates are given,
>   And wisdom mortal makes its choice:
> For either hope and agitation,
>   Or for indifference and peace.
>
> Let him believe in hope alluring
>   Who's bold because his mind is young,
> Who only through conflicting rumor
>   Knows of the mockeries of fate.

Then hope, O youths with seething spirit!
    Then fly, for you are given wings;
Before you rise all brilliant projects,
    And all the heart's most flaming dreams!

But you, who've tested fate already,
    Its idle pleasures, power's griefs,
O you, who've won the truth of living,
    And in yourself its heavy lot!

Chase off their swarm all too enchanting,
    Yes! live your life in simple peace,
And guard the salutary coldness
    That's in a soul that knows no deeds.

Thus blissful in their lack of feeling,
    As corpses dead within the grave
Roused up by words from a magician
    Would rise with gnashing of their teeth—

Thus you, if warmed in soul by wishes,
    And, mad, give in to their deceit,
Will waken only to your sorrow
    To pains anew from former wounds.

In poem after poem, his disillusionments dictate a withdrawal from life, while his capacity for love and inspiration, for life's attainments and rewards, urge him to choose engagement. In "Truth" (1823) he hopes that true knowledge (and disillusionment) will not come to him before death. Whether he opts for vitality or for lifelessness, the choice is all the more painful for its transparent inadequacy. In "Death" (1828) he sees in the cessation of life a return to a natural order, an end to conflicts and turmoil. These dilemmas continued to preoccupy him through the 1830s, and in several poems he recognized introspection itself as the culprit. In other late poems he complained only of aging and of monotony. In his last poems, Baratynsky did exit from his depressions, and then he spoke not of peace, but of his practical life, of visits to Finland and Italy.

The extraordinary character of Baratynsky's intellectual poetry has caused his other poems to remain in relative obscurity. Like classicists before him, he satirized the dishonorable man, the fool, the busybody, the inconvenient neighbor. He disdained the high government official who is only the tsar's servant. Baratynsky also wrote humorous epigrams in which he attacked dull or bad writers and enemies of his poetic party. He also wrote as many love poems, or lyrics about love, as his colleagues, but he is not recalled as a lover. Some of these poems record his feelings of admiration and warmth; "A Portrait of K . . ." (1819) was written as a tribute. He also was convinced that he suffered because of his devotions. He complained that he could not trust his beloved, that he was tired of deceptions. In "To Amor" (1826) he thanks the god of love "for very little." In 1827, however, came "Stanzas," a sentimental poem in which he is glad to bring his wife and child to his patrimonial home. In the 1830s he contrasted love with art, or purity with passion. Baratynsky professed a need for friendly and for loving relationships, but in his greatest poems he is typically alone.

Baratynsky's early poems about art and literature expressed the romantic views common to the Pushkin party. In one arresting poem he wrote, unjustly, that his own muse is a "plain" girl ("Muse," 1829). A different stage of romanticism appeared as he came under Schelling's influence. He put art on a higher plane. In "On the death of Goethe" (1832) he praised the faculty of genius as a metaphysical entity that is the equal of a heaven or an earth. He found a harmony in art that places it above passion and above considerations of happiness. "The art of song does heal the ailing spirit" was written in 1835. He feared, however, for the future of civilization. In "The Last Poet" (1835) he foresees the suicide of the only remaining artist in a new iron age of reason and practicality.

Baratynsky's best poems are based on partial truths; it was his gift to make impasses intensely felt. His contrast between truth and desire led to rather geometric constructions. His voice, however, creates long, sinuous lines of thought that cross over the divisions of his contrasts with their emotional tension. His intonations are seductive and inspire confidence, and his conclusions can be powerful. His rhythms are stately and intricate, and his sense of musical sound is full and generous. His message may be of deprivations, but his poetic offerings are rich.

In his three narrative poems, Baratynsky seems to have set himself a different literary task. In each of these stories of betrayals in love, he tried to dress a literary convention in a new, realistic manner. *Eda* (1827) is a sentimental story of seduction set in Finland; his protagonists are an army officer and a Finnish farm girl; he was unable to prevail over its clichés. In *The Ball* (1838) he chose a romantic plot, a contrast between heroines, one dark, one fair. His eccentric, dark-haired Nina is superior to the shallow younger woman, but neither is finally attractive because both are self-centered. In "The Gypsy" (1842) the exotic girl is spurned and inadvertently poisons her society lover. Baratynsky's realism remained an experiment; it only robbed the tales of their inherent drama.

Iazykov

The most outspoken liberal in the Pushkin party was its youngest member, Nikolay Iazykov (1803–1847). He cultivated the light poetry that was a hallmark of the pleiad. In his Horatian epistles, he disdained signs of sentimentalism, however. His *oeuvre* is particularly autobiographical, and he is still recalled as a student poet at Dorpat University. His lyrics also include love poems and, in a later period, travel impressions. In the 1830s and 1840s he wrote verse adaptations of folk tales, narrative poems, and short verse dramas. Iazykov belonged to a gentry family of the Simbirsk area and knew Karamzin. He attended Dorpat University, a German school on Russian soil, because the political climate was felt to be more liberal there. Notoriety came with a series of seditious student drinking songs written in 1823. He addressed his love lyrics to the younger sister of Maria Protasova, Zhukovsky's beloved. In 1829 Iazykov moved to Moscow, where he entered more conservative and nationalistic circles. He was close to such future Slavophiles as

Aleksey Khomiakov and the brothers Ivan and Petr Kireevsky. Iazykov was forced by a progressive spinal paralysis to spend the years between 1829 and 1843 at German and Italian spas. His condition being incurable, he returned to Moscow and in 1844 defended the Slavophile view in xenophobic attacks on the future Westernizers.

Iazykov's outlook, especially in his epistles, derived from Horace, Tibullus, and other robust, classical minds. His virtues were candor and an instinctive sense of equality. Among his earliest poems are farewells to young friends as they depart for schools and careers; he assures them that virtue means more to him than fame. Once at Dorpat, he addressed letters to his schoolmates and to his brothers, Aleksandr and Petr. In these epistles his aired his liberal views, described his escapades, and eventually spoke of his love. He excelled at wit and satirical remarks. His ten drinking songs of 1823 include such lines as "Then let our holiness but be / Wine, and joy, and liberty!" Other poems were disparaging to the tsar. On December 20, 1825, just after the Decembrist uprising, Iazykov wrote "An Apology," which concludes with these lines:

> The times we face are cruel, harsh,
> Stupidity's enthroned in arms!
> Farewell, O poetry that's holy,
> Hello, O slavery's quietude!

Before leaving Dorpat, he praised the university as a center of enlightenment and a beacon of liberty.

Iazykov's liberal sentiments had always gone hand in hand with a generous, unthinking patriotism. In the early 1820s he experimented with historical narratives and ballads inspired by Macpherson's Ossian poems and other preromantic literature. He portrayed, as had Zhukovsky, a bard-warrior called Baian, a legendary singer named in *The Tale of Igor's Campaign.* In Iazykov's "Baian to the Russian Warrior . . . " (1823) the bard has fought against the Mongols with Dmitri Donskoy. "Evpaty" (1824) describes a citizen's defiance of the Mongols at Riazan. Other poems were devoted to Novgorod, which liberals regarded as a symbol of liberty; it was the last city to fall under the centralizing tyranny of Moscow.

As a student Iazykov addressed poignant, ambivalent love poems to Aleksandra Voeikova, *née* Protasova, whom Zhukovsky called Svetlana. Iazykov often called his love poems "elegies," but his poems were virtual travesties of that somber genre; he hated self-pity and wrote spontaneous, frank "elegies." The most ambitious poem of his student years, "Trigorskoe" (1826), was written as a thank-you letter after a summer visit to the estate of a classmate, Aleksey Wulf. The country house is described, as well as its landscapes. The family consisted of his classmate's mother and sister, and Pushkin, a neighbor at Mikhailovskoe, rode over to visit. The amusements included artistic evenings and swimming: "And bam! the water drops fly up / Like glistening rain in myriad splashes." During his student years, Iazykov praised all conviviality, and wine itself, as indicative of a love for liberty.

When he had returned to Moscow, Iazykov recalled Dorpat with nostalgia. His epistles remained an ordinary part of his relationships with new friends and new colleagues in art. The political poems that he wrote in Moscow were for more repressive times; they were "Aesopic," as Russians began to call literature with a veiled political meaning, and they counseled stoicism. "The Sailor" (1829) was popular with the radical intelligentsia throughout the nineteenth century. Iazykov also wrote adaptations of suggestive psalms, including Psalm 137, about the Jews in captivity. The love poems that he wrote in Moscow are not addressed to any object of affection comparable to Voeikova. He praised, for example, the Gypsy singer Tania, a favorite with several Russian poets. His "Insomnia" (1831) and similar poems are perhaps recollections of Voeikova.

In Moscow he began to feel the effects of his illness and to write less. He was persuaded by the Kireevsky brothers' enthusiasm for folklore to collect and imitate it himself. But his character was not suited for romantic tasks, and his verse tales are facetious. "The Tale of the Shepherd and the Wild Boar" (1835) extols wine. In "The Fire-Bird: A Dramatic Tale" (1838) the story of Ivan and the gray wolf is told with innuendos and anachronisms. The lyrics he wrote while in Italy and Germany are frankly those of a sick man visiting spas. He recorded his impressions of street scenes in Alpine towns, crossings of the Alps, and the Mediterranean seashore.

Evening

Now shades of mountains fall across the sleepy bay,
While rows of lemon, olive trees upon the shore
Are emptied; clear, the west does scarce gleam on the sea,
And soon the goodly day, so full of mirth and beauty,
With hues of fiery gold and purple will depart
From off the chastened glass of waters beyond sight.

He was often homesick. In an ode, "To the Rhine" (1840), he praises the great rivers of Russia, with their extensive landscapes and great commercial value. He also wrote three short verse dramas—"Sergeant Surmin," "Meeting the New Year," and "A Strange Occurrence"—which seem to derive from the youthful expectations that illness forced him to forgo. The works that Iazykov wrote when he returned to Moscow reflect not merely a love of country, but a hatred of things foreign. In the epistle "To Those Who Are Not Ours" (1844) he attacks the incipient Westernizers. In a medieval drama, "The Youth Viachko" (1844), he depicts an act of patriotic heroism. A narrative poem, "The Linden Trees" (1846), portrays German culture as tedious and materialistic. His moralistic urge became general. In "Earthquake" (1844) he pictures the artist as divinely inspired and soaring above the populace, an agent of his people's salvation. In "Samson" (1847) he describes the righteous man, who, although doomed, can still kill.

Iazykov's style has been described in terms of "energy" and even "fireworks." Its merit is its apparent spontaneity. He could spin out long sentences in apparently artlessly tumbling, but faultlessly articulated, syntax. This great and aggressive organizing faculty seemed to argue the presence of an unusually vigorous mind. His vocabulary was rather plain, although he used Church Slavic. When he chose to be rhetorical, as in "To the Rhine," his style was unique.

The Decembrists

The high priority that they gave to their political engagement separated the Decembrists from the Pushkin pleiad, although both groups belonged to essentially the same eclectic literary culture. The Decembrists were also closer than the Pushkin party to preromantic movements, especially to the German *Sturm und Drang*.

The liberation movements of Western Europe, especially that of Greece, had an extraordinary influence on Vilgelm Kiukhelbeker (1787–1846). Born an aristocrat in St. Petersburg, he learned about the *Sturm und Drang* poets, including the early Goethe and Schiller, from his German mother. He was educated at the Tsarskoe Selo school and was appointed to the Moscow archive of the Foreign Office, where German romantic philosophy was popular. Having gone to the West as a diplomat's secretary, he was sent home in 1821 by the Russian Embassy at Paris for having delivered revolutionary public lectures. In 1822 he served in the Caucasus, where he adopted the archaizing ideas of the playwright Aleksandr Griboedov, a liberal diplomat. Kiukhelbeker worked for the almanac *Mnemosyne* (1824 and 1825) and the literary magazine *Son of the Fatherland* before taking part in the Decembrist uprising on December 14, 1825. He spent a decade in prison and a decade in exile in Siberia, where he went blind.

Kiukhelbeker's lyrics in the 1810s were not yet civic poetry. They expressed an extreme degree of melancholia. The relentlessness of his griefs seemed excessive to the young Karamzinists, who aimed to appear more suave. Kiukhelbeker described himself as already in his coffin, and spoke of his "genius" as his only friend. The songbird he hears in "To the Nightingale" (1818) only intensifies his sorrows. He was afflicted by metaphysical anxieties and despair. His hope for immortality was faint, and symbolized by stars. He portrayed Nemesis as standing guard to punish humanity for unnamed crimes. His classical references suggested not a humanistic mentality, but pagan cults. He translated from Homer and other ancient poets their hymns to Dionysus, to Apollo, and to the earth. His nature scenes included dire portents and melancholy symbols: a solitary swan, a low sun, a prominent moon. He subscribed to the cult of art and the artist, and he saw himself as favored by Zeus but ridiculed by the crowd.

Kiukhelbeker's themes were transformed in Europe. He wrote travel impressions of Marseilles, Nice, and the Rhine, and praised Greece's struggle for independence. But in later poems he acquired an exaggerated notion of his own mission, both as a poet and as a citizen. He wrote a tragedy, *The Argives* (1823), which depicts the attempt to free ancient Corinth from tyrants. He anticipated humiliations and predicted that Nemesis, or posterity, would take revenge on those who persecute poets. In "The Fate of Poets" (1823 or 1824) he pictures a zealot whose Apollonian shafts may kill. These poems make uneasy reading and might have foretold his presence on Senate Square on December 14. He attempted to create a new high style for his civic themes through a return to Church Slavic and rhetorical syntax. The poems he wrote in prison and exile show a calmer spirit, but no change in beliefs or inclinations. In exile, Kiukhelbeker also wrote five narrative poems and three dramas about heroes and their fates, as well as a mystical novel, *The Last Column*, in 1842.

Kondraty Ryleev (1795–1826) was known as a poet and an editor before the Decembrist Revolt, when he emerged as the president of the secret Northern Society. He was the author of twenty-two narrative poems about legendary and historical Russian figures. He imitated a Ukrainian form called the *duma*. He also wrote a romantic narrative in verse, *Voinarovsky* (1824), and some agitational songs. Ryleev was a member of the gentry, a young bureaucrat who began to see in literature an instrument of cultural persuasion. He was born near St. Petersburg and educated at the Cadet Corps school, where he began to write light verse. He traversed Europe as an army officer and then married at Voronezh, in the Ukraine. In 1818 he resigned on principle from the army and moved to St. Petersburg, where he served as an assessor at the Criminal Court and then as manager of the Russian-American Company. He was an editor of the literary miscellany *The Polar Star* from 1823 to 1825. He was arrested immediately after the Decembrist Revolt in 1825 and hanged the following year.

The lyrics that Ryleev wrote between 1813 and 1820 are devoid of civic sentiments. They are the friendly and jocular poems of an eighteenth-century optimist. The majority are slight and playful poems about love, sometimes about its losses (never deeply felt), and about encounters with Delias and Doridas; one is a adaptation from Sappho. His many epistles include poems for such traditional occasions as a housewarming or a name day, and album verse to men and women. Several are adaptations from Anacreon. Only after 1820 did patriotism, citizenship, and public service become subjects for his lyrics, and only in a few. In 1824 he wrote a lament for the death of Byron, seen as a fighter for freedom. In "To Vera Nikolaevna Stolypin" (1825) he urges mothers to teach their children to die for country and for principles. Radical sentiments also appeared in epistles to Aleksandr Bestuzhev and to Prince E. P Obolensky.

Most of Ryleev's civic literature is in the form of romantic narratives about Russia's heroes and villains. His *dumy,* written between 1821 and 1823, usually depict figures described in the chronicles. The first is Oleg the Wise, who challenges Byzantium. Others include Boian of *The Tale of Igor's Campaign,* who warns of destruction and oblivion; Dmitri Donskoy, who exhorts his army into battle against the Mongol horde; Ivan Kurbsky, the high-minded boyar driven into exile by the tyranny of Ivan the Terrible; Boris Godunov as he ponders the assassination he has ordered; and the false Dmitri, who defeats Boris and becomes a worse tyrant. Modern figures include Peter the Great and Derzhavin, who is seen as a great national poet. The *duma* originated in Ukrainian songs of the sixteenth and seventeenth centuries. The influence of Ossian and of German and English ballads can be seen; may of the poems feature an ominous moon or a storm over water. Emotions run high, and scenes of outright violence alternate with rapt meditations. Ryleev's narrative poem *Voinarovsky* (1824) is a glorification of Mazeppa, the hetman of the Ukraine who betrayed Peter the Great when he joined Charles XII at the Battle of Poltava. The poem is set in Siberia, where Mazeppa's loyal nephew, Voinarovsky, has been exiled. The bleak nature scenes symbolize the blunted lives of brave citizens who have been persecuted by tyranny and injustice. Pushkin's *Poltava* (1828) was in part an answer to this poem.

Aleksandr Odoevsky (1802–1839) wrote the poetry that represents the Decembrists in exile. He was an aristocrat, an army officer, and a member of the Northern Society. After the Decembrist Revolt he was sentenced to hard labor and then to exile in Siberia; later he served in the army in the Caucasus, where he died in an epidemic. Among Odoevsky's poems is an answer to Pushkin's epistle to Siberia in 1827; he assures Pushkin that "we laugh at tears" and that chains are worn with pride. Among Odoevsky's subjects were his hardships and frustrations as a convict and exile. Other poems were patriotic; for example, he praised Russian military advances in Georgia. A narrative poem, "Vasilko" (1830), is based on a chronicle account of a Russian prince who was blinded and exiled. Odoevsky's extant poems and letters to friends have been preserved as part of the radical heritage of the nineteenth century.

The Metaphysical Poets

The metaphysical romantics did not form a distinct literary coterie, but neither did they have any strenuous opponents. Fedor Glinka (1786–1880), who was a cousin of the composer Mikhail Glinka, was a prolific poet and an army officer. His *Letters from a Russian Officer* (1806–1816) record his experiences in the Napoleonic Wars. During the 1820s he was personally close to members of the Pushkin group, and liberalism was a current in his early verse. After the Decembrist Revolt, when he was exiled to Karelia, he began to depict the rough northern scenery with a romantic sense of grandeur and awe. A religious current latent in his early verse was intensified, and it became ever stronger in the 1830s. He later sympathized with the Slavophiles. His poetry is somewhat archaic in vocabulary and slow in pace. Without offending, neither does he stimulate. He was known for his imitations of folk poetry.

Dmitri Venevitinov (1805–1827) created a small body of genuinely romantic poetry during his short life. He adhered by personal preference to the Pushkin pleiad, but his aesthetic beliefs went beyond its urbane sensibility. He was an aristocrat born in St. Petersburg. As a student at Moscow University, he was among the founders, in 1823, of the Lovers of Wisdom, the first society dedicated to the study of romantic philosophy, especially that of Schelling. In 1824 he began to work at the Moscow archives of the Foreign Office, already an early center for romantic philosophy. He was the author of critical and theoretical articles on art, music, and literature. His lyric poems number fewer than forty.

Venevitinov began, like the Pushkin poets, with friendly epistles in which he professed to prefer private pleasures to the rewards of fame and riches. He quickly began to idealize friendship; in "Epistle to Rozhalin" his friend appears as a savior after "life's shipwreck." He also wrote of love of country and of freedom. He depicted medieval battles and wrote an adaptation from Ossian. His "Song of the Greek" (1825) is a nocturnal ballad set against the background of the Greek struggle for independence from Turkey. And in "Novgorod" (1826) he asks, "Where is the bell, removed by Moscow, that signaled freedom?"

Venevitinov's real theme was the inseparability of art and earthly sorrows. He elevated artistic creation above morality, a mere sentimental value, to the most religious heights. He describes how inspiration drives the soul through shattering agonies to create works embodying an aspiration to reach the other world. His "Italy" (1826) pictures a land that has fostered this romantic creativity. His "Poet" (1826) describes a son of the divinity, racked by sadness, living in dreams, and creating mysteries. Venevitinov also idolized Byron, on whose death he wrote several fragments. He admired Goethe, the subject of "To Pushkin" (1826). He became impatient with earthly tedium and limits. He wrote, "I feel that ever burns in me / The holy flame of inspiration, / But my soul soars to its dark aims . . ." (1827). In "The Wings of Life" (1827) it is a swallow that is weary of living. There are enigmatic poems that hint at earthly mysteries; in "Favorite Color" (1826) the colors of the moon, rainbow, and dawn have a cryptic meaning, as do the aspects of love in "Three Roses" (1826). In "The Poet and the Friend" (1827) Venevitinov appears to regard himself as a mystically prescient poet. Venevitinov's early death in 1827 was widely regretted, but the promise of his poems was somewhat overrated. He was a harbinger of an idealism that was to have a wider appeal in the 1830s.

8

Romanticism
(1830–1845)

In the early 1830s the cultural climate in Western Europe began to change rapidly, but Nicholas I (1825–1855) was determined to maintain the status quo inside Russia. It was in this limiting atmosphere that Russian romanticism reached its peak during the 1830s. The July Revolution of 1830 brought Louis Philippe, the "citizen king," to the French throne, and was followed by a wave of revolts throughout Europe. A Polish insurrection erupted in 1830 and took one year to put down. Ukrainian nationalism was on the rise. In 1833 Nicholas proclaimed a general policy of Official Nationalism, whose three inalienable premises were "Orthodoxy, autocracy, and nationalism." Liberal public opinion did not lose sight of such political problems as despotism and serfdom, but they seemed to be intractable at the time. Relative to its Western counterpart, Russian romanticism was a pessimistic movement. The public itself had a taste for melancholia. A cynicism, which had its origins in Byronic nihilism, became fashionable and acquired an aura of political dissent. Notes of cosmic pessimism were found in German romantic philosophy, which simultaneously sustained a nostalgia for ideals. National pride took the form of an admiration for folklore.

The End of the Golden Age

In the countries of its origin, romanticism itself was waning. Goethe's death in 1832 was seen as the symbol of the passing of an age. Schelling's nature philosophy was to be replaced by the dialectic of Hegel, who died in 1831, as an intellectual influence in the West. In England a return to utilitarianism was in the offing. French romanticism still flourished in the works of Victor Hugo and Lamartine, but these writers raised critical questions regarding Christianity, human psychology, and the social structure. They wrote in freedom. In Russia the 1830s were perceived as the ending of the great, if eclectic, golden age. The Pushkin poets were geographically dispersed, and no new, cohesive group of poets came to replace them. The romantic generation had fewer poets than the earlier period. Among them, however, was the second-greatest poet of Russian literature, Mikhail Lermontov; he reached maturity only in 1836. Romanticism at its height was not felt to be a fully developed school in Russia. It offered little sense of spiritual attainment, moreover, or reverential awe or elation.

The Russian romantics did not share any community of aesthetic opinion, and they had almost no personal contact among themselves. Their pessimism stemmed from apparently different causes, metaphysical or social. They bore a family resemblance only in that their poetry seemed to be a general discovery of previously unsuspected deprivations, rather than of new resources. The metaphysical dimension was most strikingly seen in the works of Fedor Tiutchev, a poet of the Pushkin generation who lived in Germany and was not noticed until the 1830s. In his verse the Schellingian philosophy is inverted. The elemental aspect of the universe is feared as an inchoate menace, while it is the fragile cosmos built by man's imagination that is, like the Apollonian dream, precarious. Tiutchev also observed the human psyche's capacity to enjoy evil. He may be counted among the forerunners of Russian decadence. The greatest heir of Byron in the 1830s was Lermontov, who probed the dark side of the alienated character in his lyrics and portrayed this figure in his novel, *The Hero of Our Time*. The splenetic Byronic rebel was naturalized in Russian literature and began to symbolize social and political frustrations. Pushkin had found compassion for the antihero in *Eugene Onegin*. In the 1830s the cynical persona was seen as the product of thwarted, and perhaps noble, ambitions. The religious rebels of Lermontov's great narrative poems, *The Demon* and *The Novice*, were also derivative of Byronism. On Russian soil, ideals were sensed in their absence. It was during the romantic era that Russian authors became attached to a distant, sometimes impossible, idea of perfection.

Nationalism as an irrational sentiment was the most natural channel for a flow of affirmation. Loyalty to country took the form of an admiration for its common folk, the peasants, and for their literature. Pushkin and Zhukovsky wrote folk tales. This vogue was one reason for the success of a so-called peasant poet, Aleksey Koltsov. Finally, nationalism was to blossom into a quasi-religious doctrine, Slavophilism. The heyday of the romantic episode was brief. Semirealistic novels had appeared in France, for example, in Stendhal's *Le Rouge et le noir* (1831). Lermontov's own novel, *The Hero of Our Time*, which was published in 1840, stands at the threshold of Russian realism. Russian romanticism was overtaken by an impatience to return to realism and social engagement, as in the West.

Tiutchev

One of Russia's great metaphysical poets was Fedor Tiutchev (1803–1873). Many of his poems are mediations on the nature of the universe, and he was influenced, if indirectly, by the German romantic philosophers, particularly Schelling. Like them, he visualized the universe as a nebulous process, but beyond that beginning, his ideas were his own. In his most memorable poems he was also influenced by classical Greek myths and poetry. He spoke of a dichotomy between chaos and cosmos. In any case, his aim was not so much to describe the universe as to observe the limits of our human perceptions. He had a deep feeling for nature, a quality that separates him from earlier Russian poets. His love poetry is intense. He was a political conservative; his late poetry is pan-Slavistic and Orthodox.

Tiutchev professed to write poetry as a pastime, quite apart from his long diplomatic career in Germany. Yet he maintained a consistently high quality in his more than 200 lyrics. Born in Moscow, he was educated in an aristocratic, erudite home and at Moscow University. He was appointed to the Foreign Office and sent in 1822 to Munich, where he was to become acquainted with both Schelling and Heinrich Heine. He enjoyed the milieu of salons and was reputed to be a man of great wit. During his twenty-two years abroad, he married twice. He was released from government service in 1839, but returned to Russia only in 1844. In 1850 he began an open liaison with his daughter's governess, Elena Deniseva, which lasted until her death in 1864 and gave rise to a "Deniseva cycle" of love poems. His bureaucratic career lasted until his own death in 1873.

In his metaphysical poetry, Tiutchev portrays the psyche—or the soul, as he called it—in its intimate and scarcely perceptible reflections. Man's condition in these poems is one of vague troubles, inarticulate aspirations, dilemmas, and even perversities. In "The Ray" (1825) the soul aspires to heaven, but falls back to its earthly, troubled dreams; it is this state of ill-defined distress that is the subject of his metaphysical poems, no matter how he describes the universe. The soul's activities are not, in any case, waking preoccupations; the psyche is aroused at dubious hours and in abnormal states, at night, during insomnias, in dreams, or over the rocking sea. Art, too, stirs the passive soul in semi-awareness; in "Vision" (1829) he writes, "Then does night thicken fast, like chaos over seas, / Oblivion, like Atlas, chokes the planet. / The Muse alone, in soul that's virgin, / Is then disturbed by gods in vatic dreams." This nighttime sphere eventually emerged in his thinking as that primordial chaos which is known from myths. In "The earthly sphere is girded like an ocean" (1830) the planet sails through an element of dreams. In one influential poem, "Silentium" (1830), he places the abyss of the ineffable not in outer spheres, but within:

> Be still, be taciturn, conceal
> What are your sentiments, your dreams—
> Across the depths within your soul
> Allow them to arise and go,
> All wordless, as though stars at night.
> Admire their passage, and be still.
>
> How can the heart express itself?
> How can another grasp your thought?
> Would he perceive by what you live?
> A thought when said becomes a lie;
> A spring is muddied when it's stirred,
> Drink of its waters, and be still.

> Then learn to live in self alone,
> Your soul holds fast a universe
> Of mystery-laden, magic thoughts—
> They're deafened by the outer din,
> Diurnal rays do them dispel—
> Hark to their singing—and be still.

Tiutchev is best remembered for those poems in which a world of seeming order and civilization rests uneasily over another sphere of the unbridled and elemental, as in "Day and Night" (1837). Our soul finds chaos irresistible. In "What means your howl, O wind, at night" (1836) he exclaims, "How avidly the soul's night world / Unto its favorite tale does harken. / It strives to burst the moral breast, / It thirsts to blend with the unbounded. . . ." As for the mere concrete world, it is unknowable. These philosophical subjects belong especially to the 1830s. During the 1840s Tiutchev wrote little, and during the 1850s he rarely wrote metaphysical poems. In addition, his perspectives were changed; in "A melody's in ocean's waves" (1865) man alone is a "thinking reed," out of harmony with nature and the universe.

A new literature of landscapes appears in Tiutchev's work. His nature poems seem to reflect a spontaneous love for the earth and to be unguarded statements. In "Spring Storm" (1828) he sees the refreshing rain as Hebe's gift. Elsewhere nature is quiet at noon because Pan is asleep. His poems reflect mere moods and aimless meditations. If they seem to verge on philosophical meanings, it is because his associations are the most natural and universal. The dew is heavenly; the spring is a time of elation, joy, and promise, while the autumn brings melancholia. He had a sense of drama and chose suggestive, pivotal times such as spring, autumn, dawn, and sunset; the storm is appealing because it disrupts. His personal views sometimes intruded on his landscapes. The Alps are compared to majestic palaces or gods, but the Baltic lands seem barren, burnt, close to insanity. Some poems seem to be suggestive because they consist of bare contrasts: the high, eternal snows are seen beside the lower, melting snows; the colorful sunset beside the cold east; the evergreen pines beside deciduous leaves. But these are purposeless, undirected reflections.

Tiutchev touched in his love poems on the dark, as well as the innocent, sides of human nature, on venality and guilt. The love poems that he wrote in Germany have no coherence as a story. They show an unconscious, and unsettling, tendency to take an aesthetic approach to relationships. He seemed drawn to portray occasions more for their emotional intensity than for the quality of the tie. He was also intrigued by states of sexual morality, such as purity or perfidy and guilt. In "I love your eyes, my friend" (1836) he depicts a transition from daytime eyes to nighttime eyes. Guilt began to be more poignant in his verse than innocence. His illicit family with Deniseva occasioned poems in which love and pain are inseparable. Among them is the well-known poem whose first line is "O how like suicide's our loving" (1851). The cycle also includes "Last Love" (1854):

> O how, as we decline, we love
> More tenderly, and more enraptured . . . .

Then shine, yet shine, O farewell light
Of our last love, the glow of sunset!

Full half our sky is seized by shade,
And just the west still holds an errant glimmer,
Then linger, yet linger, O evening day,
Then still endure, O my enchantment.

Let blood flow thin within the veins,
The heart thins not in its endearment.
O you, the last we know of love,
You are our bliss, and our undoing!

The final poems of the cycle are addressed to Deniseva in death.

Russia was not the only country whose culture Tiutchev characterized in verse. Germany is for him devoid of substance; he fears in "I love to watch the service of the Lutherans" (1834) that their meeting is only vestigially religious. He felt a spontaneous love for the Mediterranean lands; in "How long, how long, O blessed south land" (1837) he describes the spell of the ancient gods as continuing in the present. He dedicated poems to Rome, to Venice, and to Nice. His political conservatism began early; he reprimanded Pushkin for his ode called "Freedom," and he stated coldly that the Decembrists would be forgotten. Like the Slavophiles, he ascribed a profound religious feeling to the peasant population. In "These so needy little townships" (1855) he pictures Russia as favored by Christ's presence: "Crushed beneath the cross's burden, / Wearing slave clothes, Heaven's King / Has traversed, O native country, / All of you and given blessing." Tiutchev also wrote anti-Catholic poems and predicted the decline of the West.

Tiutchev wrote of the intimate life as of the inchoate stuff of universal existence and of cultures as though he knew the future. His style is solemn or rhetorical, and sometimes relies on an eighteenth-century wit. His early poems were especially hieratic and sometimes archaic in vocabulary. In time he became less old-fashioned, but his voice was always elevated. His verse is rich in musical sound. In his late poems, he invented long, compound adjectives; these were adopted by the neoromantic poets who followed him. In his sense of the intimate as a sharing of the universal, Tiutchev was a forerunner of the Russian symbolists of the turn of the century.

Lermontov

Mikhail Lermontov (1814–1841) is popularly considered Russia's second poet after Pushkin and the most characteristic embodiment of Russian romanticism. His lyrics reflect both the dark and the ethereal poles of romanticism. He gave expression to the splenetic and cynical impulses of Byronism, and he felt a nostalgia for ideals. As the age inclined toward prose, he found a new voice verging on realism. He was the author of twenty-seven romantic narrative poems, two of which are among the best-known in the language. His novel, *The Hero of Our Time,* was instrumental in shaping that genre in Russia and in delineating its typical hero. Lermontov also attempted dramas, some in verse, but none is memorable, and some were left in fragments.

An aristocrat and a minor army officer, Lermontov became a celebrity who grasped the desire of Russians to see their frustrations aired. Born in Moscow, he was reared, after his mother's death, by wealthy female relatives. He was educated at Moscow University and at the army cadet school in St. Petersburg; he graduated as a hussar in 1834. He had a contentious personality and was prone to unrequited attachments to women. He reached a wide audience in 1837 with "Death of a Poet," an angry exposé of Pushkin's influential enemies. He was "exiled" to the Caucasus because of this poem, but allowed to return a year later. Two volumes of poems appeared in 1840, as did *The Hero of Our Time*. He joined with fellow officers in a secret debating society called The Sixteen. After a duel with the son of the French ambassador, he was again exiled to the Caucasus and demoted. He was killed at age twenty-seven in a duel at Piatigorsk with a former schoolmate.

Lermontov wrote more than 300 lyrics before he reached his mature stride in the late 1830s. By age fourteen he was already an erudite young man, composing in accordance with the conventions of the golden age. His poems recall such poets as Zhukovsky, Pushkin, Byron, and Schiller. He wrote Anacreontics, elegies, epistles, ballads, songs, and epigrams. His subjects in these poems were love, friendship, melancholia, nature, art, and, finally, Caucasian impressions. He was fond of dramatic scenes and had a taste for high passion and romantic sins. His Byronism appeared in 1830, when he was going on sixteen. His mind is poisoned by an ill-defined sickness; he is given to self-recriminations and occasionally to religious defiance; he complains of boredom and seeks an audience for his gloom. An aspiration to the heavenly, sometimes symbolized by stars, appeared simultaneously in Lermontov's lyrics. At age eighteen he wrote "The Angel" (1832), in which a newborn soul is carried to the grieving world. In the same year, his Byronic bitterness reached new heights, and he began to be preoccupied with inevitable doom, especially his own. In "The Sail" (1832) he pictures a solitary boat that seeks fulfillment in storms. He began to write political verse, and the Caucasian setting became an increasingly important aspect of his work.

Lermontov would not have been forgotten had he written only these early poems; they lack only the noble distinction of his later work. Many of their traits, such as the Byronic core, were to endure. He learned to write poems that are novelistic, as though monologues and dialogues taken from larger stories. He also perfected in them the voice of inner monologue, with pauses, tangents, and an intimate vocabulary. He found images that were to recur throughout his poetry and prose: the boat, the mountains of the Caucasus, a grave, a solitary female, the sky at night, storms, stars. When he moved to St. Petersburg to become a cadet, however, he all but ceased to write lyrics for several years.

The mature verse began to appear in 1836, and in 1837 a steady flow began; the poems were to number fewer than 100, but many are memorable. His central vision is altered; he no longer strives to outdistance the reader, although he remains striking and original in himself. The public responded enthusiastically to "Death of a Poet," in which his target is the *haut monde*. A similar sense of public indignation appeared in several other poems. In "Meditation" (1838) he indicts his entire generation, naming as its faults its wasted talents, self-indulgence, excessive irony, and ultimate emptiness—the traits of a Childe Harold. In "Poet" (1838) even the contemporary artist is useless, like a dagger hung on a wall as mere decoration. In "How often when surrounded by a festive throng" (1840) he remembers his pure and spontaneous childhood while in the midst of a noisy New Year's Eve celebration. These and other poems appealed to the intelligentsia, and Lermontov's idealism became a measure of the nation's morality.

Yet the center of Lermontov's mature lyrics was precisely that frustrated persona that was derived from the earlier Byronic poems. In this guise, he is a creature of contradictions in whom the habit of melancholia is entrenched. His cynicism is epitomized in this poem written in 1840:

> It's tedious, sad, and there's no one to touch with your hand
>> At times when your heart is in anguish . . .
> And striving! for what do we idly, eternally strive?
>> And years pass us by—all the best of our lifetime!
>
> And love . . . but for whom? if in passing, it's not worth the pain,
>> And love that's forever is hearsay.
> If inward you look, you discover no trace of your past;
>> No joys and no sorrows—there's nothing that matters.
>
> What's passion? for early or late that so pleasant disease
>> Will vanish when reason has spoken:
> And life, if you look with cool candor at what's on all sides,
>> Is, O, what a joke that is stupid and vapid. . . .

He declares in other poems that he is isolated from society, like a cliff, or "damnable," like an overripe fruit. He is obsessed, as in the earlier poems, by the inevitability of fate. His last poems include the famous "Dream" (1841), in which he lies dead of a bullet wound in hot Dagestan, while at a party in St. Petersburg a young woman can see that corpse in her mind's eye.

There was in Lermontov's mature verse a growing readiness to respond to signs of religious meaning, virtue, and idealism. In "Flower of Palestine" (1837) the pressed flower reminds him of what Jerusalem stands for: "All's full of peace and full of gladness / That is around you and above you." In "Prayer" (1839) his soul is moved to tears by the ritual of religious words. In "When grain fields that have turned to yellow sway" (1841) he feels a flow of religious affirmation; he communes with the stream and sees God in the heavens. In "Out upon the road alone I exit" (1841) he wishes in death to remain attentive to the oak and hear its sounds.

Lermontov was reluctant to allow real human relationships to be inferred from his verse. He wrote about human ties in enigmatic poems and ascribed human emotions to nature. His poems about love reflect complex, novelistic situations; most are recollections of the past. In "To the Child" (1840) a cast-off widower speaks words that might have been those of Lermontov's own estranged father to him. In poems about nature, he tended to sympathize with the victims of abuses, losses, and injustices. The trees in "Three Palms" (1839) are destroyed by the men who owed them gratitude. In "The Cliff" (1841) the massive rock is pathetic; it pines for the cloud that has left its brow. Opposites are forever attracted, but separated; a northern pine dreams of a southern palm, an oak leaf is rejected by the luxurious plane tree. In some of his later poems, Lermontov portrays military men. An enlisted man in "The Testament" (1840) instructs his comrade to spare his parents the news of his death, but to tell the neighbor: "So do not spare her empty heart, / And let her cry a little . . . / It wouldn't hurt her any!" In several poems of this kind Lermontov was on his way to realism.

A love for Russia and its common people appeared only in the mature verse. In "Borodino" (1837) a simple soldier describes his part in the decisive battle that saved Russia. Lermontov's adaptation from an ethnic song, "Cossack Lullaby" (1840), suggests his sympathy for a warlike people in their perils. And in "Homeland" (1841) he shows his affection for Russia's unspectacular landscapes:

> I love my country, but with love that seems eccentric!
> My reason cannot conquer it at all.
> No glory, which by blood is purchased,
> Nor peace replete with self-assurance and with pride,
> Nor yet the fateful testaments of dim past ages
> Can stir in me those daydreams that are filled with gladness.
>
> And yet I love, for what, I cannot say—
> Her steppe lands that are filled with frigid silence,
> Her forests with their ever boundless swaying,
> The currents of her rivers, broad as any seas;
> I like to ride my wagon through the country byways,
> And pierce with sleepy eye the shadows of the night
> To meet on every side, as I sigh for a lodging,
> The trembling lights of melancholy little towns.
>
> I love the smoke of burning stubble,
> The caravans in steppes at night,
> And on the hill in yellow grain fields—
> A pair of birches that show white.
> With gladness still unknown to many
> I look upon the harvest stored,
> The hut whose roof with straw is covered
> Whose windows have their shutters carved,
> And, holiday, on dewy evenings
> I love to watch 'til midnight comes
> The dancing, and the stamping, whistling,
> The while that drunken peasants talk.

Lermontov was among the first in Russian literature to portray the peasant without idealization.

In Lermontov's lyrics, the romantic ego develops in freedom, and the psyche may be poisoned and sick, and precious because it is unique. Yet his images are reassuringly ordinary. His stars, for example, are as simply symbolic as they were in the poems of such earlier romantics as Zhukovsky. Lermontov's stanza forms are for the most part conventional, but intelligently varied. His vocabulary is unassuming and his syntax rather like that of the spoken language, seemingly careless. His style is deceptively plain. If Lermontov is sometimes underestimated, it is probably because of the utter accessibility of his speech.

Lermontov's narrative poems have many of the conventions of romantic literature—protagonists of heroic proportions; exotic settings, either in medieval Russia or in the Caucasus; and an abundance of picturesque qualities. The hero of "Hajji Abrek" (1835) is an outcast native of the Caucasus who has been exiled as a murderer. The son of the people is victimized by the tyrant in "Song of Tsar Ivan Vasilevich, of the Young Bodyguard and the Brave Merchant Kalashnikov" (1838): the merchant is killed in a boxing match. "The Boyar Orsha" (1842) is set in the sixteenth-century wars with Livonia. In spite of its conventions, *The Novice* (1840) is one of Lermontov's most powerful works; it depicts a Caucasian native who has run away from a monastery. He is a rebel whose bitterness is justified by the stultifying tyranny of the institution. Nature becomes, during his brief, free life in it, his true religion. Dying from wounds inflicted by a leopard, which had seemed to be his own alter ego and brother, he curses the religious father who had kept him from a genuine life. *The Demon* (1841) stems from earlier Byronic inspirations and occupied Lermontov during his entire mature career. The Demon is Lucifer, the fallen angel; he loves a mortal, a native princess of the Caucasus; in effect, he loves earth, nature, and a life in reality, which he cannot, by his origin, possess.

The Hero of Our Time, the novel, is a respectful imitation of Pushkin's *Eugene Onegin* and at the same time an embodiment of the persona of Lermontov's lyric poetry. Like *Eugene Onegin,* the work has a narrator of wider perspectives, an editor, who sheds light on the perniciousness of the hero, a dandy and outcast. But the warning does nothing to dispel the readers' interest in and sympathy for the doomed hero. The novel is set in Piatigorsk, where Lermontov was soon to die in a duel that unfolded like a tragic parody of the novel.

Koltsov

Aleksey Koltsov (1809–1842) was a son of the soil in the same sense that Robert Burns had been in the eighteenth century. His poetry is that of a largely self-educated man, but at the same time a reflection of the literature of sensibility. Koltsov owed his popularity to his many imitations of the "drawn-out" folk song. For this reason he was considered a "peasant poet." These semi-educated poets were sometimes popular in Russia, and Koltsov was the first major example. They were by no means always peasants, but they remained close to the countryside in taste and sentiments. Peasant poets were to return to favor in the avant-garde era, when primitive art was popular. Koltsov was a merchant, the son of a Ukrainian cattle dealer in Voronezh. He was introduced to literary circles in Moscow and St. Petersburg by a local landowner, Nikolay Stankevich, who was an influential man of letters. Koltsov counted Krylov, Viazemsky, and Pushkin among his friends and longed for a life in the literary capitals. Not all his lyrics were imitations of folk songs.

The keynote of Koltsov's lyrics is a wistfulness, sometimes a resentment, that is close, even in his literary genres, to that of the "drawn-out" folk song. This sorrow gave coherence to his simple *oeuvre*. Koltsov's sadness at first had conventional causes, such as autumn or being on the road. But the mood became a constant outlook on life; in "Disillusionment" (1829) he has lost hope in humanity, in family, in friends. In "The Last Battle" (1838) he is determined to go down before fate fighting, and a late poem is called simply "A Cry of Pain" (1840). His literary poems include a number on love; they appear to emanate primarily from the imagination. He wrote of unrequited love, of love lost through death, of jealousies; he wrote as women, as men, as young and old people. Some of the later poems are dramatic, even violent. Like any other man of letters, Koltsov wrote epistles and occasional poems for friends; among these is "A Sign on the Grave of Venevitinov" (1830). Certain philosophical poems, called *dumy,* are manifestly out of keeping with his *oeuvre;* these are attempts to come to grips with Schelling's ideas, probably as they were discussed in Stankevich's Moscow circle. Koltsov also wrote a portrait of a Cossack, ballads, Anacreontics, and even an adaptation, "From Horace" (1842). "To the Benefactor of My Nation" (1842) shows a liberal political consciousness. Koltsov's literary verse has an attractive, forthright tone and a natural delicacy.

His imitations of folk songs are the lyrics of a conscientious poet or even of an ethnographer. His love poems in the folk style are about forced marriages, innocent lovers, or violent acts of jealousy and revenge. This song was written in 1834:

Rustle not, O rye,
Your full, ripened ears.
Mower, sing not songs
Of the wide, wide steppe.

Now I have no cause
To collect rich goods.
There's no cause for me
To be wealthy now.

For the youth stored up,
Laid up all his goods
For his soul that's gone,
For his soul, his girl.

O how sweet for me
To look in her eyes,
In her eyes, so full
Of love's tender thoughts!

And those eyes so clear
Ceased to shed their light.
In the grave's deep sleep
Sleeps my pretty girl!

Worse than mountain's weight,
Or than midnight dark,
Is the black, black gloom
That fell on my heart!

Koltsov's social commitment is evident in his liking for the poor man's lament, seen, for example, in "The Meditation of a Villager" (1837), which begins, "I shall sit down / And give thought a while." The men's songs also include those of the robber, the runaway serf, and the rebellious youth. In time, Koltsov wrote ever more folk songs and fewer literary poems. His *oeuvre* was then less personal, but he knew how to express his own feelings in the folk form: "Forest" (1837) is his response to the death of Pushkin; the trees lament the death of a folk hero, Bova. Koltsov's peasant songs are as much literary compositions as are those by Sumarokov and other eighteenth-century poets. His style is coherent and polished. His rhythms are related to, but not identical with, those of folk songs; his line endings are dactylic, and often unrhymed. But in romantic times, such songs were no longer the hobby of the gentry, and they were perceived as the contribution of a rustic folk. Many of Koltsov's songs were set to music by such composers as Rimsky-Korsakov, Mussorgsky, and Balakirev.

Minor Romantic Poets

The lesser poets of the age also reflect its inherent diversity. Contemporaries identified Aleksandr Polezhaev (1804/1805–1838) with the Byronic current. An army officer, he was sentenced to service in the ranks because of a spoof of Pushkin's *Eugene Onegin* called *Sashka* (1825); the poem seemed to be atheistic. Polezhaev deserted once, was transferred to the Caucasus, and died of tuberculosis. His fewer than 100 lyrics are those of a man who believes he has been unjustly condemned and is thirsting for revenge. His imagination is violent and dramatic. "The Song of the Captive Iroquois" (1828) was admired for its defiant attitude. He sees himself as a live corpse in one of his lyrics and as demonically inspired in others. The Caucasus is the setting of a number of poems; he describes its picturesque landscapes and the exotic life of its primitive tribes, peoples given to passions and warlike behavior. His dozen narrative poems depict fighting men in battles over matters of national, cultural, and religious principles. Most are set in the Caucasus; "The Vision of Brutus" (1830) and "Coriolanus" (1834) take place in ancient Rome. Polezhaev's style is shrill and overstated. His poetry has the drawback that it is, in essence, derivative, not only of Byron, but of Pushkin and other poets of the twenties.

Aleksey Khomiakov (1804–1860) was a leading Slavophile, an essayist and theologian of exceptional interest in the history of Russian culture. His poetry was a secondary concern, but he had a good, Biblical style, and his verse was not always at the service of his ideas. He was an aristocrat who saw military service, but who lived essentially as a man of letters. He was a member of the club called Lovers of Wisdom and later wrote for the Slavophiles' political and literary magazine, *The Moscow Herald*. In his early poems, Khomiakov spoke of nature, of friends, of art and inspiration. In the 1830s he also wrote meditations on Russian and European history, love poems, and religious observations. In time, he became the apologist of pre-Petrine Russia. As a Slavophile, he ascribed a religious superiority to native Russian culture and decried the West as spiritually inert. In the 1850s Biblical subjects, such as the resurrection of Lazarus, entered his verse. His emotions were always strongly felt and clearly stated. He also wrote two tragedies in verse on historical subjects, *Ermak* (1832) and *Dmitri the Pretender* (1833).

Vladimir Benediktov (1807–1873) was a popularizer of some poetic conventions of the 1830s; in subsequent decades, he remained a prolific poet. After serving in the army against Poland, he became a bureaucrat in the Finance Ministry. His are the elegiac themes of romantic poetry—love, nature, introspective moods, some travel impressions. He speaks in his love poems of irresistible passions and great sufferings, but the poems often depend on those graphic details, such as curls or eyes, that are reminiscent of Anacreontic verse. His nature poems, such as "Storm and Stillness" (1835), are often pretexts for the insertion of autobiographical memories or philosophical comments. His meditations generally reflect an ill-defined, melancholy view of life. His style is essentially undistinguished, but he had a taste for striking, sometimes exotic, figures of speech. There is an anonymity in his voice that readers recognized when the age for poetry had passed.

IV

THE AGE
OF REALISM

9

The Heritage of Idealism
(1840–1860)

The political stability of Russia was maintained at mid-century by the reactionary policies of Nicholas I, but the intellectuals anticipated an era of change and raised controversies about its directions. Nicholas I even endeavored through his foreign policy to prevent any political changes in Western Europe, where unrest was growing. The year 1848 brought revolutionary uprisings in the West, and then nationalistic revolts. Meanwhile, some of the Russian intelligentsia favored an accelerated Westernization, but others, the Slavophiles, argued for a return to pre-Petrine, peasant roots. Literature was enlisted in the struggle for public opinion. In Turgenev's *Sportsman's Sketches* (1852) the serfs were portrayed as human beings worthy of emancipation. Finally, Russia's defeat in the Crimean War in 1856 demonstrated to all the need for a major social reorganization. Hostilities began in 1854, when Russia intervened in the internal affairs of its historic enemy, Turkey, and ended after England and France routed the Russian army and navy on its own doorstep. In 1855 Nicholas I was succeeded by his liberal son, Alexander II, who sued for peace and set in motion policies that would lead to the liberation of the serfs in 1861.

The Decline of Poetry

In the West the public's new sociological interests were reflected in realistic fiction, rather than in poetry. Balzac's *Père Goriot* was published in 1834, and Dickens became the most prominent novelist in England. Their sociological themes, such as monetary greed and poverty, were also seen in the works of other fiction writers. Prose methods began to influence the composition of poetry. The dramatic scenes and psychological complexities of Robert Browning were novelistic. Romantic aims and premises never disappeared entirely from prose, but they began to find their stronghold in poetry. Tennyson preserved an idealistic outlook. In France, Thé-

ophile Gautier had initiated *l'art pour l'art* school in the 1830s to ward off what he
saw as a new imperative toward social engagement. In Russia the turn to realism
and to prose was even more decisive. A naturalistic school appeared in Russian
fiction of the 1840s; its goal was to call attention to the hardships of the lower
classes. Dostoevsky's "Poor Folk" (1846) was an example. The heritage of romanticism came to be associated with poetry, as in the West. Most poets felt a loss of
prestige during the 1840s and 1850s, and some were influenced by realism. An art-
for-art's-sake current arose. But a "civic" school of poetry was also born.

Those poets who wrote in the traditional, romantic manner were, furthermore,
subdued in their expressions of religious nostalgia and philosophical views. Some
adhered to the premises of German idealistic philosophy, but almost tacitly. The
greatest poet of the romantic heritage was an art-for-art poet named Afanasy Fet. He
wrote impressionistic verse in imagery that is beautiful in itself; many of his poems
are landscapes. Like the followers of Gautier, he avoided autobiographical revelations. Underlying his commitment to beauty, and silently for the most part, was a
theory of Schopenhauer's: reality is ugly, and art is an overcoming of its ties. A poet
who was influenced by the dramatic and painterly qualities of realism was Konstantin Polonsky. He was an idealist whose colorful scenes serve to illustrate his longing
for a religious faith, but he was not indifferent to social issues. The most candid
adherent to a philosophical idealism was Aleksey K. Tolstoy, a distant relative of
Leo Tolstoy. Like Schelling, he was the proponent of a principle of love and
harmony that embraces both the divinity and individuals in their relationships. He
shared with the earlier romantics a nostalgia for the medieval past. These traditional
poets as a group have been described as eclectic; they reflected various currents in
their poetry. With the exception of Fet, they had also lost the capacity for self-
criticism that had been the possession of the golden age poets.

Poets who were committed to a civic purpose appeared both among the Slavophiles and among the Westernizers. Slavophiles were usually conservative, but the
current appeared in a liberal version in the poems of Ivan Aksakov, the son of a
famous novelist. His lyrics are exhortations to altruistic work, often addressed to
himself and to his own, gentry, class. The leader of the Westernizers was Nikolay
Nekrasov, who transferred the naturalistic scenes of poverty that had appeared in
fiction to poetry. Nekrasov was also the publisher of an important leftist magazine,
The Contemporary, and a friend of the radical literary critics. The first of these,
Vissarion Belinsky, initiated a long tradition of utilitarian criticism.

Fet

Russia's only major poet of the art-for-art's-sake tendency was Afanasy Fet (1820–
1892), but he was also one of Russia's greatest poets. He wrote not only about
landscapes but also about the myths of antiquity, about life's common but elusive
joys and sorrows. His subjects are universal; he rejected the romantic preoccupation
with self as an apparent center of his *oeuvre*. Each of his poems is a self-contained
work of art. His themes seem to be less important than his impressionistic style.
Many of his lyrics are brief and appear to be slight. His compositional methods in

themselves bear the message of subjectivity. He had that style which is described as aspiring to music. His preoccupation with Schopenhauer's philosophy was serious. He published a translation of *Die Welt als Wille und Vorstellung* in 1881. Fet also wrote two volumes of memoirs, which appeared in 1890.

Fet was a provincial landowner whose delicate poetic sense seemed at odds with his inflexible and abrasive character. Leo Tolstoy, who was a friend, said of him, "Where did that country squire get the words of a great poet?" Fet's life was clouded by the fact of his illegitimate birth. He was reared to age fourteen as the son of a squire, Afanasy Shenshin, before his birth was declared to have been illegitimate and his aristocratic privileges were withdrawn. His father had been unable to marry his German mother, Charlotte Foethe, until two years after his birth. Fet was educated at a German gymnasium in Finland and at Moscow University, where he lodged with a fellow poet and future romantic literary critic, Apollon Grigorev. Fet's first collection of poems, *Lyrical Pantheon,* was published in 1840. In a vain effort to regain his gentry rights, he served for eight years in the army near the Black Sea town of Kherson. He refused to marry the woman he loved in this town, apparently for reasons of ambition. In 1853 he was transferred to St. Petersburg, where he became the friend of Turgenev and other literary men and married the sister of a liberal critic. After publishing a defense of pure art in an essay of 1859 on Tiutchev, he was excluded by Nekrasov from *The Contemporary.* His 1863 collection of verse was attacked by its radical critics, and during the remainder of the 1860s and the 1870s he was unable to publish at all. He retired to a country estate and devoted himself to farming. In 1873 a tsar's decree restored his father's name and rights. In the 1880s Fet was welcomed back into literature and esteemed as the most illustrious poet of the new era. His collections of verse, beginning in 1883, were called *Evening Lights.*

Fet's early lyrics, written when he was a university student, reflect the life of a landed squire. He describes the landscapes seen on one provincial estate throughout all the seasons of the year. The country life of the gentry landowner is portrayed as nearly idyllic. His joys are many, and his melancholias few and passing. The winter holidays bring such peasant entertainments as mummery, games, and fortune telling. In the summer, there are rowing excursions on a nearby river. The poet and his family are anonymous; there are plausible domestic touches, such as a child with his toys and a neighbor who has a caged nightingale. Some poems are records of love's encounters. This example from the year 1843 may still be Fet's most famous poem:

> I have come to you in greeting,
> Come to say the sun has risen,
> Say it trembles on the foliage,
> That its light is hot and burning;
>
> Come to say the woods are waking,
> Waking all, in every sapling,
> And in every bird has quivered,
> Filled with avid, vernal thirsting;
>
> Come to say my love is equal
> To what yesterday I brought you,

That my heart is bound in service
Still to you and our good fortune;

Come to say that I feel rapture
Waft on me from every quarter,
What my song shall be I cannot
Know, but sense a song is rising.

The drama and the passions of living were not to be found in these studiously
reticent early poems. The more ardent sides of life did appear, however, in lyrics
that were literary references—for example, in a cycle called "To Ophelia" (1840s).
Fet was inspired by classical antiquity, as were the postromantic French poets. His
public particularly admired "Diana" (1847), in which he described a statue so
lifelike that it "might walk towards Rome." Fet also found passions in the myths. In
"Golden curled Phoebus on quitting his dew-bedecked bed and departing" (1847)
the god encounters the corpse of Endymion, whom the moon has loved. Fet sometimes wrote imitations of the ancients that consisted in detached observations on
nature and other subjects. Fet's predecessors in his early poems included Goethe and
Schiller. He was especially close to the Heine who wrote such unassuming poems as
"Du bist wie eine Blume, / So hold und schon and rein. . . ." Heine was devoted to
French poetry, imitated it, and was its interpreter to the Germans.

After Fet's move to Kherson, his poetry was less specifically tied to the Russian
provinces. His lyrics acquired their universal character and at the same time became
more intimate, as though the inner thoughts of anyone. The world of nature replaced
the provincial estate as the ordinary locale of human life. Landscapes became even
more important to his poetry. He usually described simple northern scenes. For the
most part, only his responses to nature convey any sense of his own identity. Some
of his most memorable poems portray the ecstasies that he felt on May nights. He
often describes the sky. He had the same warm regard for stars that Novalis,
Zhukovsky, and Lermontov once had. In his descriptions of the open land and the
Milky Way in "The Steppe at Night" (1854) there is a foretaste of Pasternak. In
"Southern Night, Upon a Haystack" (1857) Fet created the sensation of falling
upward into the sky. He was also moved to joy in poems set in the dead of an icy
winter. Sorrows had no more personal cause than joys; they emanated from the
undramatic low-lying scenes typical of Russia. In "Willows and Birches" (1843–
1856) the trees symbolize two varieties of grief. A number of poems are set by the
sea, but they, too, are devoid of autobiographical signs. In "Storm in the Sky on an
Evening" (1842) the seascape seems to instill a sense of gloom and foreboding. In
this picture of the shore at dawn, written in 1857, he feels the delight that is more
characteristic of his poems:

O, how fine your damp wreath, Amphitrite,
Does appear in the morning's first gleam,
And how striking the fire and sheer nacre
That Aurora bestows on the east;

In its infinite coils lies the seaweed,
That the wave has washed high on the beach.

> Heaven's arch in the water is capsized,
> So it speckles the bay with its rose,
>
> And an island drifts over green shadows;
> Not a movement, or sound, in this calm,
> And the reeds with their tips bending over
> The salt sea, stand in drops that are large

Nature is often described at times of change—morning, evening, the storm. Always a pantheist, Fet was not openly philosophical until his later period. The ecstasies of these years seem to stem simply from gratitude for the gift of life. In the 1870s he began to reveal his outlook. In the "May Night" of 1870 nature is linked with eternal spheres. The rose, a flower so long symbolic of ideals, appears as the subject of several of his later poems. In other poems, it is butterflies and moths that are symbolic of an aimless beauty that is transient and fragile. Through his poems, the butterfly was to become a familiar emblem of art-for-arts-sake poetry.

Fet was to emerge as a private person in the sphere of love. He addressed a number of his poems as though to a lover, although the poems are not necessarily about love. They are fragments of dialogues in intimate, or domestic, circumstances to which we are not privy, but which seem familiar. These poems are almost devoid of idealization, and he seldom drew portraits. At the most he would recall one graphic detail; often it is a tress of hair. The later poems about love are all memories, and they are pervaded by an awareness of failure or of an irrevocable loss. These poems seem to originate in his love for Maria Lazich, whom he refused to marry, and who may have died by suicide. The cycle culminated long after her death in "Alter Ego" (1878), where he writes, "And I know at those times when I look at the stars, / That when you and I gazed at them, we were like gods."

The joys of Fet's early poems gave way gradually to a melancholia in the later poems. There came a time when his gloomy moods took a prominent place beside his ecstasies. In the later poems his pessimism leads to religious thoughts. His world of beauty and happiness had been fragile. In "Worn out by life, fickle hope's deceptions" (1864?) he finds a refuge in his pantheistic faith: all creation is said to be the rays of the same cosmic sun, and so he hopes to meet his love in the afterlife. The poem has an epigraph from Schopenhauer: "Wir Alle in denselben Traum versenkt sind." He believed in the Eternal Feminine when he wrote "Evocative and yet in vain, and wearing" (1871). The same period also brought metaphysical anxieties and fear of death. In "O do not trust the noisy crowd" (1874–1886) he has come to rely only on "the transient," "the present only." An "iron fate" precludes both happiness and freedom in "All, all is mine, what is, and all that was" (1887).

Fet's poems about art place him in the practical world of artists; they yield little of an aesthetic. He recognized his closeness to decadence when he said of his muse that she is drawn to "late flowers" and "fragmentary speech" ("The Muse," 1854). He recognized the dispute over utilitarian art in "You're right, for we grow old, and winter's not far off" (1860), where he urged: "drink of Hebe's cup, / For in it there is art for art's sake." He continued to praise the art of antiquity, for example in "Venus de Milo" (1856) and "Apollo Belvedere" (1857). He wrote eulogies for Schiller (1854) and Tiutchev (1866), as well as for composers—Beethoven,

Chopin, Tchaikovsky. His tacit association of art with a religious ideal appeared in "To My Muse" (1882), where he wrote, "And you are still the same, a sacred goddess," in a "crown of stars."

Fet's impressionistic style was recognized by his contemporaries as foreign, and they often linked him with Heine. Fet's aim was to make *objets d'art* out of experience, whereas his Russian contemporaries were more concerned with the experience itself. Fet's poems are elusive; he himself spoke of the inadequacy of rational discourse in "How poor we are in words!—I want and yet I can't" (1887). He had a painter's eye; he described both sweeping panoramas and minute details. His language is musical in its sounds and yet unassuming, almost primitive, in its vocabulary and syntax. His poems resemble the *romances sans paroles* of French poetry. He was aggressively innovative in versification. He sometimes rhymed only odd lines, as in English poetry, and he experimented with *vers libre*. His poems give the impression of distance and fragility, but they originated in a stubborn, and unhappy, mind.

Lesser Pure Art Poets

All the poets who rejected utilitarianism in art were called "pure art poets" by their contemporaries. In fact, some were philosophical idealists, while others belonged to the art-for-art's-sake current. Apollon Maikov (1821–1897) bore a close resemblance to the art-for-art's-sake poets of France. He curbed the romantic impulse to write autobiographical verse and to display emotions. He wrote with a classical kind of detachment and precision, and he was often inspired, like the followers of Gautier, by Classical antiquity. He was a descendant of the eighteenth-century poet Vasily Maikov; his father was a painter, and his brother a literary critic. He was educated in St. Petersburg and studied art in France and Italy between 1842 and 1844. On his return to Russia, he began to work for the Rumiantsev Museum in Moscow.

Maikov captured the essences of exotic cultures in his verse. He was also to show an awareness of history in its unfolding. His early poems, written in the late 1830s and 1840s, were inspired by ancient Greece and Rome. He paraphrased poems by Sappho, Horace, and others. He stylized his own observations on art and nature so that they might have been written by ancient Greeks. Later he wrote travel impressions of modern Europe. In *Sketches of Rome* (1847) he included portraits of contemporary street figures, such as a Capuchin monk and elsewhere a beggar. In other works he described Normandy, the Alps, and Naples. Maikov the man can be seen in his rather straightforward responses to nature in its various seasons. His recollections of love, his only private poems, tend to be pagan in spirit—unsentimental and graphic. In the 1850s Maikov's choice of historical periods was diverse and unusual. He wrote dramatic scenes from the Spanish Inquisition, composed the diary of a fictitious ancient Syrian, and made imitations of Provençal romances. Russian culture and history also drew cycles from him. He adapted stories from chronicle legends and accounts of Ivan the Terrible and Peter the Great. Among his landscapes of contemporary Russia was "Haymaking" (1856), a favorite with his readers:

Hay's aroma fills the meadows . . .
Happy is the heart in song.
Rakes in hand, in rows, the women,
Circling, pull the hay around.

All the dry is gathered yonder,
Then the men surround the pile,
Toss it high up on the wagon,
Like a house, up, up it soars . . .

As he waits, the skinny stallion
Stands as though he were dug in . . .
Ears apart, and legs in arches,
Sleeping, maybe, standing up . . .

But the lively dog goes dashing
Through the hay, that rocks like waves,
He goes flying, he goes plunging,
Jumping, barking in his haste.

Maikov's Russian poems include a modern version of *The Tale of Igor's Campaign* (1889). The pathos of all his work is present in a long narrative, "Two Worlds" (1880); it depicts a confrontation between ancient Roman culture, still great but facing a decline, and the early Christians, still unaware of their strength. His poems are without sentimentality, but his *oeuvre* is not without passion.

Lev Mey (1822–1862) was similar to Maikov in his perception of cultures as historical entities and eventually in his admiration for Classical art. He was known primarily as a translator, particularly of Anacreon and of Heinrich Heine. The son of an army officer, Mey was educated at Tsarskoe Selo and began a bureaucratic career, but became a school inspector. At first he wrote conventional, melancholy lyrics, sometimes devoted to nature or to love. He was an imitator of "drawn-out" folk songs and of historical songs as well. "The Town Bell of Novgorod" (1840) was popular for its liberal sentiments. He translated *The Tale of Igor's Campaign* (1850) before Maikov did. In the 1850s Mey began to write imitations of Classical poetry and poems illustrating myths. His historical plays, including a verse drama, *The Maid of Pskov* (1860), were popular in the 1860s. Mey's lyrics were set to music by Glinka, Borodin, Tchaikovsky, Rimsky-Korsakov, Mussorgsky, and Rachmaninoff.

Polonsky

The romantic tendencies preserved in the lyrics of Iakov Polonsky (1819–1898) were old-fashioned and rather limited. For the most part, he was content with spectacle, or local color, and with a nostalgia for religious security and faith. Like the realists, he was an observer of society, which he depicted in dramatic scenes and portraits. His subjects, however, are colorful, diverse, and out of the ordinary. His world is not realistic, but it is exhilarating, as well as cruel and sad. He longed for social order and for a sense of transcendental values that had vanished with an earlier age. He regrets that the universe is now perceived as a random, haphazard place. Polonsky had little to say about himself. His first collection was *Scales* (1844). In addition to his lyrics, he wrote long verse narratives, of which the best-known is "The Grasshopper Musician" (1859). He published some civic poetry during the 1860s and 1870s, when art without a utilitarian purpose was not well received, but he still did not escape the attacks of radical critics. He also wrote plays in verse and prose, as well as novels, essays, and memoirs, none of which is widely remembered.

Polonsky belonged to the lesser gentry and was active in both bureaucratic and library spheres. He was born in Riazan and attended Moscow University, where he knew both Fet and the future poet and critic Apollon Grigorev. He held civil service positions in Odessa and Tiflis, where many of his exotic poems are set. While there, he published three collections of verse and began to write ethnographic feuilletons and plays. From 1851 on he lived in St. Petersburg, where he contributed to *The Notes of the Fatherland* and *The Contemporary*. He was an editor of *The Russian Word* in 1859 and 1860. From 1860 to 1896 he served in an office for the censorship of foreign literature.

Polonsky's portraits are of the striking and unique individuals that make up a romantic literature. Usually his characters face some misfortune, and some are already sunk in meditative sorrow. He pictured, for example, a blind preacher who is tricked by his lazy helper, lovers who sit together on a grave and reflect on death, a prisoner who dreams that lightning will strike the walls of his prison and set him free, and a family that is entangled in a domestic drama of unknown cause. The world as Polonsky presents it contains good and evil, beauty and ugliness, but in a bewildering disorder. The divinity has withdrawn from it and left mankind alone, and the earth is empty. Polonsky spoke openly of his loss of religious faith. In "The holy church bell has a festive, solemn sound," he wrote, "And I do wish to pray, but now a doubt oppressive / Obscures my soul's whole impetus to holy deeds, / And life—our life drags on, a dream not understood." The cynical light he throws on society is also explained in other poems. In "Shades" (1840s) he speaks of the "heavy thoughts" that afflict "mankind's heart." Although a pessimist, Polonsky does not surrender to a mood of resignation. He had an energetic spirit that is demonstrated in the richness of his imagination. In "The Challenge" (1850s) he called his melancholia out in a duel.

During most of his career, Polonsky wrote picturesque poems in which the philosophical message is quite clear. In "The Georgian Girl" (1840s) he drew the lesson himself:

> The Georgian girl that you first saw but yesterday
> > Stood on a roof all strewn with carpets.
> In silks she was adorned, and lace, and airy gauze,
> > Transparent, soared above her shoulders.
> Today—how poor she is; beneath her white yashmak
> > She scampers, mountain paths ascending,
> A broken wall she enters, bearing on her head
> > A patterned pitcher, to a wellspring.
> Wayfarer weary, hasten not to follow her—
> > Be not led on by idle fancies!
> For no mirage will quench your fever's painful thirst,
> > Nor babble like your dream's sweet waters.

It was romantic fiction writers like E. T. A. Hoffmann and Gogol who warned that sinister or humdrum realities may be hidden beyond intriguing glimpses. Other exotic, southern figures who appeared in Polonsky's portraits included the Persian singer, the street beggar, and the Tatar girl. In later years, the travel scenes that he recorded included the Finnish shore, Lake Geneva, the Italian coastline, and Sorrento. Polonsky's pessimism led him to ironies, most often in poems devoted to love or lovers. These poems contain, in fact, some of the cruelest lessons about life. In "The Meeting" (1840s) he encounters a former lover who became a fallen woman and has aged before her time. In "The Recluse" (1840s) he confesses to keeping trysts with a lady who lives in a world of fantasy, perhaps insanity. In "The Grasshopper Musician" the unfortunate insect loves a short-lived butterfly; Polonsky's tone is frivolous, although the story is sad.

The poems that Polonsky wrote during the 1860s and 1870s were less conducive to philosophical interpretations, and in some he addressed social and political issues. His viewpoint was liberal. He shows the tsar's official to be self-serving in "To tell you the truth, I've forgotten, my friends" (1860s). In "The Fugitive" (1860s) he describes a runaway prisoner who loves his family and land, but is forced to hide in the forests, fearing a punishment that is perhaps unmerited. Polonsky returned in the 1880s and 1890s to metaphysical suggestiveness. In "The Swan" (1890s) he describes the death of a noble bird next to a shabby amusement park. The poem belies the Greek belief, so loved by romantics, that the swan's death song is a hymn of mystic joy. In "Shades and Dreams" (1890s) life's difficult realities are shown to be interwoven with its precarious illusions.

Polonsky longed for divine justice in a world of unordered relativity. His religious protest remains empty and ultimately frustrating. His ironies appear because his figures are essentially powerless. His tone, moreover, is needlessly didactic. His language was praised by contemporaries for its colloquial and unassuming character. In contrast, his verse lines are intricately patterned and reveal in themselves his constant artistic awareness. His poems were set to music by Tchaikovsky, Dargomyzhsky, and Rachmaninoff.

Tolstoy

The guardian of German romantic idealism in Russia poetry of the mid-century was Aleksey K. Tolstoy (1817–1875). He is remembered as the author of a trilogy of historical verse dramas set in the time of Ivan the Terrible and his immediate successors, including Boris Godunov. Tolstoy's lyrics have not had as wide an audience, but they were influential among poets. He was deeply committed in all his art to his transcendental beliefs, but he was not essentially nostalgic. The world was for him an arena where good and evil constantly contend. He often portrayed Kievan culture because he believed that it had embodied certain chivalric virtues that the nation had subsequently lost. In his dramatic trilogy he depicts the beginning of the rule of tyranny and violence in the Muscovite era. The separate plays are *The Death of Ivan the Terrible* (1866), *Tsar Fedor* (1868), and *Tsar Boris* (1870). In his early career, Tolstoy collaborated with three of his cousins (Zhemchuzhnikovs) in a literary escapade, the creation of the works of a fictitious author, a ridiculous conservative philistine named Kozma Prutkov.

Tolstoy was a wealthy aristocrat who idolized the Pushkin poets and viewed art, as he believed they had, as a civilizing process. He was born in St. Petersburg, but reared in the south by his mother and her brother, Aleksey Perovsky, who was the author of Gothic tales under the pseudonym Anton Pogorelsky. Tolstoy learned his idealism and his craft from Perovsky and began to write verse at age sixteen. He was educated at Moscow University, appointed to the Foreign Office, and served in Frankfurt from 1837 to 1840. On his return he published a Gothic tale, "The Vampire." He resumed publication only in the 1850s with his own poems and others attributed to Prutkov. In 1861 he retired to his estate in the south and in 1863 married Sofia Miller, the inspiration of many poems. His first collection of verse appeared in 1867, when he was fifty years old.

Tolstoy's first public renown came with the appearance of the comic poems attributed to Prutkov. The poems showed Prutkov to be a reprehensible bureaucrat and an incomparably bad author. Tolstoy wrote several harmless parodies of his own romantic tendencies. "From Heine" (1854) is a senseless lyric about the end of summer, and "The Desire to Be Spanish" (1854) extols impetuous behavior. The jointly authored Prutkov poems express reactionary political views. In the system of Tolstoy's *oeuvre,* Prutkov is a representative of evil in its practical aspect.

Tolstoy's transcendental idealism is most persuasively seen in his love lyrics. The poems are patently addressed to one lifelong love, his wife. She can be recognized by her constant and unexplained sadness. "And your sad eyes, whose grieving has not ended, / Regarded me in that still evening hour," he wrote in "The hot day paled by fine degrees at evening" (1856). His affectionate love for her is in part protective; he shields her like a young tree, and thinks of her as a flower. His love for her is unutterable in this poem written in 1858:

> Autumn. Now our barren park—wears a coat of leaves.
> Faded yellow leaves take sail—floating on the wind.
> Beauty is but distant now—at the valley's end,
> Where the withered rowan trees show their bright red twigs.
> Happiness and bitterness vie within my heart.
> Silently I warm your hand, press it in my own,
> When I look into your eyes, silent, I shed tears,
> For I cannot say in words—all my love for you.

Eventually her inalterable sadness is understood: it originates in her deep sensitivity to life's ordinary suffering. She comprehends that the real is distant from the ideal. Another beacon of the transcendental was art. He speaks of the "Word" in the poem "In darkness and in dust to me" (1851 or 1852). He wrote elsewhere about the mission of the prophet and about Raphael's Madonna. He believed that poetry originates in the sphere of the eternal ("Artist!—you vainly suppose you're the author of all your creations!" 1856).

Tolstoy portrays himself as a creature in whom moral strengths and weaknesses are exaggerated. He is overcome by melancholia in "Here in my room it is lonely. For I sit apart at my fireplace" (1851). He urges himself to rise to activity in "I have been sleeping, my head hanging" (1858). He compares his potential power to a volcano spewing lava in "My sternest friend, O do have patience" (1858). He had a romantic sympathy for extremities of behavior, as signs of spontaneity and free will. In 1854 he wrote, "If you love, then show no reason, / If you threaten, then no joking, /If you curse, then make it hot." Tolstoy's own character can be recognized in his responses to nature. He wrote about the dramatic features that appeal to the imagination—the storm, the exotic Mount Ayudag, the ocean. Like the Pushkin poets, he described the picturesque landscapes of the Crimea. His "Crimean Sketches" (1856–1858) include warm personal memories, usually of outings with his wife.

The arena for the struggle between good and evil in Tolstoy's verse was often Russia as a nation. Contemporary Russia is seen in dismal images. In "The Empty House" (1849) he hints at the passing of a culture. Poverty is his subject in "Along the old boardwalk that's shaking" (1840s), where he describes an ugly river bank, a ragged Jew, a boy who is fishing, and a tumbledown mill. "The Convicts" (1850) depicts gloomy men marching in chains. The past, in contrast, is the object of boundless enthusiasm. He praises the Kievan *bogatyr* and the historic Ukraine, whose capital is Kiev. He imagines that the older culture fosters a sense of honor and a love of freedom. He believes in a timeless Russian spirit, whose essence is expansiveness. He sees in the Russian character a Gypsy strain. In this unassuming poem of 1856 he evokes a primitive Russia:

> O my land, my native land—
> Horses swift in freedom—
> Eagles' cries, and flocks on high—
> Wolves' howls on the lowlands!
>
> Hallo there! my native land,
> Hallo! sleeping forests!
> Nightingales in song all night,
> Steppe, and winds, and storm clouds!

"And I once also had a country" (1856) is a candid imitation of Heine's "Ich hatte einst ein schones Vaterland." Tolstoy often imitated the "drawn-out" folk song, sometimes for ethnic portraits. In "O tell me why have you, my evil fate" (1858) a woman has been mismatched above her class; the poem is unmetered except for its dactyl line endings, and is unrhymed.

Tolstoy wrote a number of narrative poems, many of which were akin to folklore and which he called ballads, *byliny*, and tales. They encompass both his nostalgia for the past and his political views. The chivalric virtues that he found in Kievan culture were usually those admired by contemporary Westernizers. The tyranny that characterized the Muscovite period always seems in his poems to be a reference to the present. In "Prince Mihailo Repnin" (1840s) he portrays an independent and courageous boyar as he is killed by an angry Ivan the Terrible. Tolstoy's imitations of *byliny*, written over two decades, include "Tugarin the Serpent," "Ilia Muromets," "Alesha Popovich," and "Sadko." Tolstoy also wrote literary narrative poems; they were less popular than his imitations of folklore, and they were usually religious or philosophical statements. "The Sinful Woman" (1857) is a Biblical story of a conversion. "John Damascenus" (1859), a story about an eighth-century saint, contains a prayer for the dead that was well known for its sustained magnificence. "The Portrait" (1873) tells of a boy's love for an eighteenth-century lady. In "The Dragon" (1875) a monster emanates from the struggle in Italy between the Guelfs and the Ghibellines.

The trilogy of plays in verse was preceded by a Scottian novel, *Prince Serebriany* (1862), in which Ivan the Terrible is again portrayed as a villain. The fictitious hero, "the silver prince," represents the independent, but doomed, culture of Old Russia. The plays of the trilogy are indebted in form to French romantic tragedies, but their stories were derived from Karamzin's *History of the Russian State*. Tolstoy's moral supposition throughout is that of Karamzin (and Pushkin)—that power brings retribution on those who are not fit to wield it. In *The Death of Ivan the Terrible* the tsar is shattered inwardly by the defeats he deserved. In *Tsar Fedor* the forces of conservatism contend with Boris Godunov, the upstart and bearer of Western ideas. In *Tsar Boris* the ruler is doomed by his own guilt in the assassination of Fedor's heir. Historical novels and plays enjoyed a particular vogue in the 1860s, when "serious" literature was contemporary in setting.

Tolstoy had a cosmopolitan view of literature and its capabilities. The sentiments which seem to inspire his *oeuvre* are appealing, especially his self-confidence and forthright manner. If he had a drawback, it was a facile style; his words tend to come in ready clumps and to verge on clichés. Tolstoy was the favorite poet of many in his utilitarian age, and his lyrics kept transcendental idealism alive for the succeeding era. His poems were set to music by Liszt, Rimsky-Korsakov, Rubenstein, Mussorgsky, Rachmaninoff, and Gliere. Tolstoy translated Byron, Chenier, Goethe, and Heine, and wrote poems himself in both French and German.

Lesser Idealists

The "pure poets," if both art-for-art's-sake writers and idealists are taken together as a group, constituted the majority of poets. The two groups shared, moreover, a tendency to melancholia. Karolina Pavlova (1807–1893) was among those for whom poetry was a manifestation of an elevated spirituality, a vehicle for the cultivation of the imagination and of love. She was an erudite poet, the daughter of a professor at Moscow University; she was acquainted with such golden age poets as Pushkin, Baratynsky, Iazykov, and Venevitinov. She wrote in three languages, Russian, French, and German; her contribution to literature was, in part, her translations among these languages. *Das Nordlicht* (1833), her first book, includes both original lyrics and translations from some Russian poets into German. Her husband, Nikolay Pavlov, was also a writer; together they maintained a literary salon in Moscow before they separated in 1853. During the 1850s she traveled in Europe, and eventually settled in Dresden.

Pavlova's poetry is dedicated to what she called "the dream," the lofty aim to which all should aspire. Her work is to a great extent a moral autobiography, a record of her attempts to achieve her ideals. The heights of the "dream" could be realized in art, in exalted sexual love, in friendship, and in compassion for others. Life, however, is daunting in her view of it. In "The Pilgrim" (1843) a wanderer exclaims in the wilderness, "Where are you, O my promised land, / The single aim of my desire?" Pavlova sometimes wrote about her personal dramas in epistles to friends and lovers or fellow artists, who included Ivan and Sergey Aksakov. She wrote warm letters to young women, and was fond of warning them that much of their youthful capacity for the "dream" would be taken from them by society. Her poems about lovers include perplexed memories of the Polish poet Adam Mickiewicz. Her philosophical poems include "The Moth" (1840), in which she describes the poet as free from earthly ties. Her religious faith appears in other poems to be unquestioning and childlike. She also wrote on historical and cultural subjects. She felt at home in the Mediterranean lands. In "Roman Festival" (1855) she depicted the moral disintegration of a great society. Her travels in the 1850s brought descriptions of Naples, Venice, Dresden, and Marseilles. She was the author of an innovative novelette about love and marriage called *A Double Life* (1848). It is a record of the inner struggle of a young woman who knows the truth in her spirit, but who is pressed by her mother to make a conventional, and profitable, marriage. Her daytime thoughts proceed in prose, but she meditates in verse as she falls asleep each night. Pavlova's poetry was described by her contemporaries as cold and rational, even virtuoso. She was relatively unable to create the illusion of experience, and her defense of the emotional life is abstract. Her poems are also marred by her high opinion of her own sensitivity and courage.

Apollon Grigorev (1822–1864) was a literary critic well known for what he called an "organic theory" of literature. He believed that the relationship between a nation and its literature is mystical and inevitable. His poetry was not unambitious; it has perhaps been somewhat discounted because of the popularity of his guitar songs. He was also the author of a memoir, *My Literary and Moral Wandering* (1862–1864), which has its own literary merit. Born in Moscow, he was the son of a minor bureaucrat. He studied law at Moscow University; his family housed his fellow student Afanasy Fet. Much of Grigorev's literary criticism appeared in the Slavophile magazine, *The Muscovite* (1850–1856), and in Dostoevsky's magazines, *Time* and *The Epoch* (1861–1865). Grigorev, Dostoevsky, and Dostoevsky's brother Mikhail formed an intellectual group, called the Men of the Soil, for the advocacy of a liberal variant of Slavophilism. Grigorev lived the unsettled life of an urban bohemian, was alcoholic, and died in a debtors' prison. In his essays, he described Pushkin as the best embodiment of the nation's spirit. He popularized the plays of his friend Aleksandr Ostrovsky, who originated, as he had, in Moscow's merchant quarter.

In his lyrics, Grigorev adopted the pose of a belated Byronic character, a Childe Harold from the middle class. His stance is clearly derived from Lermontov's Byronic pose, but Grigorev's character is more feckless, tainted, and unrestrained. Most of Grigorev's poems are about love, and some are simple cries of pain. They include his anguished Gypsy songs, among which is "Two Guitars." Several poems are addressed to George Sand's heroine Lavinia, a woman described as too experienced ever to love again. Other poems are simple expressions of melancholia; an example is "Sounds" (1845):

Again those sounds—again those tuneful dirges
        Of misery, despair—
How glad I am; instead of words they enter,
        And fill my ailing soul.

Their sounds are like those dreams that are but raving,
        That were they put in words
Were laughable, for shame could not be said,
        But which I can't dispel.

The sounds speak of a past that never happened,
        Of dreams of brighter years,
They tell of aspirations vain and dreary,
        For shades that never were. . . .

In "Epistle to My Friends" (1850s) Grigorev recalled a time when malancholia itself had been recognized as a liberal theme, a sign of "socialism" and "atheism." He showed his hatred for authoritarianism and bureaucratic stagnation, traits he attributed to a crude westernization of Russia. He predicted, in "Whenever bells in their solemnity resound" (1846), that Russia's bells, now frozen in silence, will once again be the voice of a free populace. His political ideals tend to merge with religious and artistic strivings; in his youth he was an ardent Hegelian. His Hebrew songs in "Imitations" (1852) seem to have a civic meaning. His drama, "Two Egoisms" (1845), is about his Byronic figure in love. Grigorev was a translator of lyrics by Goethe, Schiller, Heine, Beranger, Musset, and Byron. Even his apparently primitive love lyrics give evidence of his knowledge of Goethe, Schiller, Heine, and Shakespeare.

The Civic Poets

Although the critics spoke of a "civic school," the poets who were so designated included both Westernizers and liberal Slavophiles. They could not form a close group, although they were alike in their concern for the lower classes. Among the earliest of the utilitarians in poetry was the radical Slavophile Ivan Aksakov (1823–1886), the son of the famous novelist Sergey Aksakov. His brother, Konstantin, was also a prominent Slavophile. Ivan Aksakov had virtually one concern in his poetry: to urge the gentry to work for the nation. He was born near Ufa and educated in St. Petersburg. Although he was an outspoken journalist and often in the thick of contemporary controversies, he was seldom able to occupy positions of editorial responsibility because his radical views were considered suspect by the government. In the poem called "The Voice of the Age" (1844) Aksakov wrote, "But no, to serve the cause and science / You'll bring your poet's sounds and daydreams / And heat of your abundant work." His poetry has the drama of personal striving in that he confesses to temporary weaknesses. In "Andante" (1846) he attempts to overcome his soul's dejection and sloth. Aksakov still held the romantic notion that the poet has superior gifts and must lead the crowd. He anticipated the liberation of the serfs. In "There comes to meet the vatic prophet" (1860) he wrote of the "dawn."

His poetry is rhetorical, but effective. He was like Khomiakov and Kiukhelbeker in the narrowness of his purpose. His ideal of service would continue to appeal, however, to the radical intelligentsia for decades. After the emancipation of the serfs, many educated young people "went into the people." At the end of the century, Chekhov's characters still spoke of the imperative to "work."

Ivan Nikitin (1824–1861) was a self-educated poet who rose from the lower class. He was born, like Koltsov, in Voronezh. He attended a seminary, but could not afford to complete his studies. He lived as an innkeeper and bookseller and died of tuberculosis at age forty-seven. In his early poems, he wrote about nature, about his melancholia, and occasionally about his religious feelings. His career as a civic poet began with "To the Poet" (1850), where he calls for the poet to be a "herald of truth and a prophet." In other poems, art's "sacred moments" are said to touch and elevate the generation's "long work." He portrayed the life of the poor, in both urban and in rural settings. In "The Winter Road" (1853) a lush and vibrant landscape is the setting for poverty-stricken, ragged people. Some narratives tell about the desperate crimes of the poor. In "Revenge" (1853) a peasant father murders a squire because of his daughter. In "The Quarrel" (1854) an alcoholic peasant torments his family. He imitated the "drawn-out" folk song, for example in "The Inheritance" (1853), a typical song of a poor man. He wrote a new *bylina* about Ilia Muromets in "There was once a brave man" (1854). Nikitin also wrote several patriotic, indeed chauvinistic, poems. In "War for Faith" (1853) he defended Russia's intervention in Turkey on behalf of the Orthodox population. Nikitin also wrote accusatory poems in the manner of the intelligentsia poets. In "Our age in ignominy dies" (1861) he reproaches his generation for having accepted slavery. His narrative poems include "The Kulak" (1857), about the victims of oppression. Nikitin might have had a wider audience if he had belonged to one political camp or the other. His landscapes are effective. His wrenching contrasts between Russia's natural beauty and the despair of her peasants are unexpected in poetry, but defensible.

10

The Ascendancy of Civic Verse
(1860–1890)

The reign of the "Tsar-Liberator," Alexander II, brought the emancipation of the serfs in 1861 and other "great reforms" that accelerated the growth of the middle class and of trade and industry, while the fortunes of the landowning gentry declined. This was the golden age of prose; Turgenev, Dostoevsky, and Tolstoy wrote their greatest works, from *Fathers and Sons* (1862) and *War and Peace* (1869) to *The Brothers Karamazov* (1880). Liberal sentiments were viewed with considerable sympathy among the general population. The period brought a respite from the most repressive political measures. Radical trends, such as nihilism, appeared in the 1860s. In the 1870s populism had many adherents, and some young people abandoned professional careers to become teachers and artisans among the peasants. Civic poetry was popular, especially Nikolay Nekrasov's scenes of peasant life. The revolutionary movement began its continuous history. Political assassinations were perpetrated by anarchists. The assassination of Alexander II in 1881 brought a return to repressive measures by Alexander III. Radical movements began to be condemned by public opinion. Art-for-art's-sake poetry, which had been discouraged, returned, and elements of *fin de siècle* verse soon followed.

Rival Camps

A pessimistic trend was developing in the fiction of the West. Realism was to some extent replaced by naturalism. Charles Dickens was followed by Thomas Hardy, whose characters sometimes faced an inexplicably unjust fate. Gustave Flaubert's humanistic vision gave way to Émile Zola's scientific determinism. The Russian audience, however, was not prepared to accept pessimism; they preferred the view that society can ameliorate the lot of the dispossessed. While the best Russian novelists ignored the demand for social purpose in the narrow sense, they remained relatively optimistic about the capabilities of society, as well as about man's place in the universe. The civic poetry of the period was more committed to the cause of social change. It still derived its traits from the brief, and incomplete, Russian naturalism of the 1840s. Civic poetry enjoyed a short hegemony over the field in the 1860s and 1870s. It was during this period that a general sense of poetry as such reached its lowest ebb.

The tendencies of the civic "school" of poetry could all be seen by the 1850s in the works of its only major poet, Nikolay Nekrasov. Among Nekrasov's early poems were those rhetorical accusations that are addressed to the intelligentsia, to the gentry class, or the entire generation, and which stem obviously from Lermontov's legacy. In its introduction of scenes of squalor, brutality, and crime, Russian civic poetry had no counterpart in the West. The ugly aspects of reality came from prose into Russian poetry. Among the civic poets, society was always understood to be the cause of the hardships of the poor, and even of their criminality. The victim of poverty was often epitomized by Nekrasov in the figure of a woman; his most popular narrative poem, *Frost, the Red-Nosed* depicts the death by exposure of a peasant widow while gathering wood for her husband's coffin. Populist sentiment encouraged the tradition of literary imitations of folk poetry, which had, in any case, enjoyed a continuous history from classical times. Some stanzas of Nekrasov's narrative poems were widely sung as songs and believed to be anonymous. Censorship made direct expressions of political criticism and revolutionary sympathy impossible, and for this reason a nameless melancholia was often seen in the works of civic poets.

While Western fiction developed in the direction of naturalism, its poetry was undergoing a transformation toward the *fin de siècle* mentality. In 1857 Baudelaire had published *Les Fleurs du mal,* a fountainhead of decadence. The Parnassians, who flourished in the 1860s, portrayed exotic, usually antique, cultures; and mysticism was revived in English poetry by the Pre-Raphaelites. An "aesthetic revival" was to come to Russia, but not until the 1880s. Its first manifestation was a general return to art-for-art's-sake poetry. Afanasy Fet reappeared after a silence of twenty years. Precisely the lack of purpose in poetry became an admirable trait. The practical leader of the revived aesthetic school, Konstantin Sluchevsky, carried the tendency to the point of an affectation. Poets who were less aggressive wrote rather often of the fine arts. Eventually there were younger poets who imitated the European decadent malaise. They, too, revelled in beauty and found a voluptuous delight in sickness and decay.

Civic Poetry: Nekrasov

Nikolay Nekrasov (1821–1878) was the major poet of the realistic era in Russian literature. He demonstrated in poetry how far the abuses of serfdom, the effects of greed, and the hardships caused by poverty could lead. His stories were more painful and shocking than were those of contemporary fiction, and his denunciations of the gentry were more outspoken. His depictions, and his arguments, were also more one-sided. For this reason, he has been viewed by some as a naturalist, but he was separated from the more pessimistic members of that current by his belief in the possibility of progress. His purpose was to motivate changes. He created a "realistic" style of poetry and strove, in general, for a documentary authenticity. His depictions are graphic, and, when appropriate, he used the spoken language of the peasant. His best poems are perhaps those in which peasants tell their own stories in their own style. His narratives are more memorable than his meditations. His masterpieces are two long narrative poems, *The Peddlers* (1861) and *Frost, the Red-Nosed* (1863). His thoroughgoing utilitarianism has made him the subject of critical controversies.

Nekrasov was a landowner, an aristocrat who found a mission in civic poetry and was an example to the less consistent poets of his school. Born near Moscow, he was educated in St. Petersburg, but in poverty and without parental support. In 1842 he became a literary critic at *The Notes of the Fatherland,* where he was persuaded by his senior, Belinsky, to write "realist" verse. In 1846 Nekrasov became part owner and publisher of *The Contemporary,* which in his hands became the leading leftist magazine of the day. *The Contemporary* published the fiction of Turgenev, Dostoevsky, and Tolstoy and the criticism of Belinsky. Its literary critics in the 1850s were Belinsky's successors, Nikolay Chernyshevsky and Nikolay Dobroliubov. After a watershed controversy over utilitarianism in 1859 and 1860, Turgenev and other liberals deserted Nekrasov. In 1862 he was joined as a co-editor by the radical novelist Mikhail Saltykov. Nekrasov amassed a fortune as a publisher and was virtually the only poet of note who appeared in the 1860s. He lived a life of ostentation and dissipation and was accused of duplicity. In 1866 *The Contemporary* was closed, but in 1868 Nekrasov acquired *The Notes of the Fatherland,* which he co-edited with Saltykov until his death in 1878.

Nekrasov's poetry has coherence as the work of a unique personality, not simply as a collection of poems, some of which are about the poor. In his lyrical stance Nekrasov is another descendant of the Byronic character. He reveals in his introspective poems some of the faults found in the accusatory poems written by Lermontov. He is aware, for example, that he falls short of his own ideals. He bears a family resemblance to the heroes of some contemporary novels, those who were called "superfluous men" and who were also inspired by the Byronic heritage. Among Nekrasov's early poems is "My Homeland" (1842), in which his family origin is seen in a novelistic way and which seems, because of the title, to symbolize the wider social fabric of Russia. His father is said to have been a brutal squire, a tyrant who destroyed his wife, drove his daughter to leave home, terrorized his serfs, and earned the unmitigated hatred of his son. The poem concludes, "And only he alone, who crushed all other lives, / Did freely draw his breath, and have his will, and live. . . ." Nekrasov feels himself to be the natural outcome of this upbringing. He castigates himself for his idleness and for a lingering, senseless melancholia. In other poems he has become an avenger, the poet of the people's sorrows. In " 'Twas yesterday at six o'clock" (1848) he tells his muse that she must be the sister of a peasant woman whom he sees being flogged in a public square. In other poems his inspiration is called the "muse of vengeance" and of "sorrow." He is well known for having said in "The Poet and the Citizen" (1856) that "One may decline to be a poet, / But all are citizens by duty." Here is an untitled elegy of 1858:

> My verse, you are the living testimony
>   Of worlds where tears are shed!
> You have your birth in those most fateful moments
>   When storms assail the soul,
> And beat against the hearts of mankind
>   As waves beat on a cliff.

The same contradictions in character are apparent in Nekrasov's love poems. He is often apologetic, sometimes guilt-ridden; he suffers from a sense that he is unworthy; he begs not to be cursed or to be remembered well. He is compassionate when he encourages as his partner a woman with a dubious past. He is often nostalgic; he recalls a love when it is past; in several poems he encounters old letters. But his deepest anxieties are about his own spiritual inheritance. He fears, in "Why must you tear me into pieces" (1867), that the sons of corrupt fathers are always doomed to be secret slaves. In "Gloom" (1874) he is glad that his ancestral estate, the symbol of suffering, has been destroyed by fire. In the 1870s he spoke of his impending death. If Nekrasov did not create a full legend of himself in the manner of the earlier romantics, he did provide a sense of biographical cohesion among his poems. His self-assessments, however, are not devoid of sentimentality.

Some of Nekrasov's most popular poems about the poor appeared in the 1840s. He established an atmosphere suggestive of a generally dreary society in "Before the Rain" (1846):

> Mournful is the wind that's driving
> Clouds in flocks to heaven's edge.
> Groans come from a bending fir tree,
> Muffled are the dark wood's sighs.
>
> Pocked and colored is the river
> Where the leaves fly down and hit,
> Chill the air that comes attacking,
> Cutting in its draft, and dry.
>
> Twilight is on all descending.
> Flocks of ravens, jackdaws swarm,
> Flying in from every quarter,
> Cawing, circling in the air.
>
> Look, the cabriolet passing
> Has its top down, front all closed.
> And, "Get on," a gendarme rises
> Toward the driver, whip in hand. . . .

Nekrasov's subjects are the same ones seen in the naturalistic fiction of the 1840s: men are driven to drink, women are degraded, and infants suffer needless deaths. The narrator in Nekrasov's "When I go riding along a dark byway" (1847) recalls the death of a child from starvation and the departure of the mother, his lover, to the streets. Violence and crime are common in the urban poems, and both passions and calculated greed are decried. He imitated the documentary style of the feuilleton in

"On the Street" (1850) and "In the Hospital" (1855), where he supposedly recorded the typical dramas witnessed by a casual observer.

Nekrasov's rural poems are considered more characteristic of him than are his urban pieces. Early poems about the peasant include "The Unreaped Row" (1854), in which the serf responsible for this row of grain has not lived to enjoy the harvest, and "Vlas" (1856), about a kulak who has repented and become a religious pilgrim. Those poems in which the peasants are pointedly shown to be destroyed by their masters are less satisfactory. "In the Village" (1853) is one of several poems in which young men are killed accidentally in hunts that are to their owners a mere sport. In "The Forgotten Village" (1855) the masters are too busy to administer the lands on which their serfs depend for their livelihood. Those poems in which Nekrasov uses the racy language of the peasant often resemble the "drawn-out" song even when no imitation of folk rhythms is suggested. In the 1860s Nekrasov's poems about peasants became the virtual mainstay of his work. In that decade, he began to stress even more the vicissitudes endured by peasant children. They are given work beyond their strength; yet they occasionally preserve the bravery and optimism characteristic of the young. Nekrasov's two greatest narrative poems, *The Peddlers* and *Frost, the Red-Nosed,* were both written in the 1860s. In *The Peddlers* the life of peasants is seen from their own viewpoint as full of ordinary joys; the poem includes scenes of nature, towns, flirtations, and games. Episodes from this work have had the most success as anonymous, popular songs. *Frost, the Red-Nosed* is a much more literary work. The death of a peasant widow in the forest is described with reverence and detachment, and nature is made to seem monumental; yet the narrative also draws on folklore elements.

Nekrasov's analytical denunciations of Russian society had begun to appear in the 1850s. He described the provinces as stagnant, lacking in culture and activity; the charge had been made earlier by the essayist Petr Chaadaev. In "Freedom" (1861) Nekrasov warned that the liberation of the serfs would have to be followed by changes in public attitudes. In the 1860s and 1870s these more discursive poems became the vehicle of his greatest ambition. In "The Railroad" (1864) he argues that progress is not the work of those few outstanding men who are given credit, but of countless laborers, many of whom suffer and die. In "The Russian Women" (1872) he recounts stories about the wives who followed their Decembrist husbands to exile in Siberia. Two long poems were especially sweeping in their scope. In "Our Contemporaries" (1875) he portrayed the "heroes of the times" in the manner of Lermontov. "Who Lives Happily in Russia?" (1877) encompasses a vast social panorama in order to show that no one lives well in Russia.

The intensity of Nekrasov's social conscience has led some critics to pardon him for some artistic sins, especially his sentimentality. He has remained, however, a controversial poet. He opened the way for poetry that is uncomfortable and even painful. His ironies were many, and he could be sarcastic. He has always been, however unexpectedly, a poets' poet. He was praised by members of the *fin de siècle* generation, and the poets of the twentieth century owe him a debt. Yet his melancholia has been seen by some as more nearly a private impulse than a genuine response to the plight of the poor, and his utilitarian purpose has also been resented. His use of rhythms was innovative; he favored the long, lilting dactyls, amphibrachs, and anapests. They were, perhaps, not always appropriate to indignations and irony. Sometimes they seem to harbor precisely a lingering, unacknowledged sentimentality.

The civic poetry of Semen Nadson (1862–1887) was extraordinarily popular in the 1880s and thereafter for two decades. His were the passive, and elegiac, moods of the radical intelligentsia in the years of its waning confidence. His collected lyrics went through seven printings between 1883 and 1886; by 1906 they were in their twenty-second printing. His subjects are typical of the civic school—the hardships of the lower classes and the indolence of the landowning class—but his best form was the meditation. He wrote as though the social injustices of the times must be felt as personal sources of sorrow. He was born the son of a civil servant in Moscow. He served briefly in the army but resigned because of ill health and was to die young of tuberculosis. Nadson spoke for a circle of the dedicated in difficult times. He regrets in "At Sunset" (1878) that nature's beauties cannot alleviate his sadness: "Sick and full of anguish is my sorry breast." He holds out hope for some indefinite future: "This hard battle will not have been fought in vain. / When the dawn breaks, clear, a flame will light an era. / That new time will bring us truth, bright thoughts, and work." Scenes of poverty and pain flow through his meditations; burials and tears are common. In "The Mother" (1878) a tired widow faces her starving children. Historical and literary allusions appear as illustrations of the present. In "A Dream of Ivan the Terrible" (1879) he creates an atmosphere of gloomy, drunken silence that reminds of tyranny in general. The martyrdom of the early Christians at the hands of the Romans is the subject of "The Christian Warrior" (1878). He looks for signs of weakness in himself and in his generation. "In the Darkness" (1878) opens with a memory of better years: "There was a time—we entered life / With footsteps that were mighty, firm. . . ." Even Nadson's love poems speak of his prior dedication to the social struggle, for example in "I am not yours—for I am called" (1878). Only his responses to nature are free from a sense of purpose. Serenity reigns in "Currents gilded by the moonlight" (1878), where songs are heard on the river.

The poems of the 1880s are more generally pessimistic, and sometimes angry. In "The Cloud" (1880) he warns, enigmatically, that the sky's bright colors may fade. Life is compared to a prison in several poems. If he had hopes in the 1870s, they are now but daydreams. He openly declared his civic purpose for the first time in "Poetry" (1880), and he showed indignation in "Many the false phrases, puffed-up, pseudo-liberal" (1881). During the last three years of his life, his sorrow was ascribed to more cosmic causes. "Rêverie" (1883), in which he recalls his childhood, was a turning point. In other poems he wrote about such figures as Buddha and Icarus. His *oeuvre* was narrow to the point of claustrophia, but he spoke for an audience that did not want to relinquish its commitment at a time when engagement was difficult.

The Return of Poetry

The year 1880 has often served as a dividing line in the history of Russian literature. Tolstoy renounced the style of his great novels after a religious conversion. Dostoevsky died in 1881. During the reign of Alexander III (1881–1894) the magazines of the radicals were suppressed. The exhortations of utilitarian criticism began to fall on deaf ears. Short stories became more innovative than novels. Fet and other poets who had been silenced began to publish again. Civic poems disappeared from the works of some and were replaced by private or philosophical subjects. An "aesthetic revival" began to take shape that included art-for-art's-sake poets, liberal humanists, and decadents. Aleksey Zhemchuzhnikov (1821–1908), an old-style liberal, returned to literature after a tentative debut as a participant in the works of Kozma Prutkov with his brothers and Aleksey Tolstoy. Zhemchuzhnikov also wrote his own verse in the 1850s and 1860s, but did not publish, and even lived in Europe. He began to publish in the 1870s and returned to Russia in 1884; his first collection of poems appeared in 1892, when he was seventy-one years old. He was an intelligent and outspoken cultural critic. In the 1850s he criticized the patriotism of the Slavophiles as exaggerated and ridiculed their adulation of "primitive" customs. He used such words as "rotten" and "cowardly" to describe Russia in the 1870s and 1880s. In "Autumn Cranes" (1871) he laments that his homeland is a country of "darkness, poverty, anguish, bad weather, and mud." After returning to Russia, he wrote "Homeland" (1884), in which he rediscovers his love for its natural landscape, but still feels hatred for its people. His poems have a matter-of-fact tone and ironic touches that recall the parodies he wrote for Kozma Prutkov. Among his later poems are some tributes to the country, to Derzhavin, and to Fet.

Aleksey Apukhtin (1841–1893) was the most legitimate heir of the poetry of the 1840s, a close link with the past. His work encompasses a common range of interests, from the fine arts to social issues. He was a member of the gentry; he was educated at the Petersburg Institute of Jurisprudence, where he was a classmate of Peter Tchaikovsky, and served in the Ministry of Justice until 1862. In that year he declared himself to be among the "pure poets," and he was subsequently excluded from the press. He returned to publishing in the 1880s, and his first collection of verse appeared in 1886. In his last years, he wrote prose stories, which were published posthumously.

Apukhtin's poems typically have the tone of reverie; they are usually about love, nature, and art. His subjects are less important than his aura of well-bred sensitivity. He is moody and changeable. "Life" (1853) is both hedonistic and Christian: we must "enjoy" existence, while we "pray, believe, and love." But in a later poem, also called "Life" (1856), existence has become a "distant" song, an "unbroken chain of tears and suffering." His love poems are tender but sad, as in this example from 1867:

> No answer, not a word, and not a greeting,
> The world, a wilderness, between us lies.
> My pondering, its question without answer,
> Weighs hard upon my heart and brings me fear.
>
> Then will our past, between the hours of anguish
> And of anger, slip by without a trace?
> Like airy notes of songs that are forgotten,
> Or like a star that falls into the night?

Apukhtin's landscapes are always seen in a melancholy mood. He describes scenes that are beautiful in themselves—flowers lit by moonlight. But even spring is sad: "My soul is sickened by my constant grief," he wrote in a cycle called "From Spring Songs" (1860). His impressionistic style was part of his character. "From a Long Poem—The Last Romantic" (1860s) consists of a series of fragments.

Other themes appeared more fleetingly. Apukhtin's social conscience is reflected in poems about the victims of war and poverty. "A Soldier's Song about Sevastopol" (1860s) was his response to the Crimean War. In "The Orphan" (1855) a poor child speaks on the grave of its mother. His interest in art overshadowed his social concerns, however. He addressed a number of poems to musicians, among them Dargomyzhsky and Tchaikovsky. He published his translations of Heine, Byron, Chenier, Alfred de Musset, and Sully-Prudhomme among his own lyrics. His travel impressions include Russian and European scenes. "The Village Road" (1858) shows a love for the primitive Russian countryside, while "Venice" (1873) is an appreciation of a lively, and old, civilization. His range of subjects is broad, but his attitudes are somewhat predictable. His impulses are laudable, but he shows few signs of an authentic individuality. His style is accomplished and exceptionally musical from the standpoint of sound.

The poets who reached maturity in the 1870s and 1880s had unbroken careers, but they belonged to an obscure and transitional generation. Arseny Golenishchev-Kutuzov (1848–1913) wrote traditional poetry that was never constrained by utilitarianism. His subjects were love of country, private hopes and disappointments, nature, and social problems. He was an aristocrat, born at Tsarskoe Selo and educated at St. Petersburg University. He held bureaucratic positions, but was always close to musicians and writers, including Mussorgsky, Fet, and Polonsky. His first noteworthy collection was *Calm and Storm* (1878). He wrote fantasies that reflect folklore, but his most deeply felt responses were to nature. Certain poems, which are set on the Adriatic or in Russia on white nights, describe ecstasies that recall Fet and contain a hint of Pasternak. His poetry grew increasingly optimistic during his lifetime.

New "Aesthetic" Trends

Konstantin Sluchevsky (1837–1904) was a standard-bearer for the poetry of the "aesthetic revival" and a pioneer of Russian decadence. He wrote as a literary dandy and hedonist. His first poems, published in 1860, resulted in a controversy over his indifference to civic issues. In 1861 he went to Europe, where he spent five years studying at the Sorbonne and at the universities of Berlin and Heidelberg. On his return, he worked at first in the Foreign Office and then in the Government Properties Office. A novel, *From Kiss to Kiss,* appeared in 1872. His first collection of verse came in 1880, and in 1887 he published fiction in *Thirty-Three Stories.* In the 1890s the young symbolists attended his salon.

Sluchevsky maintained a slight air of stylization and playful pretense in all his verse. The distance between art and reality is always apparent. In "We Are Two" he confesses to a double identity: one side is the visible man, and the other side is the "dreamer." It is the fantasies we see in his poems. His work is more like the mask of a poet than the self-expression of a man. He is a relativist in philosophy, a disbeliever in truths; he loves the kaleidoscopy of change. In "Forms and Profiles" he delights in nature's ever-varying shapes. In "Lux Aeterna" his subject is not the eternal light, but a dream world suggested by moonlight. He is more concerned for the state within than for objective reality:

> Our mind at times is like a battle, ending.
> We hear—retreat is sounded loud and clearly.
> The ranks are shrunk through losses and, closed up, depart.
> And everywhere is gore in bloody tracks still seen.
> The grass is crushed and blades are flashing on it.
> These heaps are corpses here, and those are dying.
> A male nurse comes; attentive to each sound, he works.
> A priest administers his dispensations—
> The smoke from final rites stands round in layers . . .
> Then nature's little bird reveals his priceless gift,
> The holy gift of song that brings back living.
> He sits upon a bayonet still wet with blood
> And sings in happiness—he sings of peace and love.

It is the images of beauty, peace, and love that prevail in Sluchevsky's verse. He was fascinated, like other modernists, by transience. He wrote poems on nonce perceptions, such as a doll that falls as though alive ("The Doll"), and on ephemeral events, such as forget-me-nots that bloom during a storm ("Near a river, here and there where they may fall"). His few love poems are as unrealistic as idylls; they are pastoral celebrations of an unclouded harmony enjoyed in carefree leisure. He compares his love to a white swan, to a gentle dove, and to a fiery ruby. His stubborn opposition to utilitarianism in literature is nowhere plainer than in a cycle of farcical poems devoted to Mephistopheles. The demon is pictured as a capricious imp, "virtuously lying and sinfully praying." Mephistopheles, too, is an utter relativist; he consigns an abandoned child to a good life so as to further diversity in the world ("On a World"). Sluchevsky himself shows many qualities of the imp; he is often bored by the mundane, as in a cycle called "The Diary of a One-Sided Man."

Travel impressions and cosmopolitanism became a hallmark of the aesthetic poets. Among Sluchevsky's landscapes is a cycle devoted to the south of Russia— hot and abundant—and another to the extreme north—Murmansk. Here he pictures the barren Arctic:

> At those brief times when the horizon here is clear,
> And sunshine strikes upon the sandbanks and the shallows,
> Then neither Adriatic wave nor Hellespont
> Can gleam like that, with emerald turning ever darker.
>
> Nor can they yet possess that blue line's density
> That marks where heaven is divided from the ocean . . .

For here eternity, where beauty is severe,
Sank down to rest at peace, and breathes in open spaces.

In other poems he describes the Volga region and the Crimea. His European poems include impressions of Wiesbaden, Strasbourg, and Normandy. Allusions to the West and its works of art appear throughout his poems. His last book, *Songs from a Corner* (1902), shows the hedonist in a new pose: now he has grown old and is eager to shield his corner, a beautiful garden, from the outside world and its anxieties. He will savor his lively mental capacities, his imagination, and his memories.

Sluchevsky was a prolific poet, and perhaps somewhat facile and careless in style. His work is most damaged, however, by an absence of self; he is all mask. Yet his ability to return the playful imagination to art was salutary in his own time. Like art-for-art's-sake poets before him, he made effective use of insignificant details, such as tiny field flowers. Sluchevsky's style was occasionally marred by disturbingly prosaic notes, usually of a scientific nature.

Konstantin Fofanov (1862–1911) eagerly adopted the manner, the images, and the philosophies of European decadence, or symbolism. He resembles the West's extreme romantics and eccentrics, like Novalis, Gérard de Nerval, and Oscar Wilde. He was a pantheist, but he also cultivated the art of the elusive and the love of the corrupt. His innovative subjects in no way precluded some social criticism. Fofanov was born in St. Petersburg, the son of petty merchants of peasant origin. His first collection appeared in 1887, and his best, *Shades and Secrets,* in 1892. He was subject to periods of mental illness. In the 1900s he was published in the magazines of the symbolist movement, although he was not a member of its inner circles.

Fofanov's early poems are philosophical and religious; among them is a statement of pantheism: "In me the world abides, and I'm within its soul" (1880). He also wrote adaptations from the Bible. His later subjects were moods, however, which he placed in natural settings, as in this example from 1883:

A sad and a roseate sunset
Is gazing through shaggy fir branches.
My soul is engulfed in its sorrow—
Love's sounds in it no longer echo.

It's still in my soul, like a graveside,
My heart suffers pain in this silence—
It thirsts, and so deeply, like torment,
So deeply, for sobs and for singing.

His pantheism is not joyous, but sad: "It's all the same to me—be it my vision, / Or I its dream—its pain is close to me," he wrote in "Melancholia" (1889). The yearnings of the spirit are juxtaposed with what is tainted and decaying: he brings together faded flowers, graves, tales, and miracles in "The oak grove that is half denuded" (1881). A forget-me-not that is growing in a swamp ("Within the sphere of mist and evil," 1881) is a symbol of the ideal. Like other decadents, Fofanov discovered dualities, both in the world and in himself. In "Two Worlds" (1886) a vision of moonlight and fairies is contrasted with the hardships of reality. In "Sky and Sea" (1886) the starry heavens are addressed as "You," while he is the dark ocean. In "The Double" (1887) his melancholia is his alter ego. Fofanov borrowed Western imagery, as in the grottoes, statues, silvery darkness, tulips, jasmine, and lilies that he describes in "The waves and the grasses were sleeping" (1885). He was also open to the influence of Russian folk tales and wrote, for example, about house sprites. His style is characterized by lilting rhythms, alliterations, and vowel harmonies. He had a pervasive influence on the symbolists who appeared in the 1890s.

V

SYMBOLISM

11

The *Fin de siècle* (1890–1905)

From the 1890s onward the Russian monarchy, first under Alexander III and then under Nicholas II (1894–1905), was to pursue those reactionary policies that had met with resistance in the past. The nation was facing the end of a stable era both in its political and in its cultural life. Changes in its social structure were rapid. The declining gentry was challenged by a new middle class. The peasant population was partially transformed into an urban labor force, but still plagued by a daunting poverty. Strikes and organized protests were increasingly common throughout the 1890s and into the new century. New realist writers who looked more closely at social issues appeared beside Chekhov, who remained, however, the most distinguished author. The writers of the *fin de siècle* camp sensed that time was on their side; a change was crossing Europe that would alter Russian tastes as well. The turn of the century, in fact, brought a remarkable renaissance in Russian literature and the arts. In public moods, the anticipation of "aesthetic" changes was linked with the expectation of political amelioration. When Russia was defeated in the Russo-Japanese War, the event precipitated the abortive Revolution of 1905.

The Rise of Symbolism

Realism or naturalism always held the widest audience in the Europe of the 1890s, while the *fin de siècle* currents altered sensibilities from an apparent position of disadvantage. Maupassant, a bleak realist, was perhaps the most respected author in France, as was Hardy in England. Meanwhile, French symbolism brought a recollection that ultimate truths, or values, are irrational in nature, perhaps religious. The school had flourished in the 1880s in the hands of Verlaine and Mallarmé. The spirit of *épater le bourgeois,* a return of romantic dandyism, was perhaps more visible in England. Oscar Wilde and his associates at *The Yellow Book* (1894–1897) assailed the moral and aesthetic conventions of the Victorian era. Symbolism appeared in Russia in the mid-1890s; it was relatively mild and philosophical in form, and at the time was always called "decadence." The first symbolist book of verse to win any public approval was *Under Northern Skies* (1894), in which Konstantin Balmont wrote about the sadness of earthly limits. The Russian symbolists were also flanked by new currents in the arts and in thought. In the years after 1900, the school assumed an exultant, "dawn" mentality. Their optimism was to last only until the collapse of the Revolution of 1905 brought an era of renewed pessimism and frustration.

The Russian "decadents" of the 1890s would have been unthinkable without the example of the French symbolists, but the Russian school was to have its own character. The French had made a break with romanticism that the Russians could not imitate. For the French symbolists the authority of religions had ended. They no longer pondered the mysteries of heaven, but sought them in the material world; the artist was no longer a seer, but an everyman. Baudelaire had seen in earthly phenomena "des forêts de symbols," and he had addressed his reader as "mon semblable—mon Frère." The Russian symbolist school was a belated romanticism; it was to be religious. The Russians wrote about the salvation of the soul and complained about the existence of evil in the world. The melancholia that Balmont typified was a frustrated idealism. Other decadents, who included Fedor Sologub and Zinaida Hippius, derived their pessimism in part from Schopenhauer or from Dostoevsky. The spirit of *épater le bourgeois* appeared, however, in the imitative poems of the future *maître d'ecole,* Valery Briusov. While still a university student, he published miscellanies called *Russian Symbolists* (1894 and 1895).

In the first years of the new century, the modernist current became respectable and began to be called symbolism. Changes were anticipated in the political sphere, and they were accepted also in the arts and in philosophical premises. It was an art magazine, Sergey Diaghilev's *World of Art* (1898–1904), that led the way, as *Die Blätter für die Kunst* once had in Germany. Balmont exemplified the change in mood when he called a collection of his verse *Let Us Be Like the Sun* (1903). Newly arisen poets joined the symbolist movement and brought with them a wave of mystical expectations. They were Viacheslav Ivanov in *Pilot Stars* (1903), Andrey Bely in *Gold in Azure* (1904), and Aleksandr Blok in *Verses About the Beautiful Lady* (1905). Some minor idealist critics began to assert that the decadents of the 1890s were not symbolists at all. In stylistic matters, the Russians were also influenced by the French, but not entirely swayed. They adopted the widespread use of metaphors that seemed to spring from Baudelaire's poem "Correspondances." But the Russians were not as committed to suggestiveness and nuances as either Verlaine or Mallarmé. The French example brought, however, a vast improvement in aesthetic standards. The Revolution of 1905 was followed by a reversal in Russian moods, but the effectiveness of Russian poetry continued to rise after that political event.

Poets of the "Aesthetic Revival"

The 1890s brought a number of new poets who were diverse, but who were perceived all together as a revival of "aestheticism," as opposed to utilitarianism. Symbolist circles were to emerge from their midst. An incalculable influence on the course of Russian symbolism was to be exerted by an Orthodox philosopher, Vladimir Solovev (1853–1900), who wrote a small body of metaphysical poems. A member of an older generation, he was never to appreciate the decadents of his time, but he bequeathed to symbolism a reverence for a concept similar to the Eternal Feminine. He believed himself to be the recipient of visions of Saint Sophia, or the Divine Wisdom, an icon of the Orthodox Church. Solovev was the son of a famous Russian historian, Sergey Solovev, who was a rector of Moscow University. He was educated at Moscow University and at the Moscow Theological Academy. He thought Saint Sophia appeared to him in 1875, when he was studying at the British Museum, and again in the Egyptian desert. He completed his doctoral dissertation at Moscow University in 1880. In a public lecture of 1881, he urged Alexander III to forgive the assassins of his father, Alexander II. Solovev's philosophy, published in books and essays, was well known and influential. Three collections of verse appeared between 1891 and 1900.

Solovev believed mankind to be progressing toward a state of "godmanhood," or consonance with the divinity, and that a Christian theocracy would ensue. Godmanhood was to be attained through mystical communion with Saint Sophia, or the feminine aspect of the divinity. The concept of the Divine Sophia had been preserved by the Byzantine Church from antiquity. The church of Hagia Sophia in Constantinople was dedicated to her, as were many Russian churches. The idea of Saint Sophia originated in a Gnostic cosmogony, of which the Russian symbolists were aware. According to this view, God had divided his being into an absolute aspect and an aspect in the state of becoming, or chaos. The second aspect, the Divine Sophia, was the spirit of the material world and of creation. Solovev, moreover, found a parallel to Saint Sophia in the Catholic Madonna.

Solovev's poetry is in no way doctrinaire. He wrote about the hopes and disillusionments attendant on the experience of becoming. In the poems of the 1870s he at times pictured Saint Sophia, or the Eternal Feminine, as a fairy-tale queen. In Cairo he wrote a poem that opens, "In a palace so high does my empress reside, / And it has seven pillars of gold" (1876). Saint Sophia is personified as a charming and infallible lover; here she speaks of his doubts and her constancy:

> And your oath you betrayed, but then could your deceit
> Ever alter my heart in affection to you?

It was this eroticized image of Saint Sophia that was to prove so attractive to several of the symbolists who followed Solovev. In his poems of the 1880s and 1890s, nature was portrayed by Solovev as the substance, not only the emblem, of the divine. His soul responds to the landscape, for example, in the poem "In the Alps" (1886). In "How can you not see, my friend" (1892) he explained his view of

earthly phenomena. Several of his poems are addressed, in affection, to the spirit of
Lake Saima in Finland; the spirit is presumably an element of Saint Sophia. "On
Saima in Winter" was written in 1894:

> Now you are wrapped in a fur that is downy,
> Silently steeped in your innocent dream.
> Death has no place here; the air is all brilliant,
> This is a silence translucent, and white.
>
> Peace, unassailable, deep, now surrounds you.
> No—not in vain did I seek you out now!
> Ever unchanged in the inner eye's image,
> Fairy—an empress of cliffs and of pines!
>
> You are as pure as the snow on far mountains,
> Deep are your thoughts, like the winter at night,
> You are as bright as the flames that are polar,
> Born of dark chaos, a daughter all light!

Solovev describes in the poem "Three Meetings" (1898) how he saw Saint Sophia,
once as a child, later in London, and again in the desert. The poem is strangely
level-headed and at times farcical—for example, when he is rescued in the desert by
incredulous Arabs. Solovev's blend of humor and mysticism was later to be seen in
the poetry of Andrey Bely. Solovev's verse was refreshing in its time for its metaphysical optimism; his somewhat naive faith is still appealing. Against a background of pessimism and decadence he saw the cosmos as benign, and he described
history and civilization as proofs of mankind's better capacities. Solovev's verse
was technically conventional, but his novel ideas resulted in phrases that appear to
be startling figures of speech.

Among the idealists was an essayist, Nikolay Minsky (real name Vilenkin;
1855–1937), in whom his contemporaries perceived a Nietzschean crosscurrent.
Having begun in the 1870s as a civic poet, he changed camps in the 1880s. His
essay *By the Light of Conscience* (1890) was influential because it argued against
utilitarianism and spoke openly of a "natural" imperative to love oneself first. He
attempted, unconvincingly, to reconcile his moral system with scientific categories
through a discussion of so-called *meons* (a term that meant "nonbeing" in Greek
and that he borrowed from Plato). Minsky was an editor of a newspaper, *The
Northern Herald,* which was the first to support the "new idealism" and the new
"decadents." Minsky's poetry appeared in four collections published between 1883
and 1907. His own spiritual quest, with its loneliness and despair, was his constant
theme. In "My Demon" (1885) the imp urges him to believe that his religious faith
is real. In "A young bacchante she appeared, when first she came" (1887) the siren
is his search for truth. Minsky's verse was conventional, and he was soon surpassed
by more innovative poets. In 1905 Minsky was associated with a Marxist periodical, *The New Life,* and was forced into permanent exile.

The first intellectual leader of the symbolists in St. Petersburg was Dmitry
Merezhkovsky (1865–1941). He was also the first of several writers to advocate a
union of Hellenism and Christianity. He was a novelist, essayist, and poet who was

indebted both to Solovev and to Nietzsche. Merezhkovsky's widest fame has rested on a trilogy of philosophical historical novels under the general title of *Christ and Antichrist* (1896–1905). He was educated at the University of St. Petersburg. In 1889 he married the writer Zinaida Hippius, who was to share in the advocacy of their common ideas and the maintenance of the couple's influential salon in St. Petersburg. Merezhkovsky was the author of the essay that is now considered the manifesto of the new school, *On the Causes for the Decline and on New Currents in Contemporary Russian Literature* (1893). In 1901 he and Hippius founded the Religious-Philosophical Society, whose aim was a renewal of Russian Orthodoxy through the infusion of Neoplatonism. The failure of the 1905 Revolution caused them to leave Russia, and they resided in France from 1906 to 1912. After the October Revolution, they were again to emigrate, and from 1921 onward they lived in Paris.

In his fiction and in his essays, Merezhkovsky predicted the arrival of a millennium in which the flesh and spirit would be reconciled in a "new religious consciousness." His trilogy of novels depicts eras in the relationship between Hellenism (the truth of the flesh) and Christianity (the truth of the spirit); the novels are entitled *Julian the Apostate (The Death of the Gods)*, *Leonardo da Vinci (The Gods Reborn)*, and *Peter and Alexis*. His chief literary essay was *Tolstoy and Dostoevsky* (1902), in which Tolstoy is the pagan seer and Dostoevsky the Christian devotee. Merezhkovsky's poems, however, have neither grand themes nor large contrasts. He writes as the melancholy and cultivated everyman whose concern is the pursuit of, not happiness, but equilibrium. His subjects are nature, the year's seasons, love and despair, the myths of antiquity, and heroes of literature, such as Faust or Job. An indicative poem is "The Parcae" (1892), a statement of existential indifference: prayer is useless, beauty silent, and truth inseparable from the lie; the threads woven by the Parcae are ever those of love and slavery. Merezhkovsky's poems are erudite and competent, but they belong, like Minsky's, to a transitional period.

Mirra Lokhvitskaya (1869–1905) made her mark as a poet of erotic love and particularly as a champion of female sensuality. Her poems share, however, in the tone of religiosity common to the new poetry of the 1890s; her protestations of love sound like litanies. She was born the daughter of a lawyer in St. Petersburg and educated in Moscow. Her *oeuvre* is extensive; it appeared in five volumes published between 1896 and 1904. Her eroticism is ornately couched in figures of speech and effusive avowals. She brought into Russian verse the decadent notes of sadomasochistic desire and the imagery of lotuses and grottoes. She also devoted some poems to religious subjects, especially to her striving for spiritual perfection; in these lyrics her imagery is that of heights, sky, mountains, and wings. She shared her love of erudition with other poets of the 1890s; a number of poems are set in exotic times and places, particularly ancient Greece. In "Lilith" she portrayed the first wife of Adam as the queen of earth, a sphere of passion and suffering. Lokhvitskaya's poems are essentially fantasies. Her preoccupation with sexual love was inherently combative, however, and in this respect she was an example to others who wished to challenge nineteenth century conventions.

The most eccentric of the new poets, both in his life and in his poetry, was Aleksandr Dobroliubov (1876–1944?), whose verse was perhaps ahead of its time.

His impulses were religious, but his outlook was primitive and his verse ornate. He was born in Warsaw and lived in St. Petersburg. He knew French symbolist poetry well and made contacts among the Russian symbolists in the mid-1890s. Then he became a religious wanderer and eventually founded his own small sect. He published a collection of poems called *Natura naturans. Natura naturata* in 1895, and another appeared in 1900. He is presumed to have died near Baku in 1944. His poems are written in both verse and prose. Some are devotional; many are about nature. He was preoccupied with love and death. His meditations have an enigmatic, dreamlike logic, and are often intimate in tone:

> Grasses do whisper from under my dreams,
> Headiness issues from each of my moments.
> Every sweet-smelling, all lives of aspiring
> —Are but dew's odor, the streams in the woods.

His style is at times folkloric, at times Biblical, and at times Nietzschean. Dobroliubov's poetry is ornately fitted out with dedications and literary allusions, sometimes to French symbolists. A number of his pieces have musical notations, such as "pianissimo" or "andante." His *oeuvre* is small, but it offers a fresh, sometimes childlike, view of the eternal circumstances of existence. His separate poems are arresting, but never deeply moving. He had little influence on the symbolist generation, but he anticipated the mentality of some futurists, for example Velemir Khlebnikov and Elena Guro.

Balmont

Konstantin Balmont (1867–1942) was a poet of metaphysical moods, but not a thinker. In the 1890s he was the leading decadent, and gave expression to the melancholia typical of religious malaise. In the early 1900s he was noted as an author beyond symbolist circles. His most successful collection, *Let Us Be Like the Sun* (1903), is filled with a pantheistic élan and with feelings of universal ties and cosmic power. Many of his lyrics are expressions of his intimacy with the natural world. He admired English and American poetry and was influenced by Poe, Shelley, Swinburne, and Whitman. His elation had, however, an amoral aspect that he derived from Nietzsche. He was the first modernist to describe Mexico and other tropical countries at first hand. His style was a novelty in its great musicality. He was a translator of English and Continental poets and the author of essays, travel sketches, plays, short stories, and a novel, all of which are scarcely known today.

Balmont posed as a spontaneous poet, but he effected a new Westernization of Russian poetry. He was born in a provincial town and entered Moscow University in 1886. His education was interrupted by a lengthy depression, a broken marriage, and a suicide attempt. He became both a translator and an original poet; literary success came with *Under Northern Skies* in 1894. In 1897 he lectured on Russian literature in England. In *Buildings on Fire* (1900) and *Let Us Be Like the Sun* he astonished his readership with his ecstasies and moral "liberation." He participated in street demonstrations during the Revolution of 1905 and afterward departed for Mexico; from 1906 to 1913 he resided in France. He prided himself on being a dandy and cosmopolitan, but he was reputed to be a poet in decline. Between 1913 and 1920 he traveled in Mexico, South Africa, and the Pacific Islands. From 1920 onward he again lived in France. He became alcoholic and was committed for insanity to a sanitarium in 1930, where he died in poverty. Over two dozen books of poetry had appeared during his lifetime.

Balmont's poetry is dedicated, throughout his several periods, to a search for cosmic oneness. In his early verse, he laments that he is, like the remainder of mankind, and all of nature, excluded from some state of beatitude. His books include, besides *Under Northern Skies, Without Bounds* (1895) and *Silence* (1898). An illustrative poem is "Sea Plants" (1894), in which the submerged vegetation knows intuitively about a world above the water, but cannot reach it:

> No light have we, no sound, nor any greeting,
> And from on high the ocean's swell sends down
> But corpses and the wrecks of broken ships.

In several poems he calls, in hopelessness, on death. His nostalgia is most intense in *Silence,* where the world's ships, its flowers, and its artists all languish in their common yearning for spiritual attainment. The same book includes a romantic rebellion in demonism: loving becomes destroying, and the material world is nightmarish. Don Juan, who was in medieval times the arch-blasphemer, the bane of innocence and holiness, is his emblem. The attainment of the spirit to which Balmont aspires in the early books is both an epiphany and a sensation—an ecstasy. In *Without Bounds* it is, for example, the Promised Land of which the ocean speaks, the truth revealed to the dying swan, the joy of dawn in the mountains. The entire early period is drawn to a close by the concluding section of *Silence,* called "The Star of the Desert," where the poet adores the Christian Lord, and in the final poems achieves heaven.

After 1900 the existential separation and striving are ended. With *Buildings on Fire* and *Let Us Be Like the Sun* the universe has become an endless process that is both good and evil. Sins are not just permitted, they are paraded. *Buildings on Fire* opens in an awareness of the loss of innocence; in a section called "Conscience" the poet writes that he has deserted to corruption, shame, and eroticism. The success of these lyrics is a measure of the public's infatuation with the notion of new freedoms. In Balmont the attitude derives from the Nietzschean injunction to perceive life as an aesthetic, rather than a moral, experience. His moods can also be sad; *Let Us Be Like the Sun* opens with a sense of cosmic elation which can, after all, fade:

> I came into this world to see the sunshine,
> > The circling arc of blue.
> I came into this world to see the sunshine,
> > And mountain heights.
>
> I came into this world to see the ocean,
> > And lusty hue of vales.

I've locked all worlds into a single vista,
    I am the king.

I overcame the coldness of oblivion,
    I made a dream instead,
My every moment brims with my elation,
    I ever sing.

It was my sorrows brought my dreams to beings,
    But I am loved for that.
Who is my equal in the gift of singing?
    No one, no one.

I came into this world to see the sunshine,
    But if the day is done,
I'll sing . . . I'll ever sing about the sunshine
    Before my death!

In other poems, the sun symbolizes both youth and eternity, the moon recalls love and dreams, and the ocean a world of nonbeing. The world also has evils, which are physical passion and death; they appear in sections called "The Enchanted Grotto" and "Danses Macabres." The arts are viewed throughout in terms of Balmont's philosophical premises. In *Buildings on Fire* he had praised artists for their visionary utopias. His pantheism lent him strength; in a poem that opens, "I am the elegance hid in our slow, Russian language" (1901), he wrote: "Ever young, like a dream, / I am strong for I love / Both myself and all else / I—am elegant verse." But he concludes *Let Us Be Like the Sun* with an acceptance of ambiguity: art is passive in its reflection of the world, and must include both beauty and pain, both good and evil.

Balmont's more worldly concerns, such as political partisanship and love of country, brought new subjects into his later books. His first departure was in *Fairy Tales* (1905), a collection written for his daughter. His response to the Revolution of 1905 was a small cycle of antimonarchical poems published in *Songs of an Avenger* (1907); his political invective is blunt and old-fashioned. During his exile in France, he turned at times to Slavic folklore and mythology for inspiration. The poems in *Evil Spells* (1906) are based on sinister incantations—curses. *The Firebird* (1907) is more balanced in mood and historical in its perspectives. It contains praise for early Slavic cultures, such as Kievan Rus under the Varangians. The most innovative book is *The Green Garden* (1909), whose poems are based on the songs of flagellant sectarians. The poems have an authentic religious intensity and air of mystery. Earthly life is passionately evoked in them, but firmly rejected for the life of heaven. Other new books by Balmont brought complaints of a tasteless boasting and an offensive eroticism. Balmont himself believed that he had reached a new era of restraint and vigor in *The Ash Tree* (1916) and *Sonnets of the Sun, Honey and the Moon* (1917), where his moods are, indeed, more somber and plausible. Before his final emigration, he published his radical verse in two books, *The Ring* and *The Song of the Worker's Hammer* (both 1920). The many books he published in France began with *The Mirage* (1922).

Balmont drew novel and imaginative conclusions from his philosophical premises. But his amorality has the ring of mischievous *épatage* and is hardly to be taken seriously. He favored the impression of irrepressible song over that of thought. His poetry introduced into Russian a mellifluousness that might have been learned from Poe and Shelley. His effect is gained largely from alliterations and vowel harmonies, which he sometimes used to excess. His verse is flawed by an apparently genuine, and unrecognized, need for self-indulgence. A number of his poems are effective, but on balance the *oeuvre* detracts from them.

Briusov

The nominal *maître* of the symbolist movement was Valery Briusov (1873–1924), but his title was earned through his organizational flair. In 1894 and 1895 he published the miscellanies, *Russian Symbolists,* which may have given their name to the school. He was a lesser, but by no means negligible, poet. His most memorable poems appeared in *Tertia vigilia* (1900) and *Urbi et orbi* (1903). His most compelling theme was the intractability of evil in human nature. He admired heroic virtues, however, and often wrote about the figures of Greek myths and of history. His predecessors in these poems were the French Parnassians. He was relatively indifferent to aesthetic doctrine. It was in part his even-handed direction at the Scorpion Publishing House that ensured the permanence of many of the best works of Russian symbolism. His literary magazine, *The Scales,* was at the heart of the movement. Briusov also wrote short stories, dramas, and historical novels.

Briusov dedicated his energies as a creative writer and as an editor to the return of Russian literature to the spheres of European intellectual life. He was born in Moscow into a merchant family. The *Russian Symbolist* miscellanies, which he issued with the aid of fellow students at Moscow University, were the butt of parodies in the press. But by 1900 he had found patronage among wealthy merchants for the Scorpion publishing enterprise, which operated until 1916. Briusov's verse in *Tertia vigilia* and *Urbi et orbi* earned him the respect of serious readers. As editor of *The Scales* (1904–1909) he popularized *fin de siècle* Western writers, printed art news, and, from 1906, published the poetry, fiction, and essays of the Russians. In 1910 he became the literary critic at a prestigious newspaper, *Russian Thought.* His most ambitious works were his novels, *The Angel of Fire* (1908) and *The Altar of Victory* (1913). Briusov embraced the October Revolution, joined the Communist Party in 1920, and held positions in the Ministry of Education until his death. His detractors have alleged that his only intellectual loyalty was to the latest cultural trend or to the future.

Briusov's poetry invites a reading in the awareness of the history of literature. Its deepest motivation seems to be the intention to build an edifice, an *oeuvre.* His first books, *Chefs d'oeuvre* (1896) and *Me eum esse* (1987), are manifestly derivative of Baudelaire and Verlaine. He borrowed from them a splenetic withdrawal from reality, and dreams, poisons. He opens *Chefs d'oeuvre* with erotic poems that are intended to be novel and shocking; they owe something to Lokhvitskaya as well as to his French predecessors. Next he turns to the primitive cultures of Africa and

Easter Island, where customs might seem savage or morals lax. He flaunts his own loss of religious ideals in a section called "The Hill of Abandoned Sanctities." In *Me eum esse* he draws sharp contrasts between the good and evil capacities in man. Erotic passion is juxtaposed with purity and innocence, especially in a section called "Moments." Heavenly visions are set beside the dreams that defile in the section "On the Road." *Me eum esse* is both provocative and sad; it has in it a current of unhappiness that seems not to be relieved by its transient eroticism and philosophical regrets.

In the collections of his mature period, Briusov found a congenial interest, which was in civilizations as such. He strove less obviously for the sensational and became the dispassionate observer of all things. The books at the peak of his career include, besides *Tertia vigilia* and *Urbi et orbi, Stephanos* (1906) and *All My Songs* (1909). *Tertia vigilia* opens with "I," a confession of an indiscriminate fascination with doctrines and credos, with "all lyceums and academies": "To me all dreams are sweet, to me all speeches precious, / And to all gods I dedicate my verse." In the same book he introduces those portraits of striking figures from myth and history who are reminiscent of the Parnassian tradition. Among the first are King Esarhaddon of Assyria, Psyche, Moses, Cleopatra, the Scythians, Mary Stuart, Napoleon. Briusov surrounds them all with an aura of power, arrogance, and passion. The Parnassians were humanists, but pessimistic, and they were antipathetical to the symbolists. Perhaps the figure with whom Briusov most wished to identify himself was Orpheus, the singer and warrior. Here is the opening of "Orpheus and the Argonauts" (1904):

> Gods! you were willing. And built is the Argo,
> Given its rope to the whims of the waves.
> Will you then stand with the daring, as warrior,
> Orpheus, charmer of cliffs?

In the early books, Briusov had expressed a nostalgia for an other-worldly ideal, but now he began to praise the accomplishments of outstanding people. In a cycle called "To My Kin," he dedicates poems to Leibnitz and Lermontov, among others. He hints, in *Urbi et orbi,* that mankind's upward struggle has been through an undeserved component of evil. The work of artists becomes self-sacrificial. His own art has been made in pain. His inspiration is pictured in the poem "In Answer" (1902) as a weary ox plowing the fields: "At night, when darkness comes to us / And closes in the circling vista, / Not I, but he, the ox—my dream—releases me himself from labor." The book *All My Songs* begins with "To the Poet" (1907), where Briusov urges the disciplined observation of one's own passions: "And know: vatic wreaths worn by poets / Are made in all ages of thorns."

The modernist urban theme, the depiction of popular culture as coarse and venal, was introduced into Russian poetry by Briusov. In *Urbi et orbi* he shows the life of the street, with its amusements, corruptions, and rasping songs. The rising tide of a wrathful, destructive revolution is reflected in *Stephanos,* in the cycle called "Contemporaneity." In the poem "Huns of the Future" (1905) Briusov salutes the passage of power that makes history (the poem is written in modern, impaired rhythms introduced by the symbolists):

> Their Eden raze, Attila.
> —Viacheslav Ivanov

Where are you, Huns of the future,
That hang o'er the world like a cloudburst?
I hear the tramp of your iron
On Pamiras as yet undiscovered.

Crash down on us like a drunken
Host from your far, dark encampments—
Give new life to our flaccid old body
In waves of blood that is flaming.

Pitch tents, O you slaves of your freedom,
At our castles, as once in past ages.
Turn the land into merry new cornfields
Where once stood throne halls and chambers.

Set books in bonfires to burning,
And dance in the light that is festive,
Befoul the grace of our temples,
For you're pure in all deeds, as are children!

And we, who are sages and poets,
The keepers of credos and secrets,
Will depart with lanterns we've lighted
Into catacombs, deserts, and caverns.

To what—in onslaughts of maelstroms,
In storms that bring all to destruction—
Will the playing fates grant survival,
To which of our hallowed creations?

Our lore may all perish, be traceless—
All we alone knew on the planet,
But you, who will come and destroy me—
I meet with a hymn and I welcome.

"The Pale Horse" (1903), a narrative depiction of the Apocalypse, forms the conclusion of *Stephanos*. In *All My Songs* Briusov added nothing to what he had already accomplished, but his talent was still firm.

Briusov's most memorable fiction pieces are studies of cultural dissolution or of individual aberrations. A novella called *The Republic of the Southern Cross* (1905) depicts the degeneration of a capitalist utopia, established at the South Pole, in bestial license. In other stories, unnamed cultures go down in sectarian orgies and conflagrations. In "The Mirror" a psychotic woman is obsessed with her own reflection. The historical novels also raise philosophical issues. The *Angel of Fire* (1908), which is set in sixteenth-century Germany, questions whether witchcraft can intervene in the course of events. *The Altar of Victory* (1913) is set in fourth-century Rome and concerns the dilemma of a young man, whether to choose the old world or the new. The fiction lacks the constructive concern for civilization that can be seen in the poetry.

After the Revolution, Briusov published verse that is not different in substance from his earlier poems, but it is less distinguished. Five small collections of poetry appeared between 1920 and 1924. Several poems are devoted to recent history and current events—to the Revolution, the famine years, the death of Lenin. Others are tributes to scientific modernity, to the automobile and the electron. The vast majority of his new poems are devoted, as before, to his self-assessments and to cultural meditations, and many are re-creations of myths. His best poems concern love and passion, his earliest subject.

Briusov's *oeuvre* is humanistic in its underlying concern—the building, rather than the destruction, of civilization. His style, too, is oddly matter-of-fact in a symbolist; his figures of speech are not mysterious, and his syntax is clear. His talent was in forcefulness; his best effects are used for the dramatic rendering of strong emotions. Briusov had, moreover, an interest in the purely technical aspects of versification; he wrote a number of poems for the sake of exotic genres or of experiments in sound. When, around 1910, a "crisis of symbolism" arose—a debate as to whether the movement should aspire to be a religion or remain a literary school—Briusov was seen as the chief exponent of the simpler path.

Sologub

Fedor Sologub (1863–1927) was the archdecadent of the Russian symbolist movement. A current of philosophical anger traverses his work and was most visible at the peak of his career. Like other symbolists, he thought of himself as a poet, but a satirical novel, *The Petty Demon* (1907), is now believed to be his masterpiece. His poetry has been described as Manichean because he created sharp contrasts between good and evil. He entertained a variety of metaphysical systems, however, as though they were transient daydreams. He wrote short stories, dramas, and several other novels. His fiction is often deceptively realistic in method; all his work is, at bottom, philosophical. His lyric dramas were among the first to be written in Russia. Some of his novels are disappointing, but his poetry seldom is, and his best poems have been described as "exquisite" in craftsmanship.

It was Sologub's dedication to aesthetic beauty, beyond the historic cause of symbolism, that made him a true decadent. He was born Fedor Teternikov in St. Petersburg and reared as the son of the maid in a merchant family that encouraged and patronized the arts. His peasant mother was sadistic and regularly beat her son and his younger sister Olga; Sologub kept this fact a secret until a deathbed confession. He was educated at the Teachers' Seminary and taught elementary school in the northwestern provinces. In 1892 he returned to St. Petersburg, where he continued as a teacher and school inspector until 1907. His literary reputation began in the mid-1890s with decadent short stories about children. In 1907 *The Petty Demon,* a Gogolian depiction of the provinces, brought him fame. In 1921 he and his wife of thirteen years attempted to emigrate, but without success, and she committed suicide. Sologub was unable to publish original works after 1923 and lived by translating. He was permanent president of the Leningrad Writers' Union when he died.

Sologub's romantic resentment of heaven was to be coupled with a fertile visual imagination. His earliest two collections, published in 1896, show little sign of his future wealth. They derive from the pastoral legacy of nineteenth-century Russian poetry. He wrote about nature and about his melancholy moods. His love for nature was genuine, however, and landscapes were to remain his best and most common subject. His sadness was to turn, at times, into spleen. In his next two collections, in 1904, Sologub emerged as a considerable fantasist. In this pastoral poem of 1897, he imagines a water nymph (*rusalka*), while the "you" whom he addresses is not identified:

> No sleep came—for a ringing
>> Past the stream,
> For a trembling, and sobbing
>> Over me.
>
> A *rusalka*, it was singing,
>> And not you.
> My past life I then pitied,
>> And my dream.
>
> Soon the dawn will come breaking—
>> How to sleep!
> I recalled my so lengthy,
>> Painful path.
>
> A *rusalka*, it was laughing
>> Past the stream—
> No, not you was it jeering
>> Over me.

In the second volume of 1896, Sologub showed a close knowledge of Verlaine and Baudelaire, especially in his escapist daydreams and in the confession of some unnamed sin. His guilt remains unconvincing, but he was to be known as "the Russian Baudelaire."

In the two volumes of 1904, Sologub invented cosmologies that vary from poem to poem. In one version of the universe, it is a unity in multiplicity. The Christian God is rarely its creator. Ordinarily this universe is an unending process without spiritual aims, a view derived from Schopenhauer's pessimism. At times the empty process is caused and ruled by an evil spirit, a Gnostic view. "In the last light of evil day" (1903) concludes with the ironic words of the cruel tyrant, "I am the only path. Love me." The sun, which gives life to the meaningless world, became for Sologub the symbol of this universal evil. "You love not, and all do slay," he wrote in "Snake who reigns above the universe" (1902). All these versions have a solipsist variant in which the poet has created the universe: "A god am I in hidden worlds, / The world itself is but my dreams," he wrote in 1896. Then it was the poet who caused multiplicity, or separated good from evil, or even desired evil.

In the Manichean view there is an ideal, whose attributes are love, harmony, and beauty, but it exists outside the physical world and is inimical to it. The ideal was associated with stars, as in the romantic era. A cycle of poems written in 1898 is devoted to an arcadian planet, Oile, which has its own star, Mair; its women dance and sing: "The twang of lyres, the fragrant scent of blossoms, / The twang of lyres, / And women's songs make one sole aspiration, / To praise Mair." He wrote of the Eternal Feminine in a poem that opens, "My love is just as pure / As bright stars in their shining" (1898). But the physical world became a place of unalleviated pain and ugliness. His rare expressions of demonism were motivated by despair; in "When I on stormy sea was sailing" (1902) he is caught in a shipwreck and dedicates his life to Satan.

Sologub's poetry reached a nadir of depression and anxiety in the post-1905 era. In *The Serpent* (1907) the reptile is a metaphor for the tyrannical sun, which must die in the sunset. The book has no political allusions, but it seems to suggest a political meaning. Sologub's philosophical anger is best reflected in *The Flaming Circle* (1908). The book opens with poems in which Sologub speaks as though in his former lives. He was the Biblical Adam, a pastoral shepherd, a medieval executioner, and other figures. The ugliness of earthly life is depicted in a cycle called "Earthly Imprisonment." In this poem of 1905 the world is a neglected zoo:

> We are beasts in our cages,
> All our barks are instinctive,
> Ageless locks shut our portals,
> We lack nerve to undo them.
>
> If our hearts are still true to our customs,
> We take solace in barking and howling.
> If our cages smell bad and are filthy—
> We don't know that, because we forgot it.
>
> And the heart, it gets used to repeating—
> We cuckoo in our monotone, dully.
> All is grey in our zoo, all is faceless;
> We long since ceased to long for our freedom.
>
> We are beasts in our cages,
> All our barks are instinctive,
> Ageless locks shut our portals.
> We lack nerve to undo them.

Other cycles are devoted to dreams and magic and to Sologub's philosophical systems. The closing section is called "The Final Consolation," and it is devoted to poems about death.

Sologub's early fiction reflects the same pessimism as the poems. His stories are almost all about children, although they seldom appear in his lyrics. They are often victims of life's cruelties and mistakes, and many are depicted as vessels of purity. Sologub's prose styles vary; his predecessors include Gogol, Dostoevsky, and Chekhov. His first novel, *Bad Dreams* (1896), describes the moral dilemmas of a schoolteacher fascinated by decadence; in substance it is a polemic against Dostoevsky's *Crime and Punishment.* The protagonist of *The Petty Demon* is a school-teacher diseased by a homicidal paranoia. The notion of demons in life stems both from Gogol and from Dostoevsky. Sologub's hero represents the world of reality in a Manichean vision of it, but his name, Peredonov, symbolized provincial stagnation in the literary criticism of the realists.

A general alleviation in mood altered Sologub's work in the years before World War I. The lyric dramas had presaged a change to optimism; technically they are reminiscent of Maeterlinck's fantasies. In 1913 and 1914 Sologub brought out a *Collected Works,* for which he rearranged his published poems, adding new lyrics, to give each volume of poetry a reconciliation with reality at its end. Sologub's most ambitious statement of his new view was a trilogy of novels called *The Legend in Creation* (1914); Russia of 1905 is contrasted with a fictitious Mediterranean nation called the United Isles. The novels suffer, however, from the transparency of Sologub's message, that reality can be transformed by the creative imagination. After the Revolution, Sologub published six small books of poems, almost all about nature, and all life-affirming. The titles of the books, which appeared between 1918 and 1922, are *Incense, The Wayside Bonfire, One Love, Panpipes, The Enchanted Cup,* and *Blue Sky.* In *One Love* he took Don Quixote as the symbol of his thesis: Quixote saw the peasant Aldonsa as the beautiful Dulcinea. Two other collections contain liberal, or radical, poetry, most of it written earlier. A final novel written after the Revolution, *The Snake Charmer* (1921), concerns a factory, its owner, and workers.

Sologub's work is diverse, and sometimes startling in its imagery, but his themes were few: his moods, first sorrow, then joy; the beauty of nature; the world order in its hopelessness, or ominousness, and the ideal beyond it. He said of himself that he always wrote about one thing, the ideal. He had a gift for stylistic changes. But he preferred to work with a small and elementary vocabulary, and he favored absolute clarity over suggestive vagueness. He had a good ear for musical sound.

Hippius

In the decadent era of the 1890s, the poetry of Zinaida Hippius (1869–1945) appeared to belong to a familiar tradition of melancholy moods and pessimistic self-assessments. She had a single, religious vision, but it was Solovevan. She accepted the doctrine of an indivisible love that binds together the earthly and the divine. After the publication of her poetry collections in 1904 and 1910, she began to be regarded as one of the most remarkable religious poets in the language. She also wrote short stories, plays, and novels, but they have been forgotten. For a time she seemed most visible as a literary figure, a female dandy, and a bohemian. She wrote literary criticism under the pseudonym Anton Krainy ("The Extremist").

Hippius viewed all culture as religious, and poetry as one of its vital aspects. The *fin de siècle* currents were a credo for her. She was born in a provincial area near Tula and educated primarily at home. In 1889 she married Dmitry Merezhkovsky, with whom she shared a sense of mission, and resided in St. Petersburg.

Their Sunday salon was one of the early circles of Russia symbolism. Her volumes of short stories began to appear in 1896. In 1901 Hippius and Merezhkovsky founded the Religious-Philosophical Society to further their ideas with clerics as well as literary people. In 1903 they started a magazine, *The New Path,* to publish the society's papers. They were joined in this enterprise by the literary critic Dmitry Filosofov, with whom they formed a *ménage à trois.* After the failure of the 1905 Revolution, they lived for more than five years in France. They welcomed the revolution of February 1917, but were later disillusioned by the Bolshevik regime and emigrated in 1921. They resided in Paris, where they were at the center of active literary and anti-Soviet circles.

Hippius relies in her poems on the drama of a struggle for moral and religious enlightenment. In an introduction to her first volume of verse she wrote that every poem, as the expression of the intuitive self, is a form of prayer. Her *oeuvre* is small and static in terms of periods. Her complaints about ennui and her guilty self-lacerations are presumably the most pertinent religious statements that she has to make. She always wrote in the masculine gender, and her moods are, indeed, universal. Hippius's 1904 volume opens with "Song" (1893), a complaint about the emptiness of a frustrated spiritual quest; she concludes: "And yet I do need what the world has not, / What the world has not." She speaks with a clarity that leads her to the use of transparent symbols; dust and rain stand for her decadent dejection. In "Dust" (1897) she begins, "My soul is in the grasp of terror." She is subject to neurotic misjudgments: in "Flowers at Night" (1894) she fears the beauty of her bouquet: "They hear all that I think, they know me. / And they aim with their poison to kill." She is preoccupied with death, both because she might choose it and because it presents a philosophical problem: Is death an absolute evil? Hippius' most dramatic poems are expressions of guilt or temptation. In "The Leeches" (1902) she is speaking about her sins: "Awful comprehension's hour—in a sunset light / Let me see that leeches cling—also on my soul." In "She" (1905) her body is imprisoned by a snake: "Within her circling rings, for she's a stubborn one, / She hugs, caresses me, she crushes tight. / This creature without life, this creature black in hue, / This creature giving fright—she is my soul!" In "Unlove" (1907) she yields to her guilty pride, which knocks on her window:

> As though wet bluster, you knock the shutters,
> A black-hued bluster, you sing: You're mine!
> I'm ancient chaos, your old companion,
> Your sole companion—so open wide!
>
> I grasp the shutter, I dare not open,
> I hold the shutter, and hide my fear.
> I keep, I coddle, I keep, I treasure
> My last faint light—my caring love.
>
> But chaos blindly, in laughter, summons:
> You'll die in shackles—break out, break out!
> You know elation, for you are single,
> Your joy's in freedom—and in Unlove.

> My blood runs colder. I now am praying,
> A prayer for loving I scarce can make. . . .
> My hands grow weaker, I lose the battle,
> My hands are weaker . . . I'll open up!

Her failures in Christian charity often result in her most moving poems.

Hippius' spiritual goal is the free acceptance of universal love. In "Dedication" an upward-bound road becomes an allegory of attainment. The moon is a symbol of the soul's capacities, both in "The Moon and the Fog," where the spirit can penetrate deceits, and in "The Goddess," where the deity is Astarte. The all-embracing cosmic love so important to Hippius' outlook is felt in "Wedding Ring," where the band is an equivalent of the cross; the doctrine is explained in "Love Is One." In "Orange Blossoms" the flowers symbolize the spiritual union of lovers in Christ. Yet all her poems about attainment have a faint air of lecturing about them. Besides, Hippius' view of the universe is usually pessimistic. The world in "The Spiders" is only the eternal spinning of webs. The poem seems to be a literary allusion to Svidrigailov's vision of the universe in Dostoevsky's *Crime and Punishment.* Hippius protests, like Dostoevsky, against the existence of evil, and particularly against the suffering of innocents. In "God's Creature" she pities even the devil, for if universal love must be indivisible, then Satan must be the obedient servant of a world order.

In Hippius' best poems, her tone is earnest and her vocabulary basic. She speaks privately, as though to herself, but her syntax is logical. She used the repetitive forms of songs, but was also intellectual. She was one of several innovators in prosody. She helped to develop the use of impaired rhythms called *dolniki* (parts). Russian verse was never to have a strong tradition of *vers libre.*

In Hippius' fiction and dramas, the doctrine of one love is not mentioned quite as often as in the verse, but its consequences for social issues are clearer. Her first book of stories, *New People* (1896), demonstrated her admiration for those characters who can cut through conventions to a spontaneous and elemental love. She was vehement about the injustices caused by class distinctions. She believed that war and political violence both cause mental illnesses. Her longer works include a play, *The Color of Poppies* (1908, written with Merezhkovsky and Filosofov), and two novels, *The Devil's Doll* (1911) and *The Prince Roman* (1913). Only one play, *The Green Ring* (1916), had any success; it depicts conciliatory meetings between members of different generations.

Hippius' post-Revolutionary career was spent in relative obscurity. Both *Last Poems* (1918) and *Poems: A Diary, 1911–1921* (1922) were published in the Soviet Union and included new antiwar poems and political verse. She anticipates a utopian future after the Bolshevik Revolution; she glorifies the color red. In emigration Hippius wrote perceptive, but whimsical, portrayals of various members of the symbolist movement, such as Sologub and Blok; the work is called *Living Persons* (1925). Her last book of verse, *Radiance* (1938), is a return to religious and philosophical themes.

Bunin

The poetry of Ivan Bunin (1870–1953) has been vastly overshadowed by his remarkable fiction. He was the best, if not the most renowned, writer in the realist camp after the death of Chekhov, and the only major realist who wrote poetry. In both fiction and verse he belonged to the same dispassionate, aesthetic current as Chekhov. His fiction was influenced, moreover, by the lyricism of the age, especially in his masterpiece, *Sukhodol* (1911). His best poems are simple descriptions of landscapes written in a restrained, classical style that is reminiscent of the golden age. Fet was also among his predecessors. His prose reveals, more than does his poetry, his essential view of the world: he marvels at the gifts of life and is saddened by the losses inflicted by time. He is inclined to be pantheistic, but ultimately not concerned with religion. His poetry does not record, as his fiction often does, the passing of the gentry way of life. Bunin was the first Russian to be awarded the Nobel Prize, in 1933.

Bunin's works are evocative of distinctive cultures, whether Russian or exotic, in the details of their atmosphere. He was born near Voronezh into a gentry family. His childhood was spent in the agricultural heartland that he so often pictured in his fiction and verse. He cut short his secondary education in order to write for provincial newspapers. His first book was a collection of verse, which appeared in 1891; some of his subsequent volumes included both fiction and poetry. In the late 1890s he joined Gorky at the Knowledge Publishing House. He began to travel in the early 1900s and visited Europe, the Middle East, North Africa, India, and Ceylon. Fame came with *The Village* (1910), a naturalistic novel describing kulaks and peasants. *Sukhodol* illustrates the decline of a gentry family in the nineteenth century. A novella, *The Gentleman from San Francisco* (1915), is a modern parable describing the death of a rich man. Bunin abhorred Bolshevism; in 1920 he moved to France, where he continued to publish fiction. His last outstanding piece was *The Life of Arsenev* (1930), a lyrical autobiography of his youth.

Bunin's early poetry is exceptionally unassuming and is perhaps more rewarding than his later verse. He wrote exclusively about the Russian countryside; his "Pleiads" (1898) is illustrative of his clarity and understatement:

> It's dark. And through the walks by ponds that now are sleepy
> I wander without aim.
> The chill that comes with fall, the leaves and fruits that ripen,
> Make rich the garden air.
>
> The foliage has grown thin—to let a starry glitter
> Shine white above the limbs.
> My gait is ever slow—for now a deathly silence
> Reigns in the dark arcade,
>
> And every step is loud. The evening air refreshes.
> How like heraldic signs
> The cold and adamantine Pleiads in their burning,
> Throughout the silent night.

In other poems Bunin described the forest or grain fields or the sky; he was fond of clouds and of the sunset. He rarely suggested any moods or thoughts; the personal aspect of his verse seems stifled by reticence. In several poems his wider interest in Russia is explicit.

Bunin's later verse was broader in that he described exotic landscapes and made allusions to the myths and the histories of other peoples, especially those of the Biblical lands. His style also became more ornate, but the heart of his verse remained relatively impersonal and classical. In his new poems, he described boats and the sea, and such exotic scenes as the sand dunes in the far north and jasmine flowers above the Terek River in the Caucasus. His precision in the description of exotic birds and animals is engaging: his eaglet hisses at the rising sun; his goat has childish, agate eyes. He often evoked Greek myths when speaking of the constellations. His poetry was complementary, finally, to his prose *oeuvre*. His very phrasing at times threatened to become prosaic. He was attentive to form, however, and wrote a number of sonnets.

12

Symbolist Idealism
(1905–1912)

After the 1905 Revolution, a limited constitutional monarchy was established with a legislative body, the Duma. An era of uneasy political peace ensued, which was the background for an intense cultural ferment. The public favored tranquility to unrest. The era of civic disturbances had been long, and the event of Bloody Sunday (January 22, 1905) disheartening. In the Duma the middle party, the Constitutional Democrats, or Cadets, prevailed. Socialism as an idea continued to gain supporters. The Marxists, the populists, and the anarchists engaged in agitation. At court, power passed to the Empress Alexandra, who herself succumbed to the sway of the peasant Rasputin. The symbolists, who were political liberals, enjoyed a brief dominance of the literary world. Their religious mysticism was epitomized in the work of a great poet, Aleksandr Blok. The movement, however, became linked in the popular mind with political pessimism. The school disintegrated as an avant-garde arose to challenge it. Meanwhile, Gorky was the single most eminent author, and he owed some of his popularity to the Marxist ideology he represented.

Symbolism in Florescence

In Europe the rift between realism and modernism in the arts was becoming permanent. In England the tide had turned against the mood of *fin de siècle*. Practical issues were in the air. Socialism inspired the plays of George Bernard Shaw, and Rudyard Kipling was preoccupied in his prose and verse with empire. But in Germany an era of mystical and aesthetic impulses parallel to symbolism in Russia still reigned in the hands of Rainer Maria Rilke and Stefan George. In Russia the animosity between realists and symbolists was always keen, because the division was also a political issue. The turn of the century had seemed to promise much for the future of the symbolist school. In the year before the 1905 Revolution, Briusov founded *The Scales,* which he edited until 1909. In 1905 a major metaphysical poet, Viacheslav Ivanov, returned from abroad because of the urgency of national affairs. The suppression of the 1905 Revolution brought an immediate reversal in the "dawn" mentality of the symbolists. Their mature works, sometimes their greatest, were brought out in an atmosphere of self-doubt, irony, and pessimism. They questioned their metaphysical principles and the purpose of the symbolist school. They were drawn by the urgency of Russia's historical moment to devote their thought to the national culture. They sometimes wrote their best works in fiction rather than in poetry.

Symbolists all too often saw a mystical significance in political events. Viacheslav Ivanov lent his authority to a populist theory of art called "mystical anarchism," and his salon dominated the creative bohemian circles of St. Petersburg from 1905 to 1907. After 1905, disillusionment, both political and mystical, was visible in the work of every symbolist but Ivanov. In 1906 Blok wrote a satirical play called *The Puppet Show* in which his target was the mystical hopes of the symbolists (including his own); the play was staged with success by Meyerhold at the Kommissarzhevsky Theater. In the same year Merezhkovsky, Hippius, and Balmont left the country because of the severity of political repressions. In 1907 Sologub published a satirical novel, *The Petty Demon,* in which the broad public saw a portrayal of reactionary Russia. (The novel, conceived before 1905, was for its author only a mirror of reality.) In the years 1908 to 1910 several doctrinaire symbolists waged controversies over the nature of the movement, particularly as to whether it was a religion or a literary school. These inner hostilities were perceived as a "crisis of symbolism," and *The Scales* ceased publication in 1909. An aura of "religiosity" or of "aestheticism" continued to be attached, however, to some poets.

After 1910 the key symbolists became more concerned with national directions and less preoccupied with personal mysticism. The country became for Blok a new hypostasis of his religious ideal. Andrey Bely emerged as the most significant observer of Russian culture. His novels revived the contention between the Slavophiles and the Westernizers of the nineteenth century. In *The Silver Dove* (1910) the educated protagonist, whose mentality is Western, is murdered by peasants whose religious sect derives from an Asiatic strain in Russian culture. In his masterpiece, *Petersburg* (1916), Bely suggests that East and West are fatefully intertwined in Russian life. Modernist writers who had never belonged to the symbolist movement simply because they were not mystics were discovered by the public. Chief among them was Innokenty Annensky, a poet who was perhaps the purest disciple of Baudelaire and Mallarmé. He became the mentor of a group of younger modernists who rebelled against symbolism. One of the most original prose writers of the era was Aleksey Remizov, a philosophical pessimist and Slavophile.

Bely

Among the most innovative members of the symbolist movement was Andrey Bely (1880–1934), who was also a millenarian extremist. His first collection of poetry, *Gold in Azure* (1904), shared in the creation of the "dawn" hopes of the new century. His collections called *Ashes* and *The Urn* (both 1909) helped to create the ensuing disillusionment. He is now best known for the novel *Petersburg,* which displays his anxieties about an absence of direction in Russian culture. The novel was seminal in the development of avant-garde fiction. Bely shattered aesthetic conventions by conducting experiments that were of personal interest to him. His earliest literary innovations were "symphonies" in prose. He also wrote short stories, dramas, and numerous articles on aesthetic and cultural subjects. In later years he popularized anthroposophical views. The influence of anthroposophy is apparent in the several lengthy novels of his early Soviet period. His memoirs, written in the 1930s, provide invaluable information about the course of the symbolist movement at the turn of the century.

Bely (whose real name was Boris Bugaev) believed that imaginative literature would inevitably be the reflection of universal truth, which he saw first in the Sophian doctrine of Solovev and later in anthroposophy. He was born in Moscow, the son of a professor of mathematics at Moscow University. As a university student he was influenced by Kant and Wagner, as well as by Vladimir Solovev, with whose family he had personal ties. Bely was recognized as a provocative symbolist after the appearance of his first two prose symphonies and *Gold in Azure.* His subsequent disillusionment was in part owing to a rejection in his love affair with Blok's wife; both writers saw in her an incarnation of Sophian love. Bely's articles on poetry and culture appeared in *Symbolism* (1910). He married in 1911 and became an adept of anthroposophy, a religious sect derived from theosophy, the study of man's mystical perception of God. The years 1912 to 1916 were spent at a retreat for anthroposophists at Dornach, Switzerland. Bely believed the Bolshevik Revolution had a mystical significance, but he was later disappointed. The first of his avant-garde novels in the Soviet period was *Kotik Letaev* (1918), an anthroposophical work still inaccessible to the general reader. In the memoirs of his last years, Bely became the first historian of symbolism.

Bely's works are the result of a strangely naive reliance on philosophical abstractions, but he often turned against them in irony. He also had a good sense of high play, or pretense and artifice. *Gold in Azure* is animated by a gentle nostalgia for mystical heights. The sunsets that open the book are memorable for their array of pastel colors and tones of awe. He anticipates dreams; in a poem of 1902 he begins:

> A distance—without end. The lazy swaying
> And sound of oats.
> My heart again awaits in its impatience
> The dreams it knows.

Other poems are tongue-in-cheek tableaux from historical periods. The rococo lovers pictured in "A Declaration of Love" (1903) recall the nostalgic scenes drawn by Verlaine in *Fêtes galantes.* Bely devoted several cycles to figures from folklore or children's literature; among them are a whimsical giant and a family of domestic centaurs. They conform to the tastes of a modern, popular art. The book also has a current of existential sadness. The closing cycle, "Royal Purple in Thorns," hints that mystical expectations may be false hopes.

Bely's prose casts light on his poetry and is inextricably linked with it in aims and periods. The four "symphonies," which he published between 1902 and 1908, are invented fairy tales, but their real subject is a spiritual ideal, or world-philosophy, as in Wagner's *Das Ring der Nibelungen.* The third symphony, called *The Return,* also contains seeds of his future fiction; a fantasy about a child and an old magician has a farcical, real-life parallel: a graduate student at Moscow University is consulting a psychiatrist. The sonata structure, the leitmotifs, and the transparent symbols of the symphonies were all to reappear in his novels. Bely's doctrinal essays, written in the years from 1904 to 1909, begin with the belief that the symbolist movement would be the vehicle of a millennium. When he became disillusioned, he began to criticize Russian culture. Europe seemed to him, as to many other Russians, lacking in spiritual depth and yet inexplicably rich in cultural achievements.

The pessimism of *Ashes* is different from that of *The Urn.* Bely's subject in *Ashes* is Russia and the despair it has caused him, while *The Urn* reflects a personal metaphysical crisis. The influence of a realist poet, Nekrasov, on *Ashes* is unmistakable, although Russia is viewed as a mystical entity. The country is seen only in its provincial areas, and in visions of poverty, crimes, and injustice. The griefs of the nation become the personal sorrow of the poet. These are the opening stanzas of "Despair" (1908), which begins the book:

> Enough, do not wait or hope longer . . .
> Begone, O my poor native race.
> Dissolve into space and be traceless,
> Each year after tormenting year!
>
> What ages of need and unfreedom!
> O let me, my poor motherland,
> Go sob in your wide open spaces,
> Your damp and your empty expanse.

The windows of the taverns at night are memorable: "The eyes that are yellow and cruel. / The eyes of your lunatic inns." In a cycle called "The Village" Bely shows that the rich are pitted against the poor; murders are committed, and women mistreated. When he talks about himself, his setting is urban. In "The City" he is a mental patient in a clown suit. In "Insanity" he sometimes imagines that he is Christ. The closing poem of this cycle is "To My Friends" (1907), an appeal from beyond the grave; it is written in impaired rhythms:

> He believed in golden sunshine,
> But shafts from the sun were his death.
> He could scan in thought the ages,
> But life—he never could learn.
>
> O ridicule not the dead poet:
> No, bring him a fresh new bloom.

On my cross is a wreath of china
That bangs, winter, summer, alike.

Its flowers now are broken.
And the icon gone dim.
My flagstones are heavy.
Will anyone lift them away?

He loved just the bells from the tower,
The low sun.
Tell me, why is it now so painful?
How am I to blame?

Please take pity, come see me;
I'll hurry to you, in my wreath,
O, I want you to love me, please love me,
For I'm, maybe, not dead, and I, maybe, will waken—

Return!

The Russian theme appears again in the poems of "The Spider Web." The book closes with the poems of "Shafts of Light," devoted to Russia's vagabonds—those forced by hardships into a life of drifting and sometimes imprisonment.

The keynote themes of *The Urn* are a personal sense of isolation and impending death. The opening poems are devoted to the poet in his lonely calling, the practice of a power that remains a mystery. The forsaken lover appears in the cycle called "Winter," whose scenes are of the frosty countryside, with a house, the stars, and wolves. Academic metaphysics is denigrated in the cycle "Philosophical Grief": books are empty, while real life means, for example, being a hunchback and awaiting death, the graveyard. Other cycles are called "Tristia" and "Meditations."

In Bely's major novels, *The Silver Dove* and *Petersburg*, the spiritual capacities of Russian civilization are under examination. The university student who is trapped and killed by peasants in *The Silver Dove* must die because he has learned the erotic secrets of a religious sect; the Eastern, instinctual, aspect of Russia is inescapable. The philosophy student who is the protagonist of *Petersburg* is engaged by revolutionaries in 1905 to bomb his father, a senator. Although the bomb explodes, nothing happens: Russia's culture is without a direction or a future. The student's love affair is a spoof of the adoration of Saint Sophia.

Bely's post-Revolutionary fiction, anthroposophical and usually avant-garde, vastly outweighs the poetry, which appeared in five small books, each different. These include the revolutionary *Christ Is Arisen* (1918), where Christ's last days on earth are seen beside Russia after the Revolution. *The Princess and the Knights. Tales* (1919) is a return to fairy tales, but his essential subject is an existential melancholia. Bely's origins as an author are celebrated in *First Meeting* (1921), a long poem depicting the Solovev family at the turn of the century. The poem recalls Vladimir Solovev's "Three Meetings," his response to the summons of Saint Sophia. Idle thoughts on metaphysical themes appear in *The Star. New Poems* (1922), while *After the Parting. A Berlin Diary* (1922) contains dreamlike lyrical episodes in free verse. The latter is a record of mental distress (he might have stayed in emigration). Bely's studies on Russian versification, made in the same period, gave impetus to the subject as a science; he compared actual rhythms with fixed meters. Bely's voluminous autobiographical writings in the early Soviet period began with *Kotik Letaev,* a lyrical work about his fetal life and infancy. His memoirs are personal in tone, but accessible; they include *On the Boundary of Two Centuries. Recollections* (1930), *The Beginning of an Age. Memoirs* (1933), and *Between Two Revolutions* (1934).

Bely's works, both in poetry and prose, are extraordinarily stimulating, but seldom genuinely tragic. It is in this respect that Bely, whatever his artistic method, was already close in spirit to the avant-garde. His talents were more narrative and dramatic than lyrical. His poems seem at times like excerpts from novels. His *oeuvre* is marked by a tendency akin to high clowning: he entertains, but he asks indulgence, too.

Blok

Aleksandr Blok (1880–1921) is believed by some to be Russia's greatest poet in the twentieth century. His evolution was shaped, as he wrote, by a mystical love for the Divine Wisdom, or Saint Sophia, an ideal revered by several Russian symbolists. His early poetry is the diary of his quest for communion, seen especially in *Verses About the Beautiful Lady.* A period of disillusionment and irony began in 1906. Before World War I the nation became an object of his mystical dedication. Under the cloud of his first metaphysical disappointment, Blok wrote the first popular lyrical dramas, beginning with *The Puppet Show* (1906). He was relatively uninterested in aesthetic controversies and symbolist doctrine. He exemplified, more than other symbolists, their tendency to interweave life with art, to live and write the same story. His character had no dandyism in it; he married young, became a celebrity, but was unhappy, and he died early. He wrote articles that are hostile to his own, gentry, class in its relationship to the remainder of the Russian population.

Blok was dedicated to art as an element of cultural history, and he viewed the latter as a process that was religious in some undefined sense. He was born in Moscow and reared in St. Petersburg by his mother, who was separated from his father, a law professor at Warsaw University. His maternal grandfather, Andrey Beketov, was rector at St. Petersburg University. His mother was close to members of the family of Vladimir Solovev, the philosopher of the doctrine of Saint Sophia. Blok married Liubov Mendeleeva, the daughter of the famous chemist, and thought of her as an earthly incarnation of divine love. His friendship with Andrey Bely began as a brotherhood in mystic faith and became a love triangle. Blok began to engage in love affairs, and in 1906 his wife left him for an unknown third man and later returned pregnant. Blok's love affairs played a key role in his poetry because he perceived them not only as a disloyalty to his wife, but also as a blasphemy of his mystic hopes. Especially poignant episodes were those with Natalia Volokhova, an actress, in 1907 and with Liubov Delmas, an opera singer, in 1914. Blok's adoration of the nation was not only as a new hypostasis of his first mystical ideal. He saw in the Russian people an embodiment of the elemental force that Nietzsche called the "spirit of music." Blok acclaimed the October Revolution in his masterpiece, a narrative poem called *The Twelve* (1918), but his new enthusiasm was also disappointed. Blok died after a famine winter in the spring of 1921.

Blok's *oeuvre* became a legend for his times, however private some of his poems were. He wrote about spiritual mistakes that were recognizable to his generation. He never wrote, moreover, as a priest of a cult, but as a mundane man. His poems appeared in small volumes over a number of years. Later, he selected and partly arranged them for the three volumes of his *Collected Works*. The first volume remains a lyrical diary of the years 1897 to 1904, years in which he sought a mystical meeting with Saint Sophia. Like Solovev before him, Blok assumes the attitudes of a lover and sometimes of a knight. The volume now has three parts: "Ante lucem," "Verses About the Beautiful Lady," and "Parting of the Ways." His short ecstasies of attainment are rare. His setting is often a benign edge of town, at times in the sunset. In "Parting of the Ways" he is already aware of triangles, of his propensity to betrayals, and of an ominous and blasphemous "double." His imagery is sometimes of masquerade balls, where the commedia dell'arte figures Pierrot, Columbine, and Harlequin are seen. Blok's early poems are intriguing as a whole collection, and indispensable to an understanding of his mature work, but his single poems are not as yet memorable.

Blok's disillusionment was not so much in the concept of the Divine Wisdom as in the mystical quest for her. His period of irony is dominated by an enigmatic female figure whom he calls "the stranger" and who appears at night in St. Petersburg; she is a distorted memory of the Divine Sophia. The second volume of the *Collected Works* opens with a farewell poem to the Beautiful Lady, who recedes as her poet turns to earthly spheres. The Solovevan optimism is belied in a poem that begins, "High in a choir loft a maiden was singing" (1903); her song is about the safe return of distant ships, but a cherub is sobbing: "Because he knew—no one ever comes back." Blok's first confession of an erotic temptation appears in a narrative poem called "The Nocturnal Violet" (1906). The poem called "The Stranger" (1906) has remained his most famous piece. Too long to quote in full, it pictures the outskirts of town, now a sinister setting, and the tavern where the poet salutes his "only friend," his image reflected in his glass.

> Obscure the secrets I've been given,
> A sun not mine rests in my care,
> And all my soul's dark inner windings
> Are entered by the bitter wine.

He observes the woman of the night, whose "blue eyes" are flowers that bloom on "a distant shore." His painfully ironic conclusion is an echo of the drunken call around him: "In vino veritas." Under the spell of Natalia Volokhova, Blok wrote, in January 1907, the thirty poems that form the cycle called "Snow Mask." The poems, written in fifteen days, record the ominous blandishments of an alluring woman who assumes the blue and starry attributes of Saint Sophia. She promises ecstasy and demands servitude. In all his periods, Blok wrote about Russia, about war, and about social injustices, but in the first two volumes these subjects are not yet well developed.

Blok's lyric dramas, *The Puppet Show* and *The Stranger,* both of which he wrote in 1906 for Vsevolod Meyerhold and the experimental Kommissarzhevsky Theater, are self-lacerating works. The principal figures in *The Puppet Show* are Pierrot, Columbine, and Harlequin. Other characters include a group of foolish Petersburg mystics who are awaiting the angel of death; they confound her with Columbine, who turns out, anyway, to be a mere "cardboard bride." Blok's mystical aspirations in *The Stranger* are represented by a poet and by an astrologer; the two men adore a woman or a fallen star named Maria, but they fail to recognize her when she appears. Blok's other plays include *The King on the Square* (1906), an antigovernment statement, and *The Song of Fate* (1908), another reflection of his infatuation with Volokhova; the latter play includes notes of populist sentiment.

The poems of Blok's third volume are his greatest. They are more richly motivated, they reflect his searching intelligence, and they are more balanced in theme. Art is recognized, in the opening poem, "To the Muse" (1912), as service not to a mystical ideal, but to a beauty that is amoral. This spiritual ambiguity is a new source of suffering for the poet: "For all others the Muse is a wonder. / But for me You're a torment and hell." The first cycle in the book, called "The Terrible World," contains one of Blok's best-loved poems, a simple statement of ennui written in 1912:

> It's night, the street, a street light, drugstore,
> A senseless and an obscure light.
> You'll live perhaps two score and over—
> It's all like that. There's no way out.
>
> You'll die and then begin all over,
> All is repeated—as it was:
> Night. The canal has icy ripples.
> A drugstore and a street light, street.

The cycle "Retribution" is about his derelictions from his Neoplatonic love for the Divine Sophia. His "blasphemies" are always perceived in an agony of guilt. In this poem of 1908 he is the unworthy husband:

> That fame exists, and deeds, and knightly valor
> In this so saddened world, I had forgot
> When still your face, whose frame was always simple,
> Before me shone upon my table top.
>
> There came a time, you from this house departed.
> I threw my blessed ring into the night.
> Your fate you then entrusted to another,
> And I forgot the beauty in your face.
>
> The days flew by, a cursed swarm encircling . . .
> And wine and lust made torment of my life . . .

And I remembered you before the altar,
I called you, as I would have called my youth.

I called to you, but you did not look backwards,
I wept for you, but you did not relent.
You sadly wrapped your dark blue cape around you,
Into the damp of night you left this house.

I know not where your pride has found a shelter
For you who are so gentle and so dear . . .
My sleep is sound. I see your dark blue cape in slumber—
The cape you wore into the damp of night . . .

I dream no more of gentleness or glory,
For all has passed away, my youth is gone.
I took your face, still in its frame so simple,
With my own hand from off my table top.

Several of Blok's most effective poems are similar in meaning. In "The Steps of the Commander" (1912) a Don Juan is about to be slain by the statue he has invited. Blok suggests, like Pushkin in "The Stone Guest," that the profligate and murderer has discovered a higher vision and died repentant. Blok's Juan may be transfigured in death through his love: "At your death will Donna Anna waken. / Anna at your death will rise."

Blok was concerned in many poems with the eternal dilemma of the Neoplatonist: perfection is other-worldly, beyond death, whereas life has vital joys. In 1909 he wrote the cycle "Italian Poems," the result of a trip made with his wife to begin their marriage anew. The cycle opens with "Ravenna," where a sensuous life seems to lie buried with the passionate figures of Italy's past. Only Dante, who created in his idealization of Beatrice a vision of eternal life, can speak to the present: "The shade of Dante, eagle-profiled, / *La Vita Nuova* sings to me." But his victory is not complete, and in other poems neither death nor vitality can win. *The Rose and the Cross* (1912), Blok's best play, and the only one written in verse, is also about Neoplatonic love. The wife of a medieval count of Languedoc, Izora, yearns for the mystic songs of a distant trouvère; she never suspects that the self-effacing old knight who guards the castle bears for her a love that is pure and perfect.

In the cycle "Carmen" (1914) Blok's betrayal of his Neoplatonic love is committed in the name not only of life, but also of art. The poems are dedicated to the affair with Delmas, who, as the singer who played Carmen in Bizet's opera, was not a temptress only, but a fellow artist; she too knew the ambiguous power of beauty. In 1913 Blok had lamented in "The Artist" that poetry is always incomplete in its attainment, like the caging of a bird that was once free: "Bird that had wanted to take away death, / Bird that had wanted to rescue the soul . . . ." In Bizet's opera Delmas impersonated a beauty that is doomed, and she came very near to being for Blok an incarnation of art. But the allure of art was viewed more sternly in a narrative poem, "The Nightingale Garden" (1915). The laborer who tarries in the garden that stops time emerges to find that his ass is dead and his house in ruins.

Blok placed his poems dedicated to Russia, a country lacerated by violence, at the end of his third volume. The most memorable are the five poems of the cycle "On Kulikovo Field," written in 1908. The battle of 1380 in which Dmitry Donskoy defeated the Mongols appears to be taking place around the poet. The scenes of steppes, warriors, and horses are intermingled, however, with the present, and Blok foresees a similar challenge in the future: "My horse's mane again is rising, / Swords do call beyond the wind." He addresses Russia throughout as his wife, lover, and ideal. The images recall medieval epics, especially *The Tale of Igor's Campaign* and its imitation, the *Zadonshchina*.

The revolution that would destroy his own class is the subject of three of Blok's narrative poems. "Retribution," at which he worked from 1910 to 1921, remained unfinished. Blok explains the aim of the poem in a terse prose introduction: he wants to depict three generations of a genteel, liberal family as they bring the revolution ever nearer; the last child will grasp the rudder of history. The portraits that follow are unexpectedly warm and humorous (they were drawn from the Beketovs). *The Twelve* has in it the ardor of his Sophian dreams; it was written in two days in January 1918. The accidental shooting of a prostitute, the last hypostasis of the Beautiful Lady, by her former lover, a Red soldier, is its chief event. The poem is set in the streets of Petrograd where red banners hang, and the receding past is symbolized by a fat priest and a hungry dog. At the poem's end, the Reds shoot at an unseen figure who emerges as Jesus Christ:

> Soft his step above the snowstorm,
> Pearly-hued his snowy dusting,
> White the roses of his crown—
> Jesus Christ walks out ahead.

Christ's presence is in no way explained. The rhythms of the poem were derived from urban popular songs, particularly the *chastushka*, the factory song. *The Twelve* was followed by a lesser poem, "The Scythians" (1918), in which Blok warns the West against any intervention in Russia's civil war. His tone is angry and arrogant. Blok's last play, *Ramses* (1919), is a short but suggestive statement; it depicts the betrayal and death of the king of Thebes under Ramses II.

Blok's articles were the customary vehicle of his populist sympathy. Beginning with "The Populace and the Intelligentsia" (1908), he had seen the country as divided into those two hostile camps, both sincere in desiring to serve Russia. Guided in part by Nietzsche, he had come to believe that the culture of the educated class, built up by history, was not in any sense vital, whereas the populace represented a religious force. In "The Intelligentsia and the Revolution" (1918) he emphasizes his debt to Nietzsche by his references to the "spirit of music."

Blok combined a great intelligence with a passionate, meditative character. His writing appears to spring from the spontaneous needs of a rich, but unordered inner life; he wrote almost as though the victim of his own talent. He possessed, however, a nearly inviolable tastefulness, or tact. His style is deceptive in its simplicity, at times casual and ordinary. It was first learned from Zhukovsky and Lermontov, rather than from Baudelaire, or even Verlaine. Blok also retained a capacity for redemption that separated him from the French *poètes maudits*. He was adept at *dolniki,* the impaired rhythm that the Russian symbolists invented under the influence of French *vers libre,* which they almost never imitated. Blok's themes have been seen by Russians in terms of a mythic development—from the Lady to the Stranger and then to Russia—that encapsulates the progress of a segment of the intelligentsia from religious faith to irony and on to love of country. Blok was complex, however, and did not sustain two divisive crises. His themes traverse his work in counterpoint, emerging in varying emphases, and each one always in evolution.

Ivanov

The spirit of joy was uncommon as an underlying motivation for Russian symbolists. Yet it is a metaphysical optimism that inspired the poems of Viacheslav Ivanov (1866–1949). He had a streak of robust paganism in his thinking, and in general he gave credence, as a Classical scholar, to the myths of antiquity. For him they embodied the same divine and eternal principles as the mystical traditions of Christianity. His first book of verse, *Pilot Stars,* appeared in 1903; his major collection was *Cor ardens* in 1911. He wrote a number of erudite and polemical articles on art and culture that first appeared in *By the Stars* (1909). In his poetry he was a twentieth-century master of the grand style. He was affectionately known to critics as "Viacheslav the Magnificent." He followed Nietzsche in the belief that poetry originated in drama, and ultimately in Dionysian rites. He was the author of classical tragedies (*Tantalus,* 1905; *Prometheus,* 1916) that are now forgotten.

Ivanov was ever guided by the idea that literature is a religious activity—a search for the divine in individual perceptions. He was born in Moscow and educated at Moscow University. He earned a graduate degree at the University of Berlin in 1899 before turning in his research to the cult of Dionysus. He traveled extensively, but his collections of verse, *Pilot Stars* and *Translucence* (1904), were published in Russia before his return in 1905. In St. Petersburg he took over the position of leadership that had belonged to Merezhkovsky. Ivanov's Wednesday salon was maintained with his second wife, the writer Lydia Zinoveva-Hannibal, until her death in 1907. His sixth-floor apartment was called "The Tower." In 1907 he moved to Moscow, and his influence declined after he married his stepdaughter. In 1923 he defended a doctoral dissertation at Baku University and became a professor there. In 1924 he defected in Italy; in 1926 he converted to Catholicism and began to teach Russian literature at the University of Pavia. He had become known in Western literary spheres before he died in 1949.

In *Pilot Stars* and *Translucence* Ivanov both explains his beliefs and glorifies their substance, and his premises were never to change. His poetic presence was immediately felt to be powerful. The world is, in his view, a place of mysteries that promise paradise. *Pilot Stars* is devoted to aspects of the Dionysian view of existence. The opening cycle pictures landscapes in terms of the unity in multiplicity that is the universe. Dionysus, or Pan, is equated with Christ in a poem called "The Earth": at the Crucifixion nature itself responded. In further cycles earth, or the earthly, yearns for the fulfillment of the divine. In the poem "Voices" Ivanov suggests that we are stirred by nature in the Mediterranean area to recall its gods: "Why then do the shades in smoky auras / Sway, as though they were the very gods? Why do they call us back to native shores?" In "Thalassia" the seas long for the divine, and in "Oreads" it is the mountains. Man's aesthetic urge, too, is prompted by the gods within him, and the arts are his striving to reach the sacred. The cycle "Italian Sonnets" includes "Taormina" (1901), in which an altar to Dionysus still smokes in the ruins of an ancient theater on Sicily. Ivanov uses archaic designations—Ausonia for Italy, Evia or Evius for Dionysus, and Pontus for the sea:

> Ausonia is still dark, but eastern skies turn red.
> And snowcapped Etna sends an amber smoke ascending.
> Its snow turns pink and burns. A purple light does shimmer,
> Descending from its head, like unction fit for kings,
>
> To silent slopes of oaks, and to the peace of fields,
> To groves of olive trees; the shore is yet in twilight,
> But soon the Pontus dim, when struck with airy azure,
> Will gleam between the ruins of once sacred gates.
>
> In shards the stage does sleep. The orchestra is muted.
> And yet your snowbound altar lifts its smoke unceasing,
> O you who are to come at day's east, holy age!
>
> And from your citadel Melpomene does ever
> In tears, O Evius, observe this desert arc,
> And Tartarus, who breathes, beneath a garden trapped.

The closing cycles are "Evia," in which the Dionysian ritual symbolizes the reconciliation of all matter in the earthly rounds of death and resurrection, and "Suspiria," where the soul is transfigured in death.

In *Translucence,* published one year later, Ivanov was more attentive to the actual experience of earthly life, particularly in its eroticism and pain. His allusions to Greek myths (or the figures of history) have less abstract, more everyday, purposes. In "Pan and Psyche" the woman, still human, draws new notes of sorrow from the panpipes of the god. Ivanov urges artists, in "The Nomads of Beauty" (1904), ever to destroy the old and create the new:

> Their Eden raze, Atilla—
> Through new and empty lands
> Your stars will rise ascendant—
> The blossoms of your wilds.

Cor ardens is a far more imposing and less ingratiating accomplishment. The volume is deeply mystical and ornately organized. Ivanov conceived its opening part as a lament for his wife. The "burning heart" of the collection's title is discovered to be the instrument of mystical insight and the organ by which man shares his earthly and his universal love. The heart is for man what the sun is for nature. In the following cycles, Ivanov suggests the path of the soul through life.

"Speculum speculoram" is a mirror of the world at large; it is followed by "Eros" and "Love and Death." In the closing cycle, "Rosarium," he pays tribute to the rose, the flower to which mankind has attributed to many religious and symbolic meanings: it has stood both for the Virgin and for Venus. The solemnity of the work is enhanced by the many poems in set forms, such as the sonnet and the gazel. The last book that Ivanov published in Russia, *The Sweet Mystery* (1918), is devoted to the ageless joys and sorrows of a pastoral life. It includes such titles as "The Cicada," "The Fisherman's Village," and "Field Work." His metaphysical speculations are not entirely absent; "The Mirror of Hecate" is a meditation inspired by the moon.

In emigration Ivanov published *Evening Lights* (1946); it is the least ordered of his poetry volumes, but it includes two enduring cycles of sonnets. "Winter Sonnets" is religious poetry at its best; the cycle is an allegory of a winter of the soul, a season of faltering faith expressed in simple, humble words. Its poems were written in 1920 in Russia; its scenes of ice and snow are both realistic and metaphorical. The "Roman Sonnets" (1924) are a celebration of the Italian city, its art and architecture, its long history and present liveliness. "Roman Sonnet IV" begins with the permanence of a fountain sculpture:

> Now turned to stone beneath the charms of waters,
> Which rustle as they flow across the brim,
> A boat that's made to look half sunken lies;
> Young women from Campagna bring it flowers.

But the poem ends with the transience of a song:

> At night, when dark, the sighs of cavatinas
> And to the chords of velvet stringed guitars,
> The wandering strum of tunes on mandolins.

The book is closed by a diary in verse of the liberation of the city from German occupation in 1944.

Ivanov's poetry is based on ideas that are not common, but not difficult in themselves. His view of physical matter as sentient, but not quite cognizant of the god within, accounts for phrases that appear to be circumlocutions and figures of speech but are often meant literally. His lines of thought reflect a high intelligence in their fluid length and complexity. His syntax is straightforward, however; he did not speak in suggestive ellipses.

Ivanov's essays, collected in *By the Stars* and *Furrows and Boundaries* (1916), are formidable in their reasoning, but they are only discursive statements of the thoughts that are more visible in his poems. He believed that the poet is, or should be, the voice of his race, and that populations have racial memories, which the poet can fashion into new religious myths. He believed that art is created through an intricate interplay of the Dionysian will and the Apollonian dream. *A Correspondence Between Two Corners* (1922) is an exchange of letters with Mikhail Gershenzon, a literary and cultural essayist, with whom Ivanov shared a hospital room in

1920. Ivanov believed in the moral strength of culture, while Gershenzon feared a decline.

Annensky

A direct heir to the best traditions of French symbolism, Innokenty Annensky (1856–1909) remained aloof from the Russian school because he could not accept its specifically religious mysticism. His poetic *oeuvre* is small; his poems appeared in two collections, *Quiet Songs* (1904) and *The Cypress Chest* (1910). The mysteries and enigmas examined in them are those of an intensely observed inner life. Annensky was also the author of classical tragedies written in verse on mythical subjects. His plays did not enter the mainstream of Russian literature, but they were not at all irrelevant to his own world view and *oeuvre*. He was the Russian translator of the works of Euripides (1907–1921). Throughout his career, he translated French nineteenth-century poets, both symbolists and Parnassians. In the 1880s he was a literary critic, and near the end of his life he published two volumes of literary essays, called *Books of Reflections* (1906 and 1909).

Annensky was a decadent in the European sense—pessimistic, subtle, learned, and devoted to beauty. He was a teacher of Greek and Latin and of Russian literature at secondary schools, and he began publishing creative works only in his middle years. He was born in Omsk and reared in St. Petersburg, partly by an older brother who was a journalist. He was educated at St. Petersburg University and began to publish academic articles as well as literary criticism. In 1890 he traveled to Italy, and he taught for three years in Kiev before returning to St. Petersburg. His classical tragedies were his first original works. His *Quiet Songs* attracted almost no attention when it appeared in 1904, and his literary reputation began when he was "discovered" by a new wave of younger poets, the acmeists, who rebelled against symbolism. The final version of Annensky's poetry appears in *Posthumous Verse* (1923).

Annensky saw in the Classical concept of fate the same kind of irrational obstacle to happiness that seems to beset modern man. His mythical characters face devastating contests with fate. They display, moreover, the ambivalences and nuances of behavior of twentieth-century protagonists. His characters include a blinded, imprisoned mother in *Melanippa the Philosopher*, a king who desired Hera in *King Ixion*, a widow who died from grief in *Laodamia*, and a harpist who challenged Apollo in *Thamyrus Cytharoede*. The last play was staged by the experimental director Aleksandr Tairov at the Kamerny Theater in Moscow in 1916. In general, Annensky depicted bravery in the face of adversity.

Annensky's poetry is about the loneliness of the alienated everyman. He has no romantic demon, and he does not praise artistic genius or erudition. His poems are all of a piece and are seldom dated. *Quiet Songs* opens with poems that signal that his subject is the intimate experience of the self and that his awareness is existential. He assumes that his reader is acquainted with spleen. He is fascinated by nature's array of opulence and decay. A series of poems called "July," "August," "September," and "November" leads through summer heat and the golds and purples of fading gardens to the first snow. In the following poems, he writes of those private experiences that seem secret but are known to be universal. He complains of boredom, of lost hopes, of nightmares and insomnia. He excells at rendering the recognition of frustration. Like decadents before him, he is conscious of transience. He is partial in his settings to sunsets and to night.

The organizing thread of *The Cypress Chest* as a book is the passage of time. Transience without fulfillment is the subject of "Poppies":

> The happy day burns on—amid the languid grass
> Are poppies everywhere—like impotence that's avid,
> Like lips redolent of corruption and of spleen,
> Like crimson butterflies with wings outspread at fullest.
>
> The happy day burns on—the garden's mute and void.
> And long since ended its corruption and its feasting.
> The poppies now are dry—as though old women's heads,
> And sheltered by the sky with radiance from its chalice.

The poems of *The Cypress Chest* are arranged in a series of twenty-five triptychs, all with whimsical titles, such as "Temptation" and "Sentimentality," which defy logic and emphasize moods. In this book he has many more regrets for what might have been. He complains of the brevity and rare appearances of love. In "The Bow and the Strings" the ecstasy of erotic love, like that of aesthetic or spiritual heights, leads to a residual sense of poverty and pain. The opening stanza:

> What raving, O how deep and dark!
> How vague these heights and O, how lunar!
> To touch a violin for years,
> And not to know the strings by daylight!

In "The Steel Cicada" love's short duration is compared to the brief opening and shutting of a watch case; the clock's exposed movement is itself likened to the intense life of the insect, described here in two stanzas:

> Its small steel heart atremble,
> And with its wings awhir—
> Fastened, unfastened ever
> By him who did open for her . . .
>
> Ever impatient, cicadas
> Flutter their avid wings:
> Happiness, is it coming?
> Pain, is it going to end?

In a well-known poem called "The Old Barrel Organ," life is vindicated. The instrument loves to sing:

> Could the antique barrel comprehend—
> What fate means for it, and for the organ,

> Would it cease to spin, and spinning, sing—
> Because no song comes without its torments?"

Other sections of the book are called "Hinged Icons" (paired poems) and "Scattered Leaves" (single poems).

There is in Annensky's poems a pathetic tendency to self-discipline. He attributes such traits as impetuosity and ardor to flowers and to instruments, but he stifles the instinctive in himself. He seems to be a victim of his own abstractness; in "∞" he compares the mind's concept of infinity with the short moments in which it measures pain. Even the performance of art—for example, the playing of the piano—may deteriorate into mere discipline, the dancing of slave girls. He resembles Mallarmé in his capacity for exploiting the ellipsis, and he relies on the reader for sophistication and for a creative cooperation in reading the poems. The reward for the reader is the delight of discovery.

Many of Annensky's translations from French poets appeared among his own lyrics in *Quiet Songs*. He included the symbolists—Baudelaire, Verlaine, Mallarmé, and Rimbaud—whom he so obviously followed. Also present are the Parnassians Leconte de Lisle and Sully-Prudhomme, who wrote on the mythical subjects that Annensky reserved for his tragedies. He shared their humanistic sense of honor, but avoided their grandeur and was more subtle.

Annensky's critical essays in *Books of Reflections* include observations on Gogol, Dostoevsky, Turgenev, Lermontov, Heine, Ibsen, and others. In "Balmont as Lyricist" he reveals his impatience with the religious mysticism of the Russian symbolist school; Balmont was different—an amoral pantheist. Annensky's view of literature appears in an essay on Gogol's short story "The Portrait." Art was for Annensky a psychological experience, a secular avenue of spiritual elevation. The same view would be found later among members of the avant-garde.

VI

POSTSYMBOLIST
MODERNISM

IV

13

Tradition and Acmeism (1912–1925)

The prewar period of peace was followed, in the experience of much of the intelligentsia, by the two revolutions of 1917 and then by years of a devastating civil war. Any general political tendency that had been shared by the intelligentsia was dissolved in factional differences. The monarchy was weakened in the prewar years by the opposition of the gentry. In that era the modernists took their literary cues from Western Europe, however. Symbolism gave way to new, antimystical currents. There arose in Russia a moderate group that called itself acmeism and that tended toward political conservatism. The radicals in literature and politics were the futurists. Immediately after its entry into the war, the nation suffered military setbacks. By March 1917 Nicholas II had abdicated, and in November the Provisional Government was ended by the storming of the Winter Palace. In 1918 a civil war was begun by volunteer armies that drew mainly on the privileged classes. The Marxist regime hardened in the face of local separatist movements, the intervention of foreign powers, and a war with Poland in 1920. Many members of the intelligentsia emigrated, and some of those who remained turned against the Revolution that they had anticipated for so long, and often with sympathy. Tensions were partially relaxed by the introduction of the New Economic Policy in 1921.

Literature in Flux: Acmeism

All the new modernist currents in Europe derived something from symbolism. Even the neorealists had accepted its tendency to probe psychological nuances, and social issues had become less important than the individual. The symbolist emphasis on intuitive comprehension had made a mark on broader cultural developments. A literature devoted to the exploration of the solitary experience arose. Joseph Conrad wrote meticulously realistic observations of the individual confronted with the exotic. Marcel Proust was a neoromantic visionary of inner worlds. But both were heirs of symbolism. Their Russian counterpart was Ivan Bunin, whose works were inward-looking, sometimes exotic, and impressionistic in style. Artistic crafts-manship, likewise under the influence of symbolism, was viewed as an expression of personal traits, and the avant-garde cultivated eccentricities. In this period when Europe had great novelists, however, Russia was better endowed with poets. Boris Pasternak was once a futurist, and Osip Mandelstam was an acmeist. There were, in addition, significant independent poets who belonged to neither school. The postsymbolist era of Russian poetry was the most brilliant in its history, but it was later to be neglected by Soviet historians.

The acmeist school of poetry has been variously described as neorealist and neo-Parnassian, and it had no exact counterpart in the West. It accepted the heritage of symbolism, according to its chief manifesto, but it renounced all mystical aims. The acmeists took as the cornerstone of their common practice the simple depiction of reality, including that of the psyche, without any other-worldly symbolism. The new school was assembled by a lesser poet, Nikolay Gumilev, who himself was much indebted to the French Parnassians. Its numbers were few, but it included two of the greatest poets of twentieth-century Russia, Osip Mandelstam and Anna Akhmatova. Acmeism came into being in a series of steps. The first was the founding of the literary and art magazine *Apollo* by Gumilev and the art historian Sergey Makovsky in 1909. The new periodical replaced the symbolist magazine *The Scales,* which ceased publication in the same year. In 1911 Gumilev organized the Guild of Poets, whose title stressed the notion of craft over priestly communion. In 1912 he pub-lished his manifesto, "Acmeism and the Heritage of Symbolism," in which he called for an end to the nebulousness of German ideas and a new emphasis on French clarity and logic. The models he named for acmeist poetry were Shake-speare, Rabelais, Théophile Gautier, and François Villon.

Insofar as they made man the center of their universe, the acmeists were twen-tieth-century humanists. They also praised such individualist virtues as bravery, honor, and honesty. Gumilev was admired by his contemporaries for returning the quality of "manliness" to Russian poetry. He sometimes imitated the French Parnas-sians in their depictions of ancient Greece and Rome. Mandelstam eulogized in his poems the great accomplishments of artists of all ages, from antiquity to modern times. He was also drawn to the myths of Greece and Rome—for example, in *Tristia* (1922)—but without the direct inspiration of the Parnassians. Akhmatova at first espoused a narrow range of intimate themes, particularly the bittersweet pains of love. In *Anno Domini MCMXXI* (1921) she turned to such themes as citizenship, love of country, and the destiny of the nation. The acmeists generally claimed to esteem clarity. They also had a graphic, or painterly, emphasis that had been seen among the Parnassians. The tenor of the times made the aims of acmeism congenial to a wider spectrum of writers, some of whom remained outside the school. The acmeists anticipated some aspects of the imagist program that would be put forth by Ezra Pound in England.

Acmeist poetry did not entirely conform, however, to the aims outlined in their manifestos. Lyrical impulses were stronger in their poems than their doctrinal statements would suggest. In fact, the major acmeists all named Innokenty An-nensky, a decadent without mystical nostalgia, as their closest mentor. Annensky was a symbolist more in the French than in the Russian tradition. Gumilev's "manliness" was accompanied by a flirtation with decadence, and he sometimes posed as a dandy. While Mandelstam praised the achievements of the past, he was also sensitive to an existential sadness and to current evils; they were the reason he called his best book *Tristia*. The clarity that the acmeists extolled in their articles was in practice no more than an absence of other-worldliness. Instead, they evoked the mysteries of everyday and worldly life. Mandelstam's poems are often built on audacious metaphors, and symbols are everywhere at hand; his meanings are sometimes so closely interwoven as to approach impenetrability. Akhmatova's poems have in them the silent, unarticulated transitions of colloquial language, and she wrote as a modest "everywoman." In fact, she was an impressionist in that she allowed tangible objects to represent unspoken thoughts. Acmeism had no political program, but it did not survive long after the Revolution. In 1921 Gumilev was executed on suspicion of being a monarchist conspirator.

Gumilev

The poetry of Nikolay Gumilev (1886–1921) was in many respects more romantic than realistic. He introduced into Russian poetry the exhilaration of high adventure and danger met in distant lands, especially Africa. He discovered, like Conrad in Western prose, the dark continents of the planet and of the apparently brave spirit. His notes of decadence, his dandyism, and his early ironies were all but overlooked by many of his first readers. He began to publish his books of verse in 1905, but reached the peak of his powers in *The Quiver* (1916), where his war poems appeared. He published nine books in all. The decadence in his early verse was apparently not to be taken seriously. He also displayed a conventional faith in Orthodoxy and humility. But he began to discern a real evil in the primitive ways of Africa and other exotic areas. In the later poetry, his "manliness" lay in the capacity to face philosophical questions. He was an active literary critic. A number of plays and short stories written in his early period appeared in posthumous collections.

Gumilev devoted his life to the creation of a new direction for Russian poetry. He believed that spiritual matters are rooted in the concrete world. He was an organizer, like Briusov, and a sensible, but didactic, critic. He was born in Kronstadt, the son of a naval officer. He studied literature under Annensky at his lyceum in Tsarskoe Selo and called his first book of verse *The Path of the Conquistadors* (1905). Having studied French literature at the Sorbonne in 1907 and 1908, he returned to St. Petersburg in 1909 to cofound the magazine *Apollo*. In 1910 he married a fellow poet, Anna Akhmatova, and in 1911 he organized the Guild of Poets, which included Akhmatova, Mandelstam, Sergey Gorodetsky, and others. In the same year, he made his first trip to Africa and collected folk songs in Abyssinia. In his manifesto, "The Heritage of Symbolism and Acmeism," he spoke of an attentiveness to reality, but not of "realism." In 1913 he went to Somaliland with a group sent by the Museum of Anthropology and Ethnology. One month after the entry of Russia into World War I, he volunteered as an officer in the army. He was divorced by Akhmatova in 1918 and remarried. In 1921 he was arrested and charged with participation in a counterrevolutionary plot and executed by a firing squad.

The youthful fantasies that fill Gumilev's first two books, *The Path of the Conquistadors* and *Romantic Flowers* (1909), are dramatic and picturesque. He depicted confrontations between lovers, enemies, and stubborn rivals. In the first poem of *The Path of the Conquistadors* he is a conqueror following a star, surely on a path to love, and through storms. His air of bravura is maintained in other poems that depict Zarathustra, Fingal, Pan, and similar spirited male figures of myth and fiction. He was drawn to scenes of violence and stories of Gothic horrors, but he also described symbols of purity and perfection. Much of his imagery came from fairy tales; some poems are about kings, queens, knights, or water nymphs. In *Romantic Flowers* he introduced the tropical scenes—panthers, giraffes, and fla-mingos—that are characteristic of a modern decadence. In new moods he was tempted by self-indulgent sins and obsessed with death. He favored the vagaries of the human spirit and life's odd moments. He resembled Briusov in his poetic audacity and in his amoralism. In both early books, he allowed himself to be guided by a sense of literary play and harmless, imitative posing. He was particularly indebted to French poetry.

He was broader in cultural scope, but sadder and more pessimistic, in his next two books, *Pearls* (1910) and *An Alien Sky* (1912). In *Pearls* he was newly intro-spective and prone to dwell on his defeats, whether in love or in his contests with fate. Religious poems also appeared; in "The Gates of Paradise" he castigates the rich and the proud, and embraces modesty and humility:

> Not with seven seals that shine with diamonds
> Is the lofty gate to heaven locked,
> Neither does it tempt with light or pageant,
> And the passing people know it not.
>
> Just a door within a wall abandoned—
> Rocks and moss, and nothing more around—
> Nearby sits, as though unasked, a beggar,
> But the keys are hanging at his belt.
>
> Knights walk past him, so do men with armor,
> Trumpets blare and silver strings resound.
> But no looks are cast upon the keeper.
> Peter, the apostle blessed, is shunned.
>
> For they dream: it's at my Lord's Tomb, vaulted,
> Heaven's gate will open up for me.
> At the very foothills of Mount Tabor—
> There the clock will strike my promised hour.
>
> Thus the monster-crowd walks by at leisure,
> Trumpets wail and echo far around,
> While Apostle Peter in his tatters
> Sits as though a beggar, poor and pale.

In other poems he describes male figures, such as Dante, Don Juan, and Odysseus, who are more complicated than those in the early books. His famous depictions of derring-do, a series of poems in praise of explorers called "Captains," appears near the end of the book. *An Alien Sky* includes his first personal impressions of Africa, which he had begun to describe even before he was able to visit the continent. Both books seem to suggest that he felt caught in impasses and dilemmas.

In his mature books, which began with *The Quiver*, Gumilev's tendency to literary play and pretense was much diminished. His mythical and historical subjects were newly examined in a contemporary perspective. In "Perseus" Canova's statue of the ever victorious hero is described with irony. Perseus, who slew the Medusa and rescued Andromeda from a sea monster, now holds the head of the Medusa before him so that he cannot see its transformation: "Not he, whose soul is swept by storms, / How lovely now, and O, how human / Her eyes that had once caused but fright." Perseus is pursued by his successes: "And after him, afar, flies Victory, / For she has, like the hero, wings." Gumilev's travel impressions are included in this book. He describes Italy both in its present scenes, such as taverns, and in the Middle Ages, which he regarded, following Leconte de Lisle, as a decline from the enlightenment of pagan times. Gumilev's war poems tend to be sober and more realistic. They are morally uplifting in that they express his belief that war's dangers are conducive to spiritual growth and Christian piety. He resigns himself courageously to his fate, but in some poems, such as "The Bird," he embodies the soldier's fear.

In *The Campfire* (1918) Gumilev's subjects did not change, but they led more often to philosophical questions. In the volume's first poem, called "Trees," he discerns a moral life in unspoiled nature:

> I know that trees were given, no, not us,
> That life which is perfection and is grandeur.
> We live on this sweet earth as though abroad,
> This sister to the stars, but they are native.
>
> When stubble fields are wet with autumn's pall,
> Then copper-crimson sunsets and rich amber
> Mornings teach their colors' arts to them—
> Those airy, green, and freedom-loving nations.
>
> And there are Moses-trees among the oaks
> And Marys who are palms . . . they must in spirit
> Send quiet greetings, each to every one
> Upon hid water flowing in the darkness.
>
> And in the depths of earth, while honing gems
> Or crumbling granite, prating springs run onward
> And sing, or shout—where, broken, falls an elm,
> Where sycamores have donned their leafy clothing.
>
> I wish that I could also find a land
> Where I, with neither weeping nor with singing,
> Would only rise in silence to the heights,
> While there would pass millennia uncounted.

In the poems that follow, nature is often depicted as surpassing mankind also in ardor as well. Man, meanwhile, is tied to his physical existence. Russia's history and countryside are the subjects of new travel scenes. Although Gumilev believed Russia to be close to nature and to God, he portrayed a Rasputin in "The Peasant." In the Scandinavian lands, he sensed a nebulous metaphysical threat, as had Leconte de Lisle.

After the Revolution, Gumilev was ever more fascinated by an abstract evil and drawn to philosophical puzzles. *The Tent* (1924) embodies a spiritual nadir; its poems, all written in 1918, are all set in Africa. The animals he portrays are predators and victims, however picturesque they and their surrounding landscapes might be. *The Porcelain Pavilion* (1918) consists of paraphrases of Chinese and Indonesian lyrics; in these exercises Gumilev escaped from painful thoughts and turned to dispassionate pictures of fragile and artificial beauties. In his last book, *The Pillar of Fire* (1921), Gumilev confronted the question not asked in the acmeist aesthetic: What is, in fact, the relationship of the material world to the spiritual? He tried to discover the soul in the context of the body and reality. In "The Sixth Sense" man's agonies are perhaps like the pain of an insect in its metamorphosis to more mature forms:

> Once, in a place that's overgrown with reeds,
> There cried aloud from knowing it was helpless—
> A slimy creature, feeling on its back
> The wings that time alone would bring to being.

The book includes "The Runaway Streetcar," a frightening, dreamlike collage of travel scenes and literary allusions in which is own bloody head is displayed among others that are for sale, like cabbages, in a vegetable stall.

Gumilev's *oeuvre* has been relatively unappreciated, but he was an innovative poet, and his perspectives on poetry were generally good. His style was somewhat labored; it lacks the felicity that can attract the casual reader and create its own audience. His short stories and his plays have remained outside the mainstream of Russian literature. Most of his dozen stories appeared in his early years and reflect his decadent and exotic tendencies. He depicted unusual loves and passions, violent or mysterious deaths, and remote, sometimes African, settings. The stories were collected in a volume called *The Shadow of the Palm* in 1922. His six plays, of which most were published between 1912 and 1918, are all in verse. Their heroes include Don Juan; Acteon, who admired the goddess Diana; and Hafiz, a Persian poet. "The Poisoned Tunic" describes a rivalry between the wife and the daughter of the emperor Justinian in the sixth century A.D. A narrative poem for children, called *Mik* (1918), describes a small Abyssinian prince and his baboon in their encounter with a French child, Louis. Gumilev's approximately forty reviews are all about the works of his fellow poets.

Akhmatova

The fate of intimate poetry, especially love lyrics, in Russia is exemplified in the career of Anna Akhmatova (real surname: Gorenko; 1889–1966). Her first two books are devoted almost entirely to love, particularly to its unhappy failures. She was an innovative poet who had no obvious predecessors, although she learned from Annensky. In her early verse, she seemed to be the ideal embodiment of acmeism; her poems were devoted to worldly subjects, and her style was unassuming and apparently lucid. But her simplicity was deceptive. She created a new stylized manner reminiscent of novels and popular songs. She had a capacity for understatement reminiscent of Pushkin's, and in later years she became a Pushkin scholar. Between 1912 and 1921 she published five volumes of verse. She responded in her later poems to World War I, the civil war, the Stalinist purges, and World War II. She was seldom able to publish after 1921. A cycle called *Requiem*, which was written during the purges of the 1930s, was first published in the West. In the Thaw period she became, in part because of her intimate verse, an idol of the dissent movement and a model to young poets. Among her later works is an unfinished but widely known long poem called *Poem Without a Hero*.

Akhmatova thought of poetry as a high and exacting art, but the popular elements in her style made her a celebrity. She was born in Kherson on the Black Sea, schooled at Tsarskoe Selo, and regarded St. Petersburg as virtually her native city. She attended Ivanov's "Tower" salon, and in 1910 she married Gumilev. She saw in the acmeist aesthetic not only an artistic program but also a pledge of personal honor. She lived briefly in Paris, where she knew the young Modligliani. Her son, Lev, was born in 1912. In the same year she published her first collection, *Evening*. *The White Flock* (1917) includes some poems on her sentiments as a citizen. She divorced Gumilev in 1918 and married an Assyriologist, Vladimir Shileiko. Her son was arrested twice during the 1930s and her common-law husband, the art historian Nikolay Punin, once. During World War II she was evacuated as a prominent writer to Tashkent, and her poems began to appear in magazines after her return to Moscow. In 1946 she was ousted from the Union of Writers, as was the satirist Mikhail Zoshchenko, after critical attacks initiated by the Secretary of the Central Committee, Andrey Zhdanov. She made poetic versions of translations from Eastern languages, which she did not know. In 1958 a limited selection of poems, *The Course of Time*, appeared. She received an honorary degree from Oxford University in the year before her death. The poetry of the years 1926 to 1964 came out posthumously, as did her academic articles on Pushkin.

Her first two books include not only poems about love but also affectionately drawn cityscapes and some poems about art or about writers. Beginning with the appearance of *Evening*, her love poetry was described as a fresh view of the subject from a woman's vantage point. In fact, it is only the circumstances that are described as a woman's; the simple disappointments, and sometimes joys, that she evokes are universal. It was an innovation, however, that she wrote so unnervingly often about love's losses and regrets. "The Song of the Last Meeting" is her most widely known early poem:

> Then my heart turned to ice—I was helpless,
> But my steps as I walked were as light,
> And the glove that I took from my left hand
> I, unknowingly, put on my right.
>
> And the stairs from the porch seemed so many,

But I knew there were only three!
In the maples a whisper of autumn
Begged a favor: "Come die with me!—

I've been wronged by a sad and gloomy,
By a treacherous, evil fate."
And I answered, "O my dearest, dearest,
I was, too—I'll come die with you. . . ."

That's the song of our last, sad meeting.
I looked back at the house in the dark—
In the bedroom alone there burned candles,
With their yellow, indifferent flame.

Many of Akhmatova's poems seem, like this one, to be dramatic moments ex-cerpted from long fictions. She was further prosaic in that she did not idealize love or lovers. They are recognized as transient, and plural. Her poems about love are also apparently impersonal in that they do not cohere to make an Akhmatova "story." Each poem, so autobiographical in appearance, is separate. Her cityscapes were probably more candid; she describes in them the buildings and parks that were familiar parts of her life. Akhmatova always spoke of her own writing in terms of a stern and demanding muse. In "To the Muse" her inspiration has "taken away my gold ring."

In *The Rosary* (1914) her subjects are familiar, but her way of life has changed. She has become acquainted with an artistic bohemia whose tawdriness she professes to detest. A religious sense of guilt has appeared, which makes her speak of insomnia, suicides, and the possibility of hell. She has acquired a fame that is useless to her. In "He who indirectly praised me" she recalls her girlhood on the beach at Kherson and wants "Not to know that in fame and good fortune / Is the agent that withers the heart." The demands that her calling as an artist place on her is apparently the subject of a narrative poem, *At the Seashore* (1914), in which she again recalls her youth in Kherson. She portrays an athletic tomboy who cares only for swimming and singing and who rejects the love of a "gray-eyed boy." Her destined prince is brought to her only as he is dying. The scene is tragic, but the season is Easter. This poem exemplifies quite well the folkloric elements that are an undercurrent of many of Akhmatova's works. In general, her poems are curiously disciplined to color; she works with a muted canvas of black, white, and gray, on which she occasionally splashes a bright yellow or red.

Akhmatova's sternness with herself is a link between her intimate and her public themes. The two spheres appear side by side in *The White Flock*. Her first statement of public concern in this book is "July 1914," an ominous depiction of a drought. Other poems are set in wartime; in some she speaks of the loss of a man through war—a husband, a lover, a son. She drew stark contrasts between peacetime and wartime. In "That voice which argues with great quiet" she recalls the unsuspecting prewar years. The bohemian ways of earlier St. Petersburg seem reprehensible to her in the new context, as she wrote in "For somewhere there's a simple life, and light." The "white flock" of the title turns out to be her own poems in "I don't know if you live or have perished"; they are pure but hover like doves above disasters. Her first poems about the civil war appeared in *The Plantain Weed* (1921), but most of them reappeared in *Anno Domini MCMXXI.* She declares her decision not to emigrate in "When in suicidal anguish." She perceives, however, the contrast between Russia and the West:

> What makes our age seem worse than those before it? Maybe
> It came 'midst fumes of anguish and alarms
> And touched upon our sorest, blackest ulcer
> But brought no cure, no healing balm.
>
> Behold the Western world, the sun above keeps shining,
> Its city roofs reflect the brilliance of its rays,
> But here the void already marks our homes with crosses
> And beckons to the ravens, and the ravens come.

Anno Domini MCMXXI also includes new love poems in which marriages and alliances have replaced the bohemian art world. Her style was ever drier and more aphoristic. Some poems end with a simple graphic image; a "redbreasted bird" sits on the bronze statue of Venus at the conclusion of "In my mind I still see hilly Pavlovsk." These terse endings recall the poems of the art-for-art's-sake poet Afanasy Fet and of his French counterpart, Verlaine.

Because Akhmatova's subsequent lyrics were not published when they were written, they were subject to her revisions over the years. They are generally less stylized than the early poems and more visibly autobiographical. The posthumous canon includes a cycle called "The Reed Pipe," written between 1924 and 1940. In several of these poems, she recalled again her years in Kherson. She wrote to and about her colleagues in literature, Boris Pasternak, Osip Mandelstam, and Vladimir Maiakovsky. She used literary allusions as sources of personal symbols. She wrote about Dante as an exile, and in a poem of 1924 called "The Muse" she saw her art, or world, as an extension of Dante's:

> When I await at night for her arrival
> It seems my life is hanging on a thread.
> For what are honors, what is youth, or freedom
> Before this guest with panpipes in her hand?
>
> And now she comes. She's cast aside her veiling
> She looks with full attention in my eyes.
> I say to her: "Did you dictate to Dante
> *Inferno*'s pages? And she answers: "I."

In another poem Cleopatra is described as a suicide. A cycle is devoted to the Crucifixion and Christ's role as a redeemer.

In *Requiem,* whose poems are dated 1935 to 1940, she speaks both for herself and for a nation. She explains in a prose introduction of 1957 that the book arose from a request. She once stood in a line before a prison window where relatives could receive information about arrestees. One of the other women in that line asked whether she could record this experience. *Requiem* was her response. The lyrics are about hearing a judicial sentence read, about waiting to learn fates, about longing for death and fearing insanity. She describes Mary during the Crucifixion. The political daring of these poems recalls the rebel poems of Pushkin and of André Chenier.

Another cycle, called "The Seventh Book," forms an impressionistic autobiography of the period from the late 1930s to 1964. The opening poems are devoted to art and artists, including Pushkin and Mandelstam, as though in retrospect her poetry seems to have played the most significant role in her life. A group of poems called "In 1940" is about the wartime attacks on Paris and London. The siege of Leningrad is described in the poems of "The Winds of War." The exotic world of Tashkent is reflected in "The Moon at Zenith." The East is seen as an unchanging land of strange traditions, of Scheherazade, Biblical landscapes, warmth, and tropical fruits. After Tashkent a Soviet life opens up; its signs are tobacco, loneliness, fog, the relics of the war, and conflicting feelings of guilt and loyalty.

Akhmatova believed her masterpiece to be the long work called *Poem Without a Hero,* which is both narrative and lyric. It occupied her from 1940 to 1963 and was published posthumously. Its subject is an obsessive vision of the year 1913 in St. Petersburg as it appeared to her during the siege of Leningrad in 1940. She regrets again the sins of her bohemian life and hopes to expiate some unidentified guilt. Her former companions appear in a New Year's masquerade; at the center of these memories is a suicide at the time of a conflagration. The poem is brought to a tranquil conclusion in the refuge of Tashkent. The poem seems to record the passage of an extraordinary and irrational emotional wave. Its inspirations lie deep, but the work is flawed by the nebulousness of an implied connection between the sins of 1913 and the hardships of 1940.

Akhmatova has continued to be known primarily for her early poems and for *Requiem.* For all the distress that these works record, they seem dictated by an instinct to return to balance. They are moral poems in that they embody courage. Their impersonal character, gained through their prosaic, or popular, stylization, helps to guarantee their acceptance as universal. The later works are less compelling. They are less broadly motivated, and their wellspring sometimes appears to have been less wholesome, or even self-serving, although guilt is more prominent in them.

Mandelstam

A poet unmatched in his generation for the breadth of his cultural interests was Osip Mandelstam (1891–1938). He particularly admired the world of Greek and Roman antiquity, but he praised the accomplishments of the human spirit in every age. His subject was the legacy of European culture in the eyes of modern man. He published little more than two small volumes of verse, *The Stone* (1913), and *Tristia* (1921), yet he is one of the two greatest Russian poets in the twentieth century. His predecessors include such metaphysical poets as Tiutchev and Viacheslav Ivanov. His own poetry had a philosophical dimension. He was an acmeist in that he described man's achievements as monuments, in terms of their physical presence. He sought to represent man's perception of himself in the universe. He believed in the force of a primordial love, and he recognized that life is characteristically sad. His later, posthumously published, lyrics are pessimistic; they sometimes reflect his hatred for the authoritarian regimes that arose in the era between the wars. He wrote several volumes of autobiographical prose in which he describes the people he knew and the tenor of his times.

Mandelstam wanted his own poetry to be a monument that would bear witness to future generations of a life in his age. He was born into a Jewish family in Warsaw and reared in St. Petersburg. He spent one year in Paris and another in Heidelberg, studying Old French literature in 1909 and 1910. On his return to Russia in 1911, he entered St. Petersburg University, joined the Guild of Poets, and was baptized as a Methodist. *The Stone* established him as a poet of exceptional promise in 1913. After the Revolution his fear of arrest led him to live for long periods in the south. In Kiev he married Nadezhda Khazine, an art student who was to preserve his unpublished poems and become his biographer. He also lived in the Crimea, usually in Theodosia, and in Georgia. During the 1920s he turned to autobiographical prose because of the difficulty of publishing his poetry. His prose includes a fictionalized account of his youth, a description of his life in Theodosia, and a record of a journey to Armenia in 1930. In 1934 he was exiled for having written an anti-Stalin epigram, which was circulated in manuscript. In 1935 he was given the right to live in a larger city and settled in Voronezh. He lived in great poverty, having no legal means of support. He was arrested on May 1, 1938, and died in a distant prison camp in December of that year.

Mandelstam's earliest poems in *The Stone* are simple, primitive philosophical statements; his culturally resonant manner developed in time. In his first poems he records, for example, elementary discoveries about the self in the physical world: "I am as bare and poor as nature," he says in "The sharp ear makes its sail more taut." In "Silentium" (1910) he posited the existence of a universal love; he adores the as yet unborn Aphrodite in the sea as a primordial principle: she is the link of living things and the origin of music and words. His title, "Silentium," is a reference to the lyric in which Tiutchev spoke of the inexpressibility of first things. In other poems Mandelstam discovers an existential sadness, which he compares to a "grey, wounded bird" or a "cloudy, universal pain." Love and pain thereafter became the polar opposites of his vision. In later poems the historical achievements of European culture are viewed within their parameters. Mankind has never changed, in his view. Here is his homage to the cathedral of Hagia Sophia in Constantinople:

> Hagia Sophia—here's where God did order
> All nations and all kings to halt their march!
> For is your dome, as has a witness stated,
> Not hung as though from heaven on a chain.

> For ages all, Justinian is a model,
> Since he did seize, and that for alien gods—
> And Ephesus' Diana did allow it—
> One hundred seven columns of green stone.

But what the thoughts of your most generous builder
When he, sublime in soul and in his plans,
Did draw the lines for apses and exedrae
Directing them to west and to the east?

The temple's splendid, all in peace enfolded,
Its forty panes a victory of light.
Four archangels, beneath the dome depicted,
On pendentives, surpass the rest in art.

And so the building, round and full of wisdom
Will outlast every nation, every age,
And seraphim with all their sobs resounding
Will ever warp the darkened gilt on walls.

Mandelstam was also to praise Notre Dame in Paris and the Admiralty Building in St. Petersburg. His eulogies of buildings were for his readers the natural consequence of the acmeists' common reverence for craft, design, and effort. Mandelstam seldom described landscapes, but nature played a role in his philosophy. It reminded him, in any case, of the creations of the spirit. In "The woods have orioles, and length as seen in vowels" (1914) a lazy summer day is compared to the caesura of Homer's poetry. More important, Mandelstam believed, as he wrote in "Our nature is but Rome, and can be seen in it" (1914), that nature is the constant model for civilization and that it ever provides the tools with which to build. Mandelstam's concern with the past was also not so much for itself as for its capacity to serve as a model. His laudatory poems for Bach, Beethoven, and the *Odyssey*, for example, usually include his own interpretive comments. The Trojan War, he believes, was fought for Helen; she stood, like Aphrodite, for an unarticulated, omnipresent love that moves both history and nature.

The poems of *Tristia* describe a more personal experience of the world and some are more specific in time, but they are greater and more stimulating works. New subjects appeared among the forty-three poems, written between 1916 and 1920. In one love poem, "Solominka" (1916), passion is equated, as in the traditional metaphor, with dying. But Russia looms largest as a new concern. In 1916 Mandelstam described Moscow's Italianate architecture in the Kremlin as evidence of Russia's kinship with the Mediterranean. Later, the Revolution appears and is followed by a period of apprehensiveness about death and terror. Yet there are few political poems. In 1917 he wrote in "At ghastly heights a wandering fire is seen to glow" that the city of Petersburg-Petropolis is dying, but without any explanation. In "The twilight of freedom" (dated May 1918) his meaning is veiled; he pictures citizens as they strive to rule an all but sinking ship of state, harnessing swallows that obscure the sun. "With ten heavens we have paid the price for earth," he concludes. The piece is followed by the title poem, "Tristia" (1918), in which an ancient citizen departs reluctantly for war:

I've had to learn the science of departures
Through loose-haired grieving that is done at night.
The oxen chew and waiting lasts forever—

Until the city vigils' final hour.
And I respect that cockerel night's whole ritual,
When eyes that have been crying look afar,
And lift the sorrows of the road as burden,
When women's sobs are mixed with muse's songs.

For who can say at this one word—departure—
What kind of separation it will be,
And what the cockerel's exclamations promise
When flames in the acropolis do rise.
And at the dawn of some new life before us,
When lazily the ox chews in his shed,
Why does the herald of new life, the cockerel,
Stand on the city wall and beat his wings?

And I do love the common act of spinning,
The shuttle darts, and then the spindle hums.
But look, she comes, as though she were but swansdown,
Already Delia, barefoot, comes on wings!
O, meager is the basis of our being.
How poor our words for joy have ever been!
All went before, all will be once returning,
Just recognition's instant we find sweet.

So let it be—a small, transparent figure
Upon a clean and earthen dish does lie,
As though it were a squirrel skin extended—
Above this wax a maiden bends and stares.
It's not for us Greek Erebus to question.
For women wax, but bronze must serve for men.
Our fate is known when we have joined in battle,
But they, still telling fortunes, meet their death.

The southern lands, as sites of ancient cultures, are usually reassuring. The Georgian countryside reminds him, in 1917, of Odysseus and Penelope; Theodosia is a simple, pastoral town. Yet many poems are devoted to the theme of death. He holds this subject at a distance by speaking of it in terms of Greek myths, in references to Proserpine, to asphodels, to Lethe, to dead or blind swallows, to bees and libations of honey. The theme enters into his thoughts about country, love, history, culture, and politics. Death holds even the vibrant life of a southern culture in its frozen grasp: in "Of Venetian life, that's dark and sterile" (1920) he describes a mirror image whose frame is of cypress, ancient glass that has turned blue, and life now stilled in its "love and fear." Mandelstam believed, however, that the mythic traditions were still vital in northern theaters, although they were surrounded by snow. In "We will meet again in Petersburg" (1920) he is certain that the "blessed women" and the "meaningless word" will survive the "black velvet" of the Soviet night—because spiritual life cannot be harmed by mere physical repression. In poems near the end of the volume, the churches of St. Petersburg are a source of courageous faith.

Twenty new poems of an abruptly different character appeared in an expanded version of *Tristia* called *Poems* (1928); they were written between 1921 and 1925. The first of these pieces, "Concert at the Station" (1921), describes a grand, glass railroad station whose inner hum is the last "music" of civilization. He seldom mentions the history of culture thereafter, and Classical or Biblical allusions are rare. The poems describe a land of huts and tribal conditions. In "For some the winter brings home-brew and blue-eyed punch bowls" (1922) he speaks of treasuring for himself the warmth of "chicken dung" and "senseless sheep." In "The Age" (1923) a beast with a broken spine looks back at its useless legs. He describes himself as the cast-off shoe of a once-proud race horse in "He Who Finds a Horseshoe" (dated Moscow, 1923). And in "The Slate-Pencil Ode" (1923) he writes in mountains where goats climb. In one slight poem of 1923, a mosquito begs fate for a personal name with which to enter "Into the pregnant and deep blue." In several of the late poems, Mandelstam describes an empty sky with hostile stars.

Mandelstam kept his later, posthumously published poems in documents called the Moscow Notebook and the Voronezh Notebooks. Both collections include finished poems as well as some that are obviously trivial or experimental. His great poverty, his rancor, and his fears for his own life are abundantly clear in these pieces. His new concerns are pragmatic, and his former generous admiration for man's achievements is absent, although he still alludes at times to myths and history. He contrasts ancient Rome with modern Italy, dominated by fascism and tyranny. Without altering his philosophical views, he became pessimistic about possibilities. He still believed that mankind needs poetry; in "I'm caught within a spiderweb of light" (1937) he complains that he is distracted by the vastness of the Caucasian mountains and sky. Many of the Voronezh poems are marked by a deep ambivalence toward the flat, expansive landscapes of the steppes.

Mandelstam's autobiographical prose is crisply written, usually circumstantial, and not intended to be introspective. Its glancing style is perhaps revealing of its times. Although it is autobiographical, the prose lacks the intimate intensity of the poetry. *The Noise of Time* (1925) describes his childhood and school years in the 1890s and 1900s. In 1928 came *The Egyptian Stamp*, which includes "The Noise of Time" as well as a title story about a young writer, much like himself, called Parnok. The last part of the book is "Theodosia," an account of the Crimea during the civil war. *A Journey to Armenia* (1933) is close to a journalistic record. *The Fourth Prose* was published posthumously.

In its total effect Mandelstam's *oeuvre* is uplifting. The intelligence with which he faces both existential and historical realities is refreshing. His early poems suggest a sense of harmony with the universe. In his later poems, there is a tension that seems to arise from an offended sense of honor. His style is densely metaphorical, but always convincing. He shared with Paul Valéry a capacity to blend erudition with lyricism.

Independent Poets

The acmeist group looms large because of the great names attached to it, but it did not include all the moderate and neorealist poets of the era. There were also lesser poets who were the contemporaries of the symbolists, but whose verse had remained more traditional than theirs. These conservative poets had rejected mysticism during its heyday, they belonged to no group, and they had remained relatively unnoticed. When they also wrote about worldly life, or pictured concrete beauties in their verse, they resembled the acmeists. Among them was Maksimilian Voloshin (1877–1932), who wrote a small body of distinguished neorealist lyrics. He is now remembered chiefly for some later works, such as *The Deaf-Mute Demons* (1919), in which he decries the brutalities of the civil war. In all, he published six volumes of poems between 1910 and 1923. Voloshin was a Russian aristocrat who resided for many years in Paris. He was reared in an intellectual enclave in the southern Crimea and traveled in the West as a young man. In 1900 he was arrested and exiled for six months to Central Asia. After his release he moved to Paris, but he sometimes visited Russia, where he had ties with the symbolists, and he continued to travel throughout the Mediterranean. His first political poems were in response to the 1905 Revolution; he began to protest against violence in a book about World War I called *Anno mundi ardentis 1915* (1916). After 1917 he returned to his mother's estate near Koktebel in the Crimea. His home became a refuge for literary and artistic people of any political persuasion. He was unable to publish after 1923.

In his early poems Voloshin responds simply and directly to the world around him. He describes the scenes and events that he witnessed at home and on travels. His early cycles have such titles as "Paris," "The Cathedral at Rouen," and "Cimmerian Twilight" (the Cimmerians inhabited the Crimea before the Scythians.) His depictions give rise to brief, nostalgic reflections on history, philosophy, and culture. His poetry was more French in its roots than Russian; he acknowledged the influence of the Parnassians, particularly that of José María de Heredia. He was fond of Koktebel and its environs, which he described in somber landscapes at the seaside. Among them is the following poem of 1910:

> Frosty, gray, and brief, the day flared and ended,
> And the surf turned white—when it kissed the shoreline.
> Sobbing as they come, the waves toss up tatters—
> Wings out of spindrift.
> Meekness now embraces the heart. In silence.
> Thoughts do softly perish. An orchard olive
> Lifts aloft its branches to blind, mute heavens.
> Slaves make such gestures.

The rugged cliffs near Koktebel are described in several poems; he admired their weather-beaten vegetation, their tough grass and colorful moss. Voloshin shared with the Parnassians their atheism and pessimistic philosophy, but he took his subjects more often from the present than from the past. His early poetry was sometimes dispassionate and cold, but he was also curious and physically active.

Voloshin's repugnance toward violence gave rise in his later poems to a general religious awakening. He found a sense of Christian mission in himself, and he portrayed Russia as seized by evil powers and turned aside from its spiritual destiny. The civil war is described not only in *The Deaf-Mute Demons* but also in *Poems*

About the Terror (1923). The latter book concludes with an ironic cycle called "The Ways of Cain." In other, less topical and more philosophical poems, he wrote about sin, justice, citizenship, and the place of man in the universe. His style in the late poems is at times declamatory and at times solemn or Biblical.

One poet of the older generation who shared the literary stage with both symbolists and acmeists was Mikhail Kuzmin (1875–1936). He resembled the decadents in his idealization of artistic beauty, but he wrote as a hedonist, or epicurean, and might be called a neoclassicist. He was a prolific author of poetry, prose, and dramas. Kuzmin was born in Yaroslavl and attended St. Petersburg University. His early years were spent in religious quests to Egypt, Italy, and the sites of the Old Believer sects in northern Russia. He settled in St. Petersburg, where he contributed to Diaghilev's *World of Art* and later to the symbolists' magazine, *The Scales*. He resided at one time in Ivanov's "Tower" apartment. In 1907 he published a controversial novel, *Wings,* some of whose characters are homosexual. An article called "On Beautiful Clarity," which appeared in *Apollo* in 1910, is regarded as one of the manifestos of acmeism. He was active in the bohemian world of little theaters and had especially close ties with the cabaret called the Stray Dog. He was an accomplished artist and musician, having studied with Rimsky-Korsakov, and he sometimes illustrated his own lyrics or set them to music. He remained in the Soviet Union after the Revolution but published less creative work after 1923 and turned increasingly to literary criticism.

Kuzmin's poetry is somewhat stylized: he wrote as the epicurean whose taste is unsurpassed, and who is a dandy. He speaks throughout for the freedom to seek and talk about pleasure. His subjects include love, art, and religion, and he is acquainted with religious ecstasy. His principal theme in all his books is love. His first collection, *Nets* (1908), also has in it a nostalgia that comes of world-weariness. *Nets* includes a well-known cycle called "Alexandrian Songs," whose poems are written as though by an inhabitant of the ancient Egyptian city; he sometimes speaks of his homosexual love. This is his evocation of his metropolis, written, it seems, from memory. (The poem is written in free verse.)

> The sky at twilight on a tepid ocean,
> The fires of lighthouses in the darkened heavens,
> The smell of verbena when feasts are over,
> The freshness of dawns come after long "vigils,"
> A walk through the rows of a vernal orchard,
> The cries and the laughter of bathing women,
> The sacred peacocks at Juno's temple,
> Vendors of violets, pomegranates and lemons,
> The doves make their cooing, the sun is shining,
> O, when shall I see you, my native city!

When the speaker describes his lover, he uses the graphic details—gray eyes, dark eyebrows—that were typical of classical verse. Kuzmin enjoyed writing outright stylizations, and he often parodied the genres of the eighteenth century, an era of classical literature. His next book, called *The Carillon of Love* (1910), consists entirely of pastoral idylls, all of which he set to music. *Lakes in Autumn* (1912) also includes imitations of seventeenth-century "spiritual verse."

Kuzmin followed his own path after the Revolution and somewhat expanded his range. *The Guide* (1918) bears the name of the angel-like figure who symbolized for him the inner freedom to choose one's love. *Draped Pictures* (1920) contains humorous erotic poems in the spirit of eighteenth-century libertinism. His best collection is *Unearthly Evenings* (1923), where he wrote not only on love but also on life's purpose, on death, and on aging. In a section called "Fuji in a Teacup" there are some poems inspired by Oriental scenes and art, and another cycle is called "Poems About Italy." The book also contains erotic parodies of religious stories. Kuzmin believed that his masterpiece was a cycle of lyric poems called *The Trout Breaks the Ice* (1929), which is an autobiographical response to the return of a lover from an affair with a woman. Kuzmin's *oeuvre* combines a breathless awe, before love or before beauty, with an underlying note of fatigue, or of cynicism. His work is admittedly narrow. His tone is often light and graceful. His poems share with the art-for-art school of the nineteenth century a tendency toward escapism; evil is kept at a distance.

Kuzmin's prose is addressed to a small, artistically knowledgeable audience. The novel *Wings* describes the flirtations of urban young people in St. Petersburg and Italy; their discussions touch on the history of European culture. *The Adventures of Aimé Leboeuf* (1907) is a stylized imitation of eighteenth-century prose. *Travelers by Land and Sea* (1915) hints at the love intrigues of his contemporary bohemians in St. Petersburg. Kuzmin's dramas are comedies; the best known is *Venetian Madmen* (1915), whose setting is at carnival time in eighteenth-century Italy.

Other poets who remained outside the acmeist group were of the same generation, and similar to them, but bowed to some stronger inclination. Among those poets were Sergey Gorodetsky (1884–1967), whose first interest was in the literary romanticizing of peasant culture. The son of an ethnographer, Gorodetsky was born in St. Petersburg. While a university student, he traveled in the Pskov area observing peasant weddings and seasonal festivities. He was to be, in turn, a symbolist apprentice, an acmeist organizer, a "peasant" poet, and, after 1917, a partisan of the Revolution. He published about a dozen books of poetry and about as many of prose tales, which have never had a wide audience. In 1911 he joined with Gumilev in founding the Guild of Poets. In 1916 he established, with Aleksey Remizov, a publishing house for ethnic literature. He was a war correspondent in the Caucasus during World War I and remained for some years thereafter in the south. He repudiated his former colleague Gumilev when the latter was executed in 1921. During the 1920s Gorodetsky was active in many literary groups in Moscow. In the 1930s he began to appear as a translator.

Gorodetsky's poems are popularizations of the peasant ethos, but he followed literary fashions. His first book of verse, *Spring Sap* (1907), makes use of the cosmic imagery that was typical of some symbolists, especially of Balmont in his pantheistic moods. His opening poems are spoken by the sun, moon, and earth. Abstract principles such as birth, death, and primal kinships, including motherhood, are the speakers in the subsequent poems. His second book, *Perun* (the

name of the Slavic thunder god), was also published in 1907. In this and other books
he devoted many poems to Slavic deities, among them Stribog, the god of wind, and
lesser, and even invented, divinities. In "The Birch Tree" (1906) he describes how
Iarilo, the god of the sun, and Lel', the god of amorous love, bring the spring
season.

> One amber day I fell in love you with,
>   When, born of radiant azure heavens,
>   A languor welled and overflowed
>   From every branch, all being grateful.

> Your ivory trunk gleamed white, like headiness
>   In seething waves that cross lake waters,
>   When merry Lel' did laugh and tug
>   The raven rays that made your tresses.

> And Iarilo himself did lushly crown
>   Their net with sharply pointed foliage,
>   And then he smiled and cast aloft
>   In azure skies your bright green colors.

Gorodetsky's later poems were usually simple depictions of rural life or exercises on
peasant themes—love, nature, the seasons of the year. *Rus* (1910) stands apart
because of its descriptions of fortunetelling and of wedding rituals. *The Willow*
(1910) includes poems about the life of religious wanderers, pilgrims and the world
of monasteries, as well as several children's stories. In *The Year Nineteen Fourteen*
(1915) he depicts war in mythic terms. After the Revolution he extolled peasant
labor in heroic terms, for example in *The Sickle* (1921). He continued to publish
collections of his verse through 1964.

Vladislav Khodasevich (1886–1939) shared the acmeists' relatively conservative approach to poetry, but his outlook on life was more bitter than sad. His work
is filled with a malaise that is characteristic of the twentieth century. His forms,
however, were traditional in the early nineteenth century, and he has been regarded
as a neoclassicist. He was born in Moscow, the son of an artist of Polish descent. He
attended Moscow University, was active in literary circles, and became the friend of
acmeists. In 1920 he moved to Petrograd and is thought to have been a primary
source of a "Petersburg" current in Russian poetry. In 1922 he emigrated and lived
thereafter in Berlin, Prague, Rome, and Sorrento, where he was associated with
Gorky. In 1925 he moved to Paris and joined politically conservative émigré
groups. He eventually became more active as an editor and a literary critic than as a
poet. He was also the author of studies on Pushkin and Derzhavin, and of memoirs.

Khodasevich was unusually concerned in his poetry with the metaphysical injustices and abuses suffered by mankind in the world. He wrote with a cynicism,
and rancor, that separated him from both symbolists and acmeists. His early books,
Youth (1908) and *The Happy Cottage* (1914), are marked by an unwholesome
decadence as well. His ordinary subjects are the banal "horrors" of life: the fears of
youth, the emptiness of the would-be lover, the nebulousness of anxieties, the
inevitable end in death, and the falsity of sentimental social hypocrisy. His imagery

is of city streets, joyless landscapes, and such sights as funerals. These early poems are mannered and imitative.

Khodasevich reached maturity in *The Way of Grain* (1920) and *A Heavy Lyre* (1921). The decadence of his early work is gone, and the traditional style that he adopted is reassuring. *The Way of Grain* opens with some unexpectedly optimistic notes. In the title poem he explains that the rebirth and sprouting of grain in the spring serves as a kind of religious parable for himself. In "The Monkey" he is awakened again to spiritual life by a sign of gratitude from the animal. In subsequent poems he finds it possible to believe in "heaven, earth, love, and work." Nevertheless, his cynical views returned in later poems, which are, moreover, increasingly philosophical in nature. A frequent complaint is the indifference of the soul to the suffering and passions of material life. This poem, dated 1921, is from *The Heavy Lyre*.

The Soul

My soul is like the moon when it is full,
Its light is ever cold and ever clear.

It shines on high, it shines away at will,
And all my tears it never will make dry.

And of my woes it never feels the pain,
And never will it hear my passions's moan,

And how much anguish I have suffered here
My radiant soul thinks not worthwhile to know.

His style is often cool, detached, and somewhat conventional. In his later books, the past is compared favorably with the present. *A Collection of Poems* (1938) includes new poems, but no new departures. His studies of Pushkin are dated 1924 and 1937. In 1931 he published *Derzhavin*, his most esteemed work of literary history. His memoirs are useful; they first appeared in *The Necropolis* (1939).

14

Futurism and the Avant-Garde (1912–1925)

The cultural life of Russia was dominated by war, revolution, and civil war during most of the active years of the avant-garde. Many of its members supported the revolutionary developments with energy and enthusiasm, although others emigrated or became aloof. The successes of Marxism in the prewar period had preceded the aggressive rise to power of the lower classes. Disaffection with the monarchist government was intensified during World War I by the hardships borne by the lower classes. Russia had been so little prepared for war, for example, that in 1915 as many as one-quarter of its troops were sent into battle without weapons, and Russian fronts stretched across central Europe. The Provisional Government, which was established in February 1917, was forced from the beginning to share its power with the Soviets of Workers' and Soldiers' Deputies, and was ousted by them in November. The avant-garde writers were inclined to look with optimism on the new regime, and foremost among them were the futurists, led by Vladimir Maiakovsky. The alliance between the political left and the new art was to disintegrate during the 1920s, however. The essence of the avant-garde everywhere was the expression of the individual vision. Its audience was the privileged classes, and its nonconformist styles were relatively inaccessible to the poorly educated.

The Avant-Garde Factions

The roots of the Russian avant-garde were in the West, but it was in the course of that movement that the Russians ceased to lag behind Europe and became innovative in their turn. The European avant-garde can first be discerned in the graphic arts. It appeared in cubism as it was initiated in Paris in 1907 by Picasso and Braque, for example. The first of the avant-garde groups to be devoted extensively to literature was futurism, which was started in Italy in 1909 by Filippo Marinetti.

Manifestations of Russian avant-garde literature came in 1910, but the word *futurism* was not adopted until 1911, when Igor Severianin assembled poets in a school called ego-futurism. It was the first of the new literary coteries to attain any stability, but it was not the most important. The heart of the Russian literary avant-garde was cubo-futurism, which issued its manifesto, called "A Slap in the Face of Public Taste," in 1912. The name cubo-futurism was chosen to emphasize the close ties the group had with Russian artists. Indeed, many futurists were both writers and painters. Russian artists had, moreover, participated in the evolution of the avant-garde on European soil. Kandinsky, a Russian progenitor of nonobjective art, had resided in Munich since 1896. When Diaghilev founded the Ballets Russes in Paris in 1909, he brought Russian symbolist artists, who collaborated abroad with Picasso, Kandinsky, and others. Some Russian artists had studied abroad. Thus avant-garde art circles had already arisen in Moscow and St. Petersburg.

The factions of the Russian literary avant-garde were hostile to each other, but their programs were relatively ill-defined. Their principles were often more easily and correctly discerned in their practice than in their statements. Ego-futurism remained close to symbolism in that it was prepared to seek the spiritual in art. Its leader, Severianin, had a considerable, but transient popularity. The cubo-futurists were formally brought together by a minor painter, David Burliuk. They disclaimed any influence from the Italian futurists and did indeed differ from them. The Italians idealized technology and speed, whereas the cubo-futurists exhibited a primitivism that was pastoral and idyllic. They chose as *maître d'école* the retiring Velemir Khlebnikov, whose works embodied the utopian idealism common to all the cubo-futurists. Khlebnikov was also a master of nonobjective, or transsense, language. It was Maiakovsky who won the widest popular acceptance for nonconformist attitudes and styles. In 1913 the group mounted a notorious tour of the provinces with readings and provocative stunts. The cubo-futurists collaborated throughout their history with artists. A frequent collaborator, Kasimir Malevich, founded the suprematist school, which features nonobjective paintings utilizing geometric shapes, a manner that was to be popularized by the Bauhaus.

The cubo-futurists were opposed by more moderate avant-garde groups. The Centrifuge school, extant from 1913 to 1917 in Moscow, did not propose to reject the past, as did the cubo-futurists, but it considered the legacy of civilization to be in need of constant renovation. The group will be remembered because Pasternak adhered to it; his innovative poems in *My Sister Life* were known in manuscript in 1918. One of the major avant-garde poets, Marina Tsvetaeva, chose not to join any school. She treasured the cultural heritage, but wrote in styles resembling those of the cubo-futurists, of whom she was a coeval. A group that claimed to be more radical than futurism appeared in Moscow in 1919 and called itself imagism. It was begun, however, by a former futurist, Vadim Shershenevich. The imagists avoided pastoralism and proclaimed the importance of the latent pictures in verbal art. Paradoxically, they attracted to their ranks a leading peasant poet, Sergey Esenin.

After the 1917 Revolution some avant-gardists were inclined to anticipate productive careers in the Soviet Union, but most of these became disillusioned. Khlebnikov's work began to show signs of an ambivalence toward the Revolution before his death in 1922. Maiakovsky, a confirmed communist, tried to accommodate the "dictatorship of the proletariat"; he led the futurists into the Left Front of Literature (LEF, 1922–1927) and endorsed the "literature of fact." But his attempts at compromise (in the New LEF and REF) ended when he had to join the government-sponsored Russian Association of Proletarian Writers (RAPP) in 1930. Other cubofuturists had retired to Georgia; some returned while others emigrated. In the 1920s Pasternak turned from intimate lyrics to narrative poems, epic themes, and prose. By 1932 he had acquired a more accessible lyric style. Marina Tsvetaeva was for almost two decades the major poet of the emigration, but returned to the Soviet Union and committed suicide in 1942. In general, Russian writers were not as fortunate as the painters and musicians who could, like Stravinsky, work abroad. The writers, although often as talented, are also less celebrated now.

Ego-Futurism: Severianin

The ego-futurists were a small group of radical young men who were brought together by a more moderate poet, Igor Severianin, who soon left them. The program of the ego-futurists (1911–1914) called for the exploration of the intuitive self as the mainspring of creativity. They idealized art, as had the romantics, as a form of mystical experience. They asserted, following the Italian futurists, that the rapidly changing times necessitated a renovated language, and they experimented with neologisms. Severianin was less aggressive in this direction than some lesser members of the school. When Severianin rejected the group in 1912, the leadership was assumed by Ivan Ignatev, an organizer without much talent as a poet. The group also included a grandson of Konstantin Fofanov; he took the pseudonym Olimpov. A Moscow branch of ego-futurism, called the Mezzanine of Poetry, was initiated in 1913 by Vadim Shershenevich.

Igor Severianin (real surname: Lotarev; 1887–1941) introduced a new form of decadence into Russian poetry. He idealized the amoral and pleasure-seeking attitudes of a wealthy class devoted, apparently, to the philosophy of *dolce far niente*. Severianin was born in St. Petersburg and trained to be an engineer, but he preferred the arts and studied music. He began to publish collections of poems in 1904 and reached his stride in *Brooks Full of Lilies* (1911). Having organized ego-futurism in 1911, he crossed over in 1912 to the cubo-futurists. His next book, *The Thunder-seething Goblet* (1913), made him a celebrity, and he began to give well-attended public readings. The book had little in common, apart from its neologisms, with the work of the cubo-futurists, however. The poems are spoken by glamorous people who are usually found at tea and are often bored. They idealize their amorous romances, which are usually extramarital. They are sensitive to the glories of nature, such as sunsets, forests, and snow; they observe religious holidays and know their meanings. Yet they think more readily of their champagne. The moral lassitude embodied in these poems resembles that in the fantasies of popular fiction and was, indeed, a novelty in Russian poetry. The lack of an ethical perspective within the poems can still be felt as a flaw. Severianin remained a prolific but uninfluential poet, and he became a translator. In 1919 he emigrated to Estonia, where he lived to see the Soviet occupation of the country in 1939.

Khlebnikov

The poetry of Velemir Khlebnikov (real name: Victor; 1885–1922) was acclaimed in his own generation for its innovative aspects. He has yet to reach a wide audience, however. He was an exemplary cubo-futurist in that his poetry embodies a vision of utopian love. His uncomplicated idealism has also been the ageless dream of mankind. He published only one major collection of verse, *Creations* (1914), during his lifetime. His other poems, epics, and essays appeared in the futurist miscellanies of the period. His successes with transsense language, or *zaum*, resulted in part from his precise use of the existing parts of words—their roots, prefixes, and suffixes; but in some poems he made use of pure sound. His inspiration for other poets lay to a great extent, in the novelty of his syntax. He cut through conventional sentence structures to reveal anew the primitive relationships among words. His *oeuvre* is daunting in that quite beautiful poems appear side by side with raw experiments, and a reliable canon of finished works can never be established. His reputation as a serious poet has suffered from this disorder, as well as from the surprises among his experiments. He also wrote innovative stories and plays, which, like some of his poetry, were published posthumously. He was further known as an eccentric who had extraliterary theories about history and language.

Khlebnikov was selfless in his devotion to all his projects. His dreams were linked, moreover, through his overriding desire to bring about a better and more peaceful world. Born the son of an ornithologist in the provincial region beyond the Volga, he was educated in Kazan and in St. Petersburg. He was a participant in Ivanov's "Tower" salon and in the avant-garde groups organized by painters. The primitivism of such artists as Mikhail Larionov was influential on his work. He joined David Burliuk in the founding of cubo-futurism and signed "A Slap in the Face of Public Taste." Although he became a nominal leader of the school, he had no inclination to be a practical chief. His concerns outside poetry included an attempt to predict cycles in history, a search for the *ur*-language of the human race, and a union of "presidents" (or good men) of the globe. He carried his papers in a pillowcase, and a number of works, including poems, were lost. After the Revolution his nomadic habits and strange notions caused him to be arrested by both Reds and Whites. For several happy months, he was an administrator for the Red Army in Persia. He died in Russia in a provincial hospital of an undiagnosed disease.

In his early poems, Khlebnikov's explorations of the topic of universal love had a pastoral cast. His bucolic bias gave his poems a superficial resemblance to the sentimentalism of the early nineteenth century. But he also portrayed stark and painful brutalities. He distinguished throughout his work between his lyrics and his epic poems (*poemy*); although the basis for this division is not clear, the epics usually embody some strife. It is therefore among the lyric poems, which often seem cryptic and elusive, that his nostalgia for universal harmony can be found. The earliest poems have idyllic settings. The spirit of love is seen to include both sexual attachments and the capacity for benevolence and happiness; altruism is thus a force latent in nature. He often portrays love in some arcadian past, especially in pre-Christian, Kievan Russia. But love and a sense of cosmic belonging are possible today. In the following poem, he observes with gratitude the constellations of the zodiac:

The Crab, the Ram—I see.
The world is all a seashell
Wherein a mere touch of pearl—
Is what is wrong with me.
Rustles make whistles with knocks marching through them like "k."
Then did it seem to me that waves and our thoughts are in kinship.
Vast Milky Ways exist where here and there arise women.
Sweet custom's ways it is that
Fills this earthly dark.
When night is this way then a grave could give love
And the wines of this evening
And vast women of this evening
Are twined to make a single great wreath
Of which the young brother am I.

Khlebnikov often contrasted the grandeur of vast expanses of time and space with small, effective details. In his narrative called "A Village Friendship" he borrowed his title, his subject, and his form (the idyl) from Anton Delvig. It is in the context of his search for universal love that Khlebnikov's linguistic experiments must be seen: he hoped to find a common origin. Poems based on word plays, like the famous example of transsense called "Incantation by Laughter," may create, in addition, a spirit of effervescent play. "Wisdom in a Net" is composed mostly of bird sounds, and it concludes with the picture of a god with a baby. But Khlebnikov also wrote tragic long poems in palindromes.

In Khlebnikov's poetry the forces that constantly defeat love are sometimes societal and sometimes innate. In the epic poems of the early period, lovers are seen to arouse the antagonism of the community, and they are often persecuted. In "Maria Vechora" Khlebnikov suggests that Baroness Maria Vetsera died at Mayerling at the hands of hostile intruders. In "The Tsar's Bride" he depicts the drowning of Princess Dolgoruky immediately after her marriage; Rimsky-Korsakov used the same account for his opera. Sexual love can have treacherous undercurrents. In the epic "The Wood Nymph and the Wood Demon," which is reminiscent of Mallarmé's "L'après-midi d'un faune," the nymph despairs of the sleeping satyr and turns to human company. In other epics, love leads to cruelty, sacrifice, and self-sacrifice. And in the lyrics lovers have rivals, and the sexes are at war. Khlebnikov liked to show the return or the revenge of victims. In "The Shaman and Venus" the goddess has been exiled to Siberia, but she is recalled. In the Stone Age tale "I and E" the lovers conquer their once hostile tribe and become its triumphant rulers. In several poems Khlebnikov seemed to deplore the senseless slaughter of animals by humans. He had a reputation for pacificism, but he believed that evil must be resisted. In "The Children of the Otter" man rises above his sad world, emulates Prometheus, and can venerate the heroes of history.

Khlebnikov saw in modern times a descent into technology. The epic poem "The Crane" is about a machine that eats children. In "The Frogs' Revolt" the lowly amphibians gather to attack a train that crushes them at their crossing. In the war period, Khlebnikov recalled the carnage that man has suffered in all ages. The Mongol invasion of Russia is the subject of the following poem, "The Mound":

Whatever's touched by Tatar lances
Bends down to earth and does not murmur.
When they have left chaste women naked,
The eastern hordes spur horses eastward.

The warrior in this mound, when dying,
Grasped close the Hebrew's iron visage—
Around him steppes, a gopher's hole, his squeal, and—
Day for the mound flew ever faster.

A clan of foxes lifts its herd of noses,
A horse speeds past escaping from a Gypsy.
The Cossack mute and stern reposes
Beneath his mound through hours of ages.

Khlebnikov's protest against World War I appeared in "War in a Mousetrap."

In the poems he wrote after the outbreak of the war and during the civil war, Khlebnikov was less inclined to look back toward a primitive past and more concerned with the possibility of a utopia in the future. Some pieces show his undying sympathy for elemental nature. In his epics about Slavic water nymphs (*rusalki*) and wood nymphs (*vily*) the spirits are often menaced, exiled from festivals, or captured by hostile forces. His continuing idealization of earthiness resulted in "Three Sisters" (1920), where three young women of his acquaintance are portrayed as canny sorceresses or minor deities. Khlebnikov's travels in the east brought poems set in the Caucasus, Baku, Central Asia, and Persia. He pictures Asia as primitive in that it is poor, arid, and the home of oxen and camels. But he also found there the folklore of magic carpets and a great spirituality. On the basis of his Asian experiences, he wrote a series of outstanding poems in which nature is allied with the religions of the world. Among these are "The Koran of Spring . . . ," "Saian," a tribute to a Siberian river where an elk regards ancient runes on a mossy cliff, and "The Single Book," in which the sacred books of the world give way to the single religion of nature; he pictures large rivers and oceans. His most idealistic epic, called "The Trumpet of Gul-Mulla," consists of his impressions of Persia; he is himself the pacifistic "priest of flowers," or Gul-Mulla.

He responded, meanwhile, to the course of history. The civil war was depicted in the epic called "Night in the Trench," where "stone women," ancient symbols of fertility, watch the carnage of the war. Khlebnikov was at first sympathetic to the Revolution. He wrote an antibourgeois epic called "Ladomir." In "City of the Future" his visionary utopia is associated with a new regime; he imagines that words will be forged in factories by laborers. In his lyrics, however, he recorded the signs of civic chaos, the death of the monarch, the vanishing of friends, random shootings on the streets, and the appearance of corpses. In his later lyrics he depicted the famine; in "Volga, Volga" he protested against the cannibalism of children. His two long poems about Stenka Razin, the seventeenth-century Cossack rebel, are ambiguous; according to legend, Razin drowned his Persian bride in the Volga. Khlebnikov's political disillusionment is obvious in "The Night Search," where an icon of Christ watches as a boy is shot by Red sailors; his mother sets an avenging fire. Khlebnikov's long prose poem *Zangezi* is an autobiographical summary of his altruistic hopes and visionary themes; it was staged in 1923. Khlebnikov's poems gain from his apparent naiveté. He preserved intact a youthful indignation and a thirst for retaliation and revenge that are contagious. His verbal combinations are still startling, and still a source of exhilaration and delight.

Khlebnikov's short prose pieces and plays are dreamlike tales and sketches about the exotic and the fantastic. They are different from his poetry, and similar in their experimentalism to the work of Gertrude Stein and Samuel Beckett. Khlebnikov considered "Ka," a story about a person's relationship with his soul's aura, to be a key work in his *oeuvre*. The dramatic piece called "The Maidens' God" is about the disparity between the inclinations of young women and those of society. The adults always prevail and exile the young women's god.

Maiakovsky

A conflict between "lyricism" and "social command" proved to be the most engaging drama in the work of Vladimir Maiakovsky (1893–1930). In his early verse, he created the role of the avant-garde dandy and was a romantic rebel. After the Revolution he served the cause of the new regime, wrote outright propaganda verse, and became a virtual poet laureate of the Soviet Union. He is now chiefly remembered for a play in prose, *The Bedbug* (1928), in which he satirized both capitalist and utopian systems. He was a prolific author of lyrics; he wrote twelve narrative poems and four plays, two in verse. The collision between his desires for a private life and his need to serve the community actually traverses both periods of his work and can be seen in all his genres. He lamented his rejections in love and aired his own narcissistic loneliness. He also spoke of alleviating the sufferings of mankind and eulogized the Communist Party. The fact that much of his propaganda work is pedestrian as poetry makes his *oeuvre* difficult to assess. He retained his avant-garde style in all his work, early and late. He cultivated outrageous figures of speech, soaring fantasies, and vulgarities previously unseen in poetry. His free verse and inexact rhymes were an example to other poets. His best work, however sympathetic to the lower classes, could not create any deep affection in them; his *Bedbug* has been a favorite among intellectuals.

Maiakovsky saw in literature a vehicle for addressing society in any of his various characters—as a rebel, a martyr, or a public servant. He obviously believed at some times that he could make of literature a force for social change, but it is unclear how firm he was in this faith. He was born in Georgia, the son of a forest ranger who brought his family to Moscow in 1906. Maiakovsky became a communist agitator while still in his teens, was arrested three times, and spent six months in Butyrki Prison, mostly in solitary confinement. In 1911 he enrolled in art school, where he encountered the avant-garde circles. He chose David Burliuk, already a futurist organizer, as his mentor, and signed "A Slap in the Face of Public Taste" in 1912. In 1913 he was a prominent performer on the provincial tour of readings undertaken by the futurists. His first large work, *Vladimir Maiakovsky. A Tragedy*, was staged in 1913 as a companion piece to *Victory over the Sun* by Aleksey Kruchenykh, itself a milestone in the history of the Russian avant-garde. "A Cloud in Pants" (1915) established Maiakovsky as an independent author. In 1915 he began to associate with Osip Brik, a wealthy theoretician of the avant-garde; Brik's wife, Lili, was the object of most of Maiakovsky's love poetry. After the Revolution Maiakovsky produced propaganda posters with jingles as captions for the telegraph agency ROSTA. He founded LEF in 1922 with Brik's help. In 1924 Maiakovsky began to make nearly annual trips to Paris, and in 1924 and 1925 he visited Cuba, Mexico, and the United States. He was unsuccessful in his love for a Russian émigré woman in Paris. At home he was forced to abandon his own literary association and join the government-sponsored RAPP. In 1930 he committed suicide.

Maiakovsky's early works establish a larger-than-life image of himself, whether as dandy, rebel, martyr, or lover. In his early lyrics he swaggers with the braggadocio of the avant-gardist and sneers at society. An indicative title is "But Could You Do It" (1913). He rejects the proprieties of bourgeois conventions and describes himself as the poet of the urban poor and of the city itself, with its congested and polluted streets. He flaunts his arrogance in "A Cloud in Pants," an autobiographical poem. Here is the beginning of his introduction, which is addressed to the reader:

> Your thoughts,
> daydreaming on your soft and flabby brain
> like a fattened lackey lying on his grease-spotted couch,
> will I tease with my bloody tatters of a heart:
> I will nettle you, arrogant and biting, to my fill.

But since this is a story of a love, Maiakovsky will be a loser. He complains that despite his youth, beauty, and talents, he has been inexplicably rejected by a lover and society alike. He was able to give voice in his poetry to unabashedly juvenile fantasies. His love poems always suggest an exaggerated anguish. In "Lilichka" (1916) he compares his love-sickness to the pain of very large animals, the ox and the elephant; he scatters his verse, like fallen leaves, under her "retreating feet." Although he loved animals, he despised conventional nature poetry. "Moonlit Night" (1916) is a parody in which he debases his imagery; he sees in the moon the "silver spoon" with which God is "poking his fish soup of stars."

It was in his long works that Maiakovsky could be seen as a savior of society rather than as the detractor of middle-class conventions. In *Vladimir Maiakovsky. A Tragedy* it is the poet's mission to take away the tears of a metropolitan citizenry. In *War and the World* (1916) he assumes the guilt for the devastations of World War I; Christ is then reconciled with Cain. In *Man* (1917) Maiakovsky first saw a conflict between his need for love and his desire to change society. He describes himself as a second Christ who suffers passions and an assumption, but who returns to earth because heaven is discovered to be boring; there he is forced to see his successful rival—the husband. Maiakovsky began in his early lyrics to voice the attitudes of the working class—its resentment during the war, its hatred of the sated bourgeoisie, and its love of gambling and low life. He greeted the Revolution in tones of vengeful, antibourgeois glee.

Maiakovsky's greatest poems on private themes were written in the early 1920s.

He remains a superhuman, closer to the springs of the universe than others. In "A Good Attitude Toward Horses" (1918) he is the altruist who raises a fallen equine and tells her of the horse in all of us. He is the equal of the sun in "An Extraordinary Incident . . ." (1920), in which the orb descends in answer to his invitation to tea. His "epics" about his love are confessions in which his pain is intolerable. In "I Love" (1922) he describes his wayward childhood and desire for street knowledge, his loneliness and need to save the world; Lili's love relieves his anguished sense of self. In *About That* (1923) his grief as a lover turns him into a polar bear who floats to sea on the river of his tears; he confronts himself as a martyr for society and decides to wait for a resurrection in a better, thirtieth century. His American trip resulted in two eulogies of odic stature. One is called "The Atlantic Ocean" (1925); the other is "Brooklyn Bridge" (1925); in the latter he praises the creative spirit of the nation that erected the structure.

Meanwhile, he celebrated the triumph of the Revolution and supported its aims. He brought attention to himself as a poet of militant communism in "Our March" (1917). Here is the first stanza:

> Drum in the squares the beat of revolt!
> Higher, O plazas of proud-held heads!
> We are the Flood in its second coming,
> We will wash cities all over the world!

His communistic work tends to be arid, in part because of its didacticism. The verse drama *Mystery-Bouffe* (1918) has moments of comedy: the proletarians, "the Unclean," conquer the globe, defeating "The Clean," and storm heaven. In *150,000,000* (1920) the Russian population rises up as one giant, Ivan, who wades the Atlantic to fight Woodrow Wilson, who lives in Chicago, the quintessential American city. In *Vladimir Ilich Lenin* (1924) Maiakovsky laments the death of a mythic leader. In his lyrics he wrote on such subjects as civil war victories, the survival of bourgeois relics during the NEP, the exportation of the Revolution to Western Europe, and the production of coal and oil. Occasionally he wrote poems on the utility of poetry, which he chose to regard as a form of proletarian labor. In "A Conversation with the Tax Collector About Poetry" (1926) he argues for tax exemptions. He begged in several poems to be given a "social command," notably in "Homeward," written in 1926 at the close of his American trip.

Maiakovsky's lyric impulse was scarcely seen at all in the late 1920s. In "To Sergey Esenin" (1926) he chided the peasant poet for his suicide. The self-destructive undercurrent in Maiakovsky's own works is obscured by the grandeur of his imagination and by his humor. Some of his major works, including his masterpiece, *The Bedbug,* are fantasies about a resurrection in a distant future. *The Bedbug* is also noteworthy for its reductive image of the animal kingdom (an insect) and his fear of the zoo, once a favorite spot. In the play *The Bathhouse* (1929) an idealized feminine figure, "the phosphorus woman," comes to select good citizens to be transported in life to a utopian future. In 1927 Maiakovsky celebrated the tenth anniversary of the Revolution with *It's Good.* In *At the Top of My Voice* (1930), which remained unfinished, he declared his pride in having "stepped on the throat of my own song"; he spoke of quitting "garden" poetry for that of the streets and the proletariat. His last unfinished lyric, however, was a love poem, which includes this fragment:

> Past one. You must have gone to sleep by now
> The Milky Way's a silver river Oka
> I'm not in haste, and as for lightning telegrams
> There is no reason now to wake you and make trouble.
> And so they say the incident is over
> The boat of our love was broken against life
> Our score is now even no need have we for lists
> Of mutual hurts and insults and woes
> Look now at how still the world around's become
> For night has paid its due of stars unto the sky
> At hours like this you want to rise and speak
> To all of history's ages, all creation.

The pathos of Maiakovsky's *oeuvre* lay in its unresolved conflicts. His work is only superficially naive. He elucidated his own dilemmas: the love he craved was a part of the bourgeois world; utopian communities lead to tyrannies or to boredom, as in heaven. He recognized the link between his narcissism and his superhuman altruism. His *oeuvre* is painful, in spite of its braggadocio and comic moments.

Lesser Cubo-Futurist Poets

The cubo-futurist group included several dedicated minor artists whose concerns ranged from the sentimental idealization of pastoral life to the defiant rejection of all civilized values. Their common traits were their primitivism and their opposition to accepted conventions. One of the oldest and most dedicated to the cause of nonconformist art was Elena Guro (1877–1913), a cultivated art student who once studied with Bion Bakst. In her literary work she was a sentimental defender of the helpless and an early proponent of environmentalism. She was born Eleonora von Notenburg in St. Petersburg. Her first collection, *The Hurdy-Gurdy* appeared in 1909. In 1910 she joined a circle called Venok (the Wreath), whose membership was an initial assembling of the cubo-futurist poets. She was married to the composer Mikhail Matiushin. She died of tuberculosis in 1913, on the eve of futurism's greatest successes.

Guro was a modest visionary ahead of her time; much of the appeal of her work is in the purity of its idealism. She spoke for causes that were to become popular decades later. She advocated the full psychological development of every personality in an atmosphere of nondirective love and caring. She was pained on behalf of the polluted and mutilated natural environment. She spoke of the virtues of a bucolic life without idealizing the past. In her style she affected an innocence and naiveté. Her "poems" were written both in prose and in verse, sometimes interwoven freely. *The Hurdy-Gurdy* opens with lyric prose pieces about the inhibiting effects of city life. There follow descriptions of the irenic northern landscapes at her family dacha in Finland. Some of her verses are defenses of shy young people, especially when in love. She wanted to protect everything that is vulnerable, whether people, animals, trees, or even the inanimate beach. She spoke with nostalgia about the loss of her own baby. Two children's plays, both nonsensical in style, are included in *The Hurdy-Gurdy*. One is about the sad and clownish figure Harlequin; the second hero is a cucumber salesman. The poems of *The Little Camels in the Sky* (1914) are similar in their country settings and concern for children and teenagers. Her last poems are colored by her knowledge of her impending early death; she was grateful for the love of her husband and friends.

The pastoral life, especially in the wilderness, found another champion in Vasily Kamensky (1884–1961). He is known for *The Mud Hut* (1911), the first of several bucolic novellas written in prose interspersed with songs. Kamensky was born near Perm, the son of a gold-field inspector. His depictions of the far north were to play a large role in his work. He became the editor of a small newspaper in St. Petersburg, and then in 1910 an associate of David Burliuk. In 1913 he participated in the futurist tour of the provinces. His protagonist in *The Mud Hut* renounces urban society and his wife to live in the woods and marry a peasant. Kamensky's lyrics reflect his delight in nature, his sympathy for animals, and his feeling of being in communion with the essence of life. His poetry was somewhat influenced by the avant-garde tendency to coinages and transsense. His novel *Stenka Razin* is one of several futurist celebrations of the seventeenth-century Cossack rebel who raised the Volga area in a vast revolt. After the Revolution, Kamensky joined Maiakovsky's LEF and added Marxist themes to his work.

The primitivism of Aleksey Kruchenykh (1886–1969?) was of the kind that delights in destruction. He was the aggressive champion of the uncivilizing and irrational aspects of cubo-futurism. He was also its most productive and effective theoretician. He was born a peasant in Kherson province and graduated from an art school in Odessa. He became an associate of David Burliuk in the promotion of cubism, and signed "A Slap in the Face of Public Taste" in 1912. He wrote very little intelligible verse and much more transsense poetry. His comprehensible poetry was written early in his career and constitutes a virtual attack on every impulse toward common decency. In "The Hermit" (1913) he voices the attitudes of a predatory cave man, and in "The Hermitess" (1913) he describes the resignation of an all but defenseless creature. His poems are strange, but redeemed by humor:

> Save up your wealth and shun your dad
> Let him get on as a furniture mover
> Make safe the locks on all your doors
> He may chase after you with glares
> like those of Asian hordes on horse.
>
> And let him whisper evil spells
> and beat the door, insane,
> and let him rouse the neighborhood
> but give no credence to his grief
> and let the kids cry, so they'll learn.

He collaborated with Khlebnikov on the long poem "A Game in Hell" (1912). Kruchenykh was prolific in transsense verse; he was particularly proud of a poem that begins "dyr bul shchyl" (1913?), a sequence of sounds that is harsh, meaningless, and apparently non-Russian. He was the author of the notorious avant-garde opera *Victory over the Sun,* staged with the collaboration of the artist Malevich and the composer Matiushin in 1913. His "The Word as Such" (1913), of which Khlebnikov appears as a cosigner, is considered a seminal document of Russian futurism. He urged in it that the modern literary language should cease to be clear and pure and become painful in its effect, like a saw or a poisoned arrow. After the Revolution, Kruchenykh founded a futurist group in Tiflis with Ilia Zdanevich, and later he joined Maiakovsky's LEF. In 1929 he published a useful and sensible history of the movement called *Fifteen Years of Russian Futurism.* In the 1930s he worked for a literary museum.

Pasternak

If his famous novel *Doctor Zhivago* had never been written, Boris Pasternak (1890–1960) would still be known to literary circles outside Russia, and possibly as Russia's greatest poet in the twentieth century. That reputation was earned early in his career by two collections of verse, *My Sister Life* (1922) and *Themes and Variations* (1923). His early poetry was experimental; its metaphors are striking and its syntax is elusive. For these and other reasons, Pasternak was at home among the avant-gardists, but he chose to affiliate with a moderate faction of futurism called the Centrifuge. It advocated the continual renewal of traditions through change. In the 1920s Pasternak abandoned lyrics for long poems on recent history and short fiction. In the 1930s he published an autobiographical essay, *Safe Conduct,* and returned to lyrics. His style had become much simpler, and he repudiated his early verse. *Doctor Zhivago,* written in the 1940s, is realistic in style, but it is regarded by many as the work of a poet; it contains, moreover, the best poems of Pasternak's later years.

Pasternak believed that artistic creativity is the expression of a metaphysical force that wells up in the individual creator. It can be cultivated, he thought, but not possessed as a personal talent. His father was a well-known artist, and his mother had been trained as a pianist. He studied music with Scriabin and then philosophy at the University of Moscow, with a summer course at the University of Marburg in 1912. He joined the Centrifuge in 1914 and published a first volume of poems. He was rejected for military service, but sent to the Urals in a clerical position. The poems of *My Sister Life,* written in Moscow in 1917, established him as a major young writer even before their publication in 1922. The long poems of the 1920s were about the successes of the revolutionary movement. He believed he owed the regeneration of his lyrical powers to a 1931 trip to the Caucasus, with its freer atmosphere, in the company of the woman who was to become his second wife. The first fruits of his new style, the poems of *Second Birth,* appeared in 1932. *Doctor Zhivago* was published abroad in 1957. Pasternak rejected the Nobel Prize awarded in 1958 because of the opposition of the Soviet government. He became, however, a symbol to the world of noncompliance with authoritarian regimes.

Pasternak's verse was shaped by a sense of community he felt with the phenomena of the universe. He spoke in his poetry, he thought, for others, and he gave voice to the common experience of many or even of many things. The title of his first book, *A Twin in the Clouds* (1914), is a reference to the myth of Castor and Pollux, the twins of whom only one was immortal. Some of its poems are about that eternal aspect of the self that is a constant, but little-known, companion, whose perceptions of life are not subject to temporal considerations. Most of the other poems were reprinted in the opening section of his next book, *Over the Barriers* (1917). The first poem of his second book, "Get ink and cry—it's February," foreshadows Pasternak's attentiveness to nature and his preoccupation with an existential grief. In subsequent poems, he indicates that there is anguish in the heritage of Eden, in "feasts," and in solitary memories. The new poems of *Over the Barriers* describe in their sequence the effort of establishing a métier and a place in life. The story is symbolized by the course of nature's seasons, from autumn through winter to spring. The opening poem, "Courtyard," describes an onslaught of storms in October. Society also has its wintry vicissitudes—in war, in the strikes at Presni, in the slaughter of Huguenots on St. Bartholomew's Eve. "Urals for the First Time," with its colorful picture of a dawn, acts as a sign of awakening. The winter gives way to the ageless sadness of April and finally to the joys of spring. Several summer poems show the rain that would become so memorable in Pasternak's verse. The final poem, "Marburg," tells how he came by that heightened awareness of material objects which was to characterize his poetry.

My Sister Life, whose poems were written in the summer of 1917, is the impressionistic record of a failure in love. The book opens with an evocation of Lermontov's Demon, a creature possessed by a great and fatal passion, which Pasternak compares to an avalanche. Underlying this story is a philosopher's observation: the short-lived joys and more constant sorrows of life are rooted in our material existence. The first section includes those striking poems about animated gardens in the rain—for example, "The Weeping Garden" and "The Mirror"— which have made Pasternak seem to be the poet of impetuosity and unfettered impulse. His love appears in April and becomes overwhelming as the days pass into summer. His expectations and frustrations are seen in images of small southern train-stop towns in the steppe. A poem called "Resting Oars" embodies one moment of happiness.

> Here in my chest rocks a boat while I sleep.
> Willows hang over and kiss my still elbows,
> Collarbones, oarlocks, and O, wait a minute,
> This is what happens to everyone sometimes!
>
> This is what pleases the crowd in a song.
> This is what means, well, the ashes of lilacs,
> Wealth like the henna that's crushed in the dew,
> Lips and more lips like the stars for the asking.

> This means you reach to embrace the whole sky,
> Winding your arms 'round a heavenly Hercules.
> This means that now and for ages on end
> Squandering nights on the trilling of nightingales.

The love wanes, however, and the book ends. In "English Lessons" Desdemona and Ophelia are shown to have recognized in the moments before they died that they were one with nature. In sections called "The Study of Philosophy" and "The Definition of Creativity" Pasternak seems to suggest that our experience of existence is private and not often happy. Those poems that record ecstasies are perhaps his most memorable, but it is his rejection of a continuous optimism that makes his poetic world intelligent and persuasive.

The poems of *Themes and Variations,* written between 1916 and 1922, are a new confirmation of the same idea, that our perspectives, at least, are earthly. The themes of the poems are the same: nature, love, artistic creativity, and, occasionally, current events; the lyrics are often deeper and more complex. His opening subject is inspiration. At night, when writing is to be done, concrete objects themselves become agitated. When poems have been written, for example, by Goethe or Shakespeare, they assume a life of their own and assert their own reality. Pushkin's major inspirations are represented through dazzling zigzags between African and Russian scenes. In the following section Pasternak airs the natural complaints of the earth and of mankind, such as the arrogant refusal of the soul to participate in material life. He ends with another rejection in love, a proof that only the earthly matters. In the section called "I could forget them" he suggests that such agonies as the vanities of life, the writing of poetry, and war are the stuff of an honest awareness and cannot be forgotten. In the last, lengthy cycle, "Pleasure Park," the garden in St. Petersburg becomes a symbol for the soul, or life, for both are sometimes boring but also sometimes entertaining. The seasons are again symbolic. Here is a springtime poem:

> O spring, I'm from the street, where poplars are surprised,
> Where distances show fear, where houses shun capsizement,
> Where air is blue, just like the laundry bag
> A patient brings when hospital is over,
>
> Where evening is a void—an interrupted tale,
> Deserted, like a star without continuation,
> Which left amazed one thousand noisy eyes
> Now bottomless and reft of all expression.

The mood of the book declines through summer and autumn, when the resolution of sorrows will be in sleep.

In the long poems of the 1920s Pasternak attempted to praise the spirit of the Revolution, a plan that was alien to his notion of the nature of art. His talent, moreover, was not at home in narrative verse, and the poems have tedious passages. In "A High Malady" (1924) Lenin's decisive oratory at the Ninth Party Congress is compared favorably to the "music" of the cultural statements of the intelligentsia. The same aggressively forward tendency and impatience with triviality is ascribed to the October Revolution itself in the dedication to *The Year 1905*. The year is presented as a pivotal point in the transition from the genteel liberalism of the older generation to the angry and dangerous confrontations of the new era. The work opens with the poet's youth in a painter's apartment, where Scriabin appeared, and shows the intrusion of strikes and artillery fire, the battleship *Potemkin* at Odessa, and patrols and turmoil on the streets of Moscow. *Lieutenant Schmidt* describes the hero who led a sailors' revolt at Sevastopol during the October Revolution in terms that are both epic and sentimental. While the wealthy amuse themselves at the horse races, Schmidt is concerned for the family he is to leave behind. The novel in verse called *Spektorsky* (1931) has an epigraph from Pushkin's *Bronze Horseman* that leads us to expect a failed hero in great times. Spektorsky is a gentry intellectual who shuns political choices and thus misses the significance of the years 1912 through 1919. His circles think primarily of love affairs, of holidays and parlor games. The poem is an early preparation for *Doctor Zhivago*. Pasternak's "narrative" poem consists primarily of dramatic episodes, but they never spring to life. His characters are wooden and their words unconvincing.

The lyrics that appeared in the collections of the 1930s, 1940s, and 1950s lack the intimate vision and sense of urgency that had marked Pasternak's early work. The poems in *Second Birth* (1932), *On Early Trains* (1943), and *When the Weather Clears* (1957) now form a single volume that was published only posthumously, but that is respected as the canon desired by the author. The Caucasus is shown to have been important not only to himself but also to the history of Russia. The poem "Waves," which opens the section "Second Birth," describes the many wars that have been fought there. The lyrics of the cycle "On Early Trains" show that he was fond of the mountains with their crevices, the swift Aragva River, and semitropical fruits and flowers. The section "On Early Trains" is, however, a reflection of the 1930s and 1940s as they were lived at Peredelkino. His subjects include love, friendships, and art. His scenes show comfortable domestic interiors, and he sometimes refers to music, especially that of Chopin and Brahms. The forest at Peredelkino is seen, and the change of seasons from summer to winter. The war poems, written between 1941 and 1944, are platitudinous in their patriotism and sentimentality. "When the Weather Clears" was written during the post-Stalin Thaw of 1956 to 1959, and it is characterized by a sense of gratitude for life. The title poem describes the plenitude of nature—a lake, the sky, the grass, the wind. "In the Hospital" is a prayer of thanks to God before death. Pasternak's relatively straightforward style in these works was influenced by the reign of realism around him.

Pasternak believed that *Doctor Zhivago* was his most significant work. The characters in the novel express what were apparently his own views on religion, history, and Western culture. His earlier preparation for this prose work included an experimental short story called "The Childhood of Luvers" (1922), which portrays the emotional development of a young girl. In the autobiographical *Safe Conduct* Pasternak had described his youthful false starts in music and philosophy and his decision for poetry. Iurii Zhivago is described as a man who similarly embarks on ill-defined spiritual quests, who reflects on history and religion, and who holds a generally optimistic outlook for the future of mankind. The poems that Pasternak ascribed to his hero have been seen as somewhat distinct from his other poems of the same period. To some extent, they are also different from the fiction to which they are attached. They are more unfettered and less didactic in their assessment of the human condition. In the *Zhivago* poems, Pasternak admits again to the existence of an underlying pain and to the transience of joys. In the opening poem, "Hamlet," it is seen that life must be lived on its own terms, not those of our devising:

> Noises stopped. I entered in the limelight—
> Paused to lean against an open door.
> For I try to grasp from distant echoes
> What my age will bring as its events.
>
> Dusky night is fixed on me through lenses
> In one thousand opera glasses raised.
> If there is a way, O abba, Father,
> Let this cup not be the one for me.
>
> I adore your plan in all its strictness,
> I agree to play the role at hand.
> But this time there is another drama—
> Let me off for just this single case.
>
> But, the acts are written in their order,
> And the end is certain as is fate.
> I am one. And Pharisees surround me.
> Life, they say, is not an open field.

Nature plays, as before, an active role in man's affairs. The mute sharing of universal sorrow is the subject of "Earth"; the "calling" of the poet is to express the loneliness of the material world. Love is celebrated in "Hops" as sexual passion, while in "A Tale" the same love is an inspiration to perform feats of courage and honor. The deepest idea of love appears in "Departure," in which love is a primordial force that resembles the processes of the ocean, with its algae and shells. The Christian religion appears as a newly important theme among Pasternak's poems. The earth participates throughout in the drama of the Easter story. Nature suffers an early awakening in "Holy Week." The advance of the seasons brings a crescendo of religious awe. At Christmas a babe is born who is worshipped by kings and warmed by the breath of lowly animals, the ox and the ass. At Gethsemane, Christ speaks the prayer to be repeated by Hamlet, but Christ will be the ultimate measure of civilization.

In the *Zhivago* poems, written in the late 1940s and early 1950s, Pasternak recaptured some of the sense of urgency and the audacity of performance that can be seen in his early poems. The later lyrics are broader in that he could look with admiration and gratitude on the human gifts through which civilizations are passed from one generation to the next. In his other, less successful, late poems he was searching, under the impact of his times, for a "simpler" way of writing, and he approached realism. But in his early, and difficult, poems "simplicity" had meant for him the most direct and unreflecting route to the rendering of experience.

Lesser Centrifuge Poets

The splinter group called the Centrifuge, to which Pasternak belonged and which met in Moscow from 1913 to 1917, was small in numbers and ill-defined as to doctrine, but active in avant-garde publishing. It was hostile to cubo-futurism and other futurist extremists, and it leaned toward the spiritual interpretation of literature. Its leader was a minor poet, Sergey Bobrov (1889–1971). He was a romantic in his nostalgia for perfection, but he spoke most often of his disillusionments. He was born the son of a servant, studied archaeology, and taught mathematics. In his first book of verse, *Gardenkeepers of the Vines* (1913), he imitated the French decadents of the nineteenth century. Melancholia and death are prominent themes, but he also wrote about memories of ecstasies and he idealized the night. Some poems have medieval or mythical settings. In *The Lyre of Lyres* (1917) he abruptly changed to an avant-garde style. In the title poem he expresses his wish to discover a new beauty that would halt the march of time and encompass all of life; these were probably his aims for the Centrifuge. A number of the poems have epigraphs taken from Rimbaud. Bobrov writes in many poems about the imagination, which he calls "the dream." He believed that it was the inexpressibility of this "dream" that leads to the constant mutations of the forms of reality. He also wrote about loneliness and alienation. He was drawn to scenes of violence, whether battles or natural catastrophes. He was a prolific theoretician and historian of literature. He published, between 1915 and 1923, works on lyricism, on prosody, on Pushkin, and on N. M. Iazykov, Pushkin's contemporary. Bobrov began to write utopian novels in the 1920s, and he became a steady translator of French and English literature.

Nikolay Aseev (1889–1963) devoted his poetry to the anxieties and alarms of the twentieth century, and he was more clearly nonconformist in style than was Bobrov. He used dream logic and coined words. He was born in Moscow and reared by a grandfather who was a hunter and an amateur folklore expert. His first three volumes, published in 1914 and 1915, were his most experimental. In *The Nocturnal Flute* (1914) he speaks impressionistically of losses and regrets. His settings are urban, exotic, and medieval. His second book, *Flash* (1914), is particularly given to neologisms. *Year-Soaring* (1915) suggests, because of its folkloric and medieval Russian motifs and images, a concern with the national culture. Aseev's books became more comprehensible after he joined the army and was sent to the Far East, where he remained until 1921. In his new books he expressed apprehension about the effects of war and fear of death. He is also world-weary and afflicted by a quiet desperation. In *Oksana* (1916) he shows that the nation, which is largely peasant in population, has faced wars from early times to the present. He had presentiments of universal death, symbolized by the silence of animals. In *The Bomb* (1921) he began to write Soviet propaganda. In *The Steel Nightingale* (1922) he depicts the peasant population as wrenched into a modern world of machines and killing. By 1923 he had returned to Moscow and joined Maiakovsky's LEF. In *The Soviet of Winds* (1923) he gave up pastoral imagery for urban and proletarian scenes. He idealized Maiakovsky in the long poem "Incipit Maiakovskii" and in a number of lyrics. His last poems were free, however, from references to his avant-garde past.

Tsvetaeva

The poetry of Marina Tsvetaeva (1892–1941) was both eclectic and unique. No one literary school could claim her loyalty. She shared with some acmeists her considerable erudition and her love for the entire European heritage. But her love of country was also great, and she derived some of her inspiration from Russian folklore. She had in common with the futurists her experimental, and often primitive, style. In her earliest books, she recalled or re-created the perceptions of childhood and experiences of growing up. During the civil war, she wrote a cycle of lyrics, *The Swans' Stand* (1957), in praise of the White armies. She lived in emigration from 1922 to 1939 and published her best books, including *The Craft* (1923), abroad. Her eclectic taste could still be seen in the variety of poets to whom she wrote poems or cycles of poems: Blok, who was a symbolist; Akhmatova, an acmeist; and Pasternak, a futurist. In some of her later lyrics, she recorded the impressions of an émigré. In all, she published about ten collections of lyrics, as well as several narrative poems and plays. Her reputation has lagged behind that of other major Russian poets who remained at home and who chose a literary school.

Tsvetaeva believed the world of art to be the natural domain of a happy elite— those who possess both the gift and the will to be creative. She was born in Moscow, the daughter of a professor of graphic arts; her mother was an accomplished pianist. Her first book of verse, *The Evening Album* (1910), established her as a promising poet. Her life, which is obliquely reflected in her poetry, was lived intensely and unhappily. She married early and was devoted to her family; in 1912 a daughter, Ariadne, was born. During the civil war her husband, Sergey Efron, fought with the volunteer White Army in the Crimea. She was able to join him in the West only in 1922. They lived in Berlin, Prague, and Paris, where a son was born in 1925. Tsvetaeva was subject to exaggerated feelings of admiration for fellow poets, and sometimes to romantic infatuations, both with men and with women. Nevertheless, when Efron had been exposed as a Soviet agent and had returned to the Soviet Union with their daughter, she followed him with their son in 1939. Efron and Ariadne were subsequently arrested. During World War II, Tsvetaeva was evacuated to a small town, Elabuga, where she hanged herself.

Her early poetry was her most obviously autobiographical. In her first two books she portrays herself, with some archness, as the child of an elegant, and happy, bourgeois family. She writes about her relationships with her mama and sister, about events of family importance, and about friends, among them young men. Some poems are fantasies in which those close to her are cast in fairy-tale roles and in the conventions of literary romanticism. Her air of false innocence is somewhat sentimental, and she is at pains to show that she was a clever child. She mentions German authors and uses German words. She admits to self-indulgent regrets on leaving her sheltered childhood. She clings to the past, but she also looks forward to love. In the course of her second book, *The Magic Lantern* (1912), she shows a growing awareness of life's impending dangers and of real separations.

If she had written nothing beyond the two volumes called *Milestones*, published abroad in 1921 and 1922, her place in European poetry would have been secure. In these books, however, her love of country comes to the fore. The books create a mirror of the Russian mind, sometimes at the peasant level. The first volume opens with balladlike stories that resemble the tales of folklore. Her poems addressed to her fellow Russian poets Blok and Akhmatova are also in this volume. All the poems of the first volume were written in Russia in 1916 and were perhaps inspired by the heightened national awareness brought about by World War I. In both books she took many subjects from Russian history and the chronicles. She was particularly drawn to the figures of the false Dmitry, who seized power in the Time of Troubles, and his Polish fiancée, Marina Mniszek, the poet's namesake. Other stories come from the Bible; she apparently believed a conventional Orthodoxy to be characteristic of the Russian psyche. In any case, her poems are picturesque and dramatic, and not doctrinaire. Her style was quite new and owed much to folk songs. Her rhythms are heavily punctuated, and her vocabulary is sometimes primitive.

Between 1917 and 1922 Tsvetaeva wrote the poems of her tribute to the White Army, *The Swans' Stand;* the book was published abroad, and not until 1957. The volume is memorable for its echoes of Russia's medieval epics about the struggle against the Mongols, especially *The Tale of Igor's Campaign* and *The Zadonshchina*. In some poems she imagines the hardships of battle; in others she grieves for the fallen and praises heroes. Her strong beat and syncopations sometimes recall the factory folk song, or *chastushka*. The fighting spirit that she exhibits here did not appear only in military poems, but was latent in her character at all times.

Tsvetaeva's later books were more general in meaning and more introspective. The poems of *From Psyche* (1923) were written in the same years as those for the *Milestone* volumes, but they are not Russian in spirit. Some were written for or about her children. In others she explored the mentality of such Western figures as Don Juan and Paganini. In *The Craft* and *After Russia* (1928) her deeper concerns appear to have become the problems of living, the nature of experience, the soul. Her nationalism became more mellow and nostalgic. Here is "The Return of the Chief," plainly the fantasy of an émigré:

> The horse—lame.
> The sword—rust.
> Who—is he?
> Chief of hosts.
>
> A step—an hour.
> A sigh—an age.
> Eyes—downcast.
> Those—yonder.
>
> Foe—or friend.
> Thorns—or crown.
> All—but dreams
> —But he—horse.
>
> The horse—lame.
> The sword—rust.
> The cape—old.
> His stance—strong.

Tsvetaeva also devoted a cycle of poems to St. George, the patron saint of Russia, and the dragon. Other poems are memories of the landscapes and holidays of her homeland. Most, however, are cosmopolitan and universal in character. Many are, on the surface, literary or historical references, but she examined these subjects as symbols of the possibilities within the human mind. "Orpheus," for example, appears to be about the light and the dark within each psyche. After the death of Orpheus, his dismembered head and his lyre float down the river Helrus to the Island of Lesbos, where the Orphic Mysteries will be established. The lyre looks forward to the religious mission, but the head looks backward to earthly life. Similar vacillations have presumably always deterred Orpheus in his plans, including his failure to rescue Eurydice, whom he was to lead to the sun's light. In "Hamlet's Dialogue with His Conscience" she expands one moment in Shakespeare's play; the conscience speaks first:

> "She's down below, where silt
> And reeds grow—Off to sleep she
> Went—sleep is not there either!"
> "But I did love her more
> Than forty thousand brothers
> Could have loved her!"
> > "Hamlet!
>
> She's down below, where silt,
> Silt! . . . And her death crown floated
> On logs along the river . . . "
> "But I did love her more
> Than forty thousand . . . "
>
> > "Less yet,
> Than just one lover would have.
>
> She's down below, where silt . . . "
> "But I did—
> > (amazed)
> > > . . . love her??"

Tsvetaeva's own hardships in emigration are the subject of some other poems in *After Russia*. She also described the Alps and other European scenes. She abandoned her folkloric style for these books, but her language is still primitive, now in a personal, colloquial way. She wrote as though recording the impulsive monologues of an erudite individual.

In her several long poems, Tsvetaeva spoke of the same subjects as in her lyrics, but she used styles that were close to those of children's literature. "On a Red Steed" (1922) concludes with the thought that this peasant artistic motif has been her own "genius," or inspiration. "Crossroads," which appeared in *The Craft*, is a lament in childish language for her lost home. Her most popular long poem is a satire of a German-speaking community called "The Pied Piper" (1926); she describes the land as a utopia of trivialities. The seducer's flute speaks of an oriental satiety, and the children are lost.

Tsvetaeva's poetry is, in general, stimulating and often written with passion. At the same time, she had a tendency to function as an observer, or even as a Greek chorus. The result was a certain diffuseness. Her artistic aims—the examination of her own childhood, of the Russian psyche, and finally of the nebulous spheres of morality and desire—are not, in any visible way, inevitably linked. Perhaps her greatest drama was a search for a stable identity. Tsvetaeva's prose is more directly autobiographical than is her poetry, and perhaps contains more clues to her character. In "The Rain of Light" (1922) she praised Pasternak's *My Sister Life* for its lyricism. In *Mother and Music* (1935) she tells in whimsical tones of her youthful decision to make poetry, not music, her métier. *My Pushkin* (1937) is also about her youthful years. In it she describes how her view of the world was steadily enlarged through her expanding knowledge of Pushkin, who wrote about country and history as well as about love and friendship.

Imagism

Russian imagism (1919–1927) emerged from the cubo-futurist milieu as a faction hostile to the parent movement; its founder was the former futurist Vadim Shershenevich. The new group achieved its notoriety in part because a famous peasant poet, Sergey Esenin, joined its ranks. Esenin's easily accessible style remained quite distant from the aggressive experimentation of the avant-gardists, however. The group's manifesto, "Declaration," was issued in 1919 and signed by Shershenevich, Esenin, and Anatoly Mariengof. It advocates the recognition of a potential "image" in every word. These images were to be enhanced, they wrote, by careful attention to their mutual influence in the flow of language. The poetry of the imagists has recognizable traits. It lacks the idyllic primitivism of the cubo-futurists and resembles the rebellious posturing of street-wise urbanites. The imagists were outspoken in their criticism of society's institutions, organization, and tendencies, but they were also cynical. They praised the camaraderie of their bohemian inner circle. Imagist poetry abounds, besides, in vulgarities and in scenes of violence and gore. The imagists were active as publishers and maintained a series of cabarets, of which Pegasus' Stable was the most widely known. They prided themselves on "hooliganism" and self-advertising stunts. They began to be opposed by the government in 1924 and ceased to be a dynamic group after the suicide of Esenin in 1925.

Vadim Shershenevich (1893–1942) was more effective as an organizer than as a poet, but he published a number of small collections of verse. He devoted a great deal of energy to doctrinal statements. The son of a professor, Shershenevich was born in Kazan and educated at Moscow University. His poetry began to be taken seriously only with the publication of *Romantic Face Powder* (1913). In the same year he founded the Mezzanine of Poetry, a Moscow branch of Severianin's ego-futurism, and published his first doctrinal work, *Futurism Without a Mask*. He followed the theories and practice of Marinetti more closely than any of the other Russians; in 1914 and 1915 he published several volumes of translations of the aesthetic treatises of the Italian theorist. By 1914 he had became a cubo-futurist. In

Green Street (1916) Shershenevich articulated views on the word-image that he claimed were formulated by Marinetti and that were to provide the basis of imagism. Shershenevich's collections of poetry included *Automobile Gait* (1916), which he published as a cubo-futurist. The first of his imagist collections was *Just an Ordinary Horse* (1919), and two others were to follow. In its essentials his poetry did not change with his allegiance to new groups. He always expressed both the angry resentment of the avant-gardist and a lonely sense of alienation from society. He echoed Marinetti's admiration for technology and speed. His publications also included a long poem, *Crematorium* (1919), and two plays. During the civil war he joined Maiakovsky in producing propagandistic art for the telegraph agency ROSTA. He later wrote for the theater and cinema. He was a translator of Shakespeare, Corneille, and Brecht.

In the poetry of Anatoly Mariengof (1897–1962) there is both a nihilistic outrage and an attempt at intelligent criticism of Russia's current directions. He was born in Nizhny Novgorod and reared in Penza. He moved to Moscow in 1918 and helped to found imagism in 1919. Mariengof wrote a number of narrative-length lyric poems, an imagist genre; his best is *The Pastry Shop of Suns* (1919). In general, he portrayed, and protested against, the brutality of war and civil war. His obsessive depictions of violence and blood suggest that his anger was great, but he was also capable of irony. In other moods he depicted the carefree bohemian life of his fellow imagists. His close attachment to Esenin in the course of nearly three years is reflected in his poetry. He also made significant doctrinal statements; in *Rowdy Island* (1920) he asserted that imagism blends mysticism with realism. His play *The Conspiracy of Fools* (1922), is set at the court of Empress Anna Ivanovna in the eighteenth century; it suggests that rulers in any era devour their subjects. An autobiographical work called *A Novel Without Lying* (1927) portrays Esenin and others in their imagist milieu. His novel called *The Cynics* (1928) is a bitter and comic tale of two hedonists in the era from 1918 to 1924. Mariengof became a more conventional playwright in his later career.

Peasant Poets

The early-twentieth-century practitioners of rural verse were patronized by symbolists, but they flourished during the avant-garde era. Peasant poetry was fostered at that time both by political populism and by the new taste for the primitive. The pastoral current in Russian literature had already traversed the nineteenth century, and it cut across the barriers of schools. Bucolic life was idealized in realist novels and then in cubo-futurist verse. The peasant poets had no program, no organization, no periodicals. Their leader was Nikolay Kliuev, but it was Sergey Esenin who caught the attention of the nation with his nostalgia for a passing way of life.

The poetry of Nikolay Kliuev (1887–1937) was not limited to the mere reflection of folk songs. His verses also embodied the peasants' religious mentality, their notions of national organization and destiny, and their lore about the world at large. He was born in a peasant family of the Onega region and traveled with religious sectarians around Russia. In 1907 he obtained the patronage of Blok and other poets. Kliuev was sensitive to the differences between literary and folk styles. In *The Ringing of Pines* (1912) his lyrics are relatively literary and even include notes of a vague metaphysical grief. The poems in *Brotherly Songs* (1912) are nearly authentic sectarian pieces; some record religious exultations, while others contain far-fetched superstitious fantasies. The lyrics in *Forest Tales* (1913) and *Worldly Thoughts* (1916) are virtually restricted to folk themes, such as love, death, work, and the change of seasons; but they are written in classical meters, with the exception of the cycle called "Songs from Beyond the Onega." Kliuev hoped that a peasant utopia would appear under a communist regime and he wrote millenarian poems after the Revolution. He eulogized Lenin, whom he called a "lion" in one cycle. By 1922, however, he had come to regard the new order as a new tyranny. His disillusionment is present in his lyrics, but it can best be seen in long poems about Esenin, once his pupil and probably his lover. The most damagingly anti-Soviet of his published works was *The Village* (1927). Others were known in manuscript. He was arrested in 1933 and again in 1935. He died suddenly in 1937 while returning from exile to Moscow.

Esenin

Sergey Esenin (1895–1925) raised peasant poetry to the level of literary verse by somewhat altering its substance and its style. He created a persona that appealed to the imagination of Russians of every class—the innocent country boy spoiled by the iniquitous temptations of an urban bohemia. He was probably more widely popular than any Russian poet before him had been, yet he has been somewhat disdained by the aesthetically fastidious. His verse has been published in numerous popular editions, but it has not been the subject of scholarship. His only solid collection of poetry was *Radunitsa* (the name of a folk funeral ritual, 1916); he appeared thereafter in ephemeral publications and in readings. He also wrote long poems, which have been the least successful part of his work.

Esenin chose the role of peasant poet as an identity for himself in art and in life. He played the part with some tendency to posing, but he genuinely had no full sense of self outside his calling. He was born into a peasant family in a village in Riazan province but lived in Moscow from 1912 to 1915. In 1915 he moved to St. Petersburg and made the acquaintance of Blok, Gorodetsky, and Kliuev, who became his tutor, friend, and perhaps lover. Esenin's fame surpassed his mentor's, and in 1919 he joined Shershenevich and Mariengof in founding the imagist school. Their aesthetic was alien to his, but their hooliganism became a major theme in his verse. In 1923 Esenin married the American dancer Isadora Duncan, who spoke no Russian, and traveled with her in Western Europe and the United States. In 1924 he obtained a divorce, returned to Russia, renounced imagism, and remarried. He suffered from alcoholism but traveled extensively in the Caucasus and beyond. In 1925 he hanged himself in a hotel room in Leningrad, having written a farewell poem in his own blood.

Esenin began as an ordinary peasant poet with a somewhat anonymous voice and became a writer with an identity and a personal style. In his earliest poems, written between 1910 and 1915 in his village of Konstantinovo and in Moscow, he follows the traditions established in the nineteenth century by Koltsov and others. He is an observer of pines, birches, moonlight, and sunsets. Birds are called by their species names. A restrained undercurrent of melancholia in his poems is felt to originate in folk songs. His most stylized and impersonal poems are those about love and flirtations. Occasionally he describes religious pilgrims. In 1914 he began to emphasize Orthodox and nationalist sentiments somewhat in the manner of an observer of peasants rather than as an insider. He described monastery scenes and spoke of his landscapes as part of a vast, low-lying, sometimes bleak, poor country. He came closer to the romantic tradition of Aleksey Tolstoy. He began to cultivate picturesque figures of speech and to highlight his poems with glints of gold and gems—in one case, glass beads (*biser*) for a mother's tears.

Esenin's poetry became deeper and somewhat more mysterious after he moved to St. Petersburg in 1915. He registered a new awareness of pain, and some poems suggest a general loss of innocence. Passions are newly depicted as evil, girls are seen as crafty, and nature is sometimes devastating. A famous poem called "Song About a Dog" describes a bitch who weeps for her drowned puppies. Esenin was thereafter to show the outsider's sympathy for farm animals. He pitied dogs, cows, horses, and then cats. The narrative threads of his poems became unclear and fragmented. A pervasive ornamentalism for which he seemed indebted to modernist poets now colored his peasant poetry. Here is a poem called "Autumn" (1916):

> Silence. In the junipers atop the valley,
> Autumn—a roan mare—rubs up her name for dressing.
>
> Well above the wooded river banks—
> That's the dark blue clang her horseshoes make.
>
> Wind, a monk, walks past with wary footsteps
> Holding back the foliage on the pathways,
>
> Kissing, when he comes upon the mountain ash,
> Crimson wounds that are the marks of Christ unseen.

It was in 1916 that Esenin began to speak of a "returning" to the paternal home, from which he had become an alienated outcast. He knew he was "Esenin, Sergey," on his way to fame. This pre-Revolutionary period was the last in which he spoke freely of his own religious beliefs.

During his imagist period, between 1919 and 1922, Esenin's poetry became yet more nostalgic and bitter, and he was less productive. He wrote "I am the last village poet" (1919), and in other lyrics he anticipated the demise of his peasant culture in the age of railroads and industry. He wrote of himself as having grown old and having been passed by. He described his drinking and his fighting as an urban hooligan. His poems do not reveal that his antisocial behavior was associated with a literary movement or a sophisticated bohemia. He wrote as though he had succumbed, like the hero of "Woe-Misfortune" in the seventeenth century, to a traditional temptation. In his waywardness, he perhaps also drew on the conventional peasant idealization of the runaway nomad.

The last four years of Esenin's life brought a return to steady writing and a greater versatility in tone. His love poems became more personal, at first ecstatic and resentful, during his association with Duncan. His alienation from society acquired a finality: he wrote as a former hooligan, a former religious believer and a former village boy who may visit home but not return. In this period he wrote "A Letter to My Mother," in which he promises to visit her, and "Son of a Bitch" on finding at home the offspring of his deceased pet. He had presentiments of death. The years 1924 and 1925, however, were Esenin's most fruitful. In a cycle called "Persian Motifs" he records a new love or loves. He describes his Persian partner as formed by the exotic, hedonistic East, while he is the honest but desperate Russian. The poems of 1925 are firmly written, but they are not well known. They include a number of love poems addressed to women who remain anonymous. Other poems suggest that his homosexual ties might have been a stronger, but hidden, part of his psyche. "Farewell, Baku" was written in 1925:

> Farewell, Baku! I won't be back to see you.
> My soul is filled with grief, my soul is filled with fear.
> The heart beneath my hand is sicker, and it's nearer.
> I ever stronger sense a simple word: my friend.
>
> Farewell, Baku! Blue Turkish sea, farewell!
> The blood flows chill, and strengths are ever weaker.
> But I shall bear, like happiness, to graveside
> These Caspian waves, this Balakhany town in May.
>
> Farewell, Baku! Just like a simple folk song!
> My friend I shall enfold this one last time . . .
> So that his head, as though a rose of golden color,
> Within its lilac haze will nod to me again.

Esenin's suicide poem, "Goodbye, my friend, goodbye" (1925), contains textual echoes of the Persian cycle. Esenin also wrote long poems which have never entered into the popular image of his work and for which his talent was not suited.

VII

SOVIET
AND
ÉMIGRÉ
POETRY

15

Between the Wars
(1925–1939)

The Soviet era has been marked by a stringent economy, the threat of military involvements, and diminished avenues of communication, both internally and with the West. The late 1920s brought the first of the five-year plans and the beginning of the collectivization of agriculture. In the late 1930s came the great Stalinist purges. In the same period the call for writers to observe the "social command" became an imposition of socialist realism as an official policy. During the early five-year plans (1928–1941) factories lost during the civil war were rebuilt, and vast construction projects, often symbolized by the hydroelectric dam, were begun. These sweeping events were reflected in Soviet literature. But the underlying theme of most Soviet literature, whatever its political tendency, was the relationship between communal needs and private lives. "Proletarian" literature spoke for the rights of the former; other authors made veiled pleas for the latter. Meanwhile, the writers in emigration formed circles in France, Germany, Prague, and elsewhere. They were seldom concerned with Soviet subjects; instead, they carried on the traditions they had known in the pre-Revolutionary past.

Soviet Romanticism

Inside the Soviet Union some of the greatest poets, including Pasternak, Mandelstam, and Akhmatova, exerted only a minimal influence on the newcomers. The older poets who had not been political revolutionaries had little to say to those new poets, like Nikolay Tikhonov, who were enthusiastic in their Soviet sentiments. The young socialist poets acknowledged the lead of Maiakovsky, but in a philosophical sense they were not his heirs, either. The new Soviet romantics were political conformists, not rebels. Their romanticism consisted, first and foremost, in their ideological fervor and emotional tonality. They usually depicted the war, the Revolution, and the civil war, and their style was colorful. Thus Tikhonov described the experiences of a Red Army man in a work called *Mead* (1922). The new poets regarded military action as rough and ready; they were inclined to favor adventure stories. Their romanticism was also visible in their taste for picturesque and exotic locations. Ilia Selvinsky set his poems in Siberia, Asia, the polar north, the Crimea, and elsewhere, where he himself held odd jobs. Revolutionary poets characteristically used somewhat experimental forms during the 1920s; they were aware of their debt to futurism. The newest phase of the avant-garde, however, was constructivism. It was the new poets who in 1924 organized the Literary Center of Constructivists. Their theoretical aim was to make literature into documentary statements or into collages of documentaries.

There remained Soviet poets who belonged to the truly individualistic current of the avant-garde, but they did not thrive. They did not write about military or revolutionary subjects, and their perceptions of the world were transformed into unrealistic visions. Foremost among them was Nikolay Zabolotsky, whose outlook was mildly absurdist and whose styles were often grotesque. He belonged to an obscure school called the Oberiu (1927–1930), whose name was an approximate acronym for the Association for Real Art. The theories and practice of the group stemmed from futurism in its more irrational aspects, including transsense language, or *zaum*. Its leaders were the minor poets Daniil Kharms and Aleksandr Vvedensky. These more extreme avant-gardists were sometimes to find a place at Detgiz, the publishing house for children's literature, under Samuil Marshak, a well-known author of juvenile poetry.

Conformity with the tendencies of socialist realism came later to poetry than to fiction, but the steps were the same. Some poets joined the state-sponsored RAPP (Russian Association of Proletarian Writers), which preceded the Writers' Union from 1928 to 1932. RAPP advocated a return to nineteenth-century realism for fiction writers; for poets the policy had to be less clear. In 1932 the Union of Writers replaced RAPP and all other literary organizations. In 1934 a meeting of the new organization was convened at which socialist realism was adopted as the inexorable policy of the state for all writers. In the 1930s some poets began to depict five-year-plan projects; Selvinsky devoted several long poems to some of these ambitious enterprises. Poetic styles that had been common before 1910 reappeared. Zabolotsky was arrested in 1938 for his nonconformist depictions of the process of agricultural collectivization in the late 1920s.

Tikhonov

A long career as a stalwart spokesman for orthodox Communist Party views was enjoyed by Nikolay Tikhonov (1896–1979). He celebrated the triumphs of the revolutionary movement and of the Soviet Union, at home and abroad. He expressed the views of the soldier. He delighted in the exotic aspects of Russia's outlying areas—the Caucasus, the Crimea, and Siberia—and described them as a curious observer. He felt no need to communicate the sense of a unique identity and never exploited the confessional genre. Tikhonov was born in St. Petersburg, the son of a tradesman, and graduated from a business school. He served as a hussar in World War I and then in the Red Army. In 1921 he joined the Serapion Brothers, a literary group that called for the preservation of artistic freedoms. His early poetry proved to be his best, especially his descriptions of the civil war in *Mead*. He traveled in Georgia, Armenia, and Central Asia during the 1920s and 1930s. He was prolific both as a poet and as a short story writer. He was active throughout his career in writers' organizations. He represented the Soviet Union in international congresses and served as Secretary of the Communist Party of the Soviet Union.

Tikhonov's *oeuvre* is a reflection of the historical fortunes of the Soviet Union as seen through the eyes of an intelligent and loyal citizen. The first of eight books that would appear in the 1920s and 1930s was *The Horde* (1921), a record of his experiences in World War I. The book shows that he had a zest for military action even before the Revolution. He finds in the act of killing and in the fear of being killed a source of exhilaration and a positive moral good in itself. He also speaks of deserving the admiration of women. *Mead,* however, is informed by a more ideological enthusiasm. The first poem expresses his elation over the victory of the Revolution in 1917:

> The years cannot be trampled out, denied—
> Our axes hewed at timber everlasting.
> But suddenly our cracking lips were scorched—
> From Timeless regions came that boiling water.
>
> We learned to fly on wings, taught by the wind.
> A fire roared up and turned our blood to amber,
> And comrades in the night did drink dark mead
> That welled with gratitude from earthly nature.
>
> Beneath a sky that started from surprise,
> It could be seen, in wild decor and simple,
> That in each glance there seethed a rising star,
> And in each stride our space grew ever wider.

In the subsequent poems he descends from this level of abstraction to describe the impact of raw experience on the soldier. He sees, for example, that a civil war can be especially painful because even personal relationships may turn out to be treacherous. Tikhonov had a literary mentality; he describes not only war, but landscapes and sea scenes. He alludes to Mephistopheles, the Lorelei, Thor, and the Mikado. Nevertheless, the Party line became Tikhonov's guide in *The Quest for a Hero,* whose poems were written between 1923 and 1926. He disdains the foes of the Soviet Union, such as the Finns, Estonians, British, Americans, and Armenians, as "Lilliputians" or as oppressors. His ideal, or hero, he discovers in the Soviet man on the street. Tikhonov's long poems include a eulogy of Lenin called *Face to Face* (1924). It was in his picturesque poems about southern and eastern areas that his love of beauty and his lyrical feeling could be found. In *Yurga* (1930) and *Poems About Kakhetia* (1935) he showed his affection for mountainous terrain, local color, and the music of foreign names, like Shiram and Dzhugan Tsinandeli.

The poems Tikhonov wrote during the era of World War II were devoted in one way or another to the effort to win. Many were simply about the allies and enemies of the Soviet Union. He began to recall the Western allies of World War I in the years before World War II. *The Shade of a Friend* (1936) includes sympathetic descriptions of some national holidays in the West, and even of the events they commemorate. His title is a reference to a poem by Batiushkov. The first signs of World War II come in *Autumn Strolls* (1940), in which he hears that Paris is burning, that London is shaken by attacks. Most of his wartime poems are devoted to the heroism of Russians, first in the war against Finland in 1940 and later during the siege of Leningrad, in 1942. Many postwar poems are descriptions of Yugoslavia and the Ukraine. He enjoyed the magnificence of their landscapes, and he described the suffering and modest accomplishments of their ordinary people.

Tikhonov did not respond immediately to the Thaw. His first recognition that his nation had been engaged in a reappraisal of the past came in *Times and Paths* (1969). In "The Sun's Inspection" he describes how a rebirth may result from a simple event: the entry into a house of a sunset ray that illuminates the entire interior in a new way. His other poems are comments on aspects of history and culture. He recalls the hardships of such cities as Leningrad and Warsaw. He praises the accomplishments of Peter the Great. He describes Georgia and Azerbaidzhan as though in travelogue scenes. Tikhonov's last lyrics were written in the spirit of a search for peace, harmony, and a reconciliation with the past. Tikhonov was by preference an observer, and portrayed himself as both modest and ordinary. He chose for his poetry the role of citizen.

Selvinsky

Ilia Selvinsky (real name: Karl; 1899–1968) was a quixotic, and prolific, creator of lyrics, tales, and verse plays on widely diverse and colorful topics. His underlying subject was, however, the class struggle. His many topics reflected his own life of adventure as well as his lively imagination. He was born the son of a furrier in the Crimea. He worked on the docks and in a circus, graduated from Moscow University, and became, in 1924, a founder and leader of the constructivist literary school. His first book of lyrics, *Records,* appeared in 1926, and his most successful epic, *The Ulialaev Uprising,* in 1927. He subsequently taught fur farming in Kirghizia, participated in a polar expedition, traveled in Europe and Asia, and served as an officer in World War II. His themes included man's life among the animals, the commercial instinct, and military confrontations. He was fond of Asian settings and of dialect renderings. His popularity was at its height from the 1930s through the 1950s.

Selvinsky's early works reveal the natural defiance of a rebel character. Moreover, he was at first confident that the avant-garde rebellion and the political revolution were to go hand in hand. His early poetry was, accordingly, experimental and sometimes witty. His first book, *Records,* opens with "Transitionals," a poem in which he describes with satisfaction Europe's horror of the new Soviet barbarians. He attacked the commercial tendencies of the NEP period. He identified himself, as Maiakovsky had, with the deprived, and he espoused utopianism. That done, he turned to whimsy—in Gypsy songs, "anecdotes" about a comical Turkish philosopher, and an exotic cycle called "A Crimean Collection." His early poems include, however, the gripping "Report" (1924), which describes the death of a proud White Army officer:

> To the President of the Troika,
>   Mister Dolinin,
>   From the Cavalry Captain Bravin,
>   A REPORT:
> By the order of the Kronstadt regional
>   Kommandant
> Of the fourth bastion (Southwest),
> For my having commanded during the intervention
>   of Karelia
> The White armored train "Roarer"—
> On the eve of the third—I was shot
> And buried in a ditch.
> To uphold the honor of the Russian flag,
> I request that the poor marksmen responsible be held to account,
> And that I should be, on the same spot, by that rock,
>   *Shot to death.*
>   The signature: Bravin.
>   Lucerne Township.
>   March 3.
> The number of the entry and the decision:
> No objection. Granted.

Aside from being gruesome, the poem was intended to illustrate the constructivist dictum that an entire epic poem, with great historical and social sweep, could be encompassed in the length of a lyric poem. The poem was also typical of Selvinsky's obvious interest in the subject of deliberate killings, whether of people or of animals.

Selvinsky's reflections on the acquisitive impulse included a hidden sympathy, which he relinquished in time. In his epic called *The Ulialaev Uprising* he described with verve and admiration the fortunes of a kulak, Ulialaev, who seized an estate from its pre-Revolutionary owner and was later defeated in an anarchist rebellion by the Red Army. Selvinsky's depictions are folkloric. The hero's wife, first taken from the landowner, is brutally murdered, her corpse dragged by a horse, and her head impaled on a spear by the Red commander. Ulialaev himself is shot and decapitated. In the 1950s this tale had to be rewritten, and its hero became Lenin. Other narratives by Selvinsky included *The Fur Trade* (1929), a production epic for the five-year-plan era. In this work he attacked liberals, émigrés, "inside émigrés," and other enemies. In his style he combined literary allusions, often to Byron, with Soviet acronyms and some avant-garde distortions.

Selvinsky's attitudes, as well as his styles, became progressively more conventional from the 1930s through the 1950s. His plays describe attempts to socialize the primitive. They include *Pao-Pao* (1932), about an ape who is enlightened through work, and "Umka the Polar Bear" (1933), about the modernization of an Arctic tribe. The lyrics he wrote in the 1930s include travel impressions, often quite biased, of Japan, Paris, Poland, and England. World War II brought expressions of pride in the history of his nation. He also wrote accounts of his own sleeplessness and deprivations as an officer, and of the sight of corpses and mourners. His postwar lyrics include a belated confrontation with the theme of lovesickness, and then quiet celebrations of family life and poems on love of country. In general, the teeming variety of Selvinsky's works stemmed from what seemed at first to be a genuinely irrepressible character. But his imagination was superficial, and the lessons of his works were in the end predictable.

Bagritsky

Signs of a dual loyalty, to art and to state, can be seen in the works of Eduard Bagritsky (real surname: Dziubin; 1895–1934). In some poems he typified the socialistic verve so often found in works celebrating the Revolution. He was invited to rewrite his 1926 civil war epic, *The Lay of Opanas,* as a libretto for an opera. Yet his first love in literature was the preromantic era in Europe, and his own best lyrics were intensely private in inspiration. He was born in Odessa, into a Jewish family, fought in the civil war, and settled in Moscow in 1925. There he joined Pereval, a literary group that was dedicated to communist principles, but that put a refined interpretation on the notion of "social command." Later he joined the constructivists, and in 1930 he entered RAPP. His first collection of lyrics was *The Southwest* (1932). His successful career was cut short by tuberculosis.

Bagritsky attempted in his major works to adapt the genres of early Western romanticism to Soviet circumstances. The title of his first book, *The Southwest,* points not only to his origin in Odessa but also to his sympathy for the European west. He opens the book with adaptations from Western legends, including a Till Eulenspiegel story, and from the works of such English authors as Robert Burns and Walter Scott. Bagritsky's "Melon" traces the progress of the fruit to market in the style of sentimental poems on how grain becomes bread. His "Contrabandists" is a merry smuggler's song, and his "Autumn" is a grand elegy celebrating the plenitude of life on the southern seashore. It was in this context that his *The Lay of Opanas,* ostensibly an imitation of the Ukrainian folk narrative genre, appeared. His hero, Opanas, is a Ukrainian rebel who joined the forces of the separatist Makhno and incurred the personal enmity of the Red commissar Kogan, a Jew. The style of the piece owes much to the *byliny.* Here he sets the stage for a duel:

> Poplars in a gray flock standing,
> Poplar scented breezes . . .
> O Ukrainian land, our mother,
> O this song of home! . . .
> Steppe land stretching far and yonder,
> Grasses dry and bending,
> Tumbleweed that whistles, rolling,
> Crows' caws, loud and raucous . . .

> Lo, the sun of battle rises
> On a meadow pathway,
> On that road but two men enter—
> Opanas and Kogan.

Later comes the elegiac epilogue:

> Gone are now the years of duels
> From Ukrainian pastures.
> Early waters rise no longer
> With their din and rustle . . .
> I know not now where our hero's
> Bones do lie if buried:
> Maybe in a bank of willows,
> Maybe in a graveyard. . . .

He concludes the poem with praise for both contenders. In "The Cigarette Box" Bagritsky celebrates, in sentimental fashion, a friendship between men. And in a lyric poem called "Lines About a Nightingale and a Poet" he complains about having to write utilitarian poems for newspapers.

Bagritsky shared with his readers, as Laurence Sterne once had, his anticipation of his impending death from tuberculosis. *The Victors* (1932) opens with "Origins," a poem in which he describes the loveless Jewish family in which he was first awakened by youth to wholesome ambitions, to love, and to philosophical questions. There follow poems in which human professions are cast in painful perspectives. In "Cyprinna Carpio" he surrounds the fish farmer with the interwoven imagery of reproduction and of knives. In "Spring, the Veterinarian, and I" he describes the doctor's thankless dedication to animals. Bagritsky's own profession as a poet has brought the accusations of literary critics. In "TB" he describes the physical sensations that stifle the already sick man who learns that he will die. His next book, *The Last Night* (1932), is plainly the work of a man condemned by disease. In the title poem he recalls the "last night" of his youth. In the last poem he describes the closeness between a dying girl and her grieving mother.

Bagritsky requested that these three volumes of lyrics remain intact, without the intrusion of his other poems, which have a wide variety of subjects, sometimes patriotic, and sometimes propagandistic. His cynicism about professions perhaps went beyond the scope of sentimentalism and romanticism in the early nineteenth century; but his poems remained quite traditional in form, and his style was lovingly old-fashioned.

Lesser Socialist Poets

The general level of competence among poets was high in the late 1920s and the early 1930s. A great period had recently passed, and the amount of verse still written and published was considerable. The socialist camp included a number of deserving poets. Among them was Vera Inber (1890–1972), who was perhaps better known as a journalist and memoirist. She began with poetry, however, and was the author of a popular long poem, *The Pulkov Meridian* (1943), about the blockade of Leningrad during World War II. She was born the daughter of a publisher in Odessa, and spent the years 1910 to 1917 in Paris. She was in Odessa during the civil war years and moved in 1922 to Moscow, where she became a staunch constructivist. In the late 1920s she worked as a journalist in Paris, Brussels, and Berlin, and turned to prose sketches, short stories, and autobiographical works.

Inber's first three books of poetry, beginning with *The Wine of Melancholia* (1914), were published under the influence of French and Russian symbolists. Her realistic publications began with *The Aim and the Way* in 1925. In *To the Son I Do Not Have* (1927) she began to exploit the sentimental side of communal life. Her title poem is a lullabye patterned on the folk form. She cultivated a simple style that can be seen in her commemoration of the death of Lenin, "Five Nights and Days"; she describes the mourning of the crowds of average people. She recognized her own contribution to Soviet styles in "Sotto voce," a quiet celebration of the 1932 anniversary of the October Revolution. She described the blockade of Leningrad in several of her books; in each one she shows how the common people rise to heroism. Her lyrics appeared in *The Soul of Leningrad* (1942). In her "epic," *The Pulkov Meridian,* she depicts such momentous scenes as the first artillery fire; her style is studiously unassuming and everyday throughout. In 1946 Inber published a well-known prose account of the blockade called *Almost Three Years*. In the 1950s she wrote both prose and poetry for children, and in 1960 she published a book of poems about Lenin called *April*. The modesty of her voice is everywhere at odds with her real sophistication and wide experience as a European correspondent.

Vladimir Lugovskoy (1901–1957) wrote conventional military and socialist verse that is now overshadowed by the imaginative lyrics about everyday life that he wrote during the Thaw. He was born in Moscow, the son of a teacher of Russian literature. He completed the Military Pedagogical Institute in 1921 and served in the Red Army during the civil war. In 1926 he joined the constructivists and in 1930, RAPP. Lugovsky's experiences in the civil war appear in *Lightning* (1926) and *Muscle* (1929). "The Song of the Wind" embodies a typically revolutionary fervor, but landscapes and love poems also appear among his early verse. During the Stalin years he traveled in Central Asia, with the fleet in the Mediterranean, and in Central Europe. Many poems reflect these exotic places, particularly those of *To the Bolsheviks the Deserts and Springs* (three volumes in 1931, 1933, and 1948). In *Life* (1933) he became more personal and philosophical. And in the 1950s he published his most original books, *The Sun's Orbit* (1956), *Blue Spring* (1958), and *Mid-Century* (1958). Among the most popular poems of these books is "The Bear," a little ballad about a teddy bear who tries at night to return to the forest: "Just because, without our midnight stories, / Life is dull, for people and for beasts." "The Girls' School Vengerka" describes a graduation dance in the ominous year 1919. Both poems had been written in 1939. The title poem of his last book, *Mid-Century,* is an elegy set in the country on an autumn night. In his last period, he also wrote reflections on history and on the future. His comments on philosophical and private subjects are not deep, but they are free from any utilitarian purpose. His verse is usually traditional, but some poems are laddered in the style of Maiakovsky.

Pavel Antokolsky (1896–1978) made no apparent distinction between a dedication to art and service to the state. He had a romantic taste for the bizarre, but his essential concern was for the history and growth of cultures as such. He regularly depicted France and Germany, but he also dealt without constraint with themes dictated by socialist realism. He was born in St. Petersburg, the son of a lawyer. He began as an actor, and became a director in Evgeny Vakhtangov's experimental theater. An early collection was called *The West* (1926), and many lyrics in it reflect his sympathy for Europe. Even in the era of the five-year plans, he wrote historical epics set in the West while his colleagues wrote about Russia. He demonstrated in his narratives, however, that revolutionary zeal can also be found abroad; his first significant epic poem was *The Commune of 1871* (1933), and another depicts the Weimar Republic. In a long poem called *François Villon* (1934) he celebrated the rebel character as such. Antokolsky's view that art contributes to the process of civilization is reflected in such lyrics as "The Craft," where poetry is seen as a form of dialogue, and in "Shakespeare," where the playwright's work is immortal because it will always admit of new interpretations and insights. In the 1930s Antokolsky conformed more closely to socialist realist norms for poetry, and during World War II he wrote patriotic lyrics. His best work, however, is a lament, *The Son* (1943), written after the death of his son. In the postwar period he published new epics, including *Eighteen-Hundred Forty Eight* (1948), set in Europe. *The Strength of Vietnam* (1960) was written to praise the common folk, but the work is an experimental mélange combining descriptions with commentary and verse with prose. In the lyric "Marina" (1962) he paid tribute to the poet Tsvetaeva and professed again his undiminished awe before the capacity of poetry to endure.

Unconventional Soviet Poets: Zabolotsky

The work of those poets who preserved the heritage of the radical avant-garde was very similar to that of the expressionists and surrealists abroad. The Russians were brought together to some extent in the group called Oberiu, but the times would not have allowed the full development of any avant-garde school. The most visible of the new avant-gardists was Nikolai Zabolotsky (1903–1958), whose first and best book was *Columns* (1929). His work is like that of the moderate futurists of the pre-Revolutionary era: the events he describes are commonplace, but his perception of them is distorted and fantastic. He was born in Kazan, the son of an agronomist. He completed the Herzen Pedagogical Institute in Leningrad in 1925 and later joined the Oberiu. *Columns* was followed in 1930 by a satirical long poem, "The Celebration of Agriculture" (1930), for which he was severely criticized. He was employed thereafter by Detgiz, the publishing house for children's literature, both as an author and as a translator; his version of *Till Eulenspiegel* appeared in 1934. In 1938 he was arrested, and after his release in 1946 he was prohibited from living in Moscow or Leningrad. He settled in Tarusa and returned to translating and to writing, but in a more sober vein.

In the poems of *Columns* Zabolotsky often describes sights that are familiar, either from public or from private life. He observes, for example, the crowds at a tavern, at the farmer's market, at church, or in the museum. He responds to such popular events as the death of a sports hero. These harmless subjects are turned by him into grotesques; the events become meaningless in themselves, but disturbing in an undefined way. The people in these scenes live through them in great passions and agonies. The tavern is a Bedlam; a tempestuous Gypsy singer feels the Caucasian river Aragva in her breast. In the following poem, a corpse performs its own funeral procession:

Eau forte

Through all of the deafening hall came the shout:
The dead man ran out of the house of the tsar!

The dead man walks proudly along all the streets
And tavern guests lead him along by the bit.
He chants in a trumpeting voice his own prayer
And raises his arms to the skies.
His pince-nez is bronze, and holds on to his nostrils,
He's filled to the throat with the water of swamps.
The birds, made of wood, make a knocking above him—
They shut on the wings of the doors.
What a din, like a thunder, and crackling of top hats,
The sky's curly-headed, and lo—
There's a vault in the town with a wide open door,
And with rosemary at its small panes.

Zabolotsky intensifies the realities in his poems through a ridiculous accumulation of excesses. An artillery man is shot not once but repeatedly, as if in a frenetic dream. The heaps of food laid out at a wedding become revolting. His scenes are deliberately painful, distressing, or tasteless. His beggars at the market are amputees or blind. His crowds include people who are sexually aroused. The plants in his landscapes are animated, and his scenes often include dogs. Zabolotsky's language itself is breathless and obsessive. Without making any philosophical statement whatsoever, he creates a world in which the activities of humans are perceived as heated, but lacking in any reasonable motivation. In the long poem called "The Celebration of Agriculture" Zabolotsky satirizes a conference at a collective farm where a soldier, not a farmer, presides and controls events. The very animals complain of their treatment. At the end, a false harmony is achieved, and even the arts are said to flourish on the farm.

The poems Zabolotsky published in A Second Book (1937) were apparently unchanged in subject, but their underlying tonality is different. He became less satirical. Although his manner was as witty and picturesque, the curiosity he had once displayed about life was reduced to superficial questions. He became sentimental and he turned more often to landscapes and to abstract topics, such as death. The poems he wrote after his release from prison in 1946 were dramatically different from all his earlier work. In the new poems, his cynicism was completely gone, replaced by expressions of a great joy. He delighted in the dawn, in storms, in Beethoven's music, in the wisdom of Socrates. "The Testament" tells of his gratitude for life. In other poems he described the exotic scenes of the Caucasus, the Urals, the steppe. Love was not a common topic for Zabolotsky in his lyrics, but it plays a large role in his unfinished long poem "Lodeinikov," the name of his protagonist.

The Oberiu group, which came into being in 1927, resulted from an attempt to bring together the avant-garde writers and painters in Leningrad. Its two leaders, Daniil Kharms and Aleksandr Vvedensky, were active poets and playwrights, and Kharms wrote fiction. Oberiu stood in literature for the tendency to depict concrete things and to disassociate them from their ordinary contexts. The writers were influenced by such modernist painters as Pavel Filonov in their distortions and fragmentations of reality. The Oberiuty thought of themselves as "leftists" in art and in life, but their art was denigrated by Marxist critics. They ceased to be active in 1930, and the group was nearly forgotten. When its publications and manuscripts came to light in the Thaw period, the Oberiu had become an unofficial literature in the hands of dissidents and circulated in *samizdat*. The impact of the lyrics written by Daniil Kharms (real surname: Iuvachev; 1905–1942) was slight; he was more successful at cameo pieces of fiction. He was born in St. Petersburg, the son of an unsuccessful writer. He began to appear at poetry readings in 1925 and published his poetry, prose, and plays in ephermeral brochures. The essence of his work is its insistence on the illogical. His pieces are usually dreamlike fantasies. He also wrote in transsense language, or *zaum*. He coined neologisms and made use of syntactically disrupted sentences. The following poem is dated 1928:

> On Tuesdays up above the streets
> A gas balloon did empty fly.
> It soared in silence through the air;
> And in it someone smoked a pipe,
> He gazed at squares and yards below,
> He gazed in peace 'til Wednesday came,
> On Wednesday he would douse the lamp,
> And say, ah well, the town's alive.

For all their illogical procedures, Kharms's poems are explorations of human relationships, in urban and in country settings. Their opaque quality suggests not only the tomfoolery of experimental art, but also an inclination to defiance. Yet some poems are quite successful at rendering moods and insights. Kharms became a children's author, writing for Detgiz and for the magazines *Ezh* (*Hedgehog*) and *Chizh* (*Siskin*) edited by Samuil Marshak. In 1931 Kharms was arrested on the grounds that transsense poetry constituted a distraction from socialist construction. He returned to Leningrad in 1932, but he was arrested again in 1941 and died of starvation in prison.

The poetry of Aleksandr Vvedensky (1904–1941) was even more obscure than that of Kharms. Vvedensky was born in St. Petersburg, the son of an economist, and spent his short life in avant-garde circles, especially those of painters. He wrote lyric poems, short dramatic poems, and plays. His best work, the avant-garde play "Christmas at the Ivanovs'" (1938), is a durable work; in its latent anger it resembles the earlier plays of Alfred Jarry in France. Vvedensky also wrote children's literature and contributed to *Ezh* and *Chizh*. He moved to Kharkov in 1936, was arrested in 1941, and died the same year.

The men who took children's literature upon themselves during this era also deserve to be remembered. Foremost among them was Korney Chukovsky (1882–1969). He worked primarily as an editor, organizer, essayist, and academic scholar. He began to write for children in 1916 and became well known for his fairy tales in verse. His book of comments on children, called *From Two to Five,* has been translated into English and other languages. Samuil Marshak (1887–1964) began to write for children in 1923 and founded the state children's publishing house, Detgiz, as well as several magazines for children, including *Ezh* and *Chizh*. His own poetry for children was so imaginative and well written that it often attracted adults as well. Marshak once studied at the University of London and was influenced by English, as well as Russian, folklore. He also wrote poetry for adults and was known as a translator of English poetry.

Trends in Emigration: The Parisian Note

Émigré Russian poetry was notably lacking in topical subjects and was seldom inspired by the notion of art as a utilitarian activity. The wars themselves were reflected only infrequently, and Soviet developments in poetry were ignored. The émigré poets carried forward the currents that were familiar to them from the past; they tended, moreover, to be meditative and philosophical. The finest poet in exile was Marina Tsvetaeva, but she was no more a leader, or even a practical guide, than Pasternak was in the Soviet Union. Vladislav Khodasevich was admired as a poet, and he fostered, as an influential editor, a current of pessimism and restraint. But the majority of the poets who first flourished in emigration were indebted more directly to the acmeist tradition. These émigré circles found a principal leader in Georgy Adamovich (1884–1972), who was an editor, a literary critic, and a minor poet. In the early 1930s he organized a new school called the Parisian Note. This circle took a dark view of the cosmos and of the capacities of human nature. They rejected the optimistic humanism of their predecessors, the acmeists. In style they were traditionalists, and they favored a plain and simple manner based on concrete imagery. The major representative of the Parisian Note was Georgy Ivanov, who had been a minor poet in St. Petersburg. This skeptical school had adamant opponents, who formed their own coteries. Among them were those poets who remained faithful to religious tendencies, whether Christian or Jewish; their spokesman was Iury Terapiano. Others valued the heritage of the Western cultural tradition or its newest poetic techniques.

Several modernist schools were traversed by Georgy Ivanov (1894–1958) before he came to rest in the Parisian Note. He was close to the acmeists in that his major concern throughout his work was, as it had been for them, the place of man in the universe. His skeptical statements sometimes placed him as close to the *fin de siècle* decadents as he was to the Parisian Note. He was born in a provincial town in western Russia and enlisted as a young man in the elite St. Petersburg Cadet Corps. He appeared very early in literary circles and published his first collection, *Depar-*

ture for the Isle of Cythera, in 1912. In the same year he joined the acmeist Guild of Poets. In 1921 he married the poet Irina Odoevtseva, and in 1923 they emigrated to Paris. There he joined the Green Lamp, a literary group led by the symbolists Dmitri Merezhkovsky and Zinaida Hippius. But Ivanov found a more congenial place with Georgy Adamovich in the Parisian Note. He matured as a poet in emigration, and his audience has been limited primarily to Russians abroad. He published with some regularity; his best poems appeared in *Roses* (1931). During World War II, he and Odoevtseva lived in Biarritz. He died in ill health and in poverty in southern France.

However often Ivanov denied his love for pre-Revolutionary Russian culture, his poetry was always a deliberate expression of its traditions. His first six books, published in Russia before his emigration, show him to have been a willing participant in nearly every current around him. In *Departure for the Isle of Cythera* he is plainly an ego-futurist and much under the influence of the urbane decadence of Igor Severianin. Ivanov is another world-weary figure preoccupied with introspective reflections, or with love's incidents; he is amoral and sad. He differed from his mentor, however, in his reliance on the conventions of a classical mentality, on allusions to such mythical figures as Diana and Icarus. He imitated the pastoral idyll, the triolet, the ghazel, and other venerable genres, even including an acrostic.

In his acmeist period Ivanov made much of his attachment to the substance and signs of European, and global, culture. The lyrics of *The Chamber* (1914) are about historical events and exotic places. *The Monument of Glory* (1915) consists of patriotic responses to World War I. His poems are anthems, short narratives about soldiers, and expressions of gratitude to the Allied nations, including France and England. *Heather* (1916) shows the love of the connoisseur and collector for the artifacts and symbols of Western culture. His poems are about various *objets d'art,* maps, engravings, and small paintings, particularly Flemish. His knowledge of the arts and of arcane subjects is intimate and unabashedly precious. He admires Watteau. The closed sphere he creates in these poems is simplified in emotions, yet intricate in design, warm, tasteful, and always peaceful. His escapism suggests a residual nostalgia, but his tone is tender and soft-spoken. No great step was needed to arrive at the poems of *Gardens* (1921) and *The Icon Lamp* (1922), where he imitated the *fin de siècle* mentality. Like Verlaine or Innokenty Annensky, Ivanov spoke of his sadness, his loves, and the landscapes of his imagination. He drew on the imagery of nightingales, moonlight, and shepherd's horns.

Once he was abroad, Ivanov's sadness began to seem philosophically motivated, and it emerged as a bitter pessimism. He portrayed himself as living still in comfort and plenty, and amid natural beauties such as sunsets. Yet he is cold inside; he now professes an indifference (never believable) to history and to his distant homeland. The following poem illustrates his pleasure in emptiness:

> How good it is—without a Tsar.
> How good it is—without our Russia.
> How good it is—without a God.
>
> Only just the yellow dusk.
> Only just the icy starlight.
> Only just a million years.

> How good it is—that nothing is,
> How good it is—that no one is,
> Now it is so black and dead,
>
> That a death could be no deeper,
> That no black could be more black,
> That no one will ever help us—
> We ourselves don't ask for help.

Ivanov speaks in other poems of his loves, his changing moods, and the landscapes he observes. His usual voice is intimate and low-keyed. His other books include *A Portrait Without Resemblance* (1950) and *1943–1958 Poems* (1958). The world of Ivanov's poetry is somewhat disconcertingly narrow, but it is finely crafted and effective. It strikes no new notes; his melancholia is familiar, as is his notion of a world without meaning.

The poets of the Parisian Note were relatively explicit about their premises. They were religious skeptics, and they no longer trusted in the fabric of civilization; but they espoused, like the acmeists, a high morality. They aimed at simplicity in style, and in particular they avoided figures of speech. They admired the work of the decadent Annensky without resembling him. A resonant sense of culture and history is absent from the small *oeuvre* of Anatoly Steiger (1907–1944). His complaints are elementary, but his poems are more than usually convincing. His acquaintance with culture is visible in his mastery. He was born Baron Steiger near Kiev. He had to stay in an orphanage in Constantinople after 1917. His family was reunited in Prague and then went to Paris, where he joined the Parisian Note. He was a journalist during World War II and countered Nazi propaganda. He died of tuberculosis in Switzerland. The fullest of his four books is the posthumous *Twice Two Makes Four. Poems 1926–1939* (1950). His poems are often philosophical, despite their modest character. He spoke of an empty universe and of a world without love. Some poems are about his own pain. His style is almost primitive and can be brutal in effect. Here is his account of a loss:

> Is this parting the last one, here?
> Yes, my heart knows it is—the ending.
> It sees all. To the finish. Straight through . . .
>
> But you don't always say—"Forget."
> "Hope no more"—to a blind man, or cripple . . .

One of Steiger's most persistent complaints was of being alone, yet other poems show that he knew the closeness of family ties and the bonds of friendship. He yearned for stable links, but not for Russia as a country. He drew on difficult emotions—shock and fear—as sources of inspiration. His poems are so lacking in decorativeness that they sometimes seem to have been written more nearly for himself than for a reader. The Parisian Note was also represented by Lidiia Chervinskaia (b. 1907), whose immediate subjects were the minutiae of private existence. Her first collections, beginning with *Approaches* (1934), appeared in Paris. Her moods are usually sad; she often speaks of the failure of intimacy in love or friendship. She confronts the idea of death and other painful topics, but usually in concrete situations; she avoids abstractions as such. Her tone is delicate in its immediacy. She was intensely aware of nature without describing landscapes in themselves.

The Independent Émigrés

The Parisian Note was described as "nihilistic" by those émigré poets who had no reason to abandon their religious faith and beliefs or to reject the values of civilization. A rival group, the Union of Young Writers, was organized by Iury Terapiano (1896–1980), who espoused an Orthodox Christian faith in his own poetry. Terapiano's poems are not dissimilar in subject from those of the Parisian Note. He, too, spoke of love, nature, and such abstractions as happiness or death, but his moods and his conclusions are uplifting. He graduated from Kiev University and fought in World War I and for the White Army. He published six volumes of lyrics in emigration, beginning with *The Best Sound* (1926). He was a literary critic for *Russkaia mysl'* and published his memoirs of émigré life in *Encounters* (1953). A small poem will illustrate his emotional elasticity:

> Night again, my sleeplessness is empty.
> Recollection and opinion's hour.
> Thoughts, a flock dispersed and rudely scattered,
> Take to flight and enter endless time.
>
> Midnight strikes. The clock moves on uncaring,
> Ominous, this dark within the room:
> If my heart is too filled now for hoping,
> Still, hope has a shadow that casts light.

Terapiano's religious faith is a source of sustenance, not of doubts and defiance. His allusions are often to such religious figures as Saint Francis of Assisi. Terapiano wrote war poems that were close in sentiment to those of Gumilev: he was a moral and loyal Russian soldier. In other poems he shows his links to the great poets of French symbolism, Verlaine, Mallarmé, and Rimbaud. His poetry is appealing, but so traditional as to be nearly indistinguishable from that of Lermontov or other romantics of the nineteenth century.

Terapiano's colleagues in the Union of Young Writers included Antonin Ladinsky, who was immersed in Western Europe history, art, and culture, and Dovid Knut, a spokesman for Jewish traditions. Antonin Ladinsky (1896–1961) emigrated in 1921 and published five books of verse between 1930 and 1950. He loved the West in the manner of a nineteenth-century Russian for whom the West embodies cherished ideals. He knew the precise symbolic value in Western culture of such figures as Ann Boleyn and Ophelia. But it is plain that the author he most admired and wished to emulate was a Russian, Pushkin. Ladinsky enjoyed, as Pushkin had, making stylizations of classical and Biblical poetry. He differed from Pushkin in that he was more nostalgic. While in exile, Ladinsky published two historical novels. In

1955 he returned to the Soviet Union (having spent some time in a repatriation camp in Germany), where he continued his career as a prose writer. The poetic world of Dovid Knut (real name: David Fiksman, 1900–1955) was divided between Old Testament stories and the Paris that is symbolized by the Seine. Knut was born in Bessarabia. In emigration he became a member of the Chamber of Poets, a group formed in 1922. He published five collections of verse in Paris between 1925 and 1949. He devoted some poems to such Biblical figures as Sarah and Rachel. Others are reflections of his own earthy, and usually joyous, moods. He wrote in an elevated style that suggests exultation. An element of this style was his abandonment of classical meters for free rhythms that approximate the prose of the psalms and at the same time suggest the *vers libre* of the modernist French poets. He deserves a wider audience. His wife, the daughter of Scriabin, took part in the Jewish resistance and was executed. Knut emigrated to Israel in 1949, where he worked for the theater until his death. Among other participants in the group called the Chamber of Poets was Boris Poplavsky (1903–1935). He stands apart from his compatriots, however, because he imitated the effects of surrealism. His poems are portentous fantasies; his style is grand, whether his theme is religious or mundane. Five volumes of his lyrics appeared between 1931 and 1938. He was also the author of a novel, *The Apollo of the Ugly* (1930–1931). He was attracted in his poems to the imagery of devils and hell and, less often, of angels. His figures of speech are audacious. His demonism, however, was closer to that of *fin de siècle* decadence, or even romanticism, than to the wit and intellectualism of the Western avant-garde. In many poems he simply spoke in imaginative and tragic terms of perceptions that were private.

16

World War II and Its Aftermath (1939–1955)

The Soviet people experienced enormous devastations during World War II, and after 1946, an era of rapid reconstruction. Many authors became journalists, and a number devoted their creative writing, as well, to the war effort. The Soviet Union entered World War II by seizing, in the security of a pact with Hitler, western lands from Bessarabia to Karelia. But in 1941 Hitler invaded and advanced to within twenty miles of Moscow. The German onslaughts were repeated in 1942 and 1943, until the Red Army swept westward in 1944 and 1945 to meet the Americans at the Elbe. In the postwar period, the cold war gradually turned public opinion inside the Soviet Union against the nation's wartime allies, and Soviet authors, who were already inclined to observe a conformity, faced a renewed demand for socialist commitment. The Russians who spent the same years in exile experienced Nazi rule or the occupation of German forces. Paris, the center of émigré Russian literature, was inside Nazi territory from June 1940 until the liberation in 1944. The émigré writers were usually forced to postpone their careers, but in the postwar era they at last approached their years of florescence.

Those Soviet poets who became popular in the war years were typically older writers who had begun their careers earlier without winning a large audience. They were patriotic poets whose talents were suited to more heroic times. They were inclined by nature to write of experiences shared by the community. Their styles were increasingly realistic. The most popular literary work of the entire war was perhaps Aleksandr Tvardovsky's comic serial about a simple soldier, *Vasily Terkin* (1942–1945). The everyman, or the man on the street, was easily the hero of World War II literature. The fate of ordinary people in besieged cities like Leningrad and Sevastopol was the subject of well-known poems by Olga Berggolts. The wartime poets seldom excelled at lyrics that were intimate in the confessional sense. Poems about love and family relationships were widespread, but they were expressions of common attitudes, and many were sentimental. The narrative genres from anecdote to epic were in great favor. Observation was more appropriate than reflection and meditation. The new poets formed no literary groups. They were inclined to hold office as editors or literary functionaries, and they served at state institutions or magazines. They were rewarded with Stalin Prizes. In their later years, they sometimes turned to retrospective works recalling the heroic war years.

Tvardovsky

A man who is now remembered as a courageous editor of the Thaw period, Aleksandr Tvardovsky (1910–1971) was in his early career a pacesetter for socialist realist poets. His most successful works were his narrative poems, particularly *Vasily Terkin,* whose hero became a popular legend. Tvardovsky's epics all shared a serious subject: Russia's place in current history and the ordeals of its citizens. But his style, particularly in the beginning, was popular, unassuming, and humorous. He wrote in every case to strengthen the morale of the people in their hardships. He was somewhat more literary and less obviously didactic in his lyric poems. Tvardovsky was born in a village near Smolensk into a peasant family. His father was killed as a kulak during the period of collectivization. In the 1930s he was active as a poet and a journalist in Smolensk; his first successful long poem was *The Road to Socialism* (1931). He graduated in 1939 from the Moscow Institute of Philosophy, Literature, and History. He was a war correspondent in the Finnish campaign in 1940 and in World War II, from 1941 to 1945. His poems appeared in many collections throughout the 1940s, 1950s, and 1960s. He received four Stalin Prizes for his poetry, and in 1951 he won the Lenin Prize. He served as the editor of *Novyi mir (New World)* from 1950 to 1954 and from 1958 to 1970. At the helm of this prestigious magazine, he was a champion of controversial authors, including Aleksandr Solzhenitsyn, and of authors who had been suppressed, like Anna Akhmatova. *Novyi mir* became in his hands an object of international attention.

    In the prewar period Tvardovsky was a poet of the bucolic life. He described the land and the people in cheerful and somewhat idealized pictures. He was praised by prominent critics for his "epic" called *The Land of Muravia* (1934–1936), a piece about the collectivization of the land. It was written very much under the influence of folk tales and *byliny.* The story is about a foolish young farmer who rejects his life on the kholkhoz and sets out to seek the lost land of private ownership, called Muravia. He learns, after untoward adventures on the road, that Muravia is only a myth, and he returns with a light heart to life on the kholkhoz. With this work Tvardovsky began his revival of the genre of the comic epic. He took many of his narrative devices from the *byliny,* but he exaggerated their comic elements. The lyrics that Tvardovsky wrote in the prewar period suggest a deep affection for the countryside. He describes a flourishing land, well-kept animals, and rich harvests. He observes the strength of family ties in the villages. His scenes are attractive, but idealized. Even his few love poems are optimistic. Among his poems are comic anecdotes about a hale old man of 105 years called Danilo. The village life that Tvardovsky described was abruptly interrupted by the war. Here is his brief recognition of the change:

Not chimney smoke above the village
And not the homey creak of porch,
Not hay that smells when dawn is fresh
On needles of the frost at morning—

But smoke from fires, from mud hut's smudge,
And days on ski tracks to the forests,
The bullets' hum through air still-standing,
As though of glass—our winter's come.

From this moment onward, his sole subject in every genre became the war.

The wartime poems, long and short, all describe episodes that take place from Smolensk south into the Ukraine along the Dniepr. The hero of *Vasily Terkin* is an ordinary villager from somewhere on this western front. He is a resourceful fighter, but he is comic in the gusto with which he eats, drinks, smokes, and sleeps. The values embedded in the work are not only patriotic but also sentimental: Terkin's commander is a paternal man who invites his whole unit to dinner as combat brings them close to his modest home; he later spends the entire night chopping wood for his hard-working wife. Terkin must learn practical lessons—for example, that it is hard, but necessary, to lie still on the ground under fire. Terkin rises to epic stature. In one instance he fights a German soldier singlehanded. He is also seen to stand up to Death when wounded. He is angered by Death's refusal to allow him to return to life for the triumphal celebration:

Let me hear the victory salvos
That will ring from Moscow's guns!
Let me promenade a little
With the living on that day!
Let me tap at just one window
In the land where I was born!
If they come to see who's knocking,
Death, O Death, will you let me
Say to them one little word?
Just a half?
—No. That I can't.

Terkin started. He was freezing—
On a bed of snow he lay.

—Then go on. Your scythe take with you.
I will live to fight today.

By the close of the work, Terkin and his friends have won the day and crossed over to occupy Berlin. A less heroic and sadder narrative of the war period was *A House by the Road* (1942–1946), devoted to the lot of a woman living on the western front. Her territory constantly changes hands; she bears a child whom she must hide and witnesses her husband's pain when he returns. The "lyrics" of the war period are also stories, like those in the long poems, about soldiers near Smolensk, in Lithuania, and by the Dniepr.

In the postwar period, Tvardovsky undertook to write a verse portrait of the Soviet people across the country's vast geographical expanse. The work, called *Distance Beyond Distance* (1950–1960), is based on a journey on the Trans-Siberian Railroad across the Urals, the Siberian taiga, and regions farther east. He records conversations, reports stories, and adds his own reflections. The work is rather grand and odic, although Tvardovsky's style, partly humorous and partly sentimental, was unchanged. It was in the early 1960s that Tvardovsky reconsidered his views; apparently his new attitudes applied primarily to the ruling bureaucracy. His new Terkin work, called *Terkin in the Other World* (1963), is a satire in which Soviet situations are compared with those in hell. In "By the Right of Memory" Tvardovsky publicly revealed for the first time the fate of his own father; the poem was published abroad in 1969. Tvardovsky's tone always remained calm or stoical. He answered his critics, but without defiance. In other lyrics he returned to rural themes. He wrote poems in memory of his mother and of Lenin. His *oeuvre* is that of a steady and productive poet, a man seen as anyone would like to be remembered. He was exemplary, even when he was not didactic.

Berggolts

The most memorable subject in the poetry of Olga Berggolts (1910–1975) was the siege of Leningrad. She described the blockade in several books, beginning with *A Leningrad Notebook* (1941). She was a journalist as well as a poet. She took for granted the patriotism of Soviet citizens and went on to describe their moral courage in their various hardships. Her depictions of urban scenes are utterly realistic. She spoke of the Soviet Union as a whole in idealized terms as having already become an advanced socialist community. She was born in St. Petersburg, the daughter of a doctor, and entered literature early. She graduated from Leningrad University in 1930 and published three collections of verse before the war. Her accounts of the blockade include *Radio Leningrad* (1946), a collection of her wartime broadcasts. She won a Stalin Prize in 1951. She was also the author of a verse drama, *Loyalty* (1954), about the siege of Sevastopol. In 1959 she published a memoir of her youth and of the war called *Diurnal Stars*. Further volumes of lyrics appeared in the 1960s.

In the poem that now opens the set of her collected works, Berggolts described her poetry as the voice of the times. The lyric begins, "I shall not hide any griefs from You" (1937), and continues thus:

> You rise in me like the breath of my sighing,
> You are the froth and the still of my blood,
> I shall become what you are, O Epoch,
> And you will speak forth in the voice of my heart.

She kept her promise, and it was in this sense that her art was a service to the community. In her prewar period Berggolts wrote as a happy and romantic young girl, proud of her communal labor with like-minded companions. She dreamed of the love of estimable young men, but often their labor took them elsewhere. She was fond of Leningrad, a city with its own character and beauty. But beyond the city, she always saw "The Republic," the object of her devotion. She was inclined to sentimental recollections of her own childhood. In one long poem of the late 1930s, she described the children of wartime Spain.

The war brought a maturity to her verse. She began to speak less about her own inclinations and more about the hardships, and the heroism, of the average people around her. In the first poems of *A Leningrad Notebook* she sees soldiers in transit and recognizes the beginning of a war. She pledges her own life to the cause and exhorts the young men close to her to enter the fray. The first German attack on the city is seen in "A February Diary." In "A Leningrad Epic" she describes how the people she sees resist the temptations that arise from the deprivations of the blockade, such as the shortage of bread. In her next two collections, *Leningrad* (1944) and *Your Path* (1945), she devoted some of her lyrics to the ordeals suffered by other cities, Sevastopol and Stalingrad. Finally, she celebrates the victories of 1945. Among her shorter poems is this modest scene:

> O yes—what plain, what poor and simple words
> We uttered then—as though the first time ever.
> We spoke these words: the sun, the light, the grass,
> As others would have said: life, love, and power.
>
> Do you recall that when that skin of ice,
> Four times accursed, we peeled from off the city,
> How one old man kept stamping on the street
> And shouting out: "The asphalt, asphalt, brothers!"
>
> In olden times, when sailors saw the shore
> From off a ship, they cried: "Land ho, land ho!"

In the five collections of verse that appeared after the war, Berggolts often recalled these stirring years. She also questioned the wisdom of reviving old pains. She became the poet of healing, a long and difficult process, as she had once been of the blockade. In a number of her later poems she described southern localities, particularly the Ukraine and the Crimea, with love and admiration. Her verse play, *Loyalty,* portrays the defense of Sevastopol and the grief of its survivors. In form the piece is part epic, with long narrative settings, and part drama, divided as it is into five acts.

Simonov

The affairs of the nation and the allegiance of its citizens were equally the guiding inspirations of Konstantin Simonov (1915–1979). His perspectives were wider, however. He saw current events in the context of international relations, and battles as parts of larger strategies. He did not pose as an everyman, but showed himself as the cosmopolitan correspondent, not without glamour, that he was. He also took for granted the people's love of country, but he went on to write about the emotional gains and losses of men and women at war. He was popular both as a poet and as a fiction writer; his novel *Days and Nights* (1944) is among the outstanding accounts of the siege of Stalingrad. Simonov was born in Petrograd and graduated in 1938 from the Gorky Institute of Literature in Moscow. In 1939 he became a correspondent and traveled to the far East, the far north, and the Russian fronts in World War II. He was the author of four major novels about the war period; several collections of poems, including lyrics and long poems; and plays, his least popular genre. He received six Stalin Prizes and a Lenin Prize, and was named a Hero of Socialist Labor. He was a Secretary of the Union of Writers and a conservative editor of *Novyi mir* between 1946 and 1950 and from 1954 to 1958. After the war he traveled extensively throughout the world.

In Simonov's earliest poems, the breadth of his geographical and historical interests was already apparent. He spoke of Hungary, of Port Arthur, of the war in Spain. In *Road Poems* (1939) he can be seen living out of his suitcase, reporting now from the Caucasus, now from near Archangel. His private life suffers because neither he nor his partner is often at home. He describes life on the Trans-Siberian Railroad in 1939. He sees the approach of a war, and speaks of bombs falling in places where the houses are mere huts. He wrote six narrative poems, some of which show that his interests extended to literary history. *The Victor* (1937) is an account of the pain-wracked life of the novelist Nikolay Ostrovsky (*How Steel Was Tempered*), who was the victim of a land mine in Poland. Other narratives describe Pskov's historic "battle on the ice" with the "Germans," or Knights of the Livonian Order, in 1242. But *Far Away in the East* (1941) was written to praise the tank personnel who fight in the heat of the desert.

The poems of the war years include a number devoted to men as they face the dangers of military action, but Simonov had much more to say about human relationships behind the lines. He wrote about the loss of friends through death, the fate of family ties, and the closeness that may arise between strangers. Most of his collections bear the word "diary" in their titles. These "diaries" are in part about his own experiences, but in many of the poems he was speaking for the soldiers he saw around him. In the following poem of 1942, he speaks for the army men who met civilians fleeing from Stalingrad as they approached:

> Don't cry—the warmth of summertime
> Still lingers on the yellow meadows.
> And crowds of refugees still come,
> On foot—with children on their shoulders.
>
> Don't cry!—Although we meet them here,
> On roads from Stalingrad retreating,
> They never once lift up their eyes—
> Look not into those eyes for mercy.
>
> March on, you will not wrest a glance
> From them because of your compassion,
> Go straight to where they've been, ahead—
> No more is asked of your intentions.

The love poems that brought Simonov his widest popularity are to be found in *With You and Without You* (1942). The poem called "Wait for me, and I'll come back" was perhaps the most familiar lyric of the entire war period. Many of these poems are about departures, separations and loneliness. The following poems (1945) combines the imagery of dreams with echoes of folklore:

> It was dawn before departure,
> In my dream you were to wed,
> There's the church porch. I can see it,
> You—the bride. A beggar—I.
>
> It might happen as I dreamed it,
> Promise me if it comes true—
> You'll show mercy when you exit,
> Please don't offer alms to me.

Simonov was not guided by sentimentalism in his encounters between men and women. His lovers, wives, and husbands are both faithful and unfaithful. He praised loyalty and was grateful for freely given affection. He was realistic in the complications he was able to suggest. In the final poems he speaks for the man who has fallen out of love and will not return. One of Simonov's long poems, "The Son of an Artillery Man" (1941), describes how two men rear one child during the war.

After the war Simonov's poetry was restricted to lyrics, and those reflect his own global travels and connections. He was biased when abroad in that he tended to see people everywhere as either friends or enemies of the Soviet Union. One of his last books was *Vietnam, the Winter of '70* (1971). Simonov's work in its totality was relatively impersonal. It mattered little to his poems whether he wrote from his own experience or from observation; he touched on common ground in either case. He proved, perhaps, that the privileged are not different from the man in the street. His "lyrics" were usually narrative or dramatic in construction. He used traditional verse forms, as well as the laddered, free style of Maiakovsky.

Lesser Poets of the War Theme

The experience of World War II was overwhelming in the consciousness of the Soviet people. The war dominated the nation's literature and other arts, not only during the war, but for many years to come. Originality was not much seen among the wartime poets, however. The work of Margarita Aliger (b. 1915) was distinguished by its poignancy. Before the war she had written five-year-plan poetry. One of her major works during the war was a verse epic, called *Zoia* (1942), about a heroine of the partisan wars. In later years she wrote some poetry appropriate to Thaw themes, but she was also among those who remembered the war. Here is a small poem, "The Couple," written in 1956:

> Once more they fell to quarreling on the streetcar,
> Without constraint, before a crowd no shame . . .

But I could not conceal impulsive envy
As I looked on, uneasy, in their fight.

They cannot know how lucky they are, angry.
And thank the Lord, there is no cause to know.
For just to think!—together, both are living,
And they could make it better and see right.

Aliger has been a member of the Presidium of Writers and has written poetry reflecting her travel in foreign countries in recent years.

Other prominent writers of the war generation included Semen Kirsanov (1906–1972), who was not noted, however, for his war poems. Instead he is remembered for his unconventional genres and for having retained many elements of an avant-garde style. He was a close associate of Maiakovsky in the late 1920s and was a member of LEF. After writing five-year-plan literature, he turned in the early 1930s to science fiction in verse. He emerged as a poet with depth and power in "Your Poem," written in 1937 after the death of his wife. Kirsanov also became a war correspondent and wrote patriotic poetry. In the Thaw period he published a well-known appeal for a new moral vision in "Seven Days of the Week" (1956). The war, however, was practically the only theme of Aleksey Surkov (b. 1899). His five volumes of poems about World War II, published between 1939 and 1946, include *Russia the Avenger* (1944) and *I Sing of Victory* (1946). In the 1930s he had devoted several collections of verse to the civil war, in which he served. During World War II, he too was a war correspondent. The war continued to be his major preoccupation even in his subsequent books of essays, letters, and poems. Surkov was active at various times as an editor and a functionary; he was a Secretary of the Union of Writers and received Stalin prizes and other honors.

Delayed Careers in Exile: Ivask

The Russian poets of the same generation who went into exile during World War II were ordinarily unable to publish their books until after the war. Their personal safety was not at stake, they did not serve as war correspondents, and they were not surrounded by examples of patriotic and propagandistic Russian verse. When these poets finally appeared in the postwar period, they had relatively little to say about the war, or even about their own experiences of those years. Like the émigrés of the 1920s, they recalled the traditions of pre-Revolutionary Russian poetry and obviously wished to continue them. The cosmic pessimism seen in the Parisian Note was not a dominant influence on the new poets. Inevitably, their poems were colored by a nostalgia for Russia or for the past. They brought a new immediacy to an old theme in Russian literature, the contrast between East and West.

The metaphysical tradition that had originated with the symbolists was resumed by Iury Ivask (1907–1985) in his erudite poetry. He thought most intensely about the life of the soul, and he came close to regarding national cultures as manifestations of a worldly aspect of the spirit. He wrote about the cultural histories of Russia and of the West. His verse forms were old-fashioned and his language elegant and sometimes ornate. Ivask was born in Moscow; his family moved to Estonia after 1917, and he received a law degree from Tartu University. His first book of verse, *The Northern Shore* (1938), showed him to be a follower of the acmeists and their successors, the Parisian Note poets. He emigrated from Germany to the United States in 1949, earned a doctorate at Harvard University in 1954, and taught Russian literature at several universities, including Amherst. In addition to writing verse, he edited the works of late-nineteenth-century and early-twentieth-century Russian essayists, including those of the Tolstoy critic Konstantin Leontiev.

When Ivask resumed his literary career in the 1950s, he described cultural traditions, but he saw in them mere contexts for the experiences of the soul. He was a cultural relativist in that he found spiritual riches in various national traditions, but he felt a deeper affection for Russian culture. In *A Regal Autumn* (1953) he was a decadent to the extent that he savored what he perceived as a sweet decline before death. His setting is the golden maples and ashes that stand beside a monastery. His thoughts are not of the transfiguration of the soul, but of the brilliance of the "dead suns" that are Byzantium, Rome, and other noble empires. Russia and the West were hereafter to be the two poles of his thought. The West is praised in the poems of *Glory* (1967), while *Cinderella* (1970) shows his love for Russia. In the opening poem of *Glory* he describes the soul as taking delight in all earthly things—in the religiosity of monastic life, in the creating of boots or wine or verse. He writes in "Athos" of a monastic routine that encompasses religious adoration, the near-worship of beauty, and indulgence in sexual pleasures. The "glories" of the title are the cultural attainments of the West. Here is a eulogy called "The Acropolis":

> The sea is hazy,
> And islands to the distance fade,
> Above is marble,
> And cypress trees, but nowhere grass.
>
> On all sides columns—
> A swarthy and deep lilac grove of trees,
> And ever endless
> The vibrancy of deep blue skies.
>
> ———
>
> Geometry and cosmic being—
> The selfsame thing,
> The gold of ancient music—
> The hum of bees.

In other poems Ivask celebrates the spiritual wealth of several cities, including Salonika, Venice, Assisi, and Ravenna; he was particularly intrigued by evidences of mixed lineage. In each city he also admired the beauty of nature in its surroundings. He discovered civilizations worthy of praise at Oaxaca, Tasco, and other places in Mexico. Mexican landscapes seemed to be marvels of nature, and he enjoyed the liveliness of the Mexican people. He recalled Russian literature, but rarely. He mentioned Mandelstam's gloomy perceptions of the Soviet era.

In the title poem of *Cinderella* the lowly maid and princess of legend is a symbol of Russia in her endlessly varied roles. Russia is first seen at the pre-Lenten holiday in pre-Revolutionary times, when both the play of fantasy and the awareness of the spirit are intensified. The aspects of Russian history, culture, and literature are so diverse that they may seem incongruous. Among Ivask's contemporary subjects are Akhmatova and, in "Soccer," the rage for a sport. The medieval world is remembered in poems about the legend of the saintly lovers, Peter and Fevronia, and about the tradition of the holy fool. Those spiritual achievements of the West, like the music of Bach, which became a part of Russian culture, also have a place here. But in this book he was occasionally exasperated by the West. The Italians, the Portuguese, and the Norwegians annoyed him, and he saw a nervousness in Gothic architecture. In 1973 Ivask published a long poem, "Homo ludens," which is both an account of his spiritual evolution and a realistic record of his life, from his childhood in Moscow to his maturity in America.

Spiritual faith can also be seen in the work of a lesser poet, Dmitri Klenovsky (real surname: Krachkovsky; 1898–1976). He was an intensely religious man whose poems could not have been published in the Soviet Union. A first book of poems appeared in 1917, after which he remained silent until after he emigrated to Germany in 1943. He was born the son of a painter, attended the gymnasium in Tsarskoe Selo, and traveled in Europe. He served in the army in World War I and thereafter worked as a journalist in Kharkov. His first collection in emigration was called *The Tracks of Life* (1950); in the title poem he expresses the hope that a higher being observes his footsteps, just as he himself follows the tracks of a rabbit in the snow. Ten books followed in the next decades. He described landscapes that suggest a plenitude of natural sustenance for life. He pictured lakes, trees, the sunshine. His religious aspirations are not those of a mystic, but those of an Orthodox Christian; he struggles with doubts, guilt, and sin, and rises to the adoration of a Christ who is a distant Savior. His style is as solemn and classical as if he had written in the mid-nineteenth century or earlier.

The move from Russia to the West usually engendered a sense of loss, and sometimes a wider pessimism. The leading voice among the disappointed was that of Ivan Elagin (real surname: Matveev; b. 1918). His awareness of having made a transition from a home to the alien West is almost the sole subject of his poems. His first collection of verse was called *On the Road from There* (1947). His unhappiness in exile is usually ascribed to the density of American cities, and only occasionally to the malevolence of fate. He was born in Vladivostok and studied medicine in Kiev before the war. He began to publish in Munich. After his arrival in the United States, he taught Russian literature at New York University and at the University of Pittsburgh. Seven new books appeared between 1959 and 1982.

In a poem called "It's not in a line that sounds good" he wrote that the purpose of poetry is the "rejuvenation of the soul." The journey he records in his books, however, is one of considerable disorientation and, finally, a tardy sense of being home. In the first poems of *On the Road from There* he is seen as a promising young man, often in the pleasant countryside near Kiev. This world is disrupted by the gunfire of war, then bombs and corpses. There follow impressionistic views of a barracks life in Germany where people are herded like animals. The events in which he participates begin to seem to him the results of a struggle between God and Satan.

The first of six books about his life as an émigré in the United States was *Lights at Night* (1963). Its first poem opens with lines that suggest an accommodation:

> I do not know the pain of that nostalgia,
> I like the foreign land where I reside.

But the "lights" of his title are often the flashing neon advertisements of lower Manhattan. The trees seem to have been trapped among skyscrapers. He himself is a captive in his small apartment because he fears the onslaughts of criminals. There are poems whose plane is cosmic or philosophical; he pictures a reckless God who rolls planets like billiard balls. He sometimes commented, in *Under the Sign of the Axe* (1976), on current events in the Soviet Union. He responded to the denunciation of the "cult of personality" and to the revelations about prison camps. But in the poems of *In the Hall of the Universe* (1982) he has withdrawn into idle musing and regards the world itself as a mere empty show, like a circus. His retrospective volume, *Heavy Stars* (1986), comes to an end when he discovers that he is at home in Pittsburgh, where a squirrel appears at his window. From his earliest poems, Elagin tended to raise snows, rains, and particularly stars to a symbolic meaning. His early verse was perhaps his best: his ideals were clearer, and he was more inclined to feel generosity, gratitude, and compassion. His first moments of horror were unexpected and effective.

The substance of the poetry of Irina Odoevtseva (real name: Iraida Heinicke; b. 1901) grew out of a contrast that she chose to draw between a youthful, harumscarum, self and the sober lady she became in exile. She was, however, a prose writer who returned to poetry after almost three decades of fiction. She was born in St. Petersburg, was a member of the acmeist Guild of Poets, and always remembered Gumilev with admiration in her verse. She was married to Georgy Ivanov, with whom she emigrated in 1923, having brought out her first collection of verse in 1922. She has lived in Berlin, Paris, and the United States. After several successful novels and a number of short stores, she published *Counterpoint,* a collection of poems, in 1951. She has published sparingly since; her largest collection was *Ten Years* in 1961. She has been a fastidious craftsman, but she has not been ambitious as a poet.

The interplay in *Counterpoint* is between youthful poems about love, all undated, and introspective later poems, all dated 1950. She looks back with amusement and indulgence on her former flirtations and frivolity. In the following quatrain she pretends not to have improved before her death:

> Did you love anything that you found in the world?
> —Why, of course I was partial. You must have been jesting.
> And to what? —Let me think. To my flowers and scents!
> And to mirrors . . . but anything else I've forgotten.

In other poems, however, she hints that she now suffers from a state of spiritual emptiness. In *Ten Years* she found a new variation of the split in her character. She is still whimsical: she is the lady of a cycle called "Poems Written While Sick," whose doctor has prescribed a self-indulgent voyage to Egypt. She is also the sad and realistic émigré woman who lives in poverty and has close friends. In *Loneliness* (1965) her losses can no longer be faced with humor. She begins with grateful memories of her married love, but she ends with a cry of anguish: she fears death after the loss of a native country. All those things that have vanished are symbolized in the final poems by "my black poodle Krak." She returns to steadiness in *The Golden Chain* (1975), whose title is an allusion to the folkloric opening of Pushkin's *Ruslan and Ludmila,* where a wise cat walks a chain and tells tales. Odoevtseva had always valued the play of the imagination. This volume also includes a number of early poems dated from 1918 through 1923.

17

After Stalin
(1955–1970)

The history of the Soviet Union since the death of the dictator in 1953 is often seen as the successive ups and downs of de-Stalinization in its many ramifications. The Thaw in cultural affairs lasted from 1956 to 1966, but even the ensuing period was more liberal than the bleak Stalin years. Demands for conformity began to be less stringent in 1953, and in 1956 Nikita Khrushchev denounced the Stalinist cult of personality at the Twentieth Party Congress. The Thaw was not cloudless. The Hungarian uprising was quelled in the fall of 1956, and relations with China deteriorated. Nevertheless, the Thaw period brought the initiation of cultural exchanges with the West and more opportunities for foreign travel and Western contacts. In 1957 *Sputnik* lent a new importance to the Soviet Union in the eyes of the world. In 1962 the Cuban missile crisis alerted world opinion to a common danger from nuclear weapons. Russian émigré spheres began to prosper again, in part because of a new wave of emigrants, in part because Russian affairs commanded a new interest abroad.

Soviet literature acquired a lively component of liberal authors during the Thaw. The changes they championed were not great. The freeing of literature from social goals of an immediate nature was their first objective. They claimed the right to create some works without any ideological concerns. In addition, a call was heard for a faithfulness to experience. Inevitably, a new tendency to individualism appeared, together with the exploration of psychological realities and private themes. Poetry flourished precisely because it was lyrical, and irrational, and could be brief. Poets who were previously unnoticed became popular. Readings of poetry filled stadiums, and young leaders like Evgeny Evtushenko and Andrey Voznesensky became celebrities. The writing and recitation of poetry by the lay public became widespread. Some new poets attempted to reestablish links with the heritage of modernism that had been interrupted in the 1920s. A number looked to Maiakovsky and to Akhmatova for guidance. Some poets of the early twentieth century reappeared in print. Among them were symbolists like Blok and Bely, and eventually Sologub. The early, modernist, poems of Pasternak and others became available again. Finally, some interdicted poets, like Mandelstam, were rehabilitated, and the works of Bunin and Tsvetaeva, both well known in emigration, were published. *Samizdat,* the circulation of unpublished manuscripts, became common, and some works were secretly sent abroad for publication.

The Older Liberals

There were poets whose talents were unsuited to solemnity, heroism, or the affirmation of the conventional, and who had not met with success in the war years. They were able, however, to bring new trends into Thaw literature. Foremost among them was Leonid Martynov (b. 1905), whose poetry provided witty, often whimsical, twists on life's commonplaces. In his early works, his love for his native Siberia stood out among his themes. But his real interests were more universal. He demonstrated that a rich variety of experiences can be found in what others perceive as the ordinary world. His attitudes were irreverent, and his styles where at least unpretentious, and sometimes playful, or even clowning. He wrote both lyric and narrative verse. He was born in Omsk, the son of a railroad employee, and spent his childhood riding the Trans-Siberian Railroad in his father's train car. He became a traveling book salesman and worked at other odd jobs before becoming a journalist in Siberia. His volumes of poetry began to appear in 1939. In 1945 he was reprimanded for the idealistic fantasies of *Lukomore* (a legendary land). He began to be recognized as a significant poet only in 1955, and he continued to publish into the 1970s. His work bears the imprint of a sophisticated primitivism, both in the conception of his poems and in his style.

Martynov's earliest poetry, written in the 1920s and 1930s, shows him to have been a dreamer and a romantic. He was a self-proclaimed futurist and an avid supporter of the Revolution. His affection for Siberia was in part for its nature—the steppes, the taiga, and the sea. He was also fascinated by the past of the remote region. He admired the ancient wandering players called *skomorokhi,* the chronicles, and books of folk tales. He wrote about Siberian ancestors who were seamen, or who suffered from the inroads of the Mongol invader Batyi. In the seven long poems that Martynov wrote during the 1930s, his interests outgrew his origins. His earliest long poems are about the encounters of advanced cultures, European or Russian, with primitive areas, sometimes Siberia. At the time of the great purges, he abruptly turned, in "The Seeker of Paradise" (1937), to the subject of justice and the courts. The nature of human ideals in general is his subject in "The Homespun Venus" (1939). And "Poetry as Magic" (1939) is about the symbolist Konstantin Balmont. His narrative style was often tongue-in-cheek, and he liked to parody stilted and archaic language.

The 1940s were the nadir of Martynov's literary career. He wrote almost no patriotic poetry, although he was admired for one piece, "The Smoke of the Homeland." In 1945 came *Lukomore,* whose title poem suggests that fairy-tale dreams will come true somewhere in the northern tundra. Martynov found his most characteristic voice in the postwar period, when he was unable to publish. His new writings were both puckish and sad, and he was no longer tied to the Siberian wilderness. His subjects began to be the great universals like love and death. Here is a poem on aging:

> Still black his moustache and his brow,
> And he still dances, squatting, kicking,
> And he still brings up talk of love
> And raises ladies' hands to kiss them.
>
> —Does he still bring up talk of love,
> And raise the ladies' hands to kiss them?
> —Yes, yes, his blood, now turned to gray,
> Still bubbles on, although in ebbing.
>
> So don't deny him anything!
> Tomorrow he will sob, on seeing—
> It's not his blood alone, O no,
> It's not his blood alone that's graying . . .
> But look, he's dancing, squatting, kicking!

Here, as elsewhere, Martynov refuses to be entirely serious, even when he is sad. The topics to which he responds in his small poems are so diverse as to appear random. He writes about the weather, the circus, the ballet. His insights into time-worn subjects, like the sunset in art, are refreshing. He can stoop to silliness and verge on the absurd. He revels in repeated phrases, extended metaphors, and word plays.

During the Thaw, when Martynov won the respect he had for so long deserved, his poetry did not lose its nip of mischievousness. He became a poet of the new times, with veiled messages. Nearly every year he wrote poems about the changes that come in spring, and about the nature of change as such. In a poem of 1953 he feigns to be indignant because birds now cross borders again, as they had 100,000 years ago, and cannot be recalled by radio commands. In 1955 he wrote a small poem, "The Snowstorm," about the "desire" of the dead to return to life:

> In spring there can suddenly be a great snowstorm,
> When tram cars all stop and their arms stick up frozen,
> And everything made out of fur becomes restless,
> As though it were living, as though it were living,
> As though a desire to return to the living
> Seized everything killed—from old father raccoon
> And down to the smallest, most trivial beastie . . .
> In spring there can suddenly be a great snowstorm.

Success brought a spirit of élan and optimism that did not diminish Martynov's impishness and ironies. He became very prolific, and in time he took on such popular causes as the environment, world peace, and the resistance to nuclear arms. He also encouraged a desire for excellence and a sense of freedom. Both birds and the sun appeared as symbols. In the Brezhnev era he wrote as a man who values the cultural heritage of the West, as well as that of Russia. His literary allusions might be to Dostoevsky or to Verlaine. He wrote long poems devoted to the nineteenth-century Russian painter Aleksandr Ivanov and to the peasant poet Aleksey Koltsov. In "The Northern Lights" (1964) he talks about his own origin as an artistic alien in a technological family. He liked to mention airplanes and television in his poems, but his forte was always the capacity to return in his imagination to the primordial origins of things.

The traits that made the poetry of Evgeny Vinokurov (b. 1925) appropriate in the Thaw era were its gentleness and its continual moral decency. His essential subject, in one guise or another, has been the social cement that holds civilizations together. He has written about soldiers in World War II, about Russian village life, and about mankind in wider contexts. He was born in Bryansk, the son of a bureaucratic employee. He served when very young as an artillery officer in the war. In 1951 he graduated from the Gorky Institute of Literature and published his first book, *Poems About Duty*. He stayed on as a teacher at the Gorky Institute and has published frequently since 1956. He explored a fundamental aspect of his subject—communication—in the poems of *The Word* (1962). Some of his later lyrics reflect his travels outside the Soviet Union.

Vinokurov's constructive impulse is revealed even in his first book, *Poems About Duty,* although his subject is war. He saw the "duty" of the title as residing not only in the necessities of war but also in the order of life itself. His poems about the war are laments and expressions of compassion, shock, and horror. He shows soldiers, moreover, as humans, not heroes. They are overwhelmed by the dangers they face; when left to rest, they sew and sing. Vinokurov's love of country was deep, but calm. In his next book, *Blue Sky* (1956), he describes the provinces as a peaceful homeland. The land itself is sunny and productive. The people are good villagers, who are attached to their black bread and accordions. His first Thaw poems appeared in *Confessions* (1958), whose title was indicative of the new interest in personal lives. Vinokurov's introspective poems disclosed a thoroughly acceptable character, but he aired individualistic convictions, such as that the conscience can bite, and that art is an instinctive human activity. He initiated a common theme of the Thaw—compassion for Russian women. He established his own identity when he wrote about his father and uncle in their pioneering youth.

By the 1960s he wanted to make statements, however modest, about mankind. In *The Face of Man* (1960) his poems are still limited and sentimental. The average citizens he portrays are no longer country folk, but their attitudes are familiar and they are almost invariably admirable. Vinokurov himself confesses to preferring the old Euclidian world to the new visions of relativeness. But in *The Word,* where his subject is articulateness in itself, his moral insights are more acute and his poems more moving. He wrote about the nature of poetry, the symbolism of such public statements as statues, and about the inevitability of differences among people. The poem called "Adam" (1961) demonstrates the dangers of incomprehension:

> With lazy glance he looked at his surroundings,
> His first day here he pressed upon the grass,

He lay beneath the shade of fig trees, stretching
His hand beneath his head so he could rest.

He sweetly slept, he slept without disturbance,
Beneath the peace of Eden's bright blue skies.
. . . In dreams he saw Auschwitz, he saw its ovens,
He saw the ditches brimming with the dead.

He saw his children!
          But in Eden's splendor
The smile upon his face was unperturbed,
He drowsed and slept, he comprehended nothing,
For he knew not the evil from the good.

Vinokurov applauded every form of genuine communication, from the song of the nightingale to the stationery section in the GUM department store. In *Metaphor* (1972) he widened his range to include foreign subjects. He was interested in Indian literature and admired the poetry of Omar Khayyam. Vinokurov has written two volumes of essays on literature, *Poetry and Thought* (1966) and *Still Valid* (1979).

The voice of Boris Slutsky (b. 1919) was angry, somewhat comparable to that of the postwar "beat" generation in the West. He deplored the atrocities of the war in *Memory* (1957), his first book. In other volumes he protested against every kind of suffering. His attacks and his opinions have been relatively unpredictable. He was born in the Ukraine, graduated in 1941 from the Gorky Literary Institute, and then served as a political adviser in the army. In the mid-1950s he wrote widely known anti-Stalin poems, one called "God," and thereafter began to appear in *samizdat*. He was prevented by his dissident attitudes from publishing a collection of verse before the appearance of *Memory* in 1957. Most of the poems in it are about the men lost at war and about those who mourned for them. A number of experiences touched him personally. One of his best poems happens to be about horses rather than about people. It is called "Horses in the Ocean" (1950):

Horses do know how to swim, but
Not so well and not so very far.

Gloria, the word for Russian *Slava,*
That's a name you will remember well.

Outward sailed this ship, proud of its title,
Ocean's vast expanse it meant to cross.

Day and night there tromped one thousand horses,
Shaking their kind noses, in its hold.

One thousand horses, and four thousand horseshoes!
Happiness was never brought by them,

For a mine broke up the vessels' bottom,
As they sailed, and far away from shore.

People fled away on sailboats, lifeboats,
Horses had to swim just as they were.

What could they have done, poor things, if nowhere
Were there places on those boats for them?

One roan island swam along the ocean,
While a chestnut swam a sea of blue,

And it seemed at first that it was easy,
Ocean seemed to them a river wide.

But the other shore was still not coming,
When their equine strength began to fail.

Suddenly the horses neighed, protesting
That their people left them there to drown.

Horses sank and they were neighing, neighing,
Till there were none left above the waves,

That is all. But all the same, I'm sorry
For them, roans, who never saw the shore.

Many of the poems in *Memory* were written in obvious wrath and sorrow. Since his first book, Slutsky has published regularly, about ten books in all. He finds suffering in the life of the streets and restaurants, among everyday city dwellers. He has written about art and artists. Over time, his protests have become less pointedly social, and for that reason perhaps more inherently philosophical. But he prefers graphic images to abstractions. When he describes fine landscapes and good friendships, it is in a tone of surprise, as though he were startled by them. His blunt style is highly successful, but it has been criticized, groundlessly, for its lack of "music."

An integral part of the Thaw era was the popularity of the guitar poet Bulat Okudzhava (b. 1924), whose melancholy songs put the period of World War II in a new perspective. He had not published before the Thaw; his gentle sadness was at odds with the earlier epoch of heroism. By the 1960s Okudzhava began to describe contemporary life in the cities and villages, and he later turned to prose fiction. He was born in Moscow of mixed Georgian and Armenian descent. In 1942 he volunteered and fought at the front. He graduated from Tiflis University in 1950 and taught school near Kaluga for five years. His first collection appeared in 1956, when he began to perform with a guitar. Further collections, including *The Merry Drummer* (1964), appeared in the 1960s and 1970s. He began to publish fiction in 1961 and brought out three historical novels between 1969 and 1979.

Okudzhava's guitar songs were written for a wide audience, and the vantage point of an everyman was particularly appropriate to them. Their autobiographical nature is sometimes obvious, but he understates the capacities of his protagonist. He writes as a man who is not entirely untutored or unresourceful, but who is caught in circumstances beyond his control. The songs about the war, which were not written until between 1957 and 1959, form a cycle. In the beginning, we see a boy who was too scared to fight at his first battle; the incident was later to appear as Okudzhava's famous short story "So Long, Schoolboy." The boy becomes a soldier who is reconciled to the inevitability of dying, but sadly so, and he is not once seen as a fighting man. He loves his country, but has questions about what he sees in the war.

Other poems show how much he wants to be loved by women, how he idealizes them and sympathizes with their own lot of waiting and mourning. The cycle culminates suddenly in the song that appealed, with its irony, to a dissident generation, "The Little Paper Soldier" (1959):

> O, once a soldier lived on earth
> who was both fine and handsome,
> but he was just a children's toy:
> he was a paper soldier.
>
> He wanted to transform the world
> so everyone was happy,
> and yet his life hung on a string:
> he was a paper soldier.
>
> He would have gone through fire and smoke,
> twice died for you as duty,
> but everyone made fun of him:
> he was a paper soldier.
>
> You never would entrust to him
> your secrets so important,
> and why, I ask?
> Well, just because,
> he was a paper soldier.
>
> Artillery fire? Well, forward, go,
> And he marched when they told him,
> and there he burned from head to toe:
> he was a paper soldier.

The utopianism of the little soldier was a new note for Okudzhava, but it was a sign of his latent interests. Many of the early songs have the artless repetitions of trivial works, but Okudzhava's craftsmanship and insights were those of a serious artist. He pictured small flowers, in the manner of folk songs, but he also started to take a long view and to speak of future wars and of coming generations.

The early 1960s brought a heyday of guitar poetry, and Okudzhava was not alone as a "bard." His new songs were set in Leningrad, in Moscow, and in the provinces. This period is dominated by his search for love, a sphere in which he is, he says, more unlucky than most. People everywhere are lonely, however, and more unhappy than happy. In these songs there are no villains; fate alone is to blame. Okudzhava had ill-defined utopian ideals, symbolized, for example, by the Blue Mountains to which a Red River leads. His songs were deceptively simple in their syntax (and melodies). They were influenced by folk verse forms, but they have the casual acceptance of anguish that marks popular urban art.

In time, Okudzhava's poetry became increasingly dissident and literary in its mentality. He allowed his historical interests to show. Both Peter the Great and François Villon were portrayed as exemplary rebels. In the mid-1960s Okudzhava began to write fewer songs, and in the 1970s and 1980s he wrote as a former balladeer. He spoke, for example, of his new meetings with his old friend,

Nadezhda, the woman's name that means "hope." His love for the Moscow district called the Arbat did not fade, however. His historical novel called *Poor Avrosimov* (1969) shows his admiration for the romantic era, a period of striving for political freedoms. His protagonist idolizes a rebel, the southern leader of the Decembrists.

The New Thaw Poets: Evtushenko

The younger poets were overwhelmingly more popular than the older poets, although their verse was not intrinsically superior. It was they who drew crowds that filled stadiums in the early 1960s. The young poets were better known in the West, although the older poets also traveled abroad. The newcomers admired their elder colleagues and learned from them, but the new poets also assumed positions of leadership, as though of a political or social group. They gave more programmatic forms to such new themes as love and the possession of an individual conscience. They elevated themes to slogans. A part of their appeal was, in fact, their youthful audacity and their innocence of the past. They came of age just as the Stalin era was closing, and they appeared as social combatants to defeat the old age. They valued daring in itself, even when courage could be expressed only as whimsy or as the possession of personal "secrets" (the title of a poem by Evtushenko). They also led the way in displaying a lively curiosity about the West, although they condemned its social structure and fashions. The Thaw poets had no firsthand memories of the war. They could place their country in an optimistic, hopeful light and could not remember its sharpest pains and anxieties.

The pace for the development of Thaw poetry was set by Evgeny Evtushenko (b. 1933). He praised the common man not as the patriot but as the repository of sentimental values. He wrote defiant poems, such as "The Heirs of Stalin" (1962), and he explored the apolitical sphere of love, tenderness, and friendship. He wrote with a tinge of naiveté, as a genuine Russian provincial, born in Siberia. His familiarity with Paris and American cities seemed all the more enviable because of his origin. He encouraged an admiration for pre-Revolutionary poets, and was himself indebted to Maiakovsky. Evtushenko was born near Irkutsk, but his real childhood home was in Moscow. In 1948 he joined his father, a geologist, for several months in the field in Khazakhstan. He attended the Gorky Literary Institute between 1951 and 1954. He was praised in 1956 for "Zima Junction," a long poem about the Siberian town of his birth. By the early 1960s he had become the chief leader of the new forces in poetry. He risked disfavor and was criticized for such outspoken poems as "Babii Iar" (1961), which condemns anti-Semitism. His memoirs, *Autobiographie précoce,* were published in France rather than in Russia. He has nevertheless been a prolific poet. He has served on editorial boards and as a member of the Presidium of the Writers' Union. He has extensive connections with authors and with writers' organizations abroad.

Evtushenko popularized new themes in poetry, but he shared with the past the tendency to regard poetry as a moral platform, or guide. In the poems of the 1950s, he began to depict examples of honesty, loyalty, and other everyday virtues. He showed that they reside in the people and arise in the social fabric itself. Values do not descend, in his poems, from a state or from any higher entity. His first collection in the Thaw period was *The Third Snow* (1955), where he described the people he saw around him on trains, in parks, and at such festivities as weddings. He found them to be well-intentioned, and guiltless in whatever might be their limitations. In "Zima Junction" (1955) he presents himself as another ordinary man, with memories of summer vacations in Siberia, and of the symphony orchestra in Irkutsk. He was tactful; when he was angered by human failings, such as cowardice and hypocrisy, he spoke in generalities, or inverted his illustrations. In "Career" (1957) he supposes that Galileo had faint-hearted colleagues who protected their worldly positions by falsifying their scientific beliefs. He decried class bigotry in "The Tie Salesgirl" (1957). Somewhat later, he turned to introspection and discovered a capacity for self-criticism in "A Knock at the Door" (1959):

> "Who's there?"
>   "Old age my name.
>   I've come to you."
> "Not now.
>   Occupied.
>   I've got things to do."
> I wrote.
>   Made calls.
>   I ate my scrambled eggs.
> Went to the door,
>   but no one was around.
> Was that my friends just making fun of me?
> Or maybe it was I, misheard the name?
> Not age,
>   maturity alone was here,
> And could not wait,
>   and sighed
>   then went away?!

He captured the public's thirst for change in his poem "Fresh Things" (1959).

By the early 1960s Evtushenko had begun to stand out as a bold poet. He learned to express anger, as in "Babii Iar," which is a diatribe in the best sense. In this poem he recalls a massacre by Nazis of Kievan Jews, and he takes his countrymen to task for the anti-Semitism that allows them to ignore this atrocity. In "Heirs of Stalin" Evtushenko warns that the removal of Stalin from the mausoleum shared with Lenin will not end Stalinism in human minds. Here is the conclusion of the poem:

> And there is a reason why Stalin's heirs are at risk now
> For heart attacks. They, who
>   were once in important positions
> Don't like the new times
>   when the slave camps are empty of men,
> But halls where they listen to poems are filled,
>   overflowing.

The Party
>once told me to keep up my guard,
>>not be easy.
If someone now told me:
>Well, go easy, I wouldn't yet dare
>>to rest easy.
While Stalin still has any heirs on the earth anywhere,
It would still seem to me—
>that Stalin's in that mausoleum.

In other poems Evtushenko expressed his private emotions more freely and con-
fessed a vulnerability to sadness. He wrote about love, particularly unrequited and
unhappy loves, sometimes his own. He responded to the sights he saw abroad, but
he criticized Western "decadence" in such poems as "Verlaine" (1960) and "The
Beatnik Girl" (1961).

Since the beginning of the Brezhnev era, Evtushenko has been less sentimental
and more skeptical. In part, his critical attitude has resulted from the fact that he was
writing about Western cultures. In the mid-1960s he was in Rome. His several
poems about Spain include "When They Killed Lorca" (1967). He has written
disparagingly about New York, Beirut, and Portugal. His skepticism was usually in
abeyance when his subject was Siberia, particularly when he described the magnificent and unspoiled region of the Lena River. Nevertheless, he began to speak more
frankly about the evil around him. Like other poets of his generation, he lamented
the particular hardships of Russian women. In a reversal of his earlier opinion, he
finally expressed doubts in the universal, innate goodness of man. He became more
appreciative of the work of other artists, including Akhmatova, Blok, Pushkin, and
Charlie Chaplin. His own indebtedness to Maiakovsky never ceased; it is visible at a
glance in his laddered forms. Evtushenko was a genuine leader. He showed courage
in his verse and in his actions. His poetry suffers from its pervasive, if usually
gentle, didacticism.

The *Precocious Autobiography* that Evtushenko first published in Paris is a
plain-spoken account of the major events in his life, from his birth to the writing of
"Heirs of Stalin." The autobiography includes anecdotes about his extended visit
with his father in the field. The death of Stalin and the first "Day of Poetry," which
became an annual event, are also major occasions in his own life. The book is as
much about his times as about himself.

The first of the Soviet poets to make a clear appeal for individualism and unique
achievements was Andrey Voznesensky (b. 1933). He ignored the usual praise for
everyman and encouraged the desire to excel. He was also the first to denounce war
as such. His initial success owed much to his aggressively avant-garde style. His
verse was not so extreme as to be inaccessible, but it was certainly calculated to
startle the complacent. He is, in fact, remembered for these early poems, and not for
the later works, in which he confronted a Dostoevskian theme—the existence of evil
in the world. Voznesensky was born in Moscow, the son of an engineer. He graduated in 1957 from the Moscow Architectural Institute, but he had earlier found a
mentor in Pasternak, and he opted for a career in poetry. He published a controver-

sial first collection, *The Parabola,* in the following year. In 1963 Voznesensky was denounced by Khrushchev for "formalism." In 1967 he became a member of the presidium of the Writers' Union. He has traveled widely and has given many readings in Western countries.

In his books of the Thaw period, Voznesensky moved rapidly from a youthful vibrancy to anxieties and pessimism. In *The Parabola* he speaks as an apologist for the ambitious and unconventional. The curve described in the title poem of the book is declared to be the shortest distance to authentic achievement: Gauguin became great by retiring to Tahiti. In "Goya" (1957) he admires the Spanish artist who opposed war in his famous series of etchings called "Desastres de la guerra."

> I'm Goya!
> My eyes were plucked out of their sockets by foes who
> swept down upon fields lying barren.
>
> I'm sorrow.
>
> My voice is
> Of war, of the ashes of towns
> on the snows of the year forty-one.
>
> I'm hunger.
> My neck is
> The neck of the woman whose body once bell-like
> hung naked above the town plaza.
>
> I'm Goya!
>
> O grapes of
> Revenge! In my cannons I shot back
> the ashes of Western invaders!
> I have hammered up stars in memorial
> heavens
>
> Like nail heads.
>
> I'm Goya.

Voznesensky was often to turn to artists for illustrations of the daring qualities he admired. He favored poets, especially Pushkin, Esenin, and Maiakovsky. His first long poem, "The Master Builders" (1957), tells the story of upright medieval artisans who were cruelly betrayed by a tsar at the behest of conniving merchants. Voznesensky avoided sentimentality in the depiction of love and showed it instead to be one of the most compelling of human emotions. Passions are seen to be urgent in his poems, and the need for partnership constant. He described women not as willing martyrs, but as society's careless victims—for example, in "They Are Beating a Woman" (1960). He also idealized women; in "The Last Electric Train" (1958) a hardened girl is shown to have the capacities of a madonna. He urged everyone to desert conventional norms, and he extolled cultural variety, as seen, for example, in a bazaar in Tiflis.

Voznesensky's subsequent Thaw books lacked the same clear view of the world. He remained the defender of impulses and natural inclinations, but he now saw the future as clouded by evils, injustices, and confusion. His discovery of America in *The Three Cornered Pear* (1962) was simultaneously his introduction to evil. He saw in the United States not only a land of distressing social contrasts but also the harbinger of a dehumanizing and irresistible force. At the airport at New York he already sees a phantasmagoric wilderness. American youth are self-destructive beatniks. Other poems are about Italy, Poland, and Russia. In *Antiworlds* (1964) those alternative spheres are the never-never lands of the mind, and they can destroy anyone. The book opens in a slough of depression and proceeds to meditations on suicide. He recalls Marilyn Monroe. This volume is dominated by reflections on Paris, a city that attracted Maiakovsky, and that holds surprises, like female croupiers. *The Achilles Heart* (1966) is an argument for the exercise of the emotions, whatever the losses. His own source of agony is the absence of spiritual "wings." The world, however, is full of injustices. In "A Woman Is Beating," a maltreated female is justified in her retaliation. Elsewhere, Esenin, a poet, was driven to suicide. In the long poem *Oza* (1964) Voznesensky is obsessed by his unrequited love for a Zoia in Dubno, a city in the Ukraine.

After the Thaw, Voznesensky had much to say about the quality of modern life, which he regarded as precarious because of its dependence on technology. In the early 1970s he expected the end of the world in a nuclear holocaust. He has swung from despair to grim hope. The problem became more theoretical when he reluctantly accepted the premise that evil resides in human nature. In "Temptation," the title poem of a collection of 1978, he blames the insatiability of the individual for mankind's ventures beyond the good. If the poems of the Thaw period were in part a protest against an evil imposed from above, the later poems are a weary recognition of the complicity of all. The books of the 1970s include *The Shade of Sound* (1970), a relative withdrawal from issues, and *Oak Leaf for Cello* (1975), a volume of sad moods. Subsequent cycles bear such titles as "I Feel, Therefore I Am" and "I Shall Not Recant."

Voznesensky's style was fixed in its essentials from the first poems in print. Although he is an apologist for emotions, his poetry is intellectual at its core. He is more concerned to stimulate than to touch. He wants to make the world a more intelligent place—if need be, through a greater trust in fantasies and feelings. But he relies for his effects on the displays of wit, including word plays, that derive from the avant-garde. His forceful tone and his loose structure derive to a considerable extent from Maiakovsky. He is suggestive rather than didactic. His verse forms are free, his lines often laddered, and his rhymes prominent. Voznesensky has written a number of articles on art, artists, and autobiographical subjects.

The closest of all the Thaw poets to the lineage of the radical avant-garde was Robert Rozhdestvensky (b. 1932). He appeared to be a rebel by nature, as Maiakovsky had been. He embraced bohemian attitudes and was an enthusiast of the Revolution and of Lenin. His style is unconventional, and in fact he has never attracted the widest audiences. Rozhdestvensky was born in the Altai Mountains to military parents, both of whom served in World War II and who entrusted him to a children's home. He graduated from the Gorky Literary Institute in 1956 and published six collections of verse within the next decade. In the title poems of *The Radius of Action* (1965) he writes:

And I
> ran then away from home
>> to tear myself
>>> at last from
the radius of action
of ordinary love.

In other poems, he describes his irregular way of life and his unkempt apartment with a show of pride. He recognizes the humor of his position. In "The Watch Repair" it is his chaotic behavior that has ruined his watch, a symbol for his identity. His voice is strident. He complains to the reader about what should be his private life. He describes his failures in love, his overly lived-in room, his memories of music lessons. His humor is gone when he remembers, in "The Winter of Thirty-Eight," that his father cried, as he was to learn only twenty years later, over the innocent victims of Stalin's purges. In spite of Rozhdestvensky's visible anger, his half-serious self-pity, and his conviction that humans are generally unhappy, always waiting for the impossible, his poetry is optimistic. He believed that friendships can be trusted and that people are both strong and intelligent. He ventured an outright ideological statement in the poem "I and We," which appears in *The Radar of the Heart* (1971); any authentic love, he wrote, begins with an "I," not "we." He boasted, however, about the Revolution, which in the long poem "A Letter to the Thirtieth Century" he entrusts to posterity. "Requiem" (1962) is a tribute to the victims of World War II. His tone in all moods and for all subjects is declamatory, but his sentences are simple; he did not imitate the avant-garde in their density of metaphors and ornamental devices.

Traditionalists in the Thaw

In the Thaw era the mere writing of verse came to be a sign of enthusiasm for the new trends. Many new poets appeared, and matters of style were viewed with tolerance. The desire of the newcomers to form links with the past led some to bypass the revolutionary avant-garde and return to acmeist or classical styles. The poetry of Bella Akhmadulina (b. 1937) was the Thaw period's most distinguished example of simple, elegant, old-fashioned poetry. She did not speak self-consciously of the new themes or emulate the futurists. She was close in spirit to acmeism in that her poetry was personal in tone, modern in vocabulary, and classical in form. Akhmadulina was born in Moscow, the daughter of Italian and Tatar families, both Russified and poor. She left the Gorky Literary Institute in 1960 and published her first collection in 1962. She was a popular figure at poetry readings, but her best-known book, *A Chill* (1968), was published in Germany. She was married to Evtushenko and later to the writers Iury Nagibin and Gennadi Mamlin. She appeared in performances abroad, but she was less prolific than many other Soviet poets, and wrote even less in the 1980s.

Akhmadulina's intention was to make durable art, as was done in the past, out of life's minutiae. Personal poetry was, however, one of the cardinal issues of the

Thaw. She responds to a variety of sights—morning in the country, the crowd at a Moscow subway stop, a peasant wedding, a leopard captured for a zoo. Her own personality is elusive, but it gradually comes into focus. She speaks to the reader as though she were the familiar average observer, but she emerges as someone who is unique and colorful. She is Russian by education, but more fiery and more quickly wounded. Her imagination is especially vivid; she sees airplanes as baby chicks. Even she knows, in "The sound of rain, as though the sound of the dombra," that mere passersby stare at her on the street. Her origin is the subject of the long poem "My Genealogy" (1963). Finally, it is her fantasies and memories, her loves, her art, and her perceptions of nature that are memorable, rather than the separate events that she describes. Her loves play a role in revealing her character. She can be distressingly devoted and docile, but also unexpectedly cynical. Here is a moment of pained abstinence:

> Don't spend much time to court my company
> don't question me in depth and length.
> Don't gaze with kind and loyal eyes at me,
> and gently reach to touch my hand.
>
> When spring has come, don't track through rainy pools
> to follow where my feet have gone.
> I know—no good will come because we met—
> no issue was there from the past.
>
> You think, it's from my pride I hesitate,
> walk by and show no sign to you?
> It's not my pride, no, it's the grief I've had
> that makes me hold my head so straight.

One of her long poems, "September," is dedicated to Nagibin. Akhmadulina sometimes touched on a new theme—how to perform in the world with men without losing the right to be loved as a woman. She had a general interest in the psychopathology of illnesses, and her major book, after all, is called *A Chill*. Her poems on physical sickness seem to reflect her fears of other pains.

Akhmadulina's poetry has both a fanciful side and a bedrock morality. Her constant views are not to be gleaned from her nature poems, which reflect her moods. Her landscapes are convincing in their details, but the cold of winter may be protective if she is happy, and the promises of May are dubious if she is fearful. She seldom made moral or philosophical statements. Her convictions, and her moral lessons, are drawn from her portraits of Russian poets, particularly from Pushkin and Lermontov. Like many other Russian poets, she was fond of Georgia because of its rugged landscapes and picturesque people. She herself was exotic in temperament. In the simplicity of her style, she resembled Akhmatova.

Among other poets who were closer in tendency to acmeism than to futurism was Aleksandr Kushner (b. 1936). His verse has the ring of confessional poetry, but of an understated kind. In his preoccupations he might qualify as an everyman, but he takes a slightly ironic view and depreciates himself. He was born in Leningrad, graduated from a pedagogical institute in 1959, and taught literature in the equivalent of a high school. He has published relatively little, two books in the Thaw period and several in the 1970s, but with increasing effectiveness. In *The First Meeting* (1957) he describes his modest way of life. He reports his own rather ordinary dialogues on the telephone and explains his strange confinement to his room and small area of the city. In his imagination he is a romantic, and he has elevated ideals. But in life he ends by choosing the golden mean. Some poems are mere impersonal observations of others—boys at play, or an old man in the hospital. Kushner speaks with a wistful voice, but on reflection he accepts the workings of fate. In the title poem of *The Night Watch* (1966) he describes the dawn as finding the city, Leningrad, in no dire straits. In his later volumes, he allows himself larger statements. He speaks about humanity, about Leningrad as a city, about nature, and about literature. The poems in *The Letter* (1974) are his only reflection of a serious crisis, a failure in love. In other books his affairs are treated with romantic irony as mere trivia. His idle threat of suicide in "I shout into the telephone" (from *The Voice,* 1978), is answered with a mild rebuke:

> And that is just because, she said to me,
> You are in fact a very lucky man.

His verse forms are for the most part classical.

The poetry of Novella Matveeva (b. 1934) has been praised as the "wisdom of children." It is, rather, the active fantasy life of childhood and youth on which she draws. She was born near Leningrad and has published with increasing regularity since 1961. In many of her poems Matveeva describes quiet landscapes, often valleys with familiar birches and willows. But her scenes are richly personified by her fantasies, and she often finds moral lessons in them. In some lyrics she insists on the value of natural, unrestrained song, like that of birds, but she has also written much about art and artists. She has admired romantic English authors such as Rudyard Kipling and Robert Burns, and Americans, including Edgar Allen Poe and Mark Twain. Her poetry suffers from a rather abstemious naiveté. She has set a number of her poems to music and has performed with a guitar. Her verse shows, as does Kushner's, that Soviet poetry has outlived the trauma of World War II and the extraliterary political stimulus of the Thaw.

Brodsky

The outstanding poet of recent times, whether in the Soviet Union or in emigration, has been Joseph Brodsky (b. 1940). He was formed by currents inside the Soviet Union, although he now resides abroad and has entered Western literary spheres. His subject has been the same existential melancholia that once inspired the acmeists. Brodsky writes with philosophical premises close at hand, but he is not precisely a metaphysical poet. He has written personal poetry about his own experiences, and he has written about mankind, or his civilizations, in the universe, which he regards with some pessimism. All his collections of poetry have been published in the West including his fullest, *A Halt in the Wilderness* (1970). Some of the poems in this volume reflect his internment in a prison camp in the far north. He has not been as prolific as many Soviet poets; he has published no more than most émigrés. His link with acmeist traditions has been of the most authentic kind. He has always spoken as a participant in European culture, not only as a Soviet citizen. His early subjects include both the Biblical Abraham and John Donne. He began, like other Soviet poets, with the tones of an unassuming everyman. But he also had a faint air of self-irony, and was in fact immediately seen to be an intellectual. The poems that he wrote in the period after his arrival in the West appeared in *A Part of Speech* (1977). He also published a collection of prose essays on autobiographical and literary subjects called *Less Than One* (1986).

Brodsky has allowed his dedication to poetry to dictate the circumstances of his life, although he describes poetry, when he speaks of it, as merely an aspect of language. He was born in Leningrad, the son of a photographer and a former naval officer in a Jewish family. Without being religious, he was at first attracted to some Old Testament subjects. He left school at fifteen, worked at odd jobs, and studied foreign literatures, especially English, in private; he became a protégé of Anna Akhmatova. In 1964 he was convicted of "parasitism" and sentenced to five years of forced labor at a camp near Archangel. His sentence became an international cause célèbre and he was released in 1965. After his first two books of verse, including *A Halt in the Wilderness*, had appeared in the West, he was required, in 1972, to go into exile. He has been affiliated with the University of Michigan, Columbia University, and others. He began to write poetry and essays in English, and in 1988 he received the Nobel Prize for literature.

Brodsky's poetry has reflected throughout a concern about the imperfections of the universe. His protests have been muted and indirect, but persistent. He does not speak about social injustices. He is less inclined to anger than to irony, but he does show suffering. The long poems of his first book, *Poems and Narrative Verse* (1968), serve to illustrate the variety of his anxieties. In "Hills" his characters confront the brutal fact that evil resides in man and can result in murder. In "Great Elegy: To John Donne" Brodsky speaks to the elevated soul that means well and that suffers from the loneliness of an unintended alienation. In "Isaac and Abraham" he suggests that sacrifices, however earnestly made, have no receptor, and that salvation is nonexistent. He shows the self-crippling views of many of the figures of world literature and legend, including Don Quixote, Harlequin, and Hamlet, in "The Procession." Although Brodsky did not intentionally make social statements or limit his purview to Soviet life, several of his poems became favorites in dissident circles. Among them was "Fish in Winter"; the fish seemed to symbolize an enforced muteness and a minimal level of survival. In the following poem, his subject is a universal form of loneliness, that of the transient:

> The house is strange for him who just moved in.
> His eye slides quickly over all those objects,
> whose very shades are now so out of place,
> they feel the pain of it themselves, and languish.
> The house would like to end its emptiness.
> The lock as though was not made with that mettle,
> and cannot rise to common knowledge shared,

and clings to its resistance in the darkness.
The new one, true, does not look like that one
who brought the tables, cupboards here, and thought
that he would never more desert these walls,
but had to go away; he left and perished.
No, nothing can be said to join these two:
unlike in face, in character, or sorrow.
And yet there runs between these two a thread—
a home, it's called, in what is common parlance.

The desire, even of inanimate things, to form new ties suggests a conviction that a human thirst for love is constantly thwarted. The volume contains a few poems that were written in 1964 and have northern settings. Brodsky's somewhat weary, ironic, and colloquial style is seductive. He often used free or tonic verse and inexact rhymes.

Brodsky was unchanged in his philosophical views by his stay in the north, but deeply affected personally. Poems written before, during, and after his confinement appear in *A Halt in the Wilderness*. He gives a much more prominent place in this book to his experiences in love. His relationships are presented in glimpses of settings and in wistful addresses to women. Love is increasingly seen in its capacity to inflict its own losses and pain. In the long poem "Farewell Mademoiselle Veronica" love is, in any case, ethereal, like all the ideals that forever escape us. The warmth of actual ties is still sought in the accidents of the surrounding world. Among the poems written in the north is this small memento of affection for a fragile creature in its fitness to survive:

At Evening

The hay was powdered with snow
that fell through cracks by the roof.
I toppled the straw and there—
I met face to face—a moth.
Little moth, little moth.
It found a way not to die—
it flew up into the loft.
It lived, and winter passed.

Emerging, it slowly looks
at the steam of *die Fledermaus,*
the wall that is brightly lit
although it is made of logs.
I lift the moth to my eyes,
I see its fine little dust
more clearly than any flame,
than I can see my own palm.

And now in the evening dusk
we two are here alone.
My fingers are just as warm
as a day is in June.

In the same period Brodsky wrote "Letter in a Bottle," a long poem which suggests that he felt a need for a salvation, one that could not be foreseen. His reflections on civilization include an antiwar statement. In "Einem alten Architekten in Rom" he describes the effects of the bombing of Königsberg in World War II. The poem called "A Halt in the Wilderness" is a meditation on the razing of a Greek church in Leningrad; he concludes that every society makes its own contribution to civilization, and yet mankind is still searching for a sufficient sacrifice. His cynicism inspired a long dialogue called "Gorbunov and Gorchakov" (1965–1968), in which two "friends" in an insane asylum profess affection but engage in a cruel psychological duel. Incarceration and ill will defeat their need for companionship.

No respite from frustrations was to appear in the poems published in emigration. Brodsky's first volume after his arrival in the West, *The End of a Beautiful Epoch* (1977), contains poems that had been written in the Soviet Union. His opening poems are about his failures in love and losses by death. Many are set in the south, especially in Yalta, a vacation city, and the beach is prominent scenery. There is in these poems a hint of a surrender to decadence and idleness. In the title poem he expresses the fear that Russian culture, the result of centuries of development, will end in moral and artistic disintegration. His tone can be bitter. A philosophical dimension appears in one poem that is a dialogue with a creature of heaven. A historical resonance comes in a poem about the end of the Roman Empire. The poems that Brodsky wrote when first in the West appear in *A Part of Speech* (1977). A retelling of the Biblical story of the birth of Christ opens the book. The poem awakens a sense of adoration and new hope, but in subsequent poems he returns, after an interval of exploration, to a joyless skepticism. "A Song of Innocence, the Same—An Experiment" is an ironic parody of William Blake. In "Odysseus to Telemachus" the illustrious father cannot even remember who won the Trojan War. Brodsky discovered a multiplicity of cultures in the West, but he did not find meaningful contours. The absence of Soviet constraints did not bring a sense of inner freedom. The very diversity of his topics—from Mexico to Mary Stuart—suggests a dispersal of attention. It is only in the cycle called "A Part of Speech" that he looks within. Here is the final poem of the series:

> It is not that I'll lose my mind, but I'm tired for the summer.
> If you go for a shirt to the chest, then the day is all over.
> If only the winter would come at last and cover these over,
> all these cities and persons, but for the sake of greening.
> I shall sleep not undressing or start reading from any
> at all page in someone's book while the rest of the year ends.
> Like a dog run away from his blind man,
> they still cross the street where they ought. But freedom,
> that's when you have forgotten the middle name of the tyrant,
> and the spit in your mouth is sweeter than Shiraz halva,
> and your brain is atwist like horns on a he-goat,
> but nothing falls in drops from your eyes of azure.

The poems of this cycle are written without emphases, as though in imitation of all-over designs. The title, "A Part of Speech," suggests a lack of wholeness, perhaps of himself, or of his language, without Russia. The keenly felt nostalgia for human warmth that had made some earlier poems so appealing is more subdued in this book.

In the 1980s Brodsky tended to move beyond his memories of Russia, especially in his lyrics. *The Roman Elegies* (1982) are a tightly written cycle of small poems that reflect a life of *dolce far niente*. The temptations of decadence arise again in a new context. The ruins of the ancient Roman culture almost become a source of mere gratification; they are picturesque. In 1984 Brodsky published a spoof of this life in a humorous two-act play called *Marble*. It consists of a dialogue between two ancient Romans who voice the interests of modern-day hedonists. His prose essays in *Less Than One* (1986) include memoirs and critical pieces. "Less than one" is the value he assigned to his own identity in a typically ironic statement. He wrote appreciative essays on Akhmatova, Mandelstam, and Tsvetaeva, and on Cavafy, Montale, and Auden, to whom he has felt indebted. The memoirs reflect the same views as his poetry: the universe is a puzzle, and its inequities are offensive. No system can be discerned and no hope entertained for fundamental changes in human life. Yet his pessimism is not complete; he affirms, as does Russian verse in general, that civilizations, however defective, are worth the effort, as are individual lives.

A New Wave in Emigration

The best of the émigré poets who appeared after the war have been inspired by their metaphysical speculations or Christian convictions. Not all are young; Russian poets in exile continued to begin publishing late and often have few books to their name. On the whole, they have not been deeply affected by Western literature. They still look back to the Russian traditions of the 1920s and 1930s. One of the leading metaphysical poets is Igor Chinnov (b. 1909), whose ideas were current in an even earlier period—the symbolist era. He writes, like a Sologub or a Hippius, about the inevitably of evil, the existence of the divine, the nature of death, and the role of fantasy and of escapist dreaming. His first collection, *Monologue*, appeared in 1950. While his ideas have been constant, he has made radical changes in his style. He was born in Riga, spent his childhood in Russia, and graduated in law from the University of Riga in 1939. He fled during the war, earned a literary degree in Paris in 1947, and worked in Munich at Radio Liberty from 1953 to 1962. He then emigrated to the United States, where he was a professor of Russian literature at various universities until his retirement to Florida. Most of his poetry appeared during the 1970s.

Although Chinnov's metaphysical concerns owe much to the symbolist period, his aesthetic does not. He in no way regards the poet as a seer or purveyor of mystical insights. Like the acmeists, he believes the poet to be a craftsman pursuing a task significant in its own right. In *Monologue* (1950) he devotes some poems to protests against war, but the philosophical nature of his resentment soon becomes clear. He is angered by every killing and every pain, by the butchering of animals, and by the suffering of the old in hospitals. He holds the creating God responsible for evil. In the following poem he suggests that Orpheus should have listened to the voices of earthly things instead of charming them with his own:

He too had traversed, and alone,
The foggiest, outlying regions.
And if he had waked them from sleep . . .
And if they had given an answer . . .

And if, in the silence of fields,
The anguish, the sadness of passage,
If once only Orpheus heard
Their answer, their call, and their sorrow . . .

At nighttime the dream had no end:
It seemed that the cliff fell asunder,
It seemed that you heard a new voice
All shaken and cracked at the center.

A sobbing, and fragmented sound,
And cries that did summon and falter . . .
The dawn. And how still it all is.
Don't call for Eurydice, leave her.

The poem also illuminates Chinnov's own dilemma. Any response to the world, in life or in poetry, will arouse sympathetic pain. Should man then turn to pleasant fantasies of a painless beauty, or escape from life into dreams? or death? One decade later he took up the question of escapism in *Lines* (1960). These new poems are unexpectedly and charmingly reminiscent of *fin de siècle* decadence. He describes moonlit landscapes of the soul, perhaps with rising fountains, as in the early poems of Verlaine. He contrasts the pure and the profane, like any romantic. In some poems he describes such current events as the famines in India and the revelations about the prison camp Vorkuta. But elsewhere he describes poetry as the mere flickering of light and shade, of indifference and delight. In both books he recalls Russia with great love and in realistic detail, such as the rowan tree or the lizards of the sunny south.

An experimental and ornate style that Chinnov later adopted can be seen in *Score with Parts* (1970). His word plays and his displays of whimsy tend to cloud the meaning of these poems. His contrasts and parallels can be elaborate, his literary allusions are numerous, and he sometimes capitalizes abstractions. This intricate style was inspired by the avant-garde, but it seems also to have been tied, in Chinnov's mind, with the medieval "weaving of words" of Russian monks. In an introduction to *Pastorals* (1976) Chinnov declared that he now wished to be less angry and more appreciative of life's pleasant aspects. In this volume he turns his attention to the concrete world. He describes flamingos in Florida, some sites in New York City, and others, such as the Acropolis and the Alhambra, in Europe. His style is more colloquial and natural, even prosaic. In this book and in *Autograph* (1984) his philosophical problems are at bottom not at all changed, but their facets are more complex. His mind moves freely from the elevated to the popular, from astronomy to Mickey Mouse, and on to Greek myths and the literatures of the world. But his personality is veiled, and the poems are less lyrical and charming.

A major shift in interest took place in the poetry of Nikolay Morshen (real surname: Marchenko; b. 1917) after his emigration. His first poems reflected a life in the Soviet Union, and his focus was on social topics, but in the later poems he turned to philosophical subjects. His scientific knowledge entered into his verse, and he showed himself to be an optimist at heart. Morshen was born in Kiev, the son of a fiction writer who used the pseudonym Narokov. Morshen graduated from Kiev University with a degree in physics. In 1941 Kiev was occupied by Germany; in 1944 he became a displaced person and then emigrated to the United States. His philosophical outlook is best seen in *Two Dots, or A Colon* (1961), whose poems are often fantasies about the cosmos. Morshen was able to pose metaphysical questions in terms that are both revealing and yet familiar.

Morshen has appeared as a somewhat different poet in each of his three books, but his impulses are consistently humane and his concept of the world is spiritual. In his first book, *The Sea Lion* (1959), he is the captive of a repugnant system in a despotic country. In the title poem he wishes he were a sea lion as he recalls his acquiescence in a group decision to impose the death penalty on "enemies of the state"; sea lions can break through the ice in order to breathe. He describes the people around him in what should be casual circumstances, but he sees that everyone is subject to fear. He is especially vulnerable because he is a Christian. He also describes the beauties of nature around Kiev. In the final poems World War II has begun, and in "1943" potatoes are boiled in a field and a volume signed by Tiutchev is selected to be sold. His style is classical and indebted to acmeism. In his second book, *Two Dots, or a Colon,* Morshen's sole concern has become his spiritual thirst. He concludes in the title poem that the cosmos is an orderly place because his shadow is constant and that death, therefore, is not a single dot, or a period, but a colon. The same faith is confirmed for him the timelessness of memory in this poem:

> Not faded is last night's sunset,
> Unmelted snows that fell last year,
> Nor silent far-off nightingales
> Within my magic memory.
>
> To it—what fifteen years now past?
> What thirty years? or forty years?
> It will remember—snow or hail,
> Or laughter, sin, or color, light.
>
> O river, memory on earth,
> while here you flow both bright and wide,
> But how to find my path at dark
> To where you have your early source,
>
> Where streams still dusky splash and play
> Out of discovery's deep crevasse?

His imagination is still graphic. He can picture both a barren earth beyond life and a being in the cosmos without earth. His symbols are memorable. Death, for example, might come through causation or by chance, just as a bull might be sent either to the butcher or to the matador. The transcendence of boundaries is illustrated by the flying fish, which leaves its water and knows the air. The interplay of inspiration and concrete words, particularly in the writing of poetry, has begun to be of interest. It is this earthly side of attainment that preoccupies Morshen in his third book, *The Echo and the Mirror* (1979). He subjected his new poems to radical formal experiments, some obviously meant to demonstrate his philosophical statements. He points out that 2 squared, $2 + 2$, and $2 \times 2 = 4$; he places himself in a "fifth dimension," where time is eternity. He imitates the techniques of modern art—for example, in "White on White," about snow. He arranges some poems in parallel columns. In general, his focus seems to be on technical devices that have the effect of wit, but neither his ideas nor his poems have profited.

The poetry of Dmitri Bobyshev (b. 1936) suggests a life lived fully in an earthly sense, but within the framework of, and always shaped by, a religious understanding. His metaphysical poems reflect both a search for attainment and a warm optimism. He was born in Mariupol in the Ukraine, the son of an architect, but adopted by his stepfather, a naval engineer. His mother was a chemist, and he graduated from Leningrad Technological Institute. He was a disciple of Anna Akhmatova, together with Joseph Brodsky and others. He moved to the United States in 1979 and published a book, *Spaces* (1979), whose poems were written in the 1960s and 1970s. He teaches Russian literature at the University of Illinois. His poetry springs primarily from a spiritual quest, the need to fill the gaps in mankind's perception of divine love.

The poems of *Spaces* are arranged, regardless of date, in cycles devoted to the various aspects of human life, such as the writing of poetry, the appreciation of nature, and the experience of love. In the opening section, "Words," earthly language is linked to sacred meanings, but words are also thought to be inexact. Bobyshev's faith in the efficacy of revelation is relatively uncomplicated, like that of the early romantics, or of mystics anywhere. In cycles called "Views" he describes the world in scenes. Some poems are landscapes; others are depictions of simple folk at their modest occupations. Here, too, he intimates that correspondences exist between the heavenly and the profane. The cycle "Flowers" consists of his poems about love. It is in "Spaces" that he reflects his soul's thirst and its need to seek. The book includes five long poems on metaphysical subjects. The final poem, "Stigmata," brings poems of exultation; the devil himself is released from the bonds of the material world, and the book concludes with the triumph of the divine androgyne. Bobyshev's style is relatively accessible and classical.

A Postscript on Recent Times

The Seventies

The fortunes of Soviet literature changed again from dark to bright with the coming of Mikhail Gorbachev's policy of *glasnost* in the mid-1980s. The 1970s had been a dour period, especially during the tenure of Leonid Brezhnev as General Secretary from 1977 to 1982. The heady expectations of the Thaw were over, but the intelligentsia could be grateful that the worst repressions of Stalinist times were also gone. Literature settled into its somewhat alleviated and expanded course. The mainstream of poetry belonged to the maturing poets of the Thaw. Evtushenko and Vosnesensky remained the country's foremost poets. Others who had appeared in roughly the same years, but with less *éclat,* emerged as the new rank and file. These poets included Stanislav Kuniaev, Vladimir Tsybin, and Iunna Morits, among others. They were poets of nature and of everyday life, sometimes of the mundane. They kept alive the lyricism of intimate moods, private fantasies, and whimsy. They praised moral integrity, and they shared an inclination to sadness. The era was never without underground poets whose moral programs were more ambitious and who had difficulty publishing or even being circulated in *samizdat.* The spirit of rebellion and hopes for liberalization were kept alive for the wide public in guitar poetry, particularly in the work of the popular celebrity Vladimir Vysotsky, who was an actor and a playwright.

The guitar poets differed from Okudzhava in their outspoken voicing of social complaints; they were more bitter, grotesque, and imaginative. They were known primarily through tape recordings and by word of mouth. Aleksandr Galich (real surname: Ginzburg; 1918–1977) wrote songs about the dangers to career, well-being, and life of speaking the truth, about the government's tyranny, and about the public's reluctant silence. The rewards for compliance are seen to be material success. He was trained and practiced as a playwright, but turned to guitar poetry in the early 1960s. In 1971 he was excluded from the Writers' Union and from the Union of Cinematographers. His songs were published in *The Doomed Generation,* which appeared in Germany in 1972. The first section of that book has an ironic title, "I Choose Freedom." In general, his poems are addressed to an urban and educated audience, and include many allusions to history and literature. In a long piece called "Poem About Stalin" the life of the dictator is related as though it were the life of Christ. In 1974 Galich emigrated and settled in Munich, where he continued to write and publish. His second book of songs and lyrics appeared in Frankfurt with the title *When I Return* (1977). The book opens with the title song, a nostalgic expression of the desire to return home—to snows, the incense of church, and nightingales. Many of its poems were written in the Soviet Union, however. These are not so much songs of anger and protest as of long suffering, love, and resignation. He depicts ordinary people, those whose private lives are crossed by the hapless fate of the nation. There are religious notes among the poems of the section called "My Father's House." In the section called "The Wild West" he describes Europe as a place where he can find nothing of value and much that is absurd. "Last Poems" (1977) is a farewell to a career as balladeer. Galich's songs appeared regularly in émigré magazines, however, and he found sympathetic audiences abroad. His range is narrow and his songs are predictable, but they display a genuine wit and, except for the songs about the West, a welcome sense of appropriateness.

In the 1970s all bards were overshadowed by Vladimir Vysotsky (1938–1980), who was a star of the stage, films, television, and radio. His protests against Soviet abuses were on occasion specific, but his songs show on the whole a wider philosophical framework and awareness. During World War II, Vysotsky was evacuated to the district of Orenburg; his absent father was a colonel. He was educated in Moscow and in the German Democratic Republic before entering the studio school of the Moscow Art Theater. His songs began to appear in the early 1960s, and in 1964 he became the leading actor at the Taganka Theater, itself to become a popular center of innovative and suggestive staging under the direction of Iury Liubimov. Vysotsky became famous in the roles of Don Juan and of Hamlet. In Vysotsky's songs his awareness as a citizen had two aspects. While he deplored the repression imposed by the authorities through sentences to labor camps and insane asylums, he also remembered the ordeal of the population in World War II. The latter notes tied Vysotsky to the mainstream of public opinion and provided a channel for patriotism. In yet other poems he was a citizen of the world at large, where life is hard and sad for all, no matter what the country, and where death is the common sentence. His songs are strengthened as an *oeuvre* by his use of the first-person singular; each one emanates from a familiar viewpoint. His own situations are left in obscurity, however, and his settings are sketchy—an interior, an airport, a natural landscape. In "I live in this, the best of worlds" his tone is ironic, but his sole complaints are about the existence of rain and the absence of a horse. He often relies on the nostalgic expression of obviously false hopes. His style is relatively free of subservience to the guitar. His sentences are long and complex, and his meanings are not facile. He suffered from alcoholism and died in 1980. A two-volume posthumous collection, *Songs and Poems,* was published in New York in 1983.

Those Thaw poets who came to prominence in the 1970s had a tendency to confound private griefs with those of the land, or of the nation. Stanislav Kuniaev (b. 1932) expressed also their love for the landscapes of their native land. He was born in Kaluga, graduated from Moscow University in 1959, and worked for several years on newspapers in central Siberia. His Thaw period poetry appeared in *The Snowstorm Comes to Town* (1966). He published most extensively in the 1970s, nearly one book for every year. Among his titles are *In September and in April* (1975) and *Through the Wide World* (1978). A retrospective collection of lyrics, dating from the early 1960s to the early 1980s, appeared in 1983 under the title *The Nameless Lake*. The book opens with a sweep of poems describing wilderness landscapes in all seasons and in loving detail. His rivers, fields, and forests represent the entire land, the bountiful home. In the poems that follow, he recalls the ordeals of the people, primarily in World War II. He takes a long view of history, however, and sees in the past the many vagaries of chance. Russia becomes an enigmatic country long given to terror and to suffering that is somehow of its own making. In "Vladimir Highway" he describes the cruel immolation of a live cow for the making of the prize-winning movie *Andrey Rublev,* which celebrated a medieval painter. For Kuniaev the woes perpetrated in Russia have stretched from Rublev's time to ours. He also ponders the popularity among Russians of destructive monarchs, and the love of country of political émigrés, such as Ivan Kurbsky in the sixteenth century and Aleksandr Herzen in the nineteenth. As for himself, the poet is seen to be a wanderer, a spectator who loves change, and a gentle eccentric. In "All night the wind resounded" he dwells on the mortality of humans and the eternity of springs. A number of poems are devoted to human ties, whether of lovers or of friends; most are separated through the accidents of time. The title poem, "The Nameless Lake" (1976), describes a quiet wilderness spot that is surrounded by the rapid construction of cities and the incessant motion of airplanes. The lake is that remote place "where the soul, if it exists, might return when man dies." Kuniaev eventually touches on the far-flung geographical edges of the Soviet Union and on the possibilities for widespread mutual love and compassion. He sees the efforts of humans everywhere to pass on the fruits of civilization through various writings, papers, and books. His values are those of the sentimentalist, but he has no inclination to religion or dogma. He has an independent intelligence and is almost a loner. His style is relatively traditional in form, but his lines are sometimes without meter.

Vladimir Tsybin (b. 1932) is another intellectual who draws his strength from nature, but his poems are somewhat less taut and more given to sentiment. He was born in a small provincial town, graduated from the Moscow Literary Institute in 1958, and published *The Parent Steppe* in 1959. In the 1960s and 1970s he brought out six volumes of verse and several of fiction. *One Life* (1988) is a retrospective collection of his lyrics. The opening poems reveal the Cossack background of his family. He describes an ethnic culture in which horse racing is a holiday, the mood is often festive, and geese walk near at hand. The "One Life" of the title is not his own, but that of "Aunt Marishka," one of the many robust women of this society. The poems are not without humor and a touch of affectionate satire. In the lyrics that follow he sees the world around him as his nation, awesome in its natural beauty and vast spaces, but tragic in the lives of its people. Poets, like Pushkin, are distrusted and sacrificed. Private citizens sustain undeserved losses, such as that of a mother who has given four sons to war. Nature alone cannot assuage these griefs, and he must himself become their voice. Philosophical questions about the nature of the universe and the perception of one's own identity are raised in the section called "Distant Thoughts." These abstractions are playfully couched in the language of folklore and superstition. He speaks of mirrors, dreams, and the supernatural, but his curiosity does not seem to be naive. The cycle called "The Bells of the Soul" is a rehearsal of the claims on his heart: the ordeals of the nation, the ending of a long love, and the echoes of childhood found in the memory. All his griefs are redeemed by a great and placid gratitude for life. Nature never ceases to inform his poems, whatever their subject. His style is touched throughout by the primitivism of folklore, but is not dominated by it.

A pastoral poet who seemed to be more genuinely of the people and who had an uncomplicated style was Nikolay Rubtsov (1936–1971). His brief lyrics tell of a short, unhappy life. His misfortunes seem, again, to reflect those of the land. But he was less a spectator of suffering than was Kuniaev or Tsybin, and more nearly a victim. He was born in a small town near Archangel, grew up in orphanages, and became a stoker on fishing boats. His major theme is his love for Russia's landscapes. He describes birches, lakes and rivers, the rain, and many varieties of birds. He is a wayfarer by train, by horse, and by foot, and he observes the far-flung provincial towns of the nation. He remembers the losses of his own family. He expresses his compassion for Russia's people and for its animals, whose life he sees as a bleak physical struggle. He felt a kinship with Esenin, and in "Poetry" he seems to draw a line from Koltsov to himself. But folklore did not enter into his language as it had with those "peasant" poets. His style is simple but literary, and his meters and rhymes are firm. He spoke intimately of the land and the people, but was a loner. In 1984 a multi-volume collection called *Lyrics* began to appear.

The claims of romantic dreams and fantasies of spiritual soaring are seen in the lyrics of Iunna Morits (b. 1937). Her subjects are the hopes and memories of the intimate mind. She came from Kiev and attended the Moscow Institute of Literature until 1961. In the same year came *The Peninsula of Desire*. In the 1970s she published three collections. *Selections* (1982) is a retrospective volume spanning the years from the mid-1950s to 1981. Its opening poems are devoted to the ideals and self-indulgent hopes characteristic of youth. She longs for a full life, both in nature and among other people. She plainly enjoys her acquaintance with the Baltic coast. She often sees life, however, in terms of literature and the history of the arts; she alludes to the Bible, to Shakespeare, to Rabelais, to Bizet, and to ancient Greek myths. The title poem of one of her books, "With Stern Thread" (1973), speaks of the moral fortitude that she will need to sail through the world and on to heaven. Her many landscapes are seen in the transient seasons of rain and dramatic change, and are usually suffused with her own feelings of joy or of sorrow. She is a dedicated poet and stylist, but somewhat given to self-indulgent effusiveness. She speaks to an audience that thirsts for expressions of individualistic desire and emotional freedom.

A poet more reminiscent of the inclination of the socialist realist is Rimma Kazakova (b. 1932). She writes on the older themes as they survived the Thaw. She speaks of herself as an ordinary person, a hard-working professional with private woes. Her dual concerns are for morality and happiness, and she tends to laud patience, effort, and hard work. Born in Sevastopol, she graduated from Leningrad

University and spent seven years teaching, editing, and writing in the Far East, in Khabarovsk. She published regularly and later occupied a post in the Writers' Union. Her first notable book of the Thaw period was *Fridays* (1965). In the title poem, she pictures herself as a faithful servant awaiting the will of the Crusoes of the world. The themes that she introduced here—nature, the love of country, her memories of childhood and youth, and the role of women in love and in motherhood—were to typify the remainder of her work. In *The Green Firs* (1969) her many poems about World War II resemble the patriotic poems of an earlier generation, but these are more nostalgic in tone. The collections of the 1970s, especially *The Fair Copy* (1977), represent life as a series of ordeals and catastrophes, but she is determined to grow in character through all disasters. In her more recent poems, she often describes the scenes of her travels to Berlin, Paris, the Orient, and Peru. Her perceptions have remained those of a modest, but professional, everywoman. Her style verges on the sentimental, but her language is understated. Her poetic forms are usually traditional, but she occasionally writes without meter.

Glasnost

Since the end of the Brezhnev era, a policy of relaxed guidelines has given rise to a great influx of new literature and to expectations that bold and creative departures will be made. During the tenure in office of Iury Andropov and Konstantin Chernenko, between November 1982 and March 1985, the glum atmosphere of the 1970s was somewhat dissipated. Under Mikhail Gorbachev's policy of *glasnost,* a number of bans have been lifted. The field of literature has been enriched by the publication of little-known Russian classics, including those published earlier but forgotten, those circulated in *samizdat* or published abroad, and those written by Russians in emigration. Evgeny Zamiatin's dystopia *We* and Pasternak's *Doctor Zhivago* are now available, as is the poetry of Nikolay Gumilev and Akhmatova's lament for the imprisoned, *Requiem.* A list of Russian émigrés whose works have been published includes Aleksandr Solzhenitsyn, Vasily Aksenov, and Joseph Brodsky, the living masters. Satires of Soviet conditions, such as those by Mikhail Bulgakov, Vladimir Voinovich (now in emigration), and Georgi Vladimov have become available. Western authors, especially those of the avant-garde, such as Beckett and Ionesco, are now more widely known in translation. Nabokov's *Lolita* has appeared. Little theaters have sprung up alongside the established ones. An atmosphere of ferment has been created. Completely new works have appeared on the background of these expanded horizons. The most important—in fact, the symbol of *glasnost* opportunities—was Anatoly Rybakov's *Children of the Arbat* (1987), a record of the crimes of the Stalin era. Its popularity suggests that the taste of the 1980s was rather more for documenting the injustices of the past than for creating a new art. The tendency of recent times has also been to favor prose, and ideas, over lyrics. And even *The Children of the Arbat* has not been well received as a novel in the West.

The field of poetry has not had the spotlight, as it did in the early years of the Thaw, but it has been somewhat altered. Evtushenko, Vosnesensky, Bulat Okudzhava, and other older poets appeared often in the news, not for the publication of new collections of lyrics, but for their vigorous defense of all aspects of *glasnost*. They became organizers and spokesmen. No major poets have come to replace them. The reputations brought to the fore by *glasnost* have often been those of older poets whose manner is brighter, more individual, or more memorable than that of the poets of the 1970s. Some have been dissidents.

The oldest, Naum Korzhavin (b. 1925), was always too outspoken in his criticism of the regime to have a settled career. He suffered arrests and a Siberian exile, and he now lives in the United States. He was born in Kiev and entered Moscow's Literary Institute in 1944. He was arrested in 1947, spent eight months in prison for the circulation of manuscript poems, and was exiled to Novosibirsk. He reappeared as a dissident in the 1950s and 1960s; his first book was *Years* (1963). In 1967 a play of his was staged in Moscow, but his difficulties led him to emigrate in 1974. His third book, *Interweaving* (1981), is a retrospective collection published in Germany. In his opening lyric, "A Poem About Childhood and Romanticism" (1944), he is a dreamer whose highest goal is to become an enemy of the state, a nation whose representatives ring doorbells at night. This laconic and pungent style, with quick and effective ironies, can be seen in his earliest poems. He was far from limited to the political sphere. He has love poems; he is fond of nature and of his books and quiet refuge. His poems trace his own story through his Siberian exile, the death of Stalin, and his later travels and thoughts on Russian history. One of his famous protest poems is "The Children of Auschwitz" (1961). He also spoke often of the role of martyrdom, whether as it was played by others or as he expected it to come to him. In the early 1970s he prepared in horror for a foreign exile. His first poems written on foreign soil in 1974 are evocations of God and cries of guilt: "God took my soul for my betrayal / My eyes are stopped by muddy ice" is the opening of one poem. Further poems are set in Boston, Cape Cod, and elsewhere; his English words— "We will be happy!"—creep in with great bitterness. The title poem, "Interweaving" (1981), is nevertheless an expression of satisfaction with his strange life and its unexpected ending in the "beautiful distance." His religious view of life separated him from other Soviet poets of his generation. He was also more open to the onslaughts of emotion. His forms are usually conventional, but he also used the laddered technique seen in the followers of Maiakovsky. His fourth book, *Selected Poems*, appeared in the United States in 1983.

The poetry of Victor Sosnora (b. 1937) is marked by surrealistic fantasies. He was born in the Crimea, but was in Leningrad during the siege of World War II, and then in the Kuban during the German occupation. He lived with his father, a military officer, in Warsaw and then in Archangel. He was drafted into the Soviet army in 1955 and spent eight months in solitary confinement for a prank. Determined to become a writer, he enrolled in Leningrad University and supported himself as a factory electrician. His first book of verse was *January Downpour* (1962). He published two further books in the 1960s and was in Paris to give readings and to teach in 1965 and 1970. The books of the 1970s include *The Flying Dutchman* (1979), which contains two verse epics and a work in rhythmic prose. In 1981 he became deaf following an operation. In the 1980s, he brought out a trilogy of novels (1980–1986) and a collection of essays, *Rulers and Fates* (1986), on Classical myths and Russian history in the eighteenth century. In 1987 he visited the United States following the publication of a selection of his lyrics in Michigan. Sosnora differs from most other Soviet poets in his capacity for joys as well as sorrows. His work is characterized by a tendency to extremity in itself. In the 1960s he was known for his fanciful re-creations of Russia's medieval period, but his range was much wider. His medieval tales appeared in *The Horsemen* (1969). His lyrics of the 1960s are collected in *Poems* (1977). These include impressions of city life, but seen as though in dreams or in the imagination of a child. Birds, animals, and objects speak; crows bark and dogs caw. In other poems the life of his country appears in fantasies about its literary figures, including Pushkin; its common folk, as in "The Tractor Woman" (1960); and its trees and even insects ("The Cricket," 1964). Yet other poems are impressions of Paris. His well-known "Fantasies of the Owl" (1963) is a nightmare about arrogant feathered policemen lording it over city streets. The lyrics of *The Stork* (1972) and *Crystal* (1977) appeared again in *Lunar Song* (1982). The title poem records an ecstatic feeling of cosmic love, as though the poet has become a seraph. Sosnora's fantasies are sometimes devoted to the figures of world literature, as in his imagined moments between Hamlet and Ophelia, a confession by Daedalus, the asides of Homer, and a version of Wilde's *Ballad of Reading Gaol*. Sosnora's poems are compelling in their imagery and language. His meanings often follow the lead of similar sounds. When his fantasies are familiar, his irrational devices are especially effective.

Natalia Gorbanevskaia (b. 1936) was an outspoken dissenter in the 1960s, but her verse is lyrical, personal, and low-keyed. A typical subject was the ordinary tasks that are faced even in desperate times. She was born in Moscow and graduated from Leningrad University. Her poems circulated in *samizdat,* and she became a civil rights activist, the founder of *The Chronicle of Current Events.* In 1968 she took part in a demonstration against the invasion of Czechoslovakia, and in 1969 she was confined to a psychiatric prison in Kazan. She emigrated in 1975 and settled in France, where she began to work for Russian émigré periodicals. Her books of verse include three volumes published abroad between 1970 and 1975, and *The Wooden Angel,* a retrospective collection published in the United States in 1982. In the poems of the 1950s, she speaks about the depths of human experience that contrast, like oceans, with the two-dimensional world of repression and restrictions. Her settings are simple and her language is modest, but her poems tend to be allegorical. She describes an urban world, seen in the interiors of apartments, and on streets. She relies as an intellectual on the arts; she mentions Bartók, Mozart, and Shakespeare. She begins the poem "Sunday" with this line: "A day of verse and laundry. Over washtubs spent." The poems of 1967 bear the subtitle "The Wooden Angel." It is a year of passions, whether in love, in the enjoyment of art, or in political involvement. It is followed by a section called "Jail Poems." The poems written in the 1970s describe the ebb and flow of seasons and small joys and sorrows. She is stunned before her impending exile by the anticipation of new losses. The verse Gorbanevskaia wrote in exile has appeared, however, in at least three small volumes, published between 1983 and 1985. The poems of *Flying Over the Snow Boundary* (1979) testify to the emotional difficulty of the passage. The new world appears to her in the sad images of rain and mists over the Seine and of the monotonous views seen from trains. The story told by her *oeuvre* is pathetic, but also somewhat narrow in range. Her individual poems can be appealing, however.

The themes of Oleg Chukhontsev (b. 1938) are much the same as those of other poets of the 1970s—nature, the homeland, poetry, and love. But he preferred to perceive the world in joy rather than in sorrow, as they had. He began to appear in the magazines of the Thaw years, but he was unable to bring out a separate collection until *From Three Notebooks* in 1976. He describes storms, but dwells on the existence of blossoms. He is grateful for the gift of inspiration, and he describes his love in nights of exalted companionship. His voice is not naive, and he is aware of misfortunes, but he is more inclined to reflect on his reasons for loving life. His verse forms are traditional.

The younger poets who have appeared recently have not yet achieved the distinction of the older poets. They have tended to shun political commitment in favor of lyricism and technical experimentation. But in an era of concern for the documentation of the past and the practical acquisition of new modes of social life, they do not speak to the taste of a wide audience. The most gratifying gains have perhaps been those made by the newly recognized émigrés.

Concluding Remarks

Russian poetry has for some time flowed in two separate currents, the Soviet and the Russian émigré. It is not strange, or even unusual, that a nation's poets should be diverse, or contradictory, in their preferences. The tragedy of the Russian case is that the political aspect of the division has made the rift so deep, long-lasting, and subtle in its effects. The perception of Russian poetry as belonging to contending groups has obscured the existence of a richness that could be a guarantee of the vitality of the whole. Even during *glasnost,* Soviet and Russian émigré poetry have continued to run their separate courses, and they will probably continue to do so in the near future. Although separate, both the Soviet and the émigré currents have strong points.

Soviet poets once captured the voice of everyman, as can be seen in the works of Kushner or the early Brodsky. The accents of a modest person can be reassuring in the late twentieth century, in the West as well as in the East. Every individual entertains heroic dreams and exotic visions as the avant-garde era taught. The dreams of a seer, moreover, need no longer be expressed in radically avant-garde styles. The fanciful devices of Rozhdestvensky, or even the early Voznesensky, did not prevail in the Soviet Union, and the extremities of Sosnora are still the exception. Nor can the Soviet poet turn easily to grandeur and elevated styles. Soviet poets will probably choose, like Kuniaev, the mundane, both in substance and in style. Soviet poetry has some pitfalls. The limiting habits of socialist realism will probably continue to cast some shadow on those avenues of exploration that put an emphasis on what is unique. The nuances of psychological experience will probably not be observed in their darker sides. Sentimentally will still present a danger in the depiction of private lives. And open philosophical speculation will be a difficult path for Soviet poets to take.

Russian émigré poets have been free from any suggestions as to policy, but in the practice of the best among them the sphere of philosophy and religion have played an ever greater role. Moving poems on man in the cosmos have been written, particularly by Chinnov and Morshen. Other subjects, such as nature and love, have not been forgotten. But émigré poetry has tended to develop its own predictability. Its preoccupation with metaphysical matters suggests the presence of some motive beyond writing verse only to maintain one's own identity in an alien culture. The long-standing Russian custom of thinking about culture in literary works seems to have taken a religious turn in emigration. A spiritual emphasis may be a form of ideological opposition to the state of poetry in the Soviet Union. If the heritage of symbolism and acmeism is remembered by the émigrés, it may seem to them that metaphysical speculation was its most valuable part. The writing of a poetry may therefore seem to the émigré to be a pledge of loyalty to the best in man. For whatever reasons, the émigrés have tended to limit their explorations to formal experiments. Insofar as the innovations themselves have been derivative of an individualistic avant-garde, they have not been entirely suited to the spiritual purposes of the émigrés. The fact of experimentation indicates, however, a curiosity about the resources of Western poetry.

If an international kind of poetry written in Russian is a desirable development, then it has a pioneer of a different sort in Joseph Brodsky. His literary choices have not been identical with those of other émigrés. His voice is still relatively unassuming and intimate, especially since he claims no special identity or knowledge of the universe. His acquaintance with Western literary currents has always been extensive. He began as a participant in European culture. He found his origins in acmeism, in Biblical stories, in English poetry, and elsewhere. His capacity to confront ideas such as death, evil, and divinity derives from several poetic traditions. He too may speak of feeling alien in the West, but his muted philosophical preoccupations sound familiar to the Western ear. He has even resisted a Western temptation, that of becoming one more satiated relativist. He judges the universe, and he takes his own emotions as his measure. Brodsky also has learned a new, intellectual style in the West. It may preclude some of the direct appeal to the heart that was so attractive in his earlier verse, but it suits what he has to say in that it is low-keyed and natural. And its artistic effect derives from another offering—a steady attention to the flow of language from word to word.

Glossary

arak   an alcoholic beverage distilled from various grains.

balagan   a tent for folk puppet shows, or the show itself.

bogatyr'   The hero of a folk epic, or *bylina;* his traits are courage and physical prowess.

byliny   folk epics of a type that originated and flourished before the twelfth century.

chastushka   a type of urban, or factory, folk song with pungent words and striking rhymes.

chastaia pesnia   a fast-paced type of folk song, often used to accompany dances or games.

Dazhbog   the pagan god of the winds.

druzhina   the retinue of a medieval prince or boyar.

dukhovnye stikhi   "spiritual verse," folk songs based on Biblical or apocryphal literature.

duma   "reflection," a Ukrainian genre of folk epic.

govornyi stikh   "declamatory verse," supposedly in use by the medieval players called *skomorokhi.*

Iarilo   a pagan sun god.

istoricheskaia pesnia   a type of folk narrative poem that dealt with historical events and originated during the Mongol invasion.

kaleki   "pilgrims," wandering singers of religious folk songs.

koliadki   lyric folk songs, medieval in origin, for caroling during the winter holidays.

Lel'   the pagan god of erotic love.

maslenitsa   the pre-Lenten festival; Shrove Tuesday; Mardi Gras.

murza   a titled personage at a Mongol court in medieval times.

nadpis'   "inscription," a brief, captionlike kind of lyric written for special occasions in the eighteenth and early nineteenth centuries.

pokaiannyi stikh   "repentance verse," religious folk songs that grew out of lyrical insertions in the liturgy.

pribyl'nyi stikh   "added verse," lyrical compositions regularly inserted in the liturgy.

raeshnyi stikh   a satirical style of folk verse that originated in the folk theater.

rusaliia   a circle dance performed at spring festivities; derived from pagan rituals.

rusalka   a water nymph, a dangerous sprite in the Slavic tradition.

samizdat   "publication" by hand reproduction and distribution.

semik a folk holiday in the seventh week following Easter.

skazitel' the chanter, or "singer," of folk epics.

skomorokhi wandering players whose performances were proscribed by the Orthodox Church in medieval times.

sleptsy "blind men," wandering singers of religious folk songs.

slovo "speech," usually seen in the titles of medieval sermons, but also in the title of *The Tale of Igor's Campaign.*

stariny "old times," the folk designation for the epics called *byliny,* a term invented in romantic times.

Veles the pagan sun god.

vila a pagan Slavic wood nymph; a dangerous sprite.

virshi Russia's first literary poems, written in the seventeenth century in imitation of Polish verse.

zaum "transsense" verse, created from sounds, coinages, and syntactical experiments by avant-garde poets.

Metrical Systems

Syllabic verse requires an equal number of syllables in every line. It derived from Polish verse and was used in the seventeenth and early eighteenth centuries. It was always rhymed in couplets and made use of the caesura.

Caesura is the placement of a word division after the same syllable in every line:

————————— ‖ —————————

————————— ‖ —————————

The caesura continued to be widely used in Russia after the introduction of syllabo-tonic verse.

Syllabo-tonic verse requires a specified number of syllables in every line and the placement of stresses according to the dictates of metrical feet. It is a familiar system in wide use in Russia and the West today.

Metrical feet

Iamb:	U I	Two syllables, the second stressed.
Trochee:	I U	Two syllables, the first stressed
Anapest:	U U I	Three syllables, the third stressed
Amphibrach:	U I U	Three syllables, the second stressed
Dactyl:	I U U	Three syllables, the first stressed

In Russian the rhythm created by metrical feet may be varied by the random omission of stresses from any but the last foot of a line. This device has been in constant use in the two-syllable meters, the iambic and trochaic.

Line lengths are usually described in terms of feet. A dimeter line is made up of two feet. Further line length designations are trimeter, tetrameter, pentameter, and hexameter.

Line endings or rhyme lengths are independent of the meter of their poem.

Masculine ending or rhyme:	I
Feminine ending or rhyme:	I U
Dactyl ending or rhyme:	I U U

The Alexandrine is made up of iambic hexameter lines with a caesura after the third foot. It was rhmed in couplets:

U I U I U I ‖ U I U I U I U
U I U I U I ‖ U I U I U I U

It was used for epics and other solemn poems in the eighteenth and early nineteenth centuries and was considered by Russians to be the equivalent of the French Alexandrine.

The Dolnik meter allows for the random omission of unstressed syllables in poems based on a three-syllable metrical foot:

UU ǀ UU ǀ UX ǀ UU ǀ
UU ǀ UX ǀ UU ǀ UU ǀ

The effect is of impairment or fragmentation. The *dolnik* was widely used in the early twentieth century.

Experimentation with metrical feet, such as the regular combination of two different meters, or the imitation of ancient Greek meters, was also common in the early twentieth century.

Tonic verse, or purely accentual verse, requires a fixed number of stresses per line without any regard to the number or placement of unstressed syllables:

U ǀ U ǀ UU ǀ U
UU ǀ U ǀ UU ǀ

Tonic verse was relatively common in the early twentieth century. Three-stress tonic verse is seen in *byliny* and in other forms of folk poetry.

Free verse makes no metrical requirements. The form in Russian is closest to French *vers libre,* but it has not been widely used.

Chronology

Kievan Rus: Late 800s to 1240
Acceptance of Christianity from Byzantium: 988
Reign of Vladimir Monomakh, last great ruler: 1113–25
Defeat of Prince Igor of Novgorod-Seversk by Polovtsy: 1185
Fall of Kiev to the Mongols: 1240

Appanage Russia during the "Tatar Yoke": 1240–1533
Loss of the southwestern lands, including Kiev, to Lithuania: c. 1330–1370
Battle of Kulikovo Field, a victory over the Mongols: 1380

Muscovite Russia: 1533–1682
Reign of Ivan IV, the Terrible: 1533–1584
Time of Troubles: 1598–1613
Reign of Boris Godunov: 1598–1605
Election of Mikhail Romanov, the founder of the Romanov dynasty, as tsar: 1613
Return of the southwestern lands, as the Ukraine, from Poland: 1654
Revolt of Stenka Razin, the Cossack leader: 1670–1671

Imperial Russia through the eighteenth century: 1682–1801
Reign of Peter I, the Great: 1682–1725
  Founding of St. Petersburg as a "window on the West": 1703
  Battle of Poltava, a final victory over Charles XII of Sweden in the Great
    Northern War: 1709
Reign of Catherine II, the Great: 1762–1796
  Legislative commission called to codify the nation's laws and disbanded:
    1767–1768
  Partitions of Poland: 1772, 1793, 1795
  Pugachev Revolt, led by a Cossack, in the Ural and Volga regions: 1773–1774
  Spread of serfdom to the Ukraine: 1763–1783

Imperial Russia in the nineteenth and early twentieth centuries: 1801–1917
Reign of Alexander I: 1801–1825
  Repulsion of Napoleonic invasion and burning of Moscow: 1812
  Holy Alliance, a peacekeeping pact with Austria and Prussia: 1815
  Decembrist Revolt, an attempt to secure a constitution: 1825
Reign of Nicholas I: 1825–1855
  Crimean War, a surprise defeat by England and France: 1854–1855

Reign of Alexander II: 1855–1881
    Emancipation of the serfs: 1861
    Will of the People founded, a terrorist wing of populists: 1879
    Assassination of Alexander II: 1881
Reign of Alexander III, a period of "counterreforms" under the policy of
    "Orthodoxy, Autocracy, and Nationality": 1881–1894
Reign of Nicholas II: 1894–1917
    Defeat in the Russo-Japanese War: 1904–1905
    Revolution of 1905; Bloody Sunday, January 22, followed by uprisings and a
        massive general strike in October
    First meeting of the First Duma, a limited legislative body: 1906
    Assassination of Prime Minister Peter Stolypin: 1911
    Entry into World War I: 1914

Provisional Government following the February Revolution: 1917
    October Revolution: 1917

Soviet Union: 1917–present
    Civil War, foreign interventions, and war with Poland: 1917–1921
    New Economic Policy, a limited retreat from socialism: 1921–1928
    Death of Lenin: 1924
    Joseph Stalin as General Secretary of the Communist Party: 1924–1953
        First Five-Year Plan—industrialization and the collectivization of agriculture:
            1928–1932
        Great Purge: 1934–1938
        Nonaggression Pact with Hitler: 1939–1940
        World War II following Germany's invasion: 1941–1945
    Nikita Khrushchev as First Secretary of the Communist Party: 1953–1964
        Speech denouncing Stalin at the Twentieth Party Congress: 1956
        Invasion of Hungary: 1956
        Cuban missile confrontation with the United States: 1962
    Leonid Brezhnev as General Secretary of the Communist Party: 1964–1982
        Invasion of Czechoslovakia: 1968
    Mikhail Gorbachev as General Secretary of the Communist Party—*glasnost* and
    perestroika: 1984–present

Selected Bibliography

In each category, works in Russian precede works in Western languages. Specialized studies about each author are indented and follow the works by the author.

General Works

Anthologies

Russkie poety. 4 vols. Moscow: Izd. Det. lit., 1968.

Baring, Maurice, ed. *The Oxford Book of Russian Verse.* 2nd ed. Oxford: Clarendon Press, 1948.

Obolensky, Dmitri, ed. *The Heritage of Russian Verse.* Bloomington: Indiana University Press, 1976.

Anthologies of Translations

An Age Ago: A Selection of Nineteenth-Century Russian Poetry. Introduction by Joseph Brodsky. Trans. Alan Meyers. New York: Farrar, Straus & Giroux, 1988.

Modern Russian Poetry. Trans. Babette Deutsch and A. Yarmolinsky. New York: Harcourt, Brace, 1921.

Russian Poetry under the Tsars. Trans. Burton Raffel. Albany: State University of New York Press, 1971.

Three Centuries of Russian Poetry. Moscow: Progress, 1980.

Studies in Russian

Ginzburg, Lidiia. *O lirike.* 2nd ed. Leningrad: Sovetskii pisatel', 1974.

Istoriia russkoi poezii. 2 vols. Leningrad: Nauka, 1968.

Studies and Reference Works in Western Languages

Harkins, W. E. *Dictionary of Russian Literature.* London: Allen and Unwin, 1957. Reprint. Westport, Conn.: Greenwood Press, 1971.

Mirsky, D. S. *A History of Russian Literature.* Ed. Francis J. Whitfield. New York: Knopf, 1949.

Scherr, Barry P. *Russian Poetry: Meter, Rhythm, and Rhyme.* Berkeley: University of California Press, 1986.
Stender-Petersen, Adolf. *Geschichte der russischen literatur.* 2 vols. Munich: Litt. Beck'sche Verlagsbuchhandlung, 1952.
Terras, Victor, ed. *Handbook of Russian Literature.* New Haven, Conn.: Yale University Press, 1985.
Unbegaun, Boris. *Russian Versification.* Oxford: Oxford University Press, 1956.

The Early Period
(988–1730)

Anthologies

Adrianova-Peretts, V. P., ed. *Demokraticheskaia poeziia XVII veka.* 2nd ed. Moscow and Leningrad: Sovetskii pisatel', 1962; Biblioteka poeta, Bol'shaia seriia.
———, ed. *Russkaia sillabicheskaia poeziia XVII–XVIII vekov.* 2nd ed. Leningrad: Sovetskii pisatel', 1970; Biblioteka poeta, Bol'shaia seriia.
Astakhova, A. M., ed. *Narodnye ballady.* 2nd ed. Moscow and Leningrad: Sovetskii pisatel', 1963; Biblioteka poeta, Bol'shaia seriia.
Bazanov, V. G., ed. *Poeziia krest'ianskikh prazdnikov.* 2nd ed. Leningrad: Sovetskii pisatel', 1970; Biblioteka poeta, Bol'shaia seriia.
Bessonov, P. *Kaleki perekhozhie.* 2 vols. Moscow, 1861–1864. Reprint. London: Gregg International Publishers, 1970.
Byliny. 2nd ed. Leningrad: Sovetskii pisatel', 1957; Biblioteka poeta, Bol'shaia seriia.
Byliny. 2 vols. Moscow: GIKhL, 1958.
Gudzii, N. K. *Khrestomatiia po drevnei russkoi literature.* 8th ed. Moscow: Prosveshchenie, 1973.
Istoricheskie pesni XVII veka. 2 vols. Moscow and Leningrad: AN SSSR, 1966.
Narodnye istoricheskie pesni. Leningrad: Sovetskii pisatel', 1962; Biblioteka poeta, Bol'shaia seriia.
Narodnye liricheskie pesni. 2nd ed. Leningrad: Sovetskii pisatel', 1961; Biblioteka poeta, Bol'shaia seriia.
Prichitania. 2nd ed. Leningrad: Sovetskii pisatel', 1960; Biblioteka poeta, Bol'shaia seriia.
Putilov, B. N., and B. M. Dobrovol'skii, eds. *Istoricheskie pesni XIII–XVI vekov.* Moscow and Leningrad: AN SSSR, 1960.
Russkie narodnye pesni. Moscow: GIKhL, 1957.
Stender-Petersen, Adolf, ed. *Anthology of Old Russian Literature.* New York: Columbia University Press, 1954.

Anthologies of Translations

Chadwick, N. K., ed. *Russian Heroic Poetry.* Cambridge: Cambridge University Press, 1932. Reprint. 1964.
Hapgood, Isabel Florence, ed. *The Epic Songs of Russia.* New York: Scribner, 1916.
Zenkovsky, Serge A., ed. *Medieval Russia's Epics, Chronicles, and Tales.* New York: Dutton, 1963.

Studies in Russian

Eremin, I. P. *Lektsii po drevnei russkoi literature*. Leningrad: Izd. Leningradskogo universiteta, 1968.

Gudzii, N. K. *Istoriia drevnei russkoi literatury*. 7th ed. Moscow: Gos. Uch.-ped. izd., 1966.

Likhachev, D. S. *Chelovek v literature drevnei Rusi*. Moscow: Nauka, 1970.

―――. *Poetika drevnei russkoi literatury*. Leningrad: Nauka, 1967.

―――. *Razvitie russkoi literatury X–XVII vekov*. Leningrad: Nauka, 1973.

Orlov, A. S. *Drevniaia russkaia literatura XI–XVII vekov*. Moscow and Leningrad: AN SSSR, 1945.

Panchenko, A. M. *Russkaia stikhovornaia kul'tura XVII veka*. Leningrad: AN SSSR, 1973.

Robinson, A. N. *Bor'ba idei v russkoi literature XVII veka*. Moscow: Nauka, 1934.

Russkoe narodnoe poeticheskoe tvorchestvo. 3 vols. Moscow and Leningrad: AN SSSR, 1953–1956.

Timofeev, L. I. *Ocherki teorii i istorii russkogo stikha*. Moscow: GIKhL, 1958.

Vodovozov, N. V. *Istoriia drevnei russkoi literatury*. 3rd ed. Moscow: Prosveshchenie, 1972.

Studies in English

Brown, William Edward. *A History of Seventeenth-Century Russian Literature*. Ann Arbor, Mich.: Ardis, 1980.

Čiževskij, Dmitrij. *History of Russian Literature from the Eleventh Century to the End of the Baroque*. The Hague: Mouton, 1963.

Fennell, John, and Anthony Stokes. *Early Russian Literature*. Berkeley: University of California Press, 1974.

Gudzii, N. K. *History of Early Russian Literature*. Trans. Susan W. Jones. New York: Macmillan, 1949.

Magnes, L. A. *The Heroic Ballads of Russia*. Port Washington, N.Y.: Kennikat Press, 1967.

Pronin, Alexander. *History of Old Russian Literature*. Frankfurt am Main: Posev, 1968.

Segel, Harold. *The Baroque Poem*. New York: Dutton, 1974.

Texts and Specialized Studies

Likhachev, D. S., ed. *Slovo o polku Igoreve*. 2nd ed. Leningrad: Sovetskii pisatel', 1967; Biblioteka poeta, Bol'shaia seriia.

Jakobson, Roman, ed. *La geste du Prince Igor*. Vol. 8. New York: Annuaire de l'Institut de philologie et histoire orientales et slaves, 1948.

Mazon, Andre. *Le Slovo d'Igor*. Paris: Droz, 1940.

The Song of Igor's Campaign. Trans. Vladimir Nabokov. New York: Vintage Books, 1960.

Polotskii, Simeon. *Izbrannye sochineniia*. Ed. I. P. Eremin. Moscow and Leningrad: AN SSSR, 1953.

Prokopovich, Feofan. *Sochineniia*. Ed. I. P. Eremin. Moscow: AN SSSR, 1961.

Cracraft, James. "Feofan Prokopovich." In *The Eighteenth Century in Russia*, ed. J. G. Garrard. Oxford: Oxford University Press, 1973, pp. 75–105.

―――. "Feofan Prokopovich: A Bibliography of His Works." *Oxford Slavonic Papers* 8 (1975): 1–36.

Classicism
(1730–1800)

Anthologies

Kokorev, A. V., ed. *Khrestomatiia po russkoi literature XVIII veka.* Moscow: Pros-veshchenie, 1965.
Makogonenko, Georgii P., ed. *Russkaia literatura XVIII veka.* Leningrad: Prosveshchenie, 1970.
Poety XVIII veka. 2nd ed. 2 vols. Leningrad: Sovetskii pisatel', 1972; Biblioteka poeta, Bol'shaia seriia.
Russkaia poeziia XVIII Veka. Moscow: Izd. Khudozhestvennaia literatura, 1972.
Stikhotvornaia skazka (novella) XVIII–nachala XIX veka. 2nd ed. Leningrad: Sovetskii pisatel', 1969; Biblioteka poeta, Bol'shaia seriia.

Anthology of Translations

Segel, Harold B., ed. *The Literature of Eighteenth-Century Russia.* 2 vols. New York: Dutton, 1967.

Studies in Russian

Blagoi, D. D. *Istoriia russkoi literatury XVIII veka.* 2nd ed. Moscow: Gos. uch.-ped. izd., 1955.
Gukovskii, Grigorii A. *Russkaia literatura XVIII veka.* Moscow: Gos. uch.-ped. izd., 1939.
_____. "U istokov russkogo sentimentalizma." In *Ocherki po istorii russkoi literatury i obshestvennoi mysli XVIII veka.* Leningrad: Gos. izd. Khudozhestvennaia literatura, 1938, pp. 235–315.
Moskvicheva, G. V. *Russkii klassitsizm.* Moscow: Prosveshchenie, 1978.
Orlov, Oleg V., and V. I. Fedorov. *Russkaia literatura XVIII veka.* Moscow: Pros-veshchenie, 1973.
Serman, Il'ia Z. *Russkii klassitsizm: Poeziia—Drama—Satira.* Leningrad: Nauka, 1973.
Vinogradov, Viktor V. *Ocherki po istorii russkogo literaturnogo iazyka XVII–XIX vekov.* Leiden: Brill, 1949.

Studies in Western Languages

Brown, William Edward. *A History of Eighteenth-Century Russian Literature.* Ann Arbor, Mich.: Ardis, 1980.
Bucsela, John. "The Problems of Baroque in Russian Literature." *Russian Review* 31, no. 3 (July 1972): 760–71.
Cross, Anthony G., ed. *Russian Literature in the Age of Catherine the Great.* Oxford: Meuws, 1976.
Garrard, John G., ed. *The Eighteenth Century in Russia.* Oxford: Clarendon Press, 1973.
Lauer, Reinhard. *Gedichtform zwischen Schema und Verfall: Sonett, Rondeau, Madrigal, Ballade, Stanze und Triolett in der russischen Literatur des 18 Jahrhunderts.* Munich: Fink, 1975.
Neuhäuser, Rudolf. *Towards the Romantic Age: Essays on Sentimental and Preromantic Literature in Russia.* The Hague: Martinus Nijhoff, 1974.

Segel, Harold B. "Baroque and Rococo in Eighteenth Century Russian Literature." *Canadian Slavonic Papers* 15, no. 4 (December 1976): 556–65.

Silbajoris, Rimvydas. *Russian Versification: The Theories of Trediakovskij, Lomonosov, and Kantemir.* New York: Columbia University Press, 1968.

Authors and Specialized Studies

Ippolit F. Bogdanovich

Stihotvoreniia i poemy. 2nd ed. Leningrad: Sovetskii pisatel', 1957; Biblioteka poeta, Bol'shaia seriia.

Gavrila Derzhavin

Stikhotvoreniia. Leningrad: Sovetskii pisatel', 1957; Biblioteka poeta, Bol'shaia seriia.

Stikhotvoreniia. Moscow: Gos. izd. Khud. Lit., 1958.

   Gukovskii, Grigorii A. "Literaturnoe nasledstvo G. R. Derzhavina." In *Literaturnoe nasledstvo.* Vol. 9/10. Moscow, 1933, pp. 369–96.

   Khodasevich, Vladislav. *Derzhavin.* Paris: Sovremennye zapiski, 1931.

   Serman, Il'ia Z. *Derzhavin.* Leningrad: Prosveshchenie, 1967.

   Hart, Pierre. *G. R. Derzhavin: A Poet's Progress.* Columbus, Ohio: Slavica, 1978.

Ivan I. Dmitriev

Polnoe sobranie stikhotvorenii. 2nd ed. Leningrad: Sovetskii pisatel', 1967; Bibioteka poeta, Bol'shaia seriia.

   Khodasevich, Vladislav. "Dmitriev." In *Literaturnye stat' i i vospominaniia.* New York: Izd. im. Chekhova, 1954, pp. 25–34.

Antiokh Kantemir

Sobranie stikhotvorenii. 2nd ed. Leningrad: Sovetskii pisatel', 1956; Biblioteka poeta, Bol'shaia seriia.

Sochineniia, pis'ma i izbrannye perevody. St. Petersburg: Izd. Glazunova, 1868.

Materialy dlia biografii Kn. A. D. Kantemira. St. Petersburg: Akademia Nauk, 1903.

   Ehrhard, Marcelle. *Un Ambassadeur de Russie à la cour de Louis XV: le prince Cantemir à Paris (1738–1744).* Annales de l'université de Lyon, vol. 6. Paris: Société d'édition Les Belles Lettres, 1928.

   Grasshoff, Helmut. *Antioch Dmitrievič Kantemir und Westeuropa.* Berlin: Akademie-Verlag, 1966.

Vasilii V. Kapnist

Izbrannye proizvedeniia. 2nd ed. Leningrad: Sovetskii pisatel', 1973; Biblioteka poeta, Bol'shaia seriia.

Sobranie sochinenii v dvukh tomakh. 2 vols. Moscow and Leningrad: AN SSSR, 1960.

Nikolai M. Karamzin

Izbrannye sochineniia. 2 vols. Moscow and Leningrad: Izd. Khudozhestvennaia literatura, 1964.

Polnoe sobranie stikhotvorenii. 2nd ed. Moscow and Leningrad: Sovetskii pisatel', 1966; Biblioteka poeta, Bol'shaia seriia.

Letters of a Russian Traveler, 1789–1790. Trans. and abridged by Florence Jonas. New York: Columbia University Press, 1957.

Selected Prose. Trans. Henry M. Nebel, Jr. Evanston, Ill.: Northwestern University Press, 1969.

   Eikhenbaum, Boris M. "Karamzin." In *Skvoz' literaturu.* Leningrad, 1924.

   Anderson, Roger B. *N. M. Karamzin's Prose: The Teller in the Tale.* Houston: Cordovan Press, 1974.

   Black, Joseph L., ed. *Essays on Karamzin.* The Hague: Mouton, 1975.

————. *Nicholas Karamzin and Russian Society in the Nineteenth Century.* Toronto: University of Toronto Press, 1975.

Cross, Anthony G. *N. M. Karamzin: A Study of His Literary Career, 1783–1803.* Carbondale: Southern Illinois University Press, 1971.

Garrard, John G. "Karamzin, Mme de Stael, and Russian Romantics." In *American Contributions to the Seventh International Congress of Slavists,* ed. Victor Terras. The Hague: Mouton, 1973.

Kochetova, Natalia. *Nikolay Karamzin.* Boston: Twayne, 1975.

Nebel, Henry M., Jr. *N. M. Karamzin: A Russian Sentimentalist.* The Hague: Mouton, 1967.

Ivan I. Khemnitser

Polnoe sobranie stikhotvorenii. 2nd ed. Leningrad: Sovetskii pisatel', 1963; Biblioteka poeta, Bol'shaia seriia.

Mikhail M. Kheraskov

Izbrannye proizvedeniia. 2nd ed. Leningrad: Sovetskii pisatel', 1961; Biblioteka poeta, Bol'shaia seriia.

Mikhail V. Lomonosov

Izbrannye proizvedeniia. 2nd ed. Moscow and Leningrad: Sovetskii pisatel', 1965; Biblioteka poeta, Bol'shaia seriia.

Polnoe sobranie sochinenii. 10 vols. Moscow and Leningrad: AN SSSR, 1950–1959.

Berkov, Pavel N. *Lomonosov i literaturnaia polemika ego vremeni, 1750–1765.* Moscow: AN SSSR, 1936.

Efimov, Aleksandr I. *M. V. Lomonosov i russkii iazyk.* Moscow: Izd. Moskovskogo universiteta, 1961.

Kuznetsov, Boris G. *Tvorcheskii put' Lomonosova.* 2nd ed. Moscow: AN SSSR, 1961.

Letopis' zhizni i tvorchestva M. V. Lomonosova. Moscow and Leningrad: AN SSSR, 1961.

Menshutkin, Boris. *Zhizneopisanie Mikhaila Vasil'evicha Lomonosova* Leningrad: AN SSSR, 1947.

Serman, Il'ia Z. *Poeticheskaia stil' Lomonosova.* Leningrad: Nauka, 1966.

Zapadov, Aleksandr V. *Otets russkoi poezii: o tvorchestve Lomonosova.* Moscow: Sovetskii pisatel', 1961.

Grasshoff, Helmut. *Michail Lomonosov, der Begrunder der neueren russischen Literatur.* Halle: Verlag Sprache und Literatur, 1962.

Kudryavtsev, B. B. *The Life and Work of Mikhail Vasilyevich Lomonosov.* Moscow: Foreign Language Publishing House, 1954.

Menshutkin, Boris. *Russia's Lomonosov, Chemist, Courtier Physicist, Poet.* Trans. Jeanette Eyre Thal and Edward J. Webseter. Princeton, N.J.: Princeton University Press, 1952.

Vasetskii, G. S. *Lomonosov's Philosophy.* Trans. David Fidlon. Moscow: Progress, 1968.

Vasilii Maikov

Izbrannye proizvedeniia. 2nd ed. Moscow and Leningrad: Sovetskii pisatel', 1966; Biblioteka poeta, Bol'shaia seriia.

Mikhail N. Murav'ev

Stikhotvoreniia. 2nd ed. Leningrad: Sovetskii pisatel', 1967; Biblioteka poeta, Bol'shaia seriia.

Aleksandr Radishchev

Polnoe sobranie sochinenii. 3 vols. Moscow and Leningrad: AN SSSR, 1938–1953.

Stikhotvoreniia. 2nd ed. Leningrad: Sovetskii pisatel', 1975; Biblioteka poeta, Bol'shaia seriia.

A Journey from St. Petersburg to Moscow. Trans. Leo Wiener. Cambridge, Mass.: Harvard University Press, 1958.

Makogonenko, Georgii. *Radishchev i ego vremia*. Moscow: Gos. izd. Khud. lit., 1956.

Orlov, Vladimir. *Radishchev i russkaia literatura*. 2nd ed. Leningrad: Sovetskii pisatel', 1952.

Clardy, Jesse V. *The Philosophical Ideas of Alexander Radishchev*. London: Vision, 1964.

Evgenev, Boris. *Alexander Radishchev: A Russian Humanist of the Eighteenth Century*. London: Hutchinson, 1946.

Lang, David. *The First Russian Radical: Alexander Radishchev, 1749–1802*. London: Allen and Unwin, 1959.

McConnell, Allen. *A Russian Philosophe, Alexander Radishchev, 1749–1802*. The Hague: Martinus Nijhoff, 1964.

Aleksandr P. Sumarokov

Izbrannye proizvedeniia. 2nd ed. Leningrad: Sovetskii pisatel', 1957; Biblioteka poeta, Bol'shaia seriia.

Selected Tragedies of A. P. Sumarokov. Trans. Richard Fortune and Raymond Fortune. Evanston, Ill.: Northwestern University Press, 1970.

Berkov, Pavel N. *Aleksandr Petrovich Sumarokov, 1717–1777*. Leningrad: Iskusstvo, 1949.

Vasilii K. Trediakovskii

Izbrannye proizvedeniia. 2nd ed. Moscow and Leningrad: Sovetskii pisatel', 1963; Biblioteka poeta, Bol'shaia seriia.

Pumpianskii, L. V. "Trediakovskii." In *Istoriia russkoi literatury*. Vol. 3: *Literatura XVIII veka*, Part I. Moscow: AN SSSR, 1941, pp. 215–63.

Sensibility and Romanticism
(1800–1845)

Anthologies

Ginzburg, Lidiia, ed. *Poety 1820–1830–kh godov*. 2nd ed. 2 vols. Leningrad: Sovetskii pisatel', 1972; Biblioteka poeta, Bol'shaia seriia.

Orlov, Vladimir, comp. *Dekabristy*. Vol. 1: *Poeziia*. Leningrad: Khud. lit., 1975.

———, ed. *Poety pushkinskoi pory*. Leningrad: Gos. izd. Det. lit., 1954.

Poety 1790–1810–kh godov. 2nd ed. Leningrad: Sovetskii pisatel', 1971; Biblioteka poeta, Bol'shaia seriia.

Anthologies of Translations

Narrative Poems by Alexander Pushkin and by Mikhail Lermontov. Trans. Charles Johnston. New York: Random House, 1979.

Three Russian Poets: Selections from Pushkin, Lermontov, and Tyutchev. Trans. Vladimir Nabokov. Norfolk, Conn.: New Directions, 1944.

Studies in Russian

Gillel'son, M. I. *Ot arzamasskogo bratstva k pushkinskomu krugu pisatelei*. Leningrad: Nauka, 1977.

Gukovskii, Georgii A. *Pushkin i russkie romantiki.* Moscow: Izd. Khud. lit., 1965.

Istoriia romantizma v russkoi literature. Romantizm v russkoi literature 20–30–kh godov XIX veka (1825–1840). Moscow: Nauka, 1979.

Istoriia romantizma v russkoi literature. Vozniknovenie i utverzhdenie romantizme v russkoi literature (1790–1825). Moscow: Nauka, 1979.

Kuleshov, Vasilii I. *Literaturnye sviazi Rossii i zapadnoi Evropy v XIX veké (Pervaia polovina).* Moscow: Izd. Moskovskogo universiteta, 1965.

Russkii romantizm. Leningrad: Nauka, 1978.

Semenko, Irina M. *Poety pushkinskoi pory.* Moscow: Izd. Khud. lit., 1970.

Studies in English

Brown, William Edward. *A History of Russian Literature of the Romantic Period.* 4 vols. Ann Arbor, Mich.: Ardis, 1986.

Leighton, Lauren G. *Russian Romanticism: Two Essays.* The Hague: Mouton, 1975.

Todd, William Mills. *The Familiar Letter as a Literary Genre in the Age of Pushkin.* Princeton, N.J.: Princeton University Press, 1976.

Authors and Specialized Studies

Evgenii Baratynskii

Polnoe sobranie stikhotvorenii. 2nd ed. Leningrad: Sovetskii pisatel', 1957; Biblioteka poeta, Bol'shaia seriia.

Selected Letters of Evgenij Baratynskij. Trans. G. R. Barratt. The Hague: Mouton, 1973.

Dees, Benjamin. *E. A. Baratynsky.* New York: Twayne, 1972.

Kjetsaa, Geir. *Evgenii Baratynskii: Zhizn i tvorchestvo.* Oslo: Universitetsvorlaget, 1973.

Shaw, Thomas. *Baratynskii: A Dictionary of the Rhymes and a Concordance to the Poetry.* Madison: University of Wisconsin Press, 1975.

Konstantin Batiushkov

Polnoe sobranie stikhotvorenii. 2nd ed. Moscow and Leningrad: Sovetskii pisatel', 1964; Biblioteka poeta, Bol'shaia seriia.

Fridman, Nikolai V. *Poeziia Batiushkova.* Moscow: Nauka, 1971.

Serman, Il'ja Z. *Konstantin Batyushkov.* New York: Twayne, 1974.

Denis Davydov

Sochineniia. Moscow: GIKhL, 1962.

Popov, Mikhail. *Denis Davydov.* Moscow: Prosveshchenie, 1971.

Shik, Aleksandr. *Denis Davydov, "liubovnik brani" i poet.* Paris: Vozrozhdenie, 1951.

Anton Del'vig

Polnoe sobranie stikhotvorenii. 2nd ed. Leningrad: Sovetskii pisatel', 1959; Biblioteka poeta, Bol'shaia seriia.

Koehler, Ludmilla. *Anton Antonovič Del'vig: A Classicist in the Time of Romanticism.* The Hague: Mouton, 1970.

Nikolai M. Iazykov

Polnoe sobranie stikhotvorenii. Moscow and Leningrad: Academia, 1934.

Polnoe sobranie stikhotvorenii. 2nd ed. Moscow and Leningrad: Sovetskii pisatel', 1964; Biblioteka poeta, Bol'shaia seriia.

Vil'gelm Kiukhelbeker

Izbrannye poizvedeniia v dvukh tomakh. 2nd ed. 2 vols. Moscow and Leningrad: Sovetskii pisatel', 1967; Biblioteka poeta, Bol'shaia seriia.

Puteshestvie. Dnevnik. Stat'i. Leningrad: Nauka, 1979.

Aleksei Koltsov
   Polone sobranie stikhotvorenii. 2nd ed. Leningrad: Sovetskii pisatel', 1958; Biblioteka
      poeta, Bol'shaia seriia.
   Sochineniia. Moscow: Izd. Khud. lit., 1966.
      Moiseeva, Antonina A. *A. V. Kol'tsov: Kritiko-biograficheskii ocherk.* Moscow:
         GIKhL, 1956.
      Skatov, Nikolai. *Kol'tsov.* Moscow: Molodaia Gvardiia, 1983.
      Tonkov, Viacheslav A. *A. V. Kol'tsov. Zhizn' i tvorchestvo.* 2nd ed. Voronezh: Voro-
         nezhskii Knizhnoe izd., 1958.
Ivan Krylov
   Basni. Moscow: AN SSSR, 1956.
   Sochineniia. 2 vols. Moscow: GIKhL, 1955.
   Kriloff's Fables. Trans. C. Fillingham Coxwell. New York: Dutton, 1970.
   The Russian Fables of Ivan Krylov. Trans. Bernard Pares. Harmondsworth: Penguin
      Books, 1942.
      Stepanov, Nikolai. *Basni Krylova.* Moscow: Khud. lit., 1969.
      ———. *Ivan Krylov.* New York: Twayne, 1973.
Mikhail Lermontov
   Sobranie sochinenii. 4 vols. Moscow and Leningrad: AN SSSR, 1961–1962.
   A Lermontov Reader. Ed. Guy Daniels. New York: Macmillan, 1965.
   Major Poetical Works. Trans. Anatoly Liberman. Minneapolis: University of Minnesota
      Press, 1983.
   Selected Works. Moscow: Progress, 1976.
      Andronikov, Iraklii L. *Lermontov: Issledovaniia i nakhodki.* Moscow: Khud. lit., 1964.
      Brodskii, Nikolai. *M. Iu. Lermontov. Biografiia.* Moscow: GIKhl, 1945.
      Eikhenbaum, Boris M. *Lermontov: Opyt istoriko-literaturnoi otsenki.* Leningrad: Gos.
         izd., 1924.
      ———. *Stat'i o Lermontove.* Moscow and Leningrad: AN SSSR, 1961.
      Grigoriian, Kamar N. *Lermontov i romantizm.* Leningrad: Nauka, 1964.
      M. Iu. Lermontov v vosopominaniiakh sovremennikov. Moscow: Khud. lit., 1964.
      Kelly, Laurence. *Lermontov: Tragedy in the Caucasus.* New York: Braziller, 1978.
      Lavrin, Janko. *Lermontov.* New York: Hillery House, 1959.
      Mersereau, John. *Mikhail Lermontov.* Carbondale: Southern Illinois University Press,
         1962.
      Troyat, Henri. *L'étrange destin de Lermontov.* Paris: Plon, 1952.
Aleksandr Pushkin
   Polnoe sobranie sochinenii. 17 vols. Leningrad: AN SSSR, 1937–1959.
   The Bronze Horseman. Trans. D. M. Thomas. New York: Viking Press, 1982.
   Collected Narrative and Lyrical Poetry. Trans. Walter Arndt. Ann Arbor, Mich.: Ardis,
      1984.
   Epigrams and Satirical Verse. Trans. Cynthia A. Whittaker. Ann Arbor, Mich.: Ardis,
      1984.
   Eugene Onegin. Trans. Charles Johnston. New York: Viking Press, 1978.
   Eugene Onegin: A Novel in Verse. 4 vols. Trans. Vladimir Nabokov. Princeton, N.J.:
      Princeton University Press, 1981.
   Eugene Onegin: A Novel in Verse. 2nd ed. Trans. Walter Arndt. New York: Dutton, 1981.
   The Letters of Alexander Pushkin. 3 vols. Trans. J. Thomas Shaw. Madison: University of
      Wisconsin Press, 1967.
   On Seashore Far, a Green Oak Tower. Moscow: Raduga, 1983.
   The Poems, Prose and Plays of Alexander Pushkin. Ed. Avrahm Yarmolinsky. New York:
      Modern Library, 1936.

Pushkin on Literature. Ed. and trans. Tatiana Wolff. London: Methuen, 1971.
Pushkin's Fairy Tales. Trans. Janet Dalley. New York: Mayflower Books, 1979.
Ruslan and Liudmila. Trans. Walter Arndt. Ann Arbor, Mich.: Ardis, 1974.
Selected Works. Vol. 1: *Poetry.* Moscow: Progress, 1974.
Small Tragedies. Ed. Victor Terras. New York: Basil Blackwell, 1984.
Three Comic Poems. Trans. William E. Harkins. Ann Arbor, Mich.: Ardis, 1979.
Blagoi, Dmitrii D. *Tvorcheskii put' Pushkina (1813–1826).* Moscow: AN SSSR, 1950.
––––––. *Tvorcheskii put' Pushkina (1826–1830).* Moscow: Sovetskii pisatel', 1967.
Slonimskii, Aleksandr L. *Masterstvo Pushkina.* Moscow: GIKhL, 1959.
Tomashevskii, Boris V. *Pushkin.* 2 vols. Moscow and Leningrad: AN SSSR, 1956–1961.
Zhirmunskii, Viktor M. *Bairon i Pushkin. Iz istorii romanticheskoi poemy.* Leningrad: Academia, 1924.
Bayley, John. *Pushkin: A Comparative Commentary.* Cambridge: Cambridge University Press, 1971.
Lavrin, Janko. *Pushkin and Russian Literature.* New York: Russell and Russell, 1969.
Magarshack, David. *Pushkin: A Biography.* New York: Grove Press, 1967.
Meynieux, André. *Pouchkine: Homme de lettres et la littérature professionelle en Russie.* Paris: Librairie des cinq continents, 1966.
Mirsky, Dmitri S. *Pushkin.* New York: Dutton, 1963.
Richards, D. J., and C. R. S. Cockrell. eds. and trans. *Russian Views of Pushkin.* Oxford: Meuws, 1976.
Shaw, J. Thomas. *Pushkin's Rhymes: A Dictionary.* Madison: University of Wisconsin Press, 1974.
Simmons, Ernest J. *Pushkin.* New York: Vintage Books, 1964.
Troyat, Henri. *Pouchkine.* Paris: Perrin, 1976.
––––––. *Pushkin.* Trans. Nancy Amphoux. Garden City, N.Y.: Doubleday, 1970.
Vickery, Walter N. *Alexander Pushkin.* New York: Twayne, 1970.

Kondratii Ryleev

Polnoe sobranie sochinenii. Moscow and Leningrad: Academia, 1934.
Polnoe sobranie stikhotvorenii. 2nd ed. Leningrad: Sovetskii pisatel', 1971; Biblioteka poeta, Bol'shaia seriia.
Afanas'ev, Viktor. *Ryleev. Zhizneopisanie.* Moscow: Molodaia Gvardiia, 1982.
Tseitlin, Aleksandr G. *Tvorchestvo Ryleeva.* Moscow: AN SSSR, 1955.
O'Meara, Patrick. *K. F. Ryleev: A Political Biography of the Decembrist Poet.* Princeton, N.J.: Princeton University Press, 1984.

Fedor Tiutchev

Lirika. 2 vols. Moscow: Nauka, 1966.
Polnoe sobranie stikhotvorenii. 2 vols. Moscow and Leningrad: Academia, 1933–1934.
Polnoe sobranie stikhotvorenii. Leningrad: Sovetskii pisatel', 1957; Biblioteka poeta, Bol'shaia seriia.
Stikhotvoreniia. Pis'ma. Moscow: GIKhL, 1967.
Poems and Political Letters of F. I. Tyutchev. Trans. Jesse Zeldin. Knoxville: University of Tennessee Press, 1973.
Versions from Fyodor Tuytchev. Trans. Charles Tomlinson. New York: Oxford University Press, 1960.
Ozerov, Lev A. *Poeziia Tiutcheva.* Moscow: Khud. lit., 1975.
Pigarev, Kirill V. *F. I. Tiutchev i ego vremia.* Moscow: Sovremennik, 1978.
––––––. *Zhizn' i tvorchestvo F. I. Tiutcheva.* Moscow: AN SSSR, 1962.
Gregg, Richard A. *Fedor Tiutchev: The Evolution of a Poet.* New York: Columbia University Press, 1965.

Pratt, Sarah. *Russian Metaphysical Romanticism: The Poetry of Tiutchev and Boratynskii.* Stanford, Calif.: Stanford University Press, 1984.

Dmitrii Venevitinov

Polnoe sobranie sochinenii. Moscow and Leningrad: Academia, 1934.

Stikhotvoreniia. Proza. Moscow: Nauka, 1980.

Wytrzens, Gunther. *Dmitrij Vladimirovič Venevitinov als Dichter der russischen Romantik.* Graz: Bohlaus, 1962.

Petr Viazemskii

Izbrannye stikhotvoreniia. Moscow and Leningrad: Academia, 1935.

Sochineniia. 2 vols. Moscow: Khud. lit., 1982.

Stikhotvoreniia. 3rd ed. Moscow: Sovetskii pisatel', 1966; Biblioteka poeta, Bol'shaia seriia.

Zapisnye knizhki: 1813–1848. Ed. V. Nechaeva. Moscow: AN SSSR, 1963.

Gillel'son, Maksim I. *P. S. Viazemsii: Zhizn' i tvorchestvo.* Leningrad: Nauka, 1969.

Wytrzens, Gunther. *Pjotr Andreevič Vjazemskij.* Vienna: Verlag Notring der Wissenschaftlichen Verbande Osterreichs, 1961.

Vasilii Zhukovskii

Sobranie sochinenii. 4 vols. Moscow and Leningrad: GIKhL, 1959–1960.

Bessarab, Maiia. *Zhukovskii.* Moscow: Sovremennik, 1975.

Semenko, Irina M. *Zhizn' i poeziia Zhukovskogo.* Moscow: Khud. lit., 1975.

———. *Vasily Zhukovsky.* Boston: Twayne, 1976.

The Age of Realism
(1845–1890)

Anthologies

Poety 1880–1890–kh godov. 3rd ed. Moscow and Leningrad: Sovetskii pisatel', 1964; Biblioteka poeta, Malaia seriia.

Russkaia poeziia XIX veka. Vol. 2. Moscow: Khud. lit., 1974.

Russkie poety XIX veka. Khrestomatiia. 3rd ed. Moscow: Prosveshchenie, 1964.

General Study

Hingley, Ronald. *Russian Writers and Society in the Nineteenth Century.* 2nd ed. London: Weidenfeld and Nicolson, 1977.

Authors and Specialized Studies

Ivan Aksakov

Stikhotvoreniia i poemy. 2nd ed. Leningrad: Sovetskii pisatel', 1960; Biblioteka poeta, Bol'shaia seriia.

Kitaev, Vladimir. *Iz istorii ideinoi boy'by v Rossii v periode pervoi revoliutsionnoi situatsii: I. S. Aksakov v obshchestvennom dvizhenii nachala 60–kh godov XIX veka.* Gorky: Gor'kovskii Gos. Universitet, 1974.

Tsimbaev, Nikolai I. *I. S. Aksakov v obshchestvennoi zhizni poreformennoi Rossii.* Moscow: Izd. Moskovskogo Universiteta, 1978.

Lukashevich, Stephen. *Ivan Aksakov (1823–1886): A Study in Russian Thought and Politics*. Cambridge, Mass.: Harvard University Press, 1965.

Afanasy Fet

Polnoe sobranie stikhotvorenii. 2nd ed. Leningrad: Sovetskii pisatel', 1959; Biblioteka poeta, Bol'shaia seriia.

Stikhotvoreniia. Leningrad: Gos. izd. Khud. lit., 1956.

Vechernie ogni. Moscow: Nauka, 1971.

Blagoi, Dmitrii D. *Mir kak krasota: O Vechernikh ogniakh A. Feta*. Moscow: Khud. lit., 1975.

Bukhshtab, Boris Ia. *A. A. Fet: Ocherk zhizni i tvorchestva*. Leningrad: Nauka, 1974.

Gustafson, Richard F. *The Imagination of Spring: The Poetry of Afanasy Fet*. New Haven, Conn.: Yale University Press, 1966.

Lotman, Lydia M. *Afanasy Fet*. Trans. Margaret Wettlin. Boston: Twayne, 1976.

Apollon Grigor'ev

Izbrannye proizvedeniia. 2nd ed. Leningrad: Sovetskii pisatel', 1959; Biblioteka poeta, Bol'shaia seriia.

Literaturnaia kritika. Moscow: Khud. lit., 1967.

Vospominaniia. Moscow: Academia, 1930.

My Literary and Moral Wanderings and Other Autobiographical Material. Trans. Ralph E. Matlaw. New York: Dutton, 1962.

Apollon N. Maikov

Izbrannye proizvedeniia. 2nd ed. Leningrad: Sovetskii pisatel', 1977; Biblioteka poeta, Bol'shaia seriia.

Özata, Mehmet. *Die politische Dichtung Apollon Nikolajevic Majkovs*. Tübingen, 1972.

Nikolai Nekrasov

Polnoe sobranie sochinenii i pisem. 15 vols. Leningrad: Nauka, 1981.

Polnoe sobranie stikhotvorenii. 2nd ed. 3 vols. Leningrad: Sovetskii pisatel', 1967; Biblioteka poeta, Bol'shaia seriia.

Poems by Nicholas Nekrassov. Trans. Juliet M. Soskice. London: Oxford University Press, 1936.

Who Can Be Happy and Free in Russia? Trans. Juliet M. Soskice. London: Oxford University Press, 1917.

Chukovskii, Kornei. *Masterstvo Nekrasova*. 4th ed. Moscow: GIKhL, 1962.

Maksimov, Vladislav. *Tvorcheskii put' N. A. Nekrasova*. Moscow: AN SSSR, 1953.

N. A. Nekrasov i russkaia literatura. Moscow: Nauka, 1971.

Stepanov, Nikolai. *N. A. Nekrasov. Zhizn' i tvorchestvo*. 2nd ed. Moscow: Khud. lit., 1971.

Birkenmayer, Sigmund S. *Nikolaj Nekrasov: His Life and Poetic Art*. The Hague: Mouton, 1968.

Corbet, Charles. *Nekrasov. L'Homme et le poète*. Paris: Institut d'études slaves, 1948.

Peppard, Murray B. *Nikolai Nekrasov*. New York: Twayne, 1967.

Karolina Pavlova

Polnoe sobranie stikhotvorenii. 2nd ed. Moscow and Leningrad: Sovetskii pisatel', 1964; Biblioteka poeta, Bol'shaia seriia.

A Double Life. Trans. Barbara Heldt Monter. Ann Arbor, Mich.: Ardis, 1978.

Lettman-Sadony, Barbara. *Karolina Karlovna Pavlova*. Munich: Sagner, 1971.

Iakov Polonskii

Stikhotvoreniia. Leningrad: Sovetskii pisatel', 1957; Biblioteka poeta, Malaia seriia.

Koz'ma Prutkov (pseud. of Aleksei K. Tolstoi)
  Polnoe sobranie sochinenii. 2nd ed. Moscow and Leningrad: Sovetskii pisatel', 1965; Biblioteka poeta, Bol'shaia seriia.
Konstanin Sluchevskii
  Stikhovoreniia i poemy. 2nd ed. Moscow and Leningrad: Sovetskii pisatel', 1962; Biblioteka poeta, Bol'shaia seriia.
Aleksei K. Tolstoi
  Sobranie sochinenii. 4 vols. Moscow: Khud. lit., 1963–1964.
  A Prince of Outlaws. Trans. Clarence Manning. New York: Knopf, 1927.
  Vampires: Stories of the Supernatural. Trans. Fedor Nikanov. New York: Hawthorn Books, 1969.
    Stafeev, Gregorii I. *Serdtse polno vdokhnoveniia: zhizn' i tvorchestvo A. K. Tolstogo.* Moscow: Gos. Biblioteka SSSR im. V. I. Lenina, 1979.
    Zhukov, Dmitrii. *Aleksei Konstantinovich Tolstoi.* Moscow: Molodaia gvardiia, 1982.
    Berry, Thomas. *A. K. Tolstoy: Russian Humorist.* Bethany, W.Va.: Bethany College Press, 1971.
    Dalton, Margaret. *A. K. Tolstoy.* Boston: Twayne, 1972.
    Graham, Sheelagh Duffin. *The Lyric Poetry of A. K. Tolstoi.* Studies in Slavic Literature and Poetics, vol. 7. Amsterdam: Rodopi, 1985.

Symbolism
(1890–1912)

Anthologies

Ezhov, Ivan S., and E. I. Shamurin. *Russkaia poezii XX veka.* Moscow: Novaia Moskva, 1925. Reprint. Munich: Fink, 1972.
Hofmann, Modeste. *Poety simvolizma.* Petersburg, 1908. Reprint. Munich: Fink, 1970.

Bilingual Anthology

Markov, Vladimir, and Merrill Sparks. *Modern Russian Poetry.* Indianapolis: Bobbs-Merrill, 1966.

Anthology of Translations

The Silver Age of Russian Culture: An Anthology. Ann Arbor, Mich.: Ardis, 1975.

Study in Russian

Literaturnoe nasledstvo, vols. 27 and 28 (1937).

Studies in English

Donchin, Georgette. *The Influence of French Symbolism on Russian Poetry.* The Hague: Mouton, 1958.
Mirsky, D. S. *Contemporary Russian Literature, 1881–1925.* New York: Knopf, 1926.

Poggioli, Renato. *The Poets of Russia, 1890–1930.* Cambridge, Mass.: Harvard University Press, 1960.

Authors and Specialized Studies

Innokentii Annenskii

Knigi otrazhenii I, II. Munich: Fink, 1969. Originally published as *Kniga otrazhenii* (Petersburg, 1906) and *Vtoraia kniga otrazhenii* (Petersburg, 1909).

Stikhotvoreniia i tragedii, 2nd ed. Leningrad: Sovetskii pisatel', 1959; Biblioteka poeta, Bol'shaia seriia.

Bazzarelli, Eridano. *La poesia di Innokentij Annenskij.* Milan: Mursia, 1965.

Conrad, Barbara. *I. F. Annenskijs poetische Reflexionen.* Munich: Fink, 1976.

Ingold, Felix P. *Innokentij Annenskij; sein Beitrag zur Poetik des russischen Symbolismus.* Bern: Lang, 1970.

Setchkarev, Vsevolod. *Studies in the Life and Work of Innokentij Annenskij.* The Hague: Mouton, 1963.

Konstantin Bal'mont

Kniga razdumii. St. Petersburg, 1899. Reprint. Letchworth, Eng.: Prideaux Press, 1974.

Stikhotvoreniia. 2nd ed. Leningrad: Sovetskii pisatel', 1969; Biblioteka poeta, Bol'shaia seriia.

Althau-Schonbucher, Silvia. *Konstantin D. Bal'mont—Parallelen zu Afanasij A. Fet: Symbolismus und Impressionismus.* Bern, 1975.

Andrei Belyi (pseud. of Boris Bugaev)

Arabeski. Kniga statei. Moscow: Musaget, 1911. Reprint. Munich: Fink, 1969.

Lug zelenyil. Kniga statei. Moscow: Al'tsiona, 1910. Reprint. New York: Johnson Reprint, 1967.

Mezhdu dvukh revoliutsii. Vospominaniia. 1905–1911. Leningrad: Izd. pisatelei v Leningrade, 1934. Reprint. Chicago: Russian Language Specialties, 1966.

Na rubezhe dvukh stoletii. Vospominaniia. Moscow and Leningrad: ZiF, 1930. Reprint. Chicago: Russian Language Specialties, 1966.

Nachalo veka. Memuary. Moscow and Leningrad: GIKhL, 1933. Reprint. Chicago: Russian Language Specialties, 1966.

Peterburg. Roman. Petrograd, 1916. 2nd rev. ed. Berlin: Epokha, 1922.

Serebrianyi golub'. Moscow: Skorpion, 1910; Berlin: Epokha, 1922. Reprint of 1922 ed. Munich: Fink, 1967.

Simvolizm. Kniga statei. Moscow: Musaget, 1910. Reprint. Munich: Fink, 1969.

Stikhotvoreniia i poemy. 2nd ed. Moscow and Leningrad: Sovetskii pisatel', 1966; Biblioteka poeta, Bol'shaia seriia.

Vospominaniia ob Aleksandre Aleksandroviche Bloke. Letchworth, Eng.: Bradda Books, 1964.

Complete Short Stories. Trans. Ronald Peterson. Ann Arbor, Mich.: Ardis, 1979.

Petersburg. Trans. from 1922 ed. by Robert A. Maguire and John E. Malmstad. Bloomington: Indiana University Press, 1978.

St. Petersburg. Trans. John Cournos. New York: Grove Press, 1959.

The Silver Dove. Trans. George Reavey. New York: Grove Press, 1974.

Bugaeva, Klavdiia Nikolaevna. *Vospominaniia o Belom.* Berkeley, Calif.: Berkeley Slavic Specialties, 1981.

Christa, Boris. *Andrey Bely Centenary Papers.* Amsterdam: Hakkert, 1980.

_____. *The Poetic World of Andrey Bely.* Amsterdam: Hakkert, 1977.

Cioran, Samuel. *The Apocalyptic Symbolism of Andrei Belyi.* The Hague: Mouton, 1973.

Elsworth, John D. *Andrey Bely.* Letchworth, Eng.: Bradda Books, 1972.

Janecek, Gerald, ed. *Andrey Bely: A Critical Review.* Lexington: University Press of Kentucky, 1978.

Malmstad, John, ed. *Andrey Bely: Spirit of Symbolism.* Ithaca, N.Y.: Cornell University Press, 1987.

Maslenikov, Oleg A. *The Frenzied Poets: Andrey Biely and the Russian Symbolists* Berkeley: University of California Press, 1952.

Mochul'skii, Konstantin. *Andrei Belyi.* Paris: YMCA-Press, 1955.

Aleksandr Blok

(with Andrei Belyi) *Perepiska.* Moscow: Gos. Lit. Muzei, 1940. Reprint. Munich: Fink, 1969.

Sobranie sochinenii. 9 vols. Moscow and Leningrad: GiKhL, 1960–1965.

Zapisnye knizhki Al. Bloka. Ed. P. N. Medvedev. Leningrad: Priboi, 1930.

An Anthology of Essays and Memoirs. Trans. and ed. Lucy Vogel. Ann Arbor, Mich.: Ardis, 1982.

Selected Poems. Trans. Alex Miller. Moscow: Progress, 1981.

The Twelve and Other Poems. Trans. Anselm Hollo. Frankfort, Ky.: Gnomon, 1971.

The Twelve and Other Poems. Trans. John Stallworthy and Peter France. New York: Oxford University Press, 1970.

Blok, Liubov'. *I byl, i nebylitsy.* Bremen: K-Presse, 1979.

Dolgopolov, Leonid. *Poemy Bloka i russkaia poema kontsa XIX–nachala XX veka.* Moscow: Nauka, 1964.

Eikhenbaum, Boris. *Sud'ba Bloka.* Petersburg, 1921. Reprint. Letchworth, Eng.: Prideaux Press, 1979.

Fedorov, Andrei V. *Al. Blok—dramaturg.* Leningrad: Izd. Leningradskogo Universiteta, 1980.

Literaturnoe nasledstvo, no. 92, parts 1–4 (1980–1982).

Maksimov, Dmitrii. *Poeziia i proza Al. Bloka.* Leningrad: Sovetskii pisatel', 1981.

Mochul'skii, Konstantin. *Aleksandr Blok.* Paris: YMCA-Press, 1948.

Ob Aleksandre Bloke. Petersburg, 1921.

Orlov, Vladimir. *Gamaiun. Zhizn' Aleksandra Bloka.* Leningrad: Sovetskii pisatel', 1978.

———. ed. *Aleksandr Blok v vospominaniiakh sovremennikov.* 2 vols. Moscow: Khud. lit., 1980.

Pamiati Aleksandra Bloka. 1880–1980. London: Overseas Publications Interchange, 1980.

Rodina, Tatiana M. *Aleksandr Blok i russkii teatr nachala XX veka.* Moscow: Nauka, 1972.

Solov'ev, Boris. *Poet i ego podvig. Tvorcheskii put' Aleksandra Bloka.* Moscow: Sovetskii pisatel', 1968.

Zhirmunskii, Viktor. *Poeziia A. Bloka.* Petersburg, 1922. Reprint. Letchworth, Eng.: Prideaux Press, 1975.

Hackel, Sergei. *The Poet and the Revolution: Aleksandr Blok's "The Twelve."* Oxford: Clarendon Press, 1975.

Kemball, Robin. *Alexander Blok, A Study in Rhythm and Metre.* The Hague: Mouton, 1965.

Kluge, Rolf-Dieter. *Westeuropa und Rusland im Weltbild Aleksandr Blok.* Munich: Sagner, 1967.

Masing, Irene. *A. Blok's "The Snow Mask"; An Interpretation.* Stockholm: Almqvist and Wiksell, 1970.

Orlov, Vladimir. *Hamayun. The Life of Alexander Blok.* Trans. Olga Shartse. Moscow: Progress, 1980.

Peters, Johanne. *Farbe und Licht, Symbolik bei Aleksandr Blok.* Munich: Sagner, 1981.

Pirog, Gerald. *Aleksandr Blok's "Ital'ianski stikhi": Confrontation and Disillusionment.* Columbus, Ohio: Slavica, 1983.

Pyman, Avril. *The Life of Aleksandr Blok.* 2 vols. Oxford: Oxford University Press, 1979.

Reeve, Frank D. *Aleksandr Blok: Between Image and Idea.* New York: Columbia University Press, 1962.

Vickery, Walter N., ed. *Aleksandr Blok Centennial Conference.* Columbus, Ohio: Slavica, 1984.

Vogel, Lucy E. *Aleksandr Blok: The Journey to Italy.* Ithaca, N.Y.: Cornell University Press, 1973.

Valerii Briusov

Dalekie i blizkie. Stat'i i zametki. Moscow: Skorpion, 1912.

Dnevniki. 1891–1910. Moscow: Izd. Sabashnikovykh, 1927.

Iz moei zhizni. Moia iunost'. Pamiati. Moscow: Izd. Sabashnikovykh, 1927.

Moi Pushkin. Moscow and Leningrad, 1929. Reprint. Munich: Fink, 1970.

Ognennyi Angel. Moscow, 1909. Reprint. Munich: Fink, 1971.

Osnovy stikhovedeniia. 2nd ed. Moscow: Gos. izd., 1924. Reprint. Letchworth, Eng.: Prideaux Press, 1971.

Rasskazy i povesti. Munich: Fink, 1970.

Sobranie sochinenii. 7 vols. Moscow: Khud. lit., 1973–1975. (Does not include short fiction, theater, or diaries)

Stikhotvoreniia i poemy. 2nd ed. Leningrad: Sovetskii pisatel', 1961; Biblioteka poeta, Bol'shaia seriia.

The Diary of Valery Bryusov (1893–1905). Ed. Joan Delaney Grossman. Berkeley: University of California Press, 1980.

The Fiery Angel. A Sixteenth Century Romance. Trans. Ivor Montagu and Sergei Nalbandor. London: Neville Spearman, 1975.

The Republic of the Southern Cross and Other Stories. London: Constable, 1918.

Ashukin, Nikolai. *Valerii Briusov v avtobiograficheskikh zapisakh, pis'makh, vospominaniiakh sovremennikov i otzyvakh kritiki.* Moscow: Federatsiia, 1929.

Literaturnoe nasledstvo 85 (1976).

Maksimov, Dmitrii. *Briusov. Poeziia i positsiia.* Leningrad: Sovetskii pisatel', 1969.

Mochul'skii, Konstantin. *Valerii Briusov.* Paris: YMCA-Press, 1962.

Zhirmunskii, Victor. *Valerii Briusov i nasledie Pushkina.* Petersburg: El'zevir, 1922.

Rice, Martin P. *Valery Briusov and the Rise of Russian Symbolism.* Ann Arbor, Mich.: Ardis, 1975.

Schmidt, Alexander. *Valerii Briusovs Beitrag zu Literatur-theorie: Aus der Geschichte des russischen Symbolismus.* Munich: Sagner, 1963.

Ivan Bunin

Sobranie sochinenii. 9 vols. Moscow: Khud. lit., 1965–1967.

Stikhotvoreniia. 3rd ed. Leningrad: Sovetskii pisatel', 1961; Biblioteka poeta, Malaia seriia.

Dark Avenues and Other Stories. Trans. Richard Hare. Westport, Conn.: Hyperion Press, 1977.

Memories and Portraits. Trans. Vera Traill and Robin Chancellor. Garden City, N.Y.: Doubleday, 1951.

Stories and Poems. Trans. Olga Shartse and Irina Zheleznova. Moscow: Progress, 1979.

Afanas'ev, Vladislav. *I. A. Bunin. Ocherk tvorchestva.* Moscow: Prosveshchenie, 1966.

Baboreko, Aleksandr. *I. A. Bunin. Materialy dlia biografii s 1870 po 1917.* 2nd ed. Moscow: Khud. lit., 1983.

Literaturnoe nasledstvo 84, parts 1, 2 (1973).

Mikhailov, Oleg. *Strogii talant. Ivan Bunin. Zhizn'. Sud'ba. Tvorchestvo.* Moscow: Sovremennik, 1976.

Ustami Buninykh. 3 vols. Frankfurt am Main: Posev, 1977–1982.

Kryzytski, Serge. *The Works of Ivan Bunin.* The Hague: Mouton, 1971.

Woodward, James B. *Ivan Bunin: A Study of His Fiction.* Chapel Hill: University of North Carolina Press, 1980.

Aleksandr Dobroliubov

Sochineniia. Berkeley, Calif.: Berkeley Slavic Specialties, 1981.

Zinaida Hippius

Literaturnyi dnevnik 1899–1907. Petersburg, 1908. Reprint. Munich: Fink, 1970.

Stikhotvoreniia. Paris: YMCA-Press, 1984.

Stikhotvoreniia i poemy. Munich: Fink, 1972.

Zhivye litsa. 2 vols. Prague, 1925. Reprint. Munich: Fink, 1971.

Between Paris and St. Petersburg. Selected Diaries. Trans. Temira Pachmuss. Urbana: University of Illinois Press, 1975.

Intellect and Ideas in Action: Selected Correspondence of Zinaida Hippius. Ed. Temira Pachmuss. Munich: Fink, 1972.

Selected Works. Trans. Temira Pachmuss. Urbana: University of Illinois Press, 1972.

Zlobin, Vladimir. *Tiazhelaia dusha.* Washington, D.C.: Kamkin, 1970.

Matich, Olga. *The Religious Poetry of Zinaida Hippius.* Munich: Fink, 1972.

Pachmuss, Temira. *Zinaida Hippius: An Intellectual Profile.* Carbondale: University of Southern Illinois Press, 1971.

Zlobin, Vladimir. *A Difficult Soul: Zinaida Hippius.* Ed. Simon Karlinsky. Berkeley: University of California Press, 1980.

Viacheslav Ivanov

Borozdy i mezhi. Opyty esteticheskie i kriticheskie. Moscow: Musaget, 1916. Reprint. Letchworth, Eng.: Bradda Books, 1971.

(with M. O. Gershenzon) *Perepiska iz dvukh gulov.* Petersburg: Alkonost, 1921.

Po zvezdam. Stat'i i aformizmy. Petersburg: Ory, 1909. Reprint. Letchworth, Eng.: Bradda Books, 1971.

Sobranie sochinenii. Ed. Olga Deschartes. 3 vols. Brussels: Foyer Oriental Chrétien, 1971–1979.

Stikhotvoreniia i poemy. 3rd ed. Leningrad: Sovetskii pisatel', 1976; Biblioteka poeta, Malaia seriia.

Correspondence Across the Room. Trans. Lisa Sergio. Marlboro, Vt.: Marlboro Press, 1984.

Freedom and the Tragic Life: A Study in Dostoevsky. Trans. Norman Cameron. New York: Noonday Press, 1957.

Tschöpl, Carin. *Viačeslav Ivanov. Dichtung und Dichtungstheorie.* Munich: Sagner, 1968.

West, James. *Russian Symbolism: A Study of Vyacheslav Ivanov and the Russian Symbolist Aesthetic.* London: Methuen, 1970.

Dmitrii Merezhkovskii

Izbrannye stat'i. Reprint. Munich: Fink, 1972.

Polnoe sobranie sochinenii. 24 vols. Moscow: Sytin, 1914.

Sobranie stikhov. 1883–1910 g. Selected Poems. Reprint. Letchworth, Eng.: Bradda Books, 1969.

The Death of the Gods (Julian the Apostate). Trans. Bernard Guilbert Guerney. New York: Modern Library, 1929.

Peter and Alexis. Trans. Bernard Guilbert Guerney. New York: Modern Library, 1931.

The Romance of Leonardo da Vinci. Trans. Bernard Guilbert Guerney. New York: Modern Library, 1928.

Tolstoi as Man and Artist, with an Essay on Dostoevsky. New York: Putnam, 1902.

Hippius, Zinaida. *Dmitrii Merezhkovskii.* Paris: YMCA-Press, 1951.

Bedford, Charles. *The Seeker, D. S. Merezhkovsky.* Lawrence: University of Kansas Press, 1975.

Rosenthal, Bernice G. *Dmitri Sergeevich Merezhkovsky and the Silver Age.* The Hague: Martinus Nijhoff, 1975.

Spengler, Ute. *Merezhkovskij als Literaturkritiker.* Lucerne and Frankfurt: Bucher, 1972.

Fedor Sologub (pseud. of Fedor Teternikov)

Charodinaia chasha. Stikhi. St. Petersburg: Epokha, 1922. Reprint. Letchworth, Eng.: Prideaux Press, 1970.

Fimiamy. Stikhi. Petersburg: Stranstvuiushchii entuziast, 1921. Reprint. Letchworth, Eng.: Prideaux Press, 1972.

Koster dorozhnyi. Stikhi. Moscow and Petrograd: Tvorchestvo, 1922. Reprint. Letchworth, Eng.: Prideaux Press, 1980.

Melkii bes. Roman. Petersburg: Shipovnik, 1907. Reprint. Letchworth, Eng.: Bradda Books, 1966.

Nebo goluboe. Stikhi. Reval: Izd. Bibliofil, 1921.

Odna liubov'. Stikhi. Petrograd, 1921.

Rasskasy. Berkeley, Calif.: Berkeley Slavic Specialties, 1979.

Sobornyi blagovest. Stikhi. Petersburg: Epokha, 1921.

Sobranie sochinenii. 20 vols. Petersburg: Sirin, 1913–1914.

Stikhotvoreniia. 2nd ed. Leningrad: Sovetskii pisatel', 1975; Biblioteka poeta, Bol'shaia seriia.

Svirel'. Russkie berzherety. Petersburg, 1922.

Tvorimaia legenda. Reprint. Munich: Fink, 1972.

Velikii blagovest. Stikhi. Moscow and Leningrad: GIZ, 1923.

Voina. Stikhi. Petrograd: Izd. Zhurnala Otechestvo, 1915.

Bad Dreams. Trans. Vassar W. Smith. Ann Arbor, Mich.: Ardis, 1978.

The Created Legend. Trans. Samuel D. Cioran. 3 vols. Ann Arbor, Mich.: Ardis, 1979.

The Kiss of the Unborn and Other Stories. Trans. Murl Barker. Knoxville: University of Tennessee Press, 1977.

The Petty Demon. Trans. Samuel D. Cioran. Ann Arbor, Mich.: Ardis, 1983.

The Petty Demon. Trans. Andrew Field. New York: Random House, 1962.

Chebotarevskaia, Anastasiia, ed. *O F. Sologube. Kritika, stat'i i zametki.* St. Petersburg, 1911. Reprint. Ann Arbor, Mich.: Ardis, 1983.

Denissoff, Nina. *Fedor Sologoub. 1863–1927.* Paris: La pensée universelle, 1981.

Vladimir Solov'ev

Sobranie sochinenii. 10 vols. St. Petersburg, 1911–1913. Reprint. Brussels: Foyer Oriental Chrétien, 1966.

Stikhotvoreniia i shutochnye p'esy. 2nd ed. Leningrad: Sovetskii pisatel', 1974; Biblioteka poeta, Bol'shaia seriia.

Tri razgovora. New York: Izd. im. Chekhova, 1954.

Russia and the Universal Church. Trans. Herbert Rees. London: Bles, 1948.

A Solovev Anthology. Trans. N. Duddington. New York: Scribner, 1950.

    Mochul'skii, Konstantin. Vladimir Solov'ev. Zhizn' i uchenie. 2nd ed. Paris: YMCA-Press, 1951.

    Dunphy, William. The Religious Philosophy of Vladimir Solovyov. Chicago, 1939.

    Knigge, Armin. Die Lyrik Vl. Solov'evs und ihre Nachwirkung bei A. Belyi und A. Blok. Amsterdam: Hakkert, 1973.

    Munzer, Egbert. Solovyev, Prophet of Russian–Western Unity. London: Hollis and Carter, 1956.

    Zoubouff, Peter P. Godmanhood as the Main Idea of the Philosophy of Vladimir Solovyev. Poughkeepsie, N.Y.: Harmon, 1944.

Post-Symbolist Modernism
(1912–1925)

Anthologies of Translations

Folejewski, Zbigniew. Futurism and Its Place in the Development of Modern Poetry: A Comparative Study and Anthology. Ottawa: University of Ottawa Press, 1980.

Glad, John, and Daniel Weissbort, eds. Russian Poetry: The Modern Period. Iowa City: University of Iowa Press, 1978.

Proffer, Ellendea, and Carl L. Proffer, eds. The Ardis Anthology of Russian Futurism. Ann Arbor, Mich.: Ardis, 1980.

Study in Russian

Struve, Gleb. K istorii russkoi poezii 1910-kh nachala 1920-kh godov. Berkeley, Calif.: Berkeley Slavic Specialties, 1979.

Studies in English

France, Peter. Poets of Modern Russia. Cambridge: Cambridge University Press, 1983.

Hingley, Ronald. Nightingale Fever: Russian Poets in Revolution. New York: Knopf, 1981.

Markov, Vladimir. Russian Futurism: A History. Berkeley: University of California Press, 1968.

———. Russian Imagism, 1919–1924. Giessen: Wilhelm Schmitz, 1980.

Nilsson, Nils Åke. The Russian Imaginists. Stockholm: Almqvist and Wiksell, 1970.

Strakhovsky, Leonid I. Craftsmen of the Word: Three Poets of Modern Russia. Cambridge, Mass.: Harvard University Press, 1949.

Williams, Robert C. Artists in the Revolution: Portraits of the Russian Avant-Garde, 1905–1925. Bloomington: Indiana University Press, 1977.

Authors and Specialized Studies

Anna Akhmatova.
  Sochineniia. 3 vols. Vols. 1 and 2, Washington, D.C.: Inter-Language Literary Associates, 1967–1968; vol. 3, Paris: YMCA-Press, 1983.
  Stikhotvoreniia i poemy. Leningrad: Sovetskii pisatel', 1976; Biblioteka poeta, Bol'shaia seriia.
  The Complete Poems of Anna Akhmatova. Ed. with an introduction by Roberta Reeder. Trans. Judith Hemschemeyer. Somerville, Mass.: Zephyr Press, 1990.
  A Poem Without a Hero. Trans. Carl R. Proffer and Assya Humesky. Ann Arbor, Mich.: Ardis, 1973.
  Poems. Trans. Stanley Kunitz and Max Hayward. Boston: Little, Brown, 1973.
  Requiem and Poem Without a Hero. Trans. D. M. Thomas. Athens: Ohio University Press, 1976.
  Selected Poems. Trans. Walter Arndt and Robin Kemball. Ann Arbor, Mich.: Ardis, 1976.
  Selected Poems. Trans. Richard McKane. London: Oxford University Press, 1969.
  Way of All the Earth. Athens: Ohio University Press, 1979.
  You Will Hear Thunder. Trans. D. M. Thomas. London: Secker and Warburg, 1985.
    Chukovskaia, Lidiia. *Zapisi ob Anne Akhmatovoi.* 2nd ed. 2 vols. Paris: YMCA-Press, 1984.
    Eikhenbaum, Boris. *Anna Akhmatova. Opyt analiza.* Petersburg: Petropechat', 1923.
    Vinogradov, Viktor. *Anna Akhmatova: o simvolike, o poezii.* Petrograd, 1922. Reprint. Munich: Fink, 1970.
    _____. *O poezii Anny Akhmatovoi; stilisticheskie nabroski.* Leningrad, 1925. Reprint. The Hague: Mouton, 1969.
    Zhirmunskii, Viktor. *Tvorchestvo Anny Akhmatovoi.* Leningrad: Nauka, 1973.
    Driver, Sam Norman. *Anna Akhmatova.* New York: Twayne, 1972.
    Haight, Amanda. *Anna Akhmatova: A Poetic Pilgrimage.* New York: Oxford University Press, 1976.
    Verheul, Kees. *The Theme of Time in the Poetry of Anna Akhmatova.* The Hague: Mouton, 1971.
Sergei Esenin
  Sobranie sochinenii. 6 vols. Moscow: GIKhL, 1977.
  Selected Poetry. Trans. Peter Tempest. Moscow: Progress, 1982.
    Iushin, Petr. *Sergei Esenin. Ideino-tvorcheskaia evoliutsiia.* Moscow: Izd. Moskovskogo Universiteta, 1969.
    Marchenko, Alla. *Poeticheskii mir Esenina.* Moscow: Sovetskii pisatel', 1972.
    Naumov, Evgenii. *Sergei Esenin. Lichnost'. Tvorchestvo. Epokha.* Leningrad: Lenizdat, 1969.
    Prokushev, Iurii. *Sergei Esenin, Poet. Chelovek.* Moscow: Prosveshchenie, 1973.
    Volkov, Anatolii. *Khudozhestvennye iskaniia Esenina.* Moscow: Sovetskii pisatel', 1976.
    Auras, Christiane. *Sergej Esenin, Bilder- und Symbolwelt.* Munich: Sagner, 1965.
    Davies, Jessie, ed. *Esenin: A Biography in Memoirs, Letters, and Documents.* Ann Arbor, Mich.: Ardis, 1982.
    de Graaf, Frances. *Sergej Esenin: A Biographical Sketch.* The Hague: Mouton, 1966.
    McVay, Gordon. *Esenin: A Life.* Ann Arbor, Mich.: Ardis, 1976.
    Ponomareff, Constantin. *Sergey Esenin.* Boston: Twayne, 1978.
    Prokushev, Iurii. *Sergei Yesenin: The Man, the Verse, the Age.* Moscow: Progress, 1979.

Veyrenc, Charles. *La Forme poétique de Serge Esenin*. The Hague: Mouton, 1968.

Visson, Lynn. *Sergei Esenin: Poet of the Crossroads*. Würzburg: Jal-Verlag, 1980.

Nikolai Gumilev

Sobranie sochinenii. 4 vols. Washington, D.C.: Kamkin, 1962–1968.

On Russian Poetry. Trans. David Lapeza. Ann Arbor, Mich.: Ardis, 1977.

Selected Works. Trans. Burton Raffel and Alla Burago. Albany: State University of New York Press, 1972.

Maline, Marie. *Nicolas Gumilev, poète et critique acmeiste*. Brussels: Palais des Academies, 1964.

Elena Guro

Nebesnye verbliuzhata. St. Petersburg: Zhuravl, 1914.

Sharmanka. Petersburg: Sirius, 1909.

Little Camels in the Sky. Trans. Kevin O'Brien. Ann Arbor, Mich.: Ardis, 1983.

Jensen, Kjeld Bjørnager. *Russian Futurism, Urbanism and Elena Guro*. Arhus: Arkona, 1977.

Vasilii Kamenskii

Put' entuziasta. Avtobiograficheskaia kniga. Perm: Kn. izd., 1968.

Stikhotvoreniia i poemy. Moscow: Sovetskii pisatel', 1966; Biblioteka poeta, Bol'shaia seriia.

Gints, Savvatii. *Vasilii Kamenskii*. Perm: Kn. izd., 1968.

Daniil Kharms

Sobranie proizvedenii. 3 vols. Bremen: K-Presse, 1978–1980.

Velimir Khlebnikov

Neizdannye proizvedeniia. Moscow: GIKhL, 1940. Reprint. Munich: Fink, 1971.

Sobranie sochinenii. 4 vols. Leningrad: Izd. Pisatelei v Leningrade, 1928–1933. Reprint. Munich: Fink, 1968.

Collected Works of Velimir Khlebnikov. Trans. Paul Schmidt. Vol. 1, ed. Charlotte Douglas. Vol. 2, ed. Ronald Vroon. Cambridge, Mass.: Harvard University Press, 1990.

The King of Time: Selected Writings of the Russian Futurian Velimir Khlebnikov. Trans. Paul Schmidt. Ed. Charlotte Douglas. Cambridge, Mass.: Harvard University Press, 1990.

Snake Train: Poetry and Prose. Trans. Gary Kern et al. Ann Arbor, Mich.: Ardis, 1976.

Grigorev, V. P. *Grammatika idiostilia*. Moscow: Nauka, 1983.

Stepanov, Nikolai. *Velimir Khlebnikov. Zhizn' i tvorchestvo*. Moscow: Sovetskii pisatel', 1975.

Cooke, Raymond. *Velimir Khlebnikov: A Critical Study*. Ann Arbor, Mich.: Ardis, 1987.

Lanne, Jean-Claude. *Velimir Khlebnikov, poète futurien*. 2 vols. Paris: Institut d'études slaves, 1983.

Markov, Vladimir. *The Longer Poems of Velimir Khlebnikov*. Berkeley: University of California Press, 1962.

Mirsky, Saloman. *Der Orient im Werk Velimir Chlebnikovs*. Munich: Sagner, 1975.

Stobbe, Peter. *Utopisches Denken bei Velimir Chlebnikov*. Munich: Sagner, 1982.

Vroon, Ronald. *Velimir Khlebnikov's Shorter Poems: A Key to the Coinages*. Ann Arbor: University of Michigan Press, 1983.

Weststeijn, Willem B. *Velimir Chlebnikov and the Development of Poetical Language in Russian Symbolism and Futurism*. Amsterdam: Rodopi, 1983.

Vladislav Khodasevich

Literaturnye stat'i i vospominaniia. New York: Iz. im. Chekhova, 1954.

Nekropol'. Vosopominaniia V. F. Khodasevicha. Brussels: Petropolis, 1939. Reprint. Paris: YMCA-Press, 1976.

Sobranie sochinenii. Vol. 1. Ann Arbor, Mich.: Ardis, 1983.
Sobranie stikhov v dvukh tomakh. 2 vols. Paris: La Presse Libre, 1982.
Stat'i o russkoi poezii. Letchworth, Eng.: Prideaux Press, 1971.
Bethea, David M. *Khodasevich: His Life and Art*. Princeton, N.J.: Princeton University Press, 1983.

Nikolai Kliuev
Sochineniia. 2 vols. Germany: A Neimanis, 1969.
Stikhotvoreniia i poemy. 3rd ed. Leningrad: Sovetskii pisatel', 1977; Biblioteka poeta, Malaia seriia.
Poems. Trans. John Glad. Ann Arbor, Mich.: Ardis, 1977.

Aleksei Kruchenykh
Piatnadtsat' let russkogo futurizma. 1912–1927 gg. Moscow: Izd. Vserossiiskogo soiuza poetov, 1928.
Pobeda nad solntsem. Opera v 2 deistviiakh. Petrograd, 1919.

Mikhail Kuzmin
Proza. 6 vols. Berkeley, Calif.: Berkeley Slavic Specialties, 1984–1986.
Sobranie stikhov. 3 vols. Munich: Fink, 1977–1978.
Selected Prose and Poetry. Trans. Michael Green. Ann Arbor, Mich.: Ardis, 1972.
Wings: Prose and Poetry. Trans. Neil Granoien and Michael Green. Ann Arbor, Mich.: Ardis, 1972.

Vladimir Maiakovskii
Polnoe sobranie sochinenii. 12 vols. Moscow: GIKhL, 1955–1956.
The Bedbug and Selected Poetry. Trans. Max Hayward and George Reavey. New York: Meridian Books, 1960. Reprint. Bloomington: Indiana University Press, 1975.
The Complete Plays. Tran. Guy Daniels. New York: Washington Square Press, 1968.
Mayakovsky. Trans. Herbert Marshall. New York: Hill & Wang, 1965.
Poems. Trans. Dorian Rottenberg. Moscow: Progress, 1976.
Khardzhiev, Nikolai, and Vladimir Trenin. *Poeticheskaia kul'tura Maiakovskogo*. Moscow: Iskusstvo, 1970.
Shklovskii, Viktor. *O Maiakovskom*. Moscow: Sovetskii pisatel', 1940.
Trenin, Vladimir. *V masterskoi stikha Maiakovskogo*. Moscow: Sovetskii pisatel', 1978.
Vladimirov, Sergei. *Ob esteticheskikh vzgliadakh Maiakovskogo*. Leningrad: Sovetskii pisatel', 1976.
Bang, Jangfeldt, and Nils Åke Nilsson, eds. *Vladimir Majakovskij. Memoirs and Essays*. Stockholm: Almqvist and Wiksell, 1975.
Brown, Edward J. *Mayakovsky: A Poet in the Revolution*. Princeton: N.J.: Princeton University Press, 1975.
Charters, Ann, and Samuel Charters. *I Love: The Story of Vladimir Mayakovsky and Lili Brik*. New York: Farrar, Straus & Giroux, 1979.
Shklovsky, Viktor. *Mayakovsky and His Circle*. Trans. Lily Feiler. New York: Dodd, Mead, 1972.
Stahlberger, Lawrence Leo. *The Symbolic System of Majakovskij*. The Hague: Mouton, 1964.
Woroszylski, Wiktor. *The Life of Mayakovsky*. Trans. Boleslaw Taborski. New York: Orion Press, 1970.

Osip Mandelstam
Sobranie sochinenii. 3 vols. Washington, D.C.: Inter-Language Literary Associates, 1964–1969.
Stikhotvoreniia. Leningrad: Sovetskii pisatel', 1973; Biblioteka poeta, Bol'shaia seriia.
Stikhotvoreniia. Ann Arbor, Mich.: Ardis, 1979.

Voronezhskie tetradi. Ann Arbor, Mich.: Ardis, 1980.

The Complete Critical Prose and Letters. Trans. Jane Gary Harris and Constance Link. Ann Arbor, Mich.: Ardis, 1979.

Mandelstam's Octets. Trans. John Riley. Penanett: Grosseteste Press, 1976.

Osip Mandelstam: Selected Essays. Trans. Sidney Monas. Austin: University of Texas Press, 1977.

Osip Mandelstam's "Stone." Trans. Robert Tracy. Princeton, N.J.: Princeton University Press, 1981.

The Prose of Osip Mandelstam. Trans. Clarence Brown. Princeton, N.J.: Princeton University Press, 1967.

Selected Poems. Trans. David McDuff. Cambridge: Rivers Press, 1973.

Bushman, Irina. *Poeticheskoe iskusstvo Mandel'shtama.* Munich: Institute for the Study of the U.S.S.R., 1964.

Mandelshtam, Nadezhda. *Vospominaniia.* New York: Izd. im. Chekhova, 1970.

––––––. *Vtoraia kniga.* Paris: YMCA-Press, 1972.

Baines, Jennifer. *Mandelstam: The Later Poetry.* Cambridge: Cambridge University Press, 1976.

Brown, Clarence. *Mandelstam.* Cambridge: Cambridge University Press, 1973.

Cohen, Arthur A. *Osip Emilievich Mandelstam: An Essay in Antiphon.* Ann Arbor, Mich.: Ardis, 1974.

Harris, Jane Gary. *Osip Mandelstam.* Twayne's World Author Series. Boston: Twayne, 1988.

Mandelstam, Nadezhda. *Hope Abandoned.* New York: Atheneum, 1974.

––––––. *Hope Against Hope.* Trans. Max Hayward. New York: Atheneum, 1970.

––––––. *Mozart and Salieri.* Trans. Robert A. McLean. Ann Arbor, Mich.: Ardis, 1973.

Przybylski, Ryszard. *An Essay on the Poetry of Osip Mandelstam.* Trans. M. G. Levin. Ann Arbor, Mich.: Ardis, 1987.

Boris Pasternak

Perepiska s Olgoi Freidenberg. New York: Harcourt Brace Jovanovich, 1981.

Sochineniia. 3 vols. Ann Arbor: University of Michigan Press, 1961.

Stikhotvoreniia i poemy. Leningrad: Sovetskii pisatel', 1965; Biblioteka poeta, Bol'shaia seriia.

The Correspondence of Boris Pasternak and Olga Freidenberg, 1910–1954. London: Secker and Warburg, 1982.

I Remember: Sketch for an Autobiography. Trans. David Magarshack. New York: Pantheon, 1959.

In the Interlude: Poems, 1945–1960. Trans. Henry Kamen. London: Oxford University Press, 1962.

Letters to Georgian Friends. Trans. David Magarshack. New York: Harcourt, Brace & World, 1968.

My Sister, Life and A Sublime Malady. Trans. Mark Rudman and Bohdan Boychuk. Ann Arbor, Mich.: Ardis, 1983.

My Sister, Life and Other Poems. Trans. Olga Carlisle. New York: Harcourt Brace & Jovanovich, 1976.

Pasternak on Art and Creativity. Ed. Angela Livingstone. Cambridge: Cambridge University Press, 1985.

Poems. Trans. Eugene M. Kayden. Ann Arbor: University of Michigan Press, 1959.

The Poems of Boris Pasternak. Trans. Lydia Pasternak Slater. London: Unwin, 1984.

The Poetry of Boris Pasternak, 1919–1960. Trans. George Reavey. New York: Putnam, 1968.

Safe Conduct: An Autobiography and Other Writings. New York: New Directions, 1958.

Selected Poems. Trans. John Stallworthy and Peter France. New York: Norton, 1982; London: Allen Lane, 1983.

Aucouturier, Michel. *Pasternak par liu-meme.* Paris, Éditions du seuil, 1963.

Barnes, Christopher. *Boris Pasternak: A Literary Biography.* 2 vols. Cambridge: Cambridge University Press, 1989.

Conquest, Robert. *Courage of Genius: The Pasternak Affair.* London: Collins and Harvill, 1961; Philadelphia: Lippincott, 1962.

Davie, Donald, and Angela Livinstone, eds. *Pasternak: Modern Judgements.* London: Macmillan, 1969.

Dyck, J. W. *Boris Pasternak.* New York: Twayne, 1972.

Erlich, Victor, ed. *Pasternak: A Collection of Critical Essays.* Englewood Cliffs, N.J.: Prentice-Hall, 1978.

Fleishman, Lazar. *Boris Pasternak: The Poet and His Politics.* Cambridge, Mass.: Harvard University Press, 1990.

Gifford, Henry. *Pasternak: A Critical Study.* Cambridge: Cambridge University Press, 1977.

Hingley, Ronald. *Pasternak: A Biography.* London: Weidenfeld and Nicolson, 1983.

Hughes, Olga. *The Poetic World of Boris Pasternak.* Princeton, N.J.: Princeton University Press, 1974.

Levi, Peter. *Boris Pasternak.* London: Hutchinson, 1990.

Mallac, Guy de. *Boris Pasternak.* Paris: Éditions universitaires, 1963.

Nilsson, Nils Åke, ed. *Boris Pasternak. Essays.* Stockholm: Almqvist and Wiksell, 1976.

Payne, Robert. *The Three Worlds of Boris Pasternak.* New York: Coward-McCann, 1961.

Plank, Dale. *Pasternak's Lyric: A Study of Sound and Imagery.* The Hague: Mouton, 1966.

Proyart, Jacqueline de. *Pasternak.* Paris: Gallimard, 1964.

Igor Severianin

Ananasy v shampanskom. Poezy. Moscow: Izd. V. V. Pashukanisa, 1916; Reprint. Rockville, Md.: Kamkin, 1970.

Gromokipiashchii kubok. Poezy. Moscow: Izd. V. V. Pashukanisa, 1915; Reprint. Washington, D.C.: Kamkin, 1966.

Stikhotvoreniia. Leningrad: Sovetskii pisatel', 1975; Biblioteka poeta, Malaia seriia.

Vadim Shershenevich

Avtomobilnaia postup'. Chapel Hill, N.C., 1979.

Futurizm bez maski. Letchworth, Eng.: Prideaux Press, 1974.

Marina Tsvetaeva

Izbrannaia proza v dvukh tomakh. 1917–1937. New York: Russica, 1979.

Izbrannye proizvedeniia. Moscow: Sovetskii pisatel', 1965; Biblioteka poeta, Bol'shaia seriia.

Sochineniia v dvukh tomakh. Moscow: Khud. lit., 1980.

Stikhovoreniia i poemy v piati tomakh. 4 vols. New York: Russica, 1980–1983.

Selected Poems. Trans. Elaine Feinstein. London: Oxford University Press, 1971.

Tsvetaeva, Anastasiia. *Vospominaniia.* 3rd ed. Moscow: Sovetskii pisatel', 1983.

Karlinsky, Simon. *Marina Cvetaeva: Her Life and Art.* Berkeley: University of California Press, 1966.

———. *Marina Tsvetaeva: The Woman, Her World, and Her Poetry.* Cambridge: Cambridge University Press, 1986.

Razumovsky, Maria. *Marina Zwetajewa. Mythos and Wahrheit.* Vienna: Karolinger Verlag, 1981.

Taubman, Jane A. *A Life Through Poetry: Marina Tsvetaeva's Lyric Diary.* Columbus, Ohio: Slavica, 1989.

Maksimilian Voloshin

Stikhotvoreniia i poemy v dvukh tomakh. 2 vols. Paris: YMCA-Press, 1982–1984.

Kuprianov, Igor. *Sud'ba poeta (Lichnost' i poeziia M. Voloshina).* Kiev: Naukova dumka, 1978.

Marsh, Cynthia. *M. A. Voloshin, Artist-Poet: A Study of the Synaesthetic Aspect of His Poetry.* Birmingham: University of Birmingham Press, 1982.

Wallafen, Claudia. *Maksimilian Vološin als Kunstler und Kritiker.* Munich: Sagner, 1982.

Aleksandr Vvedenskii

Polnoe sobranie sochinenii. 2 vols. Ann Arbor, Mich.: Ardis, 1980–1984.

Soviet and Émigré Poetry
(1925–1975)

Anthologies

Ivask, Iurii P., ed. *Na zapade. Antologiia russkoi zarubezhnoi poezii.* New York: Izd. im. Chekhova, 1953.

Markov, Vladimir. *Priglushennye golosa.* New York: Izd. im. Chekhova, 1952.

Russkaia sovetskaia poeziia 50–70–x godov. Minsk: Vysheishaia shkola, 1982.

Russkaia sovetskaia poeziia. Sbornik stikhov 1917–1952. Moscow: GIKhL, 1954.

Terapiano, Iurii, ed. *Muza diaspory. Izbrannye stikhotvoreniia zarubezhnykh poetov 1920–1960.* Frankfurt am Main: Posev, 1960.

Vo ves' golos. Soviet Poetry. Moscow: Progress, n.d.

Anthologies of Translations

Milner-Gulland, R. R., ed. *Soviet Russian Verse.* New York: Macmillan, 1961.

Modern Russian Poetry. Trans. Olga Andreyev Carlisle and Rose Styron. New York: Viking Press, 1972.

Pachmuss, Temira, ed. *A Russian Cultural Revival: A Critical Anthology of Émigré Literature Before 1939.* Knoxville: University of Tennessee Press, 1981.

Reavey, George, ed. and trans. *The New Russian Poets, 1953–1968.* New York: October House, 1966.

Weissbort, Daniel, ed. *Post-War Russian Poetry.* Harmondsworth: Penguin Books, 1974.

Studies in Russian

Poltoratskii, Nikolai P., ed. *Russkaia literatura v emigratsii.* Pittsburgh: Department of Slavic Languages and Literatures, University of Pittsburgh, 1972.

Struve, Gleb. *Russkaia literatura v izgnanii.* 2nd ed. Paris: YMCA-Press, 1984.

Vykhodtsev, P. S., ed. *Istoriia russkoi sovetskoi literatury.* 3rd ed. Moscow: Vyshaia shkola, 1979.

Studies in English

Brown, Deming. *Soviet Russian Literature Since Stalin.* Cambridge: Cambridge University Press, 1978.
Kasack, Wolfgang. *Dictionary of Russian Literature Since 1917.* Trans. Maria Carlson and Jane T. Hodges. New York: Columbia University Press, 1988.
Struve, Gleb. *Russian Literature Under Lenin and Stalin, 1917–1953.* Norman: University of Oklahoma Press, 1971.

Authors and Specialized Studies

Eduard Bagritskii
  Eduard Bagritskii: vospominaniia sovremennikov. Ed. L. G. Bagritskaia. Moscow: Sovetskii pistael', 1973.
  Stikhotvoreniia i poemy. Leningrad: Sovetskii pisatel', 1964; Biblioteka poeta, Bol'shaia seriia.
    Liubareva, Elena. *Eduard Bagrtiskii. Zhizn' i tvorchestvo.* Moscow: Sovetskii pisatel', 1964.
Ol'ga Berggol'ts
  Leningradskaia poema. Poemy i stikhotvoreniia. Leningrad: Khud. lit., 1976.
  Sobranie sochinenii. 3 vols. Leningrad: Khud. lit., 1973.
    Fiedler-Stolz, Eva-Marie. *Ol'ga Berggol'ts. Aspekte ihres lyrischen Werkes.* Munich: Sagner, 1977.
    Tsurikova, Galina. *Ol'ga Berggol'ts.* Leningrad, 1966.
  Vospominaia Ol'gu Berggol'ts. Leningrad: Leninizdat, 1979.
Dimitrii Bobyshev
  Ziianiia. Paris: YMCA-Press, 1979.
Iosif Brodskii
  Chast' rechi. Stikhotvoreniia 1972–1976. Ann Arbor, Mich.: Ardis, 1977.
  Konets prekrasnoi epokhi. Stikhotvoreniia 1964–1971. Ann Arbor, Mich.: Ardis, 1977.
  Mramor. Ann Arbor, Mich.: Ardis, 1984.
  Ostanovka v pustyne. New York: Izd. im. Chekhova, 1970.
  Rimskie elegii. New York: Russica, 1982.
  Stikhotvoreniia i poemy. Washington, D.C.: Inter-Language Literary Associates, 1965.
  The Funeral of Bobo. Ann Arbor, Mich.: Ardis, 1974.
  Less Than One: Selected Essays. New York: Farrar, Straus & Giroux, 1986.
  A Part of Speech. New York: Farrar, Straus & Giroux, 1980.
  Selected Poems. Trans. George Kline. New York: Harper & Row, 1973.
  To Urania. New York: Farrar, Straus & Giroux, 1980.
    Kreps, Mikhail. *O poezii Iosifa Brodskogo.* Ann Arbor, Mich.: Ardis, 1984.
    Losev, Lev, ed. *Poetika Iosifa Brodskogo.* New York: Ermitazh, 1989.
Igor Chinnov
  Antiteza. College Park, Md., 1979.
  Avtograf. Holyoke, Me., 1984.
  Kompozitsiia. Paris: Rifma, 1972.
  Linii. Paris: Rifma, 1960.
  Metafory. New York: Novyi zhurnal, 1968.
  Partitura. New York: Novyi zhurnal, 1970.
  Pastorali. Paris: Rifma, 1976.
Ivan Elagin
  Drakon na kryshe. Rockville, Md., 1974.

Otsvety nochnye. New York: Novyi zhurnal, 1963.

Pod zvezdam topora. Frankfurt am Main: Posev, 1976.

Tiazhelye zvezdy. Tenafly, N.J., 1986.

V zale vselennoi. Ann Arbor, Mich.: 1982.

Evgenii Evtushenko

Avtobiografiia. London: Flegon, 1964.

Sobranie sochinenii v trekh tomakh. 3 vols. Moscow: Khud. lit., 1983, 1984.

Poems. Trans. Herbert Marshall. New York: Dutton, 1966.

Poems Chosen by the Author. 2nd ed. New York: Hill & Wang, 1971.

The Poetry of Yevgeny Yevtushenko. Rev. ed. Trans. George Reavey. London: Marion Boyars, 1981.

A Precocious Autobiography. Trans. Andrew MacAndrew. New York: Dutton, 1964.

Stolen Apples. Poetry. Garden City, N.Y.: Doubleday, 1971.

Georgii Ivanov

Izbrannye stikhi. Paris: Lev, 1980.

Sobranie stikhotvorenii. Wurzburg: Jal-Verlag, 1975.

Iurii Ivask

Khvala. Washington, D.C.: Kamkin, 1967.

Zavoevanie Meksiki. Holyoke, Mass.: New England Publishing, 1984.

Zolushka. New York: Mosty, 1970.

Dmitrii Klenovskii

Pevuchaia nosha. Munich, 1969.

Pocherkom poeta. Munich, 1971.

Poslednee. Munich, 1977.

Stikhi. Izbrannoe. Munich, 1967.

Teplyi vecher. N.p., 1975.

Leonid Martynov

Chudo v kovshe. Moscow: Sovremennik, 1977.

Reka tishina. Moscow: Molodaia gvardiia, 1983.

Sobranie sochinenii. 3 vols. Moscow: Khud. lit., 1976.

Uzel bur'. Moscow: Sovremennik, 1979.

Zemnaia nosha. Moscow: Sovremennik, 1976.

Zolotoi zapas. Moscow: Sovetskii pisatel', 1981.

A Book of Poems. Trans. Peter Tempest. Moscow: Progress, 1979.

     Dement'ev, Valerii. *Leonid Martynov. Poet i vremia.* Moscow: Sovetskii pisatel', 1986.

Nikolai Morshen

Dvoetochie. Washington, D.C.: Kamkin, 1967.

Ekho i zerkalo. Berkeley, Calif.: Berkeley Slavic Specialties, 1979.

Tiiulen'. Munich: Posev, 1959.

Irina Odoevtseva

Desiat' let. Stihi. Paris: Rifma, 1961.

Na beregakh Seny. Paris, 1983.

Odinochestvo. Washington, D.C.: Russkaia kniga, 1965.

Zlataia tsep'. Paris: Rifma, 1975.

Bulat Okudzhava

Arbat, moi Arbat. Moscow: Sovetskii pisatel', 1976.

Proza i poeziia. 7th ed. Frankfurt am Main: Posev, 1984.

65 pesen. Ann Arbor, Mich.: Ardis, 1980.

Stikhotvoreniia. Moscow: Sovetskii pisatel', 1984.

     Heider, Hildburg. *Der Hoffnung kleines Orchester. Bulat Okudžava—Lieder und Lyrik.* Frankfurt am Main: Peter Lang, 1983.

Boris Poplavskii
Sobranie sochinenii. 2nd ed. 3 vols. Berkeley, Calif.: Berkeley Slavic Specialties, 1980–1981.

Il'ia Sel'vinskii
Izbrannye proizvedeniia. Leningrad: Sovetskii pisatel', 1972; Biblioteka poeta, Bol'shaia seriia.
Sobranie sochinenii. 6 vols. Moscow: Khud. lit., 1971–1974.
Stikhotvoreniia; Tsarevna-Lebed'. Moscow: 1984.
    Reznik, Osip. *Zhizn' v poezii: tvorchestvo Il'i Sel'vinskogo.* 2nd ed. Moscow: Sovetskii pisatel', 1972.

Nikolai Tikhonov
Sobranie sochinenii. 7 vols. Moscow: Khud. lit., 1985.
Stikhotvoreniia i poemy. Leningrad: Sovetskii pisatel', 1981; Biblioteka poeta, Bol'shaia seriia.
    Grinberg, Iosif. *Tvorchestvo Nikolaia Tikhonova.* 2nd ed. Moscow: Sovetskii pisatel', 1972.
    Shoshin, Vladislav. *Poet romanticheskogo podviga: Ocherk tvorchestva N. S. Tikhonova.* Leningrad: Sovetskii pisatel', 1976.
    Vospominaniia o N. Tikhonova. Moscow: Sovetskii pisatel', 1986.

Aleksandr Tvardovskii
Sobranie sochinenii. 5 vols. Moscow: Khud. lit., 1966–1971.
Stikhotvoreniia. Moscow: Sovremennik, 1975.
Tyorkin and the Stovemakers. Trans. Anthony Rudolf. Cheadle, Eng.: Carcanet Press, 1974.
Vassili Tyorkin. Moscow: Progress, 1975.
    Dement'ev, Valerii. *Aleksandr Tvardovskii.* Moscow: Sovetskii pisatel', 1976.
    Kondratovich, Aleksei. *Aleksandr Tvardovskii. Poeziia i lichnost'.* 2nd ed. Moscow: Khud. lit., 1985.
    Makedonov, Adrian. *Tvorcheskii put; Tvardovskogo.* Moscow: Khud. lit., 1981.
    Murav'ev, Aleksandr. *Tvorchestvo A. T. Tvardovskogo.* Moscow: Prosveshchenie, 1981.
    Turkov, Andrei. *Aleksandr Tvardovskii.* 2nd ed. Moscow: GIKhL, 1970.

Andrei Voznesenskii
Proroby dukha. Moscow: Sovetskii pisatel', 1984.
Sobranie sochinenii. 3 vols. Moscow: Khud. lit., 1983–1984.
Antiworlds and the Fifth Ace. Trans. W. H. Auden et al. Garden City, N.Y.: Anchor, 1969.
An Arrow in the Wall: Selected Poetry and Prose. Ed. William Jay Smith and F. D. Reeve. New York: Holt, 1987.
Selected Poems. Trans. Herbert Marshall. New York: Hill & Wang, 1966.
Story Under Full Sail. Trans. Stanley Kunitz. Garden City, N.Y.: Doubleday, 1974.
    Mikhailov, Aleksandr. *Andrei Voznesenskii. Etiudy.* Moscow: Khud. lit., 1970.

Nikolai Zabolotskii
Sobranie sochinenii. 3 vols. Moscow: Khud. lit., 1983–1984.
Stikhotvoreniia. Washington, D.C.: Inter-Language Literary Associates, 1965.
Stikhotvoreniia i poemy. Moscow and Leningrad: Sovetskii pisatel', 1965; Biblioteka poeta, Bol'shaia seriia.
    Makedonov, A. *Nilolai Zabolotskii. Zhizn'. Tvorchestvo. Metamorfozy.* Leningrad: Sovetskii pisatel', 1968.
    Rostovtseva, I. I. *Nikolai Zabolotskii.* Moscow: Sovremennik, 1984.
    Vospominaniia o N. Zabolotskom. 2nd ed. Moscow: Sovetskii pisatel', 1984.

Index

Page numbers in italics refer to primary references.

Absurd, literature of the, 252
Acmeism, 5, 6, 199, 205–7, 214, 216, 218, 219, 221, 222, 241, 262–64, 275, 291–93, 299, 309
Adamovich, Georgy, 262, 263
Aeneid, 64
Aesop, Aesopian fable, 4, 25, 51, 59, 64, 98, 120
Aglaia, 85
Akhmadulina, Bella, *192, 292*
Akhmatova, Anna (pseudonym of Anna Gorenko), 206, 208, *210–16*, 241, 242, 251, 276, 279, 288, 297, 300, 305: *Anno domini MCMXXI*, 206, 213; *At the Seashore*, 212; *The Course of Time*, 211; *Evening*, 211; *The Plantain Weed*, 213; *Poem Without a Hero*, 211, 214; "The Reed Pipe," 213; *Requiem*, 211, 213, 214, 305; *The Rosary*, 212; "The Seventh Book," 214; *The White Flock*, 211, 212
Aksakov, Ivan, 140, 150, *152–53*
Aksakov, Sergey, 150, 152
Aksenov, Vasily, 305
Akundinov, Timofey, 31
Aleksey Mikhailovich (tsar), 24, 26, 32, 35
Alembert, Jean Le Rond d', 62
Alexander the Great, 10
Alexander I (emperor), 74, 79, 83, 88, 93, 104, 111, 115
Alexander II (emperor), 95, 139, 154, 169
Alexander III (emperor), 154, 159, 167, 169
Alexandreis, 10
Aliger, Margarita, *273–74*
All Sorts and Sundries, 63
Anacreon, 56, 79, 80, 145
Anacreontics, 48, 66, 68, 73, 74, 77, 78, 86, 102, 106, 108, 122, 130, 134, 136
Andropov, Iury, 305
Anna (empress), 39, 45–50, 57
Annensky, Innokenty, 187, *199–201*, 206, 207, 211, 263, 264: *Books of Reflections*, 199, 201; *The Cypress Chest*, 199, 201;

Posthumous Verse, 199; *Quiet Songs*, 199, 201; tragedies, 199
Antokolsky, Pavel, *259*
Aonides, 85
Apollo, 206, 207, 220
Apukhtin, Aleksey, *160–61*
Apuleius, Lucius, 68, 69
Archaizers, 103, 105, 121
Ariosto, Lodovico, 110
Aristotle, 25
Art for art's sake (*l'art pour l'art*), 140, 141, 143, 144, 150, 155, 160, 162, 163, 213, 221
Arzamas, 94–97, 101, 103, 106, 108, 110
Aseev, Nikolay, *240*
Auden, W. H., 297
Avraamy, *31*
Avvakum (archpriest), 24, 31, 32, 50

Bach, Johann Sebastian, 216
Bagritsky, Eduard, *256, 257*
Bakst, Lev (Leon) (pseudonym of L. S. Rosenberg), 233
Balakirev, Mili, 135
Ballad, 20, 21, 27, 60, 82, 87, 94, 95, 97, 103, 119, 122, 123, 130, 134, 149, 242, 258
Balmont, Konstantin, 168, *172–75*, 187, 201, 280: *The Ash Tree*, 174; *Buildings on Fire*, 172, 173; *Evil Spells*, 174; *Fairy Tales*, 174; *The Green Garden*, 174; *Let Us Be Like the Sun*, 168, 172, 173; *The Mirage*, 174; *The Ring*, 174; *Silence*, 173; *Songs of an Avenger*, 174; *The Songs of the Worker's Hammer*, 174; *Sonnets of the Sun, Honey and the Moon*, 174; *Under Northern Skies*, 168, 172, 173; *Without Bounds*, 173
Balzac, Honoré de, 139
Baratynsky, Evgeny, 105, *116–18*, 150
Barclay, John, 51
Barkov, Ivan, 64, *70*
Bartók, Béla, 307
Batiushkov, Konstantin, 94, 96, *100–2*, 103, 105, 106, 110, 254

Baudelaire, Charles, 5, 155, 168, 175, 179, 187, 195, 201

Beautiful Lady, 192, 195, 196. *See also* Sophia, Saint

Beckett, Samuel, 230, 305

Beethoven, Ludwig van, 143, 216, 260

Belinsky, Vissarion, 156

Belobotsky, Ian, *37, 38*

Bely, Andrey (pseudonym of Boris Bugaev), 168, 170, *187–91*, 280: *After the Parting. A Berlin Diary*, 190; *Ashes*, 188, 189; *The Beginning of an Age. Memoirs*, 191; *Between Two Revolutions*, 191; *Christ Is Arisen*, 190; *The First Meeting*, 190; *Gold in Azure*, 168, 187, 188; *Kotik Letaev*, 188, 191; *On the Boundary of Two Centuries. Recollections*, 191; *Petersburg*, 188, 190; *The Princess and the Knights. Tales*, 190; *The Return*, 189; *The Silver Dove*, 189, 190; *The Star. New Poems*, 190; *Symbolism*, 188; *The Urn*, 188, 189, 190

Benediktov, Vladimir, *138*

Beranger, Pierre-Jean de, 152

Berggolts, Olga, 267, *270–71*

Bestuzhev, Aleksandr, 122

Bion, 101

Bizet, Georges, 194, 304

Blake, William, 296

Blätter für die Kunst, Die, 168

Blok, Aleksandr, 168, 183, 186, 187, *191–96*, 241, 242, 245, 246, 280, 288: "Carmen," 194; *Collected Works*, 192; *The King On the Square*, 193; "The Nightingale Garden," 194; "On Kulikovo Field," 195; *The Puppet Show*, 187, 191, 193; *Ramses*, 195; "Retribution," 193; *The Rose and the Cross*, 194; "The Scythians," 195; "The Snow Mask," 192; *The Song of Fate*, 193; *The Stranger*, 193; *The Twelve*, 192, 195; *Verses About the Beautiful Lady*, 168, 191

Bobrov, Sergey, *240*

Bobyshev, Dmitri, *300*

Bogdanovich, Ippolit, 63, *67–69*, 80, 110: *A Collection of Russian Proverbs*, 68; *Dushenka*, 63, 67, 68, 110; *The Lyre*, 68

Boileau, Nicolas, 45–48, 50, 53, 57, 58, 60, 80

Boratynsky, Evgeny. *See* Baratynsky, Evgeny

Borodin, Aleksandr, 18, 145

"Bova the King's Son," 25

Brahms, Johannes, 238

Braque, Georges, 224

Brecht, Bertolt, 245

Brezhnev, Leonid, 282, 288, 301, 305

Brik, Lili, 231

Brik, Osip, 231

Briusov, Valery, 168, *175–78*, 186, 207, 208: *All My Songs*, 176, 177; *The Altar of Victory*, 175, 178; *The Angel of Fire*, 175, 177; *Chefs d'oeuvre*, 175; *Me eum esse*, 175, 176; *Russian Symblists*, 168, 175; *Stephanos*, 176, 177; *Tertia vigilia*, 175, 176; *Urbi et orbi*, 176

Brodsky, Joseph, 6, *293–97*, 300, 305, 308, 309: *The End of a Beautiful Epoch*, 296; *A Halt in the Wilderness*, 293; *Less Than One*, 297; *Marble*, 297; *A Part of Speech*, 296; *Poems and Narrative Verse*, 294; *The Roman Elegies*, 297

Browning, Robert, 5, 139

Bulgakov, Mikhail, 305

Bunin, Ivan, *184, 185*

Bürger, Gottfried August, 96

Burliuk, David, 225, 227, 230, 234

Burns, Robert, 133, 256, 293

Byliny, 10, *13–14*, 15, 16, 20, 21, 25, 27, 87, 98, 149, 153, 268

Byron (George Gordon, Lord), 4, 97, 104, 105–7, 109–11, 113, 122, 124, 126, 129–31, 135, 150–52, 156, 161, 255

Canova, Antonio, 209

Catherine II (the Great), 49, 51, 53, 57, 62–64, 68, 70, 71, 73, 74, 81, 83, 84, 98: *The Instruction*, 63

Cavafy, Constantine, 297

Centrifuge school, 225, 235, 240

Chaadaev, Petr, 158

Chamber of Poets, 266

Chaplin, Charles, 288

Chastushka, 195, 242

Chekhov, Anton, 153, 163, 180, 185

Chenier, André, 112, 150, 161, 214

Chernenko, Konstantin, 305

Chernyshevsky, Nikolay, 156

Chervinskaia, Lidiia, *264, 265*

Chinnov, Igor, *297, 298*, 309

Chizh (Siskin), 261, 262

Chopin, Frédéric, 144, 238

Chronicle of Current Events, The, 307

Chukhontsev, Oleg, *308*

Chukovsky, Korney, 262

Chulkov, Mikhail, 65

Civic poetry, 5, 103, 105, 121, 122, 140, 146, 152–55, 159, 160

Coleridge, Samuel Taylor, 93

Commedia dell'arte, 192

Conrad, Joseph, 205, 207

Constructivism, 252, 253, 256, 258

Contemporary, The, 105, 110, 140, 141, 146, 156

Corneille, Pierre, 59, 69, 245
Cornwall, Barry (pseudonym of Bryan Procter), 113
Correggio, Antonio Allegri da, 80
Crevier, Jean Baptiste, 52
Cubo-futurism, 5, 225–27, 233, 234, 240, 244, 245
Cyril, Saint (Apostle to the Slavs), 9
Cyril of Turov, Saint, 15

Danilov, Kirsha. *See* Kirsha Danilov
Dante Alighieri, 194, 209, 213
Dargomyzhsky, Aleksandr, 147, 161
Davydov, Denis, 94, *97, 98*, 106
Decadence, 5, 161, 168–72, 178, 181, 182, 199, 206–8, 210, 223, 240, 262, 264, 266, 275, 288, 296–98
Decembrist movement and revolt, 4, 97, 103–5, 111, 112, 115, 119, 121–23, 129, 158
Decembrist poets, 103, 105, 121, 286
Delmas, Liubov, 191, 194
Delille, Jacques, 87
Delvig, Anton, 80, *108, 109*, 110, 116, 228
Derzhavin, Gavrila, 4, 70, *73–79*, 88, 94, 122, 160, 222, 223: "The Courtier," 77; "The Crossbill," 77; "God," 76; "Gypsy Dance," 78; "Invitation to Dinner," 77; "The Monument," 77; nature poems, 77; "Nightingale in a Dream," 78; "Ode to the Wise Princess Felitsa," 74; "On the Death of Prince Meshchersky," 74; "On Transience," 78; "A Portrait of Felitsa," 74; "Russian Girls," 78; "The Swallow," 77; "To Eugene, or Life at Zvanka," 77; "To Rulers and Judges," 74; "The Vision of the *Murza*," 74; "The Waterfall," 74, 79
De-Stalinization, 6, 279. *See also* Thaw
Diaghilev, Sergey, 168, 220, 225
Dickens, Charles, 139, 154
Didelot, Charles, 110
Dederot, Denis, 59, 62, 66, 70, 71
Divine Wisdom. *See* Sophia, Saint
Dmitri Donskoy, 21, 56, 122, 195
Dmitry. *See* False Dmitry I
Dmitriev, Ivan, 82, *88, 89*, 103
Dobroliubov, Aleksandr, *171, 172*
Dobroliubov, Nikolay, 156
Dolniki, 183, 196
Domostroy. See Household Guide
Donne, John, 294
Dostoevsky, Fedor, 4, 140, 151, 154, 159, 168, 171, 180, 181, 183, 201, 282, 288
Dostoevsky, Mikhail, 151, 156
Drawn-out songs, 10, *11, 12*, 21, 28, 29, 58, 79, 108, 133, 134, 145, 149, 153, 158

Drone, The, 63, 64
Dryden, John, 80
Duncan, Isadora, 246, 248

Ecclesiastical verse, *26*
Efron, Sergey, 241
Ego-futurism, 225, 226, 244, 263
Elagin, Ivan (pseudonym of Ivan Matveev), *276, 277*
Elegy, 51, 57, 60, 70, 74, 85, 86, 94, 98, 101–3, 105, 111, 112, 114, 116, 119, 130, 136, 159, 256, 257
Eliot, T. S., 5
Elizabeth (empress), 45, 46, 50, 52, 53, 57
Émigré poets, 5, 6, 262, 265, 274, 278, 297, 308, 309
Emin, Fedor, 63
Encyclopédie, l', 62, 66
Enlightenment, 3, 4, 46, 62, 64, 66, 70, 74
Epistle, 47, 48, 51, 64, 68, 79, 80, 85, 87, 88, 94, 96, 99, 101, 102, 105, 106, 108, 115, 116, 119, 122, 130, 133, 134, 151
Epoch, The, 151
Esenin, Sergey, 225, 232, 244, 245, *246–48*, 289, 290, 304
Eternal Feminine, 143, 169, 180. *See also* Sophia, Saint
Euripides, 199
Evtushenko, Evgeny, 279, *286–88*, 291, 301, 305: "Babii Iar," 286, 287; "The Heirs of Stalin," 286–88; *Precocious Autobiography*, 286; *Third Snow*, 287; "Zima Junction," 286, 287
Ezh (Hedgehog), 261, 262

Fable, 47, 48, 51, 57, 59, 64, 66, 68, 69–72, 79, 88, 94, 98, 99, 100. *See also* Aesop, Aesopian fable
False Dmitry I, 25, 31, 111, 122, 242
Fedor III (tsar), 35
Fénélon, François de Solignac de La Mothe- (archbishop), 49, 51, 60
Fet, Afanasy, 4, 5, *140–44*, 146, 151, 155, 160, 161, 185, 213: *Evening Lights*, 141; *Lyrical Pantheon*, 141
Filonov, Pavel, 261
Filosofov, Dmitri, 182, 183
Fin de siècle, 154, 155, 158, 167, 175, 181, 186, 262, 263, 266, 298
Flaubert, Gustave, 154
Fleming, Paul, 60
Florian, Jean Pierre Claris de, 96
Fofanov, Konstantin, *163, 164*, 226
Fontenelle, Bernard le Bovier de, 97, 60
Fonvizin, Denis, 70, 82

Formalism, 289
Fouqué, Friedrich Henrich Karl de la Motte-, 97
Freemasonry, 62–64, 66, 79, 83, 85
Futurism, 5, 6, 205, 206, 224–227, 230, 233–35, 241, 252, 259, 280, 292

Galich, Aleksandr (pseudonym of Aleksandr Ginzburg), *301, 302*
Gauguin, Paul, 289
Gautier, Théophile, 140, 144, 206
Gellert, Christian Furchtegott, 59, 71
George, Stefan, 186
German (poet of the Nikon school), *31*
Gershenzon, Mikhail, 198, 199
Gessner, Salomon, 66, 82, 86
Glière, Reinhold, 150
Glinka, Fedor, 123, 145
Glinka, Mikhail, 110, 123
Gnedich, Nikolay, 101–3
Godunov, Boris (tsar), 23, 122, 147
Goethe, Johann Wolfgang von, 97, 118, 121, 124, 125, 142, 150, 152, 237
Gogol, Nikolay, 147, 178, 180, 181, 201
Golden age of Russian poetry, 4, 68, 85, 94, 100, 102, 104, 125, 126, 130, 140, 184
Golenishchev-Kutuzov, Arseny, *161*
Gorbachev, Mikhail, 301, 305
Gorbanevskaia, Natalia, *307*
Gorky, Maksim, 184, 186, 222
Gorodetsky, Sergey, 207, *221, 222*, 246
Goya, Francisco José de, 289
Gray, Thomas, 82, 94, 95
Greek Anthology, The, 102
Green Lamp (1819–1820), 108, 110
Green Lamp (1927, Paris), 263
Griboedov, Aleksandr, 121
Grigorev, Apollon, 141, 146, *151–52*
Guild of Poets, 206, 207, 215, 221, 277
Gumilev, Nikolay, 206, *207–10*, 211, 221, 265, 277, 305: *An Alien Sky,* 208, 209; *The Campfire,* 209; *Mik,* 210; *The Path of the Conquistadors,* 207, 208; *Pearls,* 208; *The Pillar of Fire,* 210; *The Porcelain Pavilion,* 210; *The Quiver,* 207, 209; *Romantic Flowers,* 208; *The Shadow of the Palm,* 210; *The Tent,* 210
Guro, Elena (pseudonym of Eleonora von Notenburg), 172, *233, 234*

Hafiz, 210
Hagia Sophia. *See* Sophia, Saint
Hardy, Thomas, 154, 167
Hegel, Georg Wilhelm Friedrich, 106, 125, 152
Heine, Heinrich, 127, 142, 145, 148–50, 152, 161, 201

Herald of Europe, The, 85, 95
Herder, Johann-Gottfried von, 85
Heredia, José-Maria de, 219
Herzen, Aleksandr, 303
Hippius, Zinaida, 168, 171, *181–83,* 187, 263, 297: *The Green Ring* and other plays, 183; *Last Poems,* 183; *Living Persons,* 183; *New People,* 183; novels, 183; *Poems. A Diary. 1911–1921,* 183; *Radiance,* 183
Historical song, 21, 25
Hoffmann, E. T. A., 147
Holberg, Ludvig, Baron, 64
Homer, 56, 80, 102, 121, 216, 307
Horace (Quintus Horatius Flaccus), 45, 48, 51, 70, 72–74, 77, 80, 115, 119, 144
Horatian ode, 47, 73, 74, 77
Horatian satire, 4, 46, 47, 59, 60, 71, 72
Household Guide (Domostroy), 37
Hugo, Victor, 125

Iavorsky, Stefan, *38, 39*
Iazykov, Nikolay, *118–20,* 150, 240
Ibsen, Henrik, 201
Ighnatev, Ivan, 226
Igor of Novgorod-Seversk (prince), 16–18, 65
Iliad, The, 38, 101, 103
Imagism, 225, 244–47
Inber, Vera, *257, 258*
Ionesco, Eugene, 305
Irving, Washington, 115
Istomin, Karion, *37*
Ivan III, 21
Ivan IV (the Terrible), 4, 9, 21, 23, 25, 63, 66, 122, 144, 147, 149, 150, 159
Ivanov, Aleksandr, 282
Ivanov, Georgy, *262–64,* 277
Ivanov, Viacheslav, 168, 177, 187, *196–99,* 211, 214, 227: *By the Stars,* 196, 198; *Cor Ardens,* 196, 197; *A Correspondence Between Two Corners,* 198; *Evening Lights,* 198; *Furrows and Boundaries,* 198; *Pilot Stars,* 168, 196; "Roman Sonnets," 198; *The Sweet Mystery,* 198; *Translucence,* 196, 197; "Winter Sonnets," 198
Ivask, Iury, *274–76: Cinderella,* 275; *Glory,* 275; "Homo ludens," 276; *The Northern Shore,* 275; *A Regal Autumn,* 275

Jarry, Alfred, 261

Kamensky, Vasily, *234*
Kamerny Theater, 199
Kandinsky, Vasily, 225
Kant, Immanuel, 85, 188
Kantemir, Antiokh, 40, *46–48,* 50, 61, 73

Kapnist, Vasily, 70, *72, 73,* 83
Karamzin, Nikolay, 66, 72, 79, 82, *84–88,* 95,
  101, 102, 105, 106, 110, 118, 150:
  "Bornholm Island," 84; *History of the*
  Russian State, 79, 85, 89, 150; *Letters of a*
  Russian Traveller, 84, 85; "Poor Liza," 82,
  84, 86
Karamzinists, 94, 96, 103, 104, 110
Katenin, Pavel, 103
Katyrev-Rostovsky, Ivan, 31
Kazakova, Rimma, *304, 305*
Keats, John, 104
Kharms, Daniil (pseudonym of Danill
  Iuvachev), 252, *261*
Khemnister, Ivan, 70, *71, 72*
Kheraskov, Mikhail, 63, 64, *65–67,* 68, 79: *The*
  Battle of Chesme, 66; *Didactic Fables,* 66;
  Didactic Odes, 66; magazines, 66; *New Odes,*
  66; novels, 67; *The Rossiad,* 63, 65–67;
  tragedies, 67
Khlebnikov, Velemir, v, 172, 225, *227–30,* 235
Khodasevich, Vladislav, *222, 223, 262*
Khomiakov, Aleksey, 119, *135, 136,* 153
Khrushchev, Nikita, 279
Khvorostinin, Ivan, 31
Khvostov, Dmitri, 109
Kipling, Rudyard, 186, 293
Kireevsky, Ivan, 119, 120
Kireevsky, Petr, 119, 120
Kirsanov, Semen, *274*
Kirsha Danilov (*Ancient Russian Poems*
  Collected by Kirsha Danilov), 12
Kiukhelbeker, Vilgelm, 105, *121,* 153
Klenovsky, Dmitri (pseudonym of Dmitri
  Krachkovsky), *276*
Kliuev, Nikolay, *245, 246*
Klopstock, Wilhelm, 51, 85
Knut, David (pseudonym of David Fiksman),
  265, 266
Koliadki, 10
Koltsov, Aleksey, 126, *133–35,* 153, 247, 304
Kommissarzhevsky Theater, 187, 193
Korzhavin, Naum, *306*
Krainy, Anton. *See* Hippius, Zinaida
Kruchenykh, Aleksey, 230, *234, 235: Victory*
  over the Sun, 230, 235
Krylov, Ivan, 82, 94, *98–100,* 103, 108, 133
Kuniaev, Stanislav, 301, *302, 303,* 304, 308
Kurbsky, Ivan, 122, 303
Kushner, Aleksandr, *292, 293,* 308
Kuzmin, Mikhail, *220, 221*
Kvashnin, Petr Andreevich, *28, 29*

Ladinsky, Antonin, *265*
La Fontaine, Jean de, 51, 59, 64, 67, 69, 96, 98

Lamartine, Alphonse de, 125
Larionov, Mikhail, 227
Leconte de Lisle, Charles-Marie-René, 201,
  209, 210
LEF (Left Front of Literature), 226, 231, 234,
  235, 240, 274
Leibniz, Baron Gottfried Wilhelm von, 52, 57,
  176
Lenin, Nikolay, 178, 246, 253, 255, 258, 270
Leontev, Konstantin, 275
Lermontov, Mikhail, 4, 126, *129–33,* 142, 155,
  156, 176, 195, 201, 236, 265, 292: "The
  Boyar Orsha," 133; *The Demon,* 126, 133,
  236; "Hajji Abrek," 133; *The Hero of Our*
  Time, 126, 129, 130; *The Novice,* 126, 133;
  "Song of Tsar Ivan Vasilevich, of the Young
  Bodyguard and the Brave Merchant
  Kalashnikov," 133
Life of Aleksandr Nevsky, The, 20
Light verse, 80, 94, 100, 101, 105, 116, 118,
  122
Liszt, Franz, 150
Literary Center for Constructivists, 252
Literary Gazette, The, 106, 108, 110
Liubimov, Iury, 302
Lokhvitskaia, Mirra, *171,* 175
Lomonosov, Mikhail, 45, 46, 49, 50, *52–57,*
  58, 73–76, 80, 84: "Evening Meditation on
  God's Greatness on the Occasion of the Great
  Northern Lights," 54; "Introduction on the
  Use of Church Books in the Russian
  Language," 52, 55; "Letter on the Rules of
  Russian Versification," 52, 55; "Letter on the
  Use of Glass," 56; "Morning Meditation on
  God's Greatness," 55; "Ode on the Day of
  Ascension . . . of Empress Elizabeth . . . ,"
  53; "Ode . . . on the Seizure of Khotin," 52,
  53; "Ode Selected from Job, Chapters 38, 39,
  40 and 41," 54; *Russian Grammar,* 52, 55;
  Short Handbook on Eloquence, 55
Lovers of Wisdom, 123, 135
Lugovskoy, Vladimir, *258*
Lully, Raymond, 38
Lvov, Nikolay, 70, 71, 72, 74, 78, *79*

Macpherson, James, 70, 75, 85, 103, 119; *see*
  also Ossian
Maeterlinck, Maurice, 181
Maikov, Apollon, *144, 145*
Maikov, Vasily, *63–65,* 69, 144: *Elisey, or*
  Bacchus Enraged, 63–65; *Fables,* 64; *The*
  Ombre Player, 64
Maiakovsky, Vladimir, 5, 213, 224, 225,
  230–33, 234, 235, 240, 245, 251, 254, 258,
  273, 274, 279, 286, 288–90, 306: *About*

Maiakovsky, Vladimir (*continued*)
  That, 232; *At the Top of My Voice*, 232; *The Bathhouse*, 232; *The Bedbug*, 230, 232; "A Cloud in Pants*," 230; *It's Good*, 232; *Man*, 231; *Mystery-Bouffe*, 232; *150,000,000*, 232; *Vladimir Ilich Lenin*, 232; *Vladimir Maiakovsky. A Tragedy*, 230–32; *War and the World*, 231
Makovsky, Sergey, 206
Malevich, Kazimir, 225, 235
Malherbe, François de, 46, 50, 53
Mallarmé, Stephan, 168, 187, 201, 228, 265
Mamai, 13
Mandelstam, Nadezhda, 215
Mandelstam, Osip, v, 5, 206, 207, 213, 214–18, 251, 275, 280, 297: *The Egyptian Stamp*, 218; *The Fourth Prose*, 218; *A Journey to Armenia*, 218; Moscow Notebook, 218; *The Noise of Time*, 218; *The Stone*, 214, 215; *Tristia*, 206, 207, 215, 216, 218; Voronezh Notebook, 218
Mariengof, Anatoly, 244, *245*, 246
Marinetti, Filippo, 224, 244, 245
Marshak, Samuil, 252, 261, 262
Martynov, Leonid, *280–82*
Marxism and Marxist criticism, 186, 205, 224, 234, 261
Matiushin, Mikhail, 233, 235
Matveeva, Novella, *293*
Maupassant, Guy de, 167
Mazeppa, 38, 113, 122
Medvedev, Silvestr, *36, 37,* 38
Mendeleeva, Liubov, 191
Men of the Soil, 151
Merezhkovsky, Dmitri, *170, 171,* 181, 182, 183, 187, 263: *Christ and Antichrist*, 171; *Julian the Apostle (The Death of the Gods)*, 171; *Leonard da Vinci (The Gods Reborn)*, 171; *On the Causes for the Decline and on New Currents in Contemporary Russian Literature*, 171; *Peter and Alexis*, 171; *Tolstoy and Dostoevsky*, 171
Methodius, Saint (Apostle to the Slavs), 9, 15
Mey, Lev, *145*
Meyerhold, Vsevolod, 187, 193
Mezzanine of Poetry, 226, 244
Mickiewicz, Adam, 151
Mikhail Romanov (tsar), 24, 29, 31, 89
Millevoye, Charles-Hubert, 82
Milton, John, 25, 80
Minsky, Nikolay (pseudonym of Nikolay Vilenkin), *170,* 171
Mnemosyne, 121
Modigliani, Amedeo, 211
Mongols, 3, 9, 12, 13, 19–21, 25, 119, 122, 195, 280

Montale, Eugenio, 297
Montesquieu, Baron de (Charles-Louis de Secondat), 47, 63
Moore, Thomas, 97
Morits, Iunna, 301, *304*
Morshen, Nikolay (pseudonym of Nikolay Marchenko), *298–300,* 309
Moscow Art Theater, 302
Moscow Herald, The, 135
Moscow Journal, The, 66, 84, 85
Mozart, Wolfgang Amadeus, 113, 307
Muravev, Mikhail, *79, 80,* 82, 101
Muscovite, The, 151
Musin-Pushkin, Count Aleksey, 18
Musset, Alfred de, 152, 161
Mussorgsky, Modest, 4, 110, 135, 145, 150, 161
Mystical anarchism, 187

Nabokov, Vladimir, 18, 305
Nadson, Semen, *159*
Nagibin, Iury, 291, 292
Nasedka, Ivan, 31
Nekrasov, Nikolay, 140, 141, 154, *155–59,* 189: "Frost, the Red-Nosed," 155, 156, 158; "Our Contemporaries," 158; "The Peddlers," 156, 158; "Russian Women," 158; "Who Lives Happily in Russia?" 158
Neledinsky-Meletsky, Iury, *79*
Nerval, Gérard de, 163
New Life, The, 170
New Path, The, 182
Nicholas I (emperor), 104, 110, 113, 125, 139
Nicholas II (emperor), 167, 205
Nietzsche, Friedrich, 170, 171, 172, 191, 195, 196
Nikitin, Ivan, *153*
Nikon, Patriarch, 24, 31, 36
Northern Flowers, 105, 108
Northern Herald, The, 70
Northern Society, 122, 123
Notes of the Fatherland, The, 146, 156
Novalis (pseudonym of Friedrich von Hardenberg), 142, 163
Novikov, Nikolay, 63, 64, 66, 79, 83, 85, 99
Novy Mir (New World), 268, 272

Oberiu (Association for Real Art), 252, 259, 261
Ode, 4, 45, 46, 48, 50–58, 60, 63–66, 70, 71, 73–76, 79, 83, 85, 86, 99, 109, 110, 113, 270
Odoevsky, Aleksandr, 122
Odoevtseva, Irina (pseudonym of Iraida Heinicke), 263, *277, 278*
Okudzhava, Bulat, *284–86,* 301, 305

Old Believers, 24, 27, 31, 50, 220. *See also* Schism, schismatics
Olenin, Aleksey, 99
Olimpov (pseudonym of Konstantin K. Fofanov), 226
Orthodoxy, 9, 20, 24, 29, 31, 36, 127, 153, 169, 171, 207, 247, 265
Ossian, 70, 75, 85, 89, 96, 98, 119, 122, 123. *See also* Macpherson, James
Ostrovsky, Aleksandr, 151
Ostrovsky, Nikolay, 272
Ovid, 25, 56, 69

Palitsyn, Avraamy, 29
Panin, Nikita, 63, 68
Parisian Note, 262–65, 274, 275
Parnassians, 5, 155, 175, 176, 199, 201, 206, 219
Parny, Évariste de, 101, 102, 105
Pasternak, Boris, v, 3, 5, 142, 161, 206, 213, 275, 226, *235–39*, 241, 244, 251, 262, 280, 288: "The Childhood of Luvers," 238; *Doctor Zhivago*, 235, 238, 239, 305; "A High Malady," 237; *Lieutenant Schmidt*, 238; *My Sister Life*, 225, 235–37, 244; *On Early Trains*, 238; *Over the Barriers*, 236; *Safe Conduct*, 235, 238; *Second Birth*, 235, 238; *Spektorsky*, 238; *Themes and Variations*, 235, 237; *A Twin in the Clouds*, 236; *When the Weather Clears*, 238; *The Year 1905*, 238
Paul I (tsar), 53, 57, 63, 74, 81, 83, 86, 99
Pavlov, Nikolay, 150
Pavlova, Karolina, *150, 151*
Peasant poets, 133, 221, 225, 232, 245, 246, 304
Pegasus' Stable, 244
Pereval, 256
Peter I (the Great), 4, 24, 26, 38, 39, 45–47, 49, 53, 84, 113, 115, 122, 144, 254, 285
Peter II (emperor), 50
Petrarch (Francesco Petrarca), 101
Petronius, 80
Petrov, Vasily, 64, 70
Phaedrus, 59, 64, 70
Physiologus, 19
Picasso, Pablo, 224, 225
Pindar, 50
Poe, Edgar Allan, 172, 175, 293
Poésie légère. See Light verse
Poètes maudits, 195
Pogorelsky, Anton (pseudonym of Aleksey Perovsky), 148
Polar Star, The, 122
Polezhaev, Aleksandr, *135*
Polonsky, Konstantin, 140, *145–47*, 161
Polotsky, Simeon, *32–36*, 37, 53: dramas, 35; *The Garden of Many Flowers*, 32–35; Psalter,

34; *The Russian Eagle*, 35; *The Rhythmologion*, 32, 35
Pope, Alexander, 56, 69, 80, 95
Poplavsky, Boris, *266*
Populism, 155, 186, 193, 195, 245
Pound, Ezra, 206
Pre-Raphaelites, 155
Preslavsky, Konstantin (bishop), 15
Primitivism, 207, 225, 227, 233, 234, 241, 244, 280, 304
Prokopovich, Feofan (archbishop), *39, 40*, 47, 50
Proletarian literature, 251. *See also* Socialist poets
Proust, Marcel, 205
Prutkov, Kozma (pseudonym of Aleksey K. Tolstoy), 148, 160
Psalter, 15, 51, 53
Pugachev, Emelian, and the Pugachev Rebellion, 26, 62, 63, 64, 74, 83, 115
Punin, Nikolay, 211
Pure art. *See* Art for art's sake
Pushkin, Aleksandr, v, 4, 28, 79, 86, 97, 103–6, 108, *109–15*, 119, 122–24, 126, 129, 130, 135, 150, 151, 194, 211, 214, 222, 223, 237, 238, 240, 244, 265, 288, 289, 292, 303, 307: *Boris Godunov*, 4, 86, 105, 110, 111; *The Bronze Horseman*, 115, 238; *The Captain's Daughter*, 110; *The Captive in the Caucasus*, 110; "Count Nulin," 111; *Eugene Onegin*, 4, 105, 109, 110, 113, 133, 135; *The Fountain of Bakhschisaray*, 106, 111; "The Gabrieliad," 111; "The Gypsies," 111, 113; "The Little House in Kolomna," 114; *Little Tragedies*, 113; *Poltava*, 105, 113, 122; "The Queen of Spades," 4, 110; *Ruslan and Liudmila*, 110; *The Tales of Belkin*, 114; "The Tale of the Golden Cockerel," 115; "The Tale of the Priest and His Servant Balda," 28, 115; "The Tale of Tsar Saltan," 115
Pushkin, Vasily, 103
Pushkin pleiad, 4, 104–6, 108, 116, 118, 121, 123, 126, 148, 149

Rabelais, François, 206, 304
Rachmaninoff, Sergey, 145, 147, 150
Racine, Jean, 59
Radishchev, Aleksandr, *82–84*
Raeshnyi verse, 28
RAPP (Russian Association of Proletarian Writers), 226, 231, 252, 256, 258
Rasputin, Gregory, 186
Razin, Stepan (Stenka), 26, 229, 234
Remizov, Aleksey, 187, 221
Repentance poetry, 22

Revolution of 1905, 5, 168, 173, 182, 186, 187, 219

Revolution of October 1917, 5, 171, 175, 178, 182, 192, 205, 207, 220, 225, 232, 235, 238, 251, 258, 280, 290

Revolutionary poets, 252. *See also* Socialist poets

Richardson, Samuel, 63

Rilke, Rainer Maria, 186

Rimbaud, Arthur, 201, 240, 265

Rimsky-Korsakov, Nikolay, 113, 115, 135, 145, 150, 220, 228

Rollin, Charles, 52

Rousseau, Jean-Jacques, 62, 70, 80, 81, 99, 111, 113

Rozhdestvensky, Robert, *290*, 291, 308

Rubenstein, Anton, 150

Rubtsov, Nikolay, *304*

Rusalii, 11

Russian Thought, 175, 265

Russian Word, The, 146

Rybakov, Anatoly, 305

Ryleev, Kondraty, 105, *122*

Rzhevsky, Aleksey, *70*

Saint Sophia, 169, 170, 188, 190–93, 195, 215. *See also* Beautiful Lady; Eternal Feminine Feminine

Saltykov-Shchedrin, Mikhail, 156

Sappho, 80, 95, 122, 144

Satirical tales of the seventeenth century, 28

Savvaty (monk and Printing Office editor), 31

Scales, The, 175, 187, 206, 220

Scarron, Paul, 64

Schelling, Friedrich Wilhelm Joseph von, 93, 105, 116, 123, 125–27, 134, 140

Schiller, Johann Christoph Friedrich von, 87, 94, 95, 97, 103, 121, 130, 142, 143, 152

Schism, schismatics, 22, 24, 32. *See also* Old Believers

Schopenhauer, Arthur, 140, 141, 143, 168, 179

Scorpion Publishing House, 175

Scott, Sir Walter, 150, 256

Scriabin, Aleksandr, 238, 266

Selvinsky, Ilia, 252, *254–56*

Serapion Brothers, 253

Severianin, Igor (pseudonym of Igor Lotarev), 225, *226*, 244, 263

Shakespeare, William, 25, 59, 80, 85, 103, 110, 111, 152, 206, 237, 243, 245, 259, 304, 307

Shakhovskoy, Semen, *30, 31*

Shaw, George Bernard, 186

Shchedrin. *See* Saltykov-Shchedrin, Mikhail

Shelley, Percy Bysshe, 104, 172, 175

Shershenevich, Vadim, 225, 226, *244, 245,* 246

Shishkov, Aleksandr S., 94, 99, 103

Shuvalov, Ivan, 56

Silver age in the arts, v, 5

Simonov, Konstantin, *271–73*

Sixteen, 130

Skomorokhi, 3, 10, 19, 24, 28, 280

"Slap in the Face of Public Taste, A," 225, 227, 230, 234

Slavophilism, 106, 118, 119, 123, 126, 129, 135, 139, 140, 151, 152, 160, 187

Sluchevsky, Konstantin, 155, *161–63*

Slutsky, Boris, *283, 284*

Smotritsky, Melety, 32, 48, 53

Social command, 230, 251

Socialist poets, 251, 257

Socialist realism, 5, 251, 252, 259, 268, 308

Society of Lovers of Russian Letters, 101

Socrates, 260

Sologub, Fedor (pseudonym of Fedor Teternikov), 168, *178–81*, 183, 187, 280, 297: *Blue Sky*, 181; *Collected Works*, 181; *The Enchanged Cup*, 181; *The Flaming Circle*, 180; *Incense*, 181; *One Love*, 181; *Panpipes*, 181; *The Petty Demon* and other novels, 178, 180, 181, 187; *The Serpent*, 180; *The Wayside Bonfire*, 181

Solovev, Sergey, 169

Solovev, Vladimir, *169, 170,* 171, 181, 188, 190–92

Solzhenitsyn, Aleksandr, 268, 305

Son of the Fatherland, 121

Sophocles, 73

Sosnora, Victor, *306, 307,* 308

Southey, Robert, 94

Stalin, Joseph, 251, 286–88, 301

Stankevich, Nikolay, 133, 134

Steiger, Anatoly, *264*

Stein, Gertrude, 230

Stendhal (pseudonym of Henri Beyle), 126

Sterne, Laurence, 85, 257

Stravinsky, Igor, 226

Stray Dog, 220

Sturm und Drang, 81, 83, 84, 96, 121

Sully-Prudhomme, René François Armand, 161, 201

Sumarokov, Aleksandr, 46, 50, 53, *57–60*, 63, 64, 66, 69, 71, 72, 108, 135: *Dmitri the Pretender* and other tragedies, 59; *Eclogues*, 57; *Fables*, 57; *The Industrious Bee*, 57; *Miscellaneous Poems*, 57; *Satires*, 57; "Two Epistles . . . ," 57, 58

Sumarokov School, 62, 63, 65, 70

Supplication of Daniil the Prisoner, The, 19, 28

Suprematism, 225

Surkov, Aleksey, *274*
Surrealism, 259, 266, 306
Swinburne, Algernon Charles, 172

Taganka Theater, 302
Tairov, Aleksandr, 199
*Tale of the Destruction of the Russian Land,
The,* 20
Tale of Igor's Campaign, The, 3, 10, 15,
16–18, 19, 96, 98, 119, 122, 145, 195, 242
"Tale of Ruff, Son of Ruff," 28
Tale of the Ruin of Riazan by Bath, The, 20
Tale of the Taking of Azov, 29
Tale of Woe-Misfortune, The, 27, 247
Tallemant, Paul, 49, 50
Tasso, Torquato, 67, 80, 102, 110
Tatars, 3, 14, 19, 56, 66. *See also* Mongols
Tchaikovsky, Peter, 4, 110, 144, 145, 147, 160,
161
Tennyson, Alfred, Lord, 5, 139
Terapiano, Iury, 262, *265*
Testament of Vladimir Monomakh, 15
Thaw, 6, 238, 254, 258, 261, 268, 279–82,
284, 286, 287, 289–91, 293, 301–5, 308.
See also De-Stalinization
Thomson, James, 46, 77, 80, 85, 107
Tibullus, Albius, 101, 119
Tikhonov, Nikolay, 251, *252–54*
Time, 151
Time of Troubles, 3, 4, 9, 23, 29–31, 59, 89,
242
Tiutchev, Fedor, 5, *126–29,* 141, 143, 214,
215, 299: "Deniseva Cycle," 127–29
Tolstoy, Aleksey K., 140, *147–50,* 160, 247:
historical plays, 150; *Prince Serebriany,* 150
Tolstoy, Fedor (the American), 106
Tolstoy, Lev, 4, 140, 146, 154, 156, 159, 171,
275
Transsense language. *See* Zaum
Trediakovsky, Vasily, 46, *48–52,* 53, 55, 58,
64: *New and Short Method for the
Composition of Russian Verse,* 48, 49, 50;
Panegyrics, 50; *The Telemachiad,* 51;
Theoptia, 51; *Voyage to the Isle of Love,* 49
Tsvetaeva, Marina, 225, 226, *241–44,* 259,
262, 280, 297: *After Russia,* 242, 243; *The
Craft,* 241–43; *The Evening Album,* 241;
From Psyche, 242; *The Magic Lantern,* 241;
Milestones, 241, 242; *Mother and Music,*
244; *My Pushkin,* 244; narrative poems, 243;
"The Rain of Light," 244; *The Swans' Stand,*
241, 242
Tsybin, Vladimir, 301, *303, 304*
Turgenev, Andrey, 101, 103
Turgenev, Ivan, 4, 139, 141, 154, 156, 201

Tvardovsky, Aleksandr, 267, *268–70: Distance
Beyond Distance,* 270; *A House by the Road,*
269; *The Land of Muravia,* 268; *The Road to
Socialism,* 268; *Terkin in the Other World,*
270; *Vasily Terkin,* 267–69
Twain, Mark, 293

Uhland, Ludwig, 94, 97
Union of Writers, 5, 252, 286, 289, 301, 305
Union of Young Writers, 265
Utilitarian literature and criticism, 5, 140, 143,
144, 146, 150, 152, 156, 158, 160, 162, 169,
170, 257, 258, 262

Vakhtangov, Evgeny, 259
Valéry, Paul, 5, 218
Venevitinov, Dmitri, *123, 124,* 134, 150
Venok (Wreath), 233
Verlaine, Paul, 5, 168, 175, 179, 188, 195,
201, 213, 263, 265, 282, 288
Viazemsky, Petr, 96, 101, *105–7,* 133
Villon, François, 206, 259, 285
Vinokurov, Evgeny, *282, 283*
Virgil, 56, 80
Virshi, 30–32
Vladimir I, Saint (grand prince), 9, 39
Voinovich, Vladimir, 305
Volokhova, Natalia, 191–93
Voloshin, Maksimilian, *219, 220*
Voltaire (pseudonym of François Marie Arouet),
46, 57, 62, 64, 66, 68, 80, 103, 110, 111
Voznesensky, Andrey, 279, *288–90,* 301, 305,
308
Vvedensky, Aleksandr, 252, *261, 262*
Vysotsky, Vladimir, *302*

Wagner, Richard, 188, 189
Watteau, Jean Antoine, 263
Westernizers, 119, 120, 140, 149, 152, 187
Whitman, Walt, 172
Wieland, Christoph Martin, 85
Wilde, Oscar, 163, 168, 307
Wilson, John, 114
Wolff, Christian von, 52
Wordsworth, William, 93
World of Art, The, 168, 220

Yellow Book, The, 168
Young, Edward, 74, 77, 80, 85, 95

Zabolotsky, Nikolay, 252, *259–61*
Zadonshchina, 18, 195, 242
Zamiatin, Evgeny, 305
Zaum, 227, 252, 261
Zdanevich, Ilia, 235
Zhemchuzhnikov, Aleksey, Zhemchuzhnikov
brothers, 147, 160

Zhdanov, Andrey, 211
Zhukovsky, Vasily, 93, *94–97*, 101, 103, 106,
   110, 115, 118, 119, 126, 130, 132, 142, 195:
   "The Bard in the Camp of Russian Warriors,"
   95, 96; "The Forest King," 97; "Ivan
   Tsarevich and the Gray Wolf," 97;
   "Liudmila," 96; "Puss in Boots," 97;
   "Svetlana," 96; "Twelve Sleeping Maidens,"
   97
Zinoveva-Hannibal, Lidiia, 196
Zola, Émile, 154
Zoshchenko, Mikhail, 211